DISTINGUISHED
GERMAN-AMERICANS

Charles R. Haller

HERITAGE BOOKS
2014

HERITAGE BOOKS

AN IMPRINT OF HERITAGE BOOKS, INC.

Books, CDs, and more—Worldwide

For our listing of thousands of titles see our website
at
www.HeritageBooks.com

Published 2014 by
HERITAGE BOOKS, INC.
Publishing Division
5810 Ruatan Street
Berwyn Heights, Md. 20740

Heritage Books by the author:

*Across the Atlantic and Beyond: The Migration of
German and Swiss Immigrants to America*

Distinguished German-Americans

International Standard Book Numbers
Paperbound: 978-0-7884-0193-0
Clothbound: 978-0-7884-9088-0

Table of Contents

List of Tables

Preface

The current essay is the second in the series of studies by the author dealing with the general subject of German-Americans. The first, *Across the Atlantic and Beyond*, published in early 1993, provides a foundation for this work which is essentially a thirty fold expansion of the chapter titled "The German-Americans" found in this earlier work.

The term German is used here in the loose sense of including all those from German-speaking areas, mainly, Germany, Austria, and Switzerland, and other satellite areas as defined in the introductory section.

The book explores in considerable detail just what contribution the various waves of German-speaking peoples made to American society. The text format is one of historical-biography with formal discussion limited to historical events and to representative individuals. For the most part, the individual and his or her role in America is placed relative to the physical and mental environment existing during his or her lifespan.

Thirteen groups, comprising more than 2,300 distinguished German-Americans, are outlined. The individuals received numerous honors. The mixture was politically cosmopolitan and included radicals, conservatives, dissidents, and many middle-of-the-roaders. Collectively, they provided a constant struggle between the forces of reform and the adherence to conservative polices.

Historically, the bulk of the seven or eight million German-speaking migrants to America were of course ordinary working people including many laborers and farmers. A relatively few were men and women of wealth and had specialized training. Those with ambition and unbounded energy contributed their fair share to American industry. First generation German-Americans tended to dominate specialized areas such as finance, the film industry, classical musical, merchandizing, larger newspapers, brewing, and certain phases of engineering. Descendants occupied many key positions in science and in government.

German-American names pervade everyday life in America and some names do so on an international basis. To name only a few, consider the Maytag washer, the Hoover vacuum cleaner, the Hershey candy bar, Smuckers jellies, Heinz ketchup, Stouffers "Lean Cuisine", the Chrysler automobile, the Schwinn bicycle, Gerber baby foods, George A. Hormel processed meats, and Brunswick bowling balls. And that ubiquitous wearing apparel known as "Levis" faced strong competition from Calvin Klein designer jeans. Of course, many businessmen were clothed in Hart, Schaffner & Marx suits.

The German-Americans were to build great industries and found fabulous fortunes based, to a strong degree, on German technology. Technology transfer often complementary and consequently ran in both directions.

Many American marketing concepts date from centuries of German experience, not the least of which were developed by the German book fairs, notably those book fairs in Frankfurt and in Leipzig. German-Americans were quick to employ a vast range of marketing techniques, and to great success.

The text abounds with interesting and colorful personalities whose life stories individually have filled hundreds of books. Dozens of household names are included. Many surprises, both large and small, were uncovered.

More than half of the family names are pinpointed precisely as to place of origin. Another large portion can be attributed to a point of origin in a broader sense of originating from a land where the German language was the primary, everday language. Many family names underwent considerable distortion in their spelling - in most cases, this distortion is clarified.

Acknowledgements

First and foremost, the library facilities at the Johannes Gutenberg-Universität (University of Mainz), as well as those at the Stadt- und Universitätsblbliothek, Frankfurt am Main, were of critical importance to this study.

Secondly, numerous corporations forwarded a large quantity of either unpublished or not widely available corporate history material. Corporate histories, where published, are noted in a special section. These corporations and their founders are acknowledged in four sections, one section being titled "Baseball, Brewers, etc.," a second section titled "Engineers and More Engineers," the third section titled "The World of High Finance and Big Business," and a fourth section titled "The World of Music." Information provided by the Archives of the New York Stock Exchange was also most helpful. Corporate-related organizations include the Beer Institute, Washington, D.C., and the National Beer Wholesalers Association, Alexandria, Va.

Data from several museums was useful. These organizations include the Auburn-Cord-Duesenberg Museum, Auburn, Ind.; the Babe Ruth Museum, Baltimore; the Winterthur Museum, Winterthur, Md.; and the Busch-Reisinger Museum, Harvard University, Cambridge, Mass.

Hall of Fame organizations include the Motorsports Hall of Fame, Talladega, Ala.; the National Inventors Hall of Fame, Akron, Oh.; and the National Baseball Hall of Fame & Museum, Inc., Cooperstown, N.Y.

Other contributing organizations include the Arthur and Elizabeth Schlesinger Library, Cambridge, Mass.; Babson College, Babson Park, Mass.; Fortune Magazine, N.Y.; the Hoover Historical Center, North Canton, Oh.; the South Carolina Dept. of Archives & History, Columbia, S.C.; and the Texas and Southwestern Cattle Raisers Foundation, Fort Worth, Tx., and various branches of the National Park Service.

Special material assistance was received also from Kevin J. Alban, Orville R. Butler, Vincent Curcio, Roberta Daymon, Paula Fink, Theresa G. Gold, Wilhelm Hamm, Stella Hook, Henry Z. Jones, Jr., Iris Carter Jones, Sister Michael Kilmer, Barbara J. Lee, Mary Medearis, Emily Miller, Herman Radloff, Alison Ryley, Irene Roughton, Charles W. Meinhardt, Christa Sammons, Richard H. Sell, Dorothy A. Stratford, Emmert Studebaker, Gregory J. Van Gasse, Marlene E. Wheatley, Frau Ursula Wöhrmann, Leonora Wolf and Frank Zabrosky.

Thanks must also go to Elisabeth C. Kinne and Nancy S. Dorsey for an introduction to the magic world of computers.

Special thanks go to Frau Inge Zöllner for a palatable (re)introduction to the fantasy world of advanced German language grammar and sentence structure.

Thanks to the staff of Heritage Books, Inc., especially Christopher Mohr and John Potter, who greatly assisted in smoothing out editorial rough spots and in dealing with the complex problem of converting from a European computer format to a usable American computer format.

Broadly Speaking, Just Who Were the German-Americans?

Reporting on the preliminary results of the 1990 U.S. Census, an article in the March 1993 issue of *Time* magazine states that some "fifty-eight million Americans, out of a total of 248 million, claim German ancestry." Thus, nearly one quarter of those living in America have German ancestors and many of these Americans can identify with one of approximately 1,900 family names in this book.

One may well ask: What constitutes a German-American? Obviously, from the German standpoint, the leading criteria, and perhaps the most important, is place of birth, in Germany, Austria, or Switzerland, and from the American standpoint, subsequent migration to, and residence in America.

The second criteria is native language, that is the German language, whether High German or Low German. Historically, the U.S. Census records, from 1790 to 1990, in combination with other population evaluations of the period from 1683 to 1790, indicate that upwards of seven or eight million German-speaking peoples have migrated to the United States.

Other criteria, in not unusual cases, are whether or not an individual considered themselves to be German even though born and raised outside of Germany, and historically, whether or not some prominent individuals were regarded by the public as German although they do not meet the standards of the first two criteria. Some literary critics use the criteria of whether or not migrants, however temporary, to America wrote in German, rather than in English, about experiences in America. This restrictive definition would exclude most 20th century writers regardless of their background.

What and Where Were the German-speaking Lands?

The second question facing the reader is: Which lands constitute Germany? For the purpose of this book, one may well take the peak German emigration period of 1850-1900 when nearly four and one half million German-speaking immigrants went to the United States. This fifty year period roughly coincides with the might of the Prussian Empire, which was centered in Berlin, and which at that time was the dominant political and military force in Europe, that is, during the era of 1871 to 1919.

Correspondingly, one may use the maps shown in the *Meyers Orts- und Verkehrs-Lexikon des Deutschen Reichs* (Bibliographisches Institut, Leipzig und Wien), printed in 1913, as indicating exactly which territories were either part of the German Reich, or under administrative control of the Reich.

Thus, in the latter part of the 19th century western German states included: Schleswig-Holstein, Mecklenburg, Hannover, Westfalen, Rheinland-Pfalz, Hessen, Baden, Württemberg, and Bayern, the latter being comprised of Franken, Ober-Pfalz, Niederbayern, and Oberbayern.

In the southwest, the states of Elsaß and Lothringen (since 1919 known as Alsace-Lorraine) were considered as part of the Reich from 1871-1919. In actuality, a German census dating from 1900 showed that 73 percent of the population in Lothringen spoke German, while 96 percent and 93 percent in Unter-Elsaß (Lower Alsace) and Ober-Elsaß (Upper Alsace), respectively, spoke German.

In the east, German states included: Pommern, Brandenburg, Sachsen with the Thüringer Wald, Westpreußen, Ostpreußen, Posen, and Schlesien. For historical purposes, this group of eastern states was administrated by German governments for the years 1793-1807, 1815-1918, and 1939-1945. After 1919, large parts of Westpreußen, Ostpreußen, Posen, and Schlesien reverted to the administrative control of Poland, that is, until the time of World War II, when they were again incorporated for a few years under German administrative control.

These German State names constitute the core of the locality names used in this study. Points of origin are taken from the records of those Germans emigrating to America in the period 1625-1949.

Who Were the German-speaking Peoples?

Data from the 1920 U.S. Census indicated that immigrants claiming a German mother-tongue were subdivided as follows: Germany - 85%, Austria-Hungary - 7.6%, Russian Empire - 3.9%, and Switzerland - 3.5%.

The much lesser number of immigrants to America from Austria came from the states of Ober-Österreich, Nieder-Österreich, Burgenland, Steiermark, Kärnten, Salzburg, Tirol, Ost-Tirol, and Vorarlberg.

The country today known as Switzerland is a complex mixture of four languages with the language of High German being overall predominant. In the center and the northeast, primarily German-speaking Kantons include: Aargau, Appenzell with Außerrhoden and Innerrhoden, Basel-Stadt, Basel-Land, the main part of Kanton Bern including the Oberland in the southeast, Glarus, Luzern, Neuenburg, St. Gallen, Schaffhausen, Schwyz, Solothurn, Tessin, Thurgau, Unterwalden with Nidwalden and Obwalden, Uri, Zürich, and Zug.

The important French-speaking Kantons of southwestern Switzerland include: Geneva (Genf), Neuchatel, and Vaud (Waadt). The Kantons of Fribourg (Friburg), and Valais (Wallis), and the area known as the Bernaise Jura are split theoretically between German-speaking and French-speaking constituents. In the southeast, The Kanton of Ticino constitutes a dominantly Italian-speaking enclave, while Kanton Graübunden (Grisons) is a politically separate Romance language area.

For purposes of this book, emigrants from all the twenty-six Kantons in Switzerland were included as being basically German. Annotation is made when family names are obviously of French or Italian origin.

Numerous geographic names are explained in somewhat greater detail in a glossary at the end of the book.

The Rise and Fall of the Hapsburg Empire

The Habsburg (English = Hapsburg) name was a condensed name of the Castle Habichtsburg, erected about 1020 near Brugg, now in Kanton Aargau, in northern Switzerland. The Habsburg family provided rulers in Austria from 1273-1918, and in Spain from 1516-1700.

When Rudolf I of the Austrian House of Habsburg defeated King Ottokar II of Bohemia at the Battle of Marchfeld in 1278, Rudolph became King and Emperor of Germany. Rudolf I thus proceeded from being ruler of the relatively small archduchy of Austria to being the leader of an empire embracing all the German peoples.

The reigns of Kaiser Karl V (1519-1556), and his brother Kaiser Ferdinand I (1556-1567), together with the reign of their close relatives in the House of Habsburg in Spain, provide intriguing probabilities that Germans often accompanied Spanish expeditions sailing to America. A prime example is the Heidelberg native and navigator Bernhard Hühne (1547-1611), who explored and charted what later was named the Gulf of California. Hühne was chief pilot on expeditions to New Spain in 1599-1600, and in 1601-1602.

Under Karl VI, who reigned from 1711-1740, the lands of the Habsburg Reich attained their maximum extent and included most of what is now Rumania, Hungary, Austria, and Bavaria, a good part of Switzerland, Belgium, and Yugoslavia, and some parts of Italy, Bohemia, and Moravia.

The Pragmatic Sanction of 1715 provided a change in law which paved the way for Maria Theresia to become ruler of the Habsburg Empire. She reigned from 1740-1780, although the early years of her rule were a period of considerable give and take between the Habsburg Empire and the Prussian might, to the north. In essence, the conflict that reached its peak in the late 18th century was between the Habsburg family and the Hohenzollern family, between Austria and Prussia, between Catholicism and Protestantism, between Maria Theresia and Frederick the Great, and between a multinational conglomerate mentality and a reich of one dominant ethnic mentality.

Queen Maria Theresia, the mother of sixteen children, proved a formidable opponent for all of the various adversaries of the Austrian part of the Habsburg Empire. She left a remarkable record including a revision of Austria's finance controls, and the start of the Stock Exchange in Wien (Vienna).

During the War of Austrian Succession (1740-1748), Friedrich II of Prussia (Frederick the Great) was partly pacified by the Austrians through the gain of administrative control of the rich province of Schlesien (Silesia). Subsequently, he integrated the Schlesien army with the Prussian army and actively promoted the occupation of Schlesien by German Protestant settlers.

The House of Habsburg was to wield enormous power over the German Empire for 528 years, or until 1806, when Emperor Franz II gave up his title of Holy Roman Emperor and renounced his association with the German Imperial Crown. However, Franz II continued to rule the hereditary empire of Austria until his death in 1835. His descendants ruled until 1918, in an ever increasingly ineffectual manner.

The Rise of Prussia

The Hohenzollern family name comes from a castle erected about 1077 on the cliffs overlooking the upper Danube River at Sigmaringen, a locality now in southern Baden-Württemberg. The family provided rulers in Brandenburg and Prussia from 1415-1918.

In 1675, when the Prussians beat the Swedes at Fehrbellen, in Brandenburg, they began a long climb towards becoming the dominant military power in northern Europe.

In 1701, Friedrich III, Elector of Brandenburg, was crowned King in Prussia under the name Friedrich I. He ruled until 1713.

The next King in Prussia was Friedrich Wilhelm I who ruled from 1713-1740. The main task of Friedrich Wilhelm I was to build the Prussian army into a fighting force, which he did successfully by raising the standing army from 40,000 to 81,000 men. More importantly, Friedrich Wilhelm I brought order to government finances. Friedrich Wilhelm I called himself King in Prussia, as distinguished from King of Prussia.

The champion of the Prussian leaders, Friedrich II (English = Frederick the Great) ruled from 1740 until his death in 1786. His rule illustrated the growing might of the Prussian forces to Europe, although the Prussian forces were still somewhat under the shadow of the Austrians. During his reign, Friederich II was able to consolidate the core states of Brandenburg, Pommern and Ostpreußen with Westpreußen, Schlesien, and Ostfriesland. He thus forged the first modern unification of Germany. The principal states outside this union were Sachsen, Hannover, and Bayern, the latter being predominantly Catholic.

Friedrich Wilhelm II was King of Prussia from 1786-1797. Toward the end of his reign, the Prussian might took a back seat to the organizational power of the revolutionary forces in France, which were in turn superceded by the Grande Armée of Napoleon. By the spring of 1807, Napoleon's forces of some 600,000 troops had overrun eastern Prussia and threatened much of Europe. As is well known, Napoleon's forces collapsed at the Battle of Waterloo in 1815, but only after having been decimated by disease, malnutrition, and a forbidding Russian winter.

Friedrich Wilhelm II was succeeded by Frederich Wilhelm III, who reigned over a struggling Prussian empire from 1797-1840. He was succeeded by Friedrich Wilhelm IV, who maintained more or less a status quo for the period of 1840-1861.

Beginning about 1820, the organization prowess of the Prussians, to the north, gradually replaced that of the Austrians. In 1848, the Austrians were barely able to supress independence demonstrations in Wien (Vienna), the capital of Austria, in Budapest, which was the capital of Hungary, and in Zagreb, the capital of Croatia. Czech nationalists in Bohemia were also supressed.

In 1861, Wilhelm I, brother of Friedrich Wilhelm IV, became King of Prussia. The century old hostility between the Prussians and the Austrians turned into armed confrontation. And in the Austro-Prussian (Seven Weeks') War of 1866, the Prussians could claim a narrow victory. The Treaty of Prague in August, 1866, sealed the political split between Austria and Germany. Wilhelm I was rewarded with the title, in 1871, of German Emperor. In 1879, however, a defensive union was formulated between Germany and the Austro-Hungarian complex. This agreement was to be utilized in 1914 with subsequent disastrous consequences for both the Habsburgs and the Hohenzollerns.

By 1871, the Prussians under Emperor Wilhelm I, who ruled from 1871-1888, were by far the dominant power in the German Empire. In this process, the center of the German Empire shifted from Wien (Vienna) to Berlin. In 1919, of course, the territorial extent and authority of both the Prussians and the Austrians was severely curtailed. Under the terms of the 1918 armistice, the German Emperor, Wilhelm II, who ruled 1888-1918, and the Austrian Emperor, Karl I, who ruled 1916-1918, gave up all rights. In essence, the Austrian House of Habsburg (actually Habsburg-Lothringen) ceased to exist. The Prussian monarchy, sometimes loosely called the House of Brandenburg or the Hohenzollern Dynasty, also lost their authority to rule.

Satellite areas included the northern part of the old Austro-Hungarian Empire, which constituted the area known for centuries as Bohemia, contained a basic German-speaking population, with many descendants eventually coming to America. Typical German family names from Bohemia are included in this study, for example Steinitz and Taussig. Following World War I, these lands became Czechoslovakia (since early 1993 the Czech Republic and Slovakia). The hilly area in the northwest of Bohemia, which was known as the Sudetenland, contained a high percentage of Germans until after World War II. At the end of World War II, many of the 3,000,000 Germans in the Sudetenland were resettled, mainly in Germany.

Beginning in 1621, there had been a massive replacement of Protestants in Bohemia and Moravia by Catholics. Most of the Catholics came from Habsburg lands or from the southern part of the German Reich, although some came from Italy and from Spain. The expelled Protestant emigrants, altogether some 36,000 families, scattered in all directions excepts towards the southwest, that is, except towards Austria.

Schlesien (Silesia) was another area which had a high percentage of Germans. Today, most of Silesia is incorporated into the southern part of Poland, and many German family and locality names have been replaced by Polish names.

Finally, historically-speaking, a few family names of obvious German origin from the eastern parts of the former Austro-Hungarian Empire known as Moravia or, in German, Mähren (in general, a southeast extension of Bohemia, but politically separate) and further southeast, Galicia are included. The country formerly known as Galicia, has been split between Poland and the Ukraine part of Russia.

Likewise, some few German family names from the area now known as Hungary are cited in this work, mainly those from capital city of Budapest. Three waves of German-speaking people moved into Hungary and down along the Danube as far southeast of Weißkirchen. These individuals formed the "Schwabenzugen" of 1717-1734, 1763-1773, and 1782-1787. The name Schwabenzugen reflects the fact that many families came from the Catholic province of Swabia in Bayern and from the Swabian Hills to the west in Württemberg.

German family names from isolated colonies in the Russian Empire, although locally important, especially in the Ukraine and on the north side of the Black Sea, are excluded. Likewise, scattered colonies of German names from areas such as Siebenbürgen, later called Transylvania, and now Rumania, in general, are excluded as being outside the scope of this study.

Who Are the German People Today?

A third question is: What constitutes a German family name? By tradition, residence over decades and centuries is an important criteria. One must consider the main mass movements of peoples into and out of Germany. Several examples, of many possibilities, of mass movement are given below.

In modern times, one of the first of the recorded mass movements of the German peoples was initiated apparently by the Habsburg Ruler of Germany, Friedrich III (1440-1493). By 1480, Friedrich III began his effort to colonize Slavic lands to the southeast with German people, especially with Catholics, in order to provide a buffer zone between Wien (Vienna) and the Turks. Thus, the vast area which became known as Austro-Hungary absorbed large numbers of German colonists. Many German family names still exist there, although most in somewhat modified form.

Under the expansion program of the Habsburgs, the ancient Bavarian family name Haller was carried to Budapest by Ruprecht Haller (1452-1513), and further southeast to Siebenbürgen by his son Peter (1500-1569). Peter Haller achieved distinction as Burgermeister of Hermannstadt (Sibiu), the main city of Siebenbürgen, in 1542-46, 1550-53, and 1554-1556; a statute in his memory existed there until recent times.

The migration of Huguenots into Germany often has been mentioned. Small groups of French-speaking peoples went to Germany in 1569, but the main groups of French Protestants went from 1685 to 1753. These constituted perhaps some 30,000 families. They formed large colonies in such places as Friedrichsdorf, near Frankfurt am Main (Hessen), in Berlin (and parts of Brandenburg), in Württemberg, in the Pfalz, and in Hamburg. Many French names were retained although in somewhat modified form, that is, Germanized. A good example is the porcelain manufacturing family of Behagel which left Flanders in the latter part of the 16th century, settled in Hanau (Hessen), and eventually took up residence in nearby Frankfurt, where it continues today. A key reference to Huguenot family names is that by Juan Zamora, 1992, entitled *Hugenottische Familiennamen im Deutschen* (Carl Winter - Universitätsverlag, Heidelberg). Oddly, few German names of Huguenot origin are represented in this text. Two rare examples, however, are Louis Jouin, cited in the Roman Catholic clergy, and the ancestors of Charles Gratiot, cited under business. Pennsylvanian Governor Beaver's immigrant ancestor was reportedly an "Alsatian Huguenot" by the name of "Jerg Bieber" who went to Philadelphia in 1744. The Huguenot origin of the governor's ancestors requires confirmation.

The Counter-Reformation of the late 16th century showed a heavy movement of Jesuits into the main university areas of Germany as far north as the large cities of Münster, Würzburg, and Prague. Likely, a number of ordinary French citizens accompanied the Jesuits and settled in the southern part of Germany.

Other Protestant-oriented groups who migrated to Germany during the Counter-Reformation include the so-called "Salzburgers" whose progressive migration lasted from 1588-1731, and the Waldensers, who were accommodated in the area of Heidelberg by political arrangement during the years 1686-1687. A notable example of the Waldsener group was the Astor family ancestors who lived in Germany for four generations before going to America, in 1783.

Also in the latter part of the 16th century, numerous Flemish and Dutch people moved into the Rhineland where they formed large colonies, for example, in Frankfurt and nearby Oberursel. Flemish and Dutch migrants sporadically continued to move into the Rhineland except during the Thirty Years' War (1618-1648). In the period 1650-1670, these Protestants were again on the move. Most of the family names are recognizable as former Flemish or Dutch names, although somewhat altered. The latter group included the German ancestors of Governor Pennypacker of Pennsylvania whose earlier Dutch ancestors bore a family name such as Pannebekker.

Also during the years 1650-1670, Swiss Protestants peacefully occupied a large part of the German states of Baden, Württemberg, and Rheinland-Pfalz. In some local areas, such as the Kraichgau, in Baden, they formed the dominant farmer element. And in Rheinland-Pfalz, an area exists south of Bad Kreuznach which calls itself the Rheinhessischen-Schweiz (Swiss district of the wine growing district of Rheinhessen). Here again, many family names have undergone some minor alteration. Good examples are the Swiss

Huber and Hershi families which settled near Landau in Rheinland-Pfalz. Descendants of the two families migrated to America in the 18th century and provided the United States with President Hoover and the Hershey candy bar. Examples of Italian names long established in Germany are the Astor and Brentano families. Descendants of both families later settled in America. The Swiss educator Pestalozzi, whose name was carried to America as a concept of primary school education, was also of Italian origin. The family name Hershey mentioned above was derived from Hershi, a name which reflects its Latin influence.

Thus, there was a relatively constant flux into and out of Germany with an ever changing ethnic population mix, however minor, and a corresponding mix of family names.

What Are German Names?

The fifth question is: How does one recognize a German family name? A ready solution is to consult one, or better yet, at least three, of the well-known German family name etymological dictionaries. One of the most universally available handbooks is that by Hans Bahlow, reprinted in several editions, the latest being 1985, with the title *Deutsches Namenlexikon* (Suhrkamp Taschenbuch, Baden-Baden). Other well-known and commonly available etymological dictionaries include those authored by Adolf Bach, by J. K. Brechenmacher, and by Max Gottschald.

Another useful book for those with some fluency in German is that by Wilfried Seibicke, published in 1982 under the title *Die Personennamen im Deutschen* (Walter de Gruyter, Berlin). Seibicke's book covers, to some extent, both personal names and family names, and bears a good bibliography of works normally accessible in larger libraries in Germany and in major libraries in the United States.

An invaluable guide to Germanic family names, as they evolved in spelling through the centuries, is Hans Jäger-Sunstenau's 1984 *General-Index zu den Siebermacher'schen Wappenbüchern, 1605-1961* (Akademische Druck - U. Verlagsanstadt, Graz). The Index organizes the entire group of Germanic nobility in a systematic matter and contains about 130,000 coats-of-arms. Most of these names are those of noble families, but the Jäger-Sunstenau book also has a good representation of bürgerlich (common citizen) names. The massive, multi-volume Siebmacher set includes noble family names from all the territories once considered to be German administrative territories, even from such isolated areas as Siebenbürgen and Croatia.

Another source for quick reference to German family names is Ottfried Neubecker's 1992 book titled *Grosses Wappen Bilder Lexikon der bürgerlichen Geschlechter Deutschlands, Osterreichs und der Schweiz* (Ernst Battenberg Verlag, München). In this book Neubecker illustrates more than 100,000 coats-of-arms, as the title states, for the ordinary citizens of Germany, Austria, and Switzerland.

A standard work on personal names is the handbook by the Dutchman J. van der Schaar and is titled simply *Voornamen* (PrismaWoordenboek, Utrecht). The 1981 edition contains dozens of variants of the usual personal names found in many countries of Europe with their corresponding geographic usuage.

Another index to European personal names was published in 1986 under the editorship of Otto Nüssler & Michael Coester. The title of this fairly expensive book is *Internationales Handbuch der Vornamen* (Verlag für Standesamtswesen, Frankfurt am Main).

Seven Basic Rules of Name Recognition

Basic rules regarding the recognition of German family names are:

First, a high percentage of German family names begin with the letters B, H, K, M, S, and W. Letter combinations, in some order of importance, are especially noteworthy: Sc(h), Be, Ha, He, Ma, St, and W. A good example is the well-known food products name of Schmucker, which in America, was often simplified to Smucker.

Germanic names very rarely start with Q, X, or Y. Moreover, certain letter combinations, such as "Wh", are English linguistic phenomena, and are totally alien to the German language. The letter combinations "Ch" and "Sh" are likewise foreign to the language, being derived from "K" and "Sch".

Second, certain vowel combinations (diphthongs) are typically German-ic. The umlaut forms ä, ö, and ü are good examples; these letters sometimes became ae, oe, and ue, and sometimes simply a, o, and u when transplanted to America. The use of vowel combinations au, aue, ie, ei, etc. is a strong hint of a Germanic name. An example is the noted Lutheran clerical family in Pennsylvania who went by the name of Mühlenberg, changing to Muehlenberg, and finally to the simplified form of Muhlenberg.

The common German letter combination ei provides an inordinate amount of problems for English writers and speakers. Most often it is transformed to ie, as in Hiester, and occasionally to y, as in Snyder. Sometimes, it is mispronounced, as in Neiman.

Third, the German-speaking people are very prone to combine words. Adjective-noun and noun-noun combinations are common, without the dash, of course. Some examples are Ackerman(n), Altgeld, Falckenstein, Hammerstein, Hellman(n), Kleinpell, Neiman(n), Nieman(n), Niehaus, Nußbaum(er) (Nusbaum), Steinmetz, and Zimmernan(n). The suffixes of German family names are important in recognizing their origin. Word suffixes such as -dorf, -heim, -man(n), and -stein normally are dead give-aways. Other noun suffixes common in German names are -bach, -bauer, -berg(er), -breit, -feld, -haus, and -müller. Prefixes include Klein, and others. Some of these, as -breit , -müller , and -stein, occur as either a prefix or a suffix, or stand alone. In America, the latter three names sometimes were translated as Bright, as Miller, and as Stone or Stine.

Another peculiarity of compound German names is the use of -er, -en, -n, and -s to separate noun-noun and adjective-noun names. Good examples are Falckenberg, Gutenberg, Habsburg (formerly Habichtsburg), Hohenzollern, Rockefeller (from the village of Rockenfeld), Rubincam (originally Rübenkamp), Rubinstein (apparently German-Russian), and Zellerbach. These "connecting forms" have essentially no meaning and serve merely to facilitate pronounciation. They do not indicate possessive, plural, or genitive, as one might assume.

Some German names in their Americanized form are deceptive. For instance, the relatively unique family name Beinecke is more likely a quaint American spelling rather than a German noun-noun combination. It does not appear to be derived from Bein (meaning leg), and Ecke (meaning corner). German variants include Behnk(e), Beinke, Beinker, Bene(ke), etc.

Unusual German/American name changes include the following: Broncard/Brokaw, Oehrle/Early, Oechslein/Exline, Tschudy/Judy, Meisser/Mizer, Rüger/Rex, Reichert/Richards, Rieth/Reed, Schleiermacher/Slaymaker, and Teisen/Tysson.

Fourth, the letter suffix -er is often attached to occupations or to localities to form family names and is termed a derivative ending. These derivative endings are common in southern Germany, Switzerland, and Austria. The suffix -er correlates with the masculine form of the "der-words" (der, dieser, welcher, jeder) in German language grammatics. Notable examples of -er endings are the prominent American family names Frankfurter, Kissinger, and Schlesinger. These three names are derived apparently from localities. The former may be associated with one of two large cities in Germany called Frankfurt (the one city in Hessen and the other in Brandenburg); the second name is likely a derivative of Kissingen, today Bad Kissingen, located in Bayern (Bavaria); the third name apparently comes from its association with the former eastern German administrative province of Schlesien (Silesia).

Other prominent German-American family names with derivative -er endings are Eisenhower and Wagner. These are occupational names, the first representing an iron-worker, formerly Eisenhauer. The second name, occurring very commonly, was shortened from wagon maker (Wagenmacher). Just as Wagner represents a shortened form, so does the common German-American name of Ziegler, which comes from Ziegelbrenner, meaning brick maker (literally brick burner).

The -er ending in the common German family name Haller shows derivation from multiple localities where rock salt was mined. Well-known salt mining localities exist in northern Austria (Hall in Tirol, Hallein, Hallstadt, etc.), in Sachsen-Anhalt (Halle), and in Baden-Württemberg (Schwäbisch Hall). The mineral halite is native rock salt and apparently stems from the New Latin term *halites*. The name Haller is an ancient family name evidently first noted in the record of a lesser noble Friedrich Haller (active 1140) living in Nürnberg, in Bayern (Bavaria), and thus is one of the very oldest family names on record in Germany. The author is not related to the noble family of Nürnberg.

Variants on the Haller name, in order of importance, include, in German-speaking lands: Heller, Holler, Höller, Hall, and Halle. In Slavic lands, a variant is Halar. The American of Hollar does not occur in European telephone books. Names with an "ig" ending are recognizable generally as being German or Swiss in origin. Examples are Gehrig and König, the latter being spelled also Koenig and Konig, and occasionally translated as King.

The adoption of family names followed both a geographic trend and an hierarchy trend. In general, family names spread from southeast to northwest throughout Germany. Family names were first adopted by the ruling families, then by the patriarch families, then the hand workers, and finally by the farmers.

The last to get family names were the farmers of the Lower Rhine and the northeastern part of Germany. Several of the families of the well-known Krefeld families (from the lower German Rhine), who formed the first permanent German settlement in America in 1683, were given fixed family names during the immigration process, for example, Op den Graaf and Kunders. In fact, the demise of the patronymic system of names, which usually involves the genitive form, did not occur in the Lower Rhine until the Napoleonic laws were adopted about 1805.

Fifth, endings with the genitive -s, -sen, and -en are typical of the lower German Rhine, but occur commonly in The Netherlands and its surrounding areas. Almost universally, these genitive endings were dropped during the process of immigration although some Dutch and Danish names kept the endings. Dutch names are also characterized by endings such as -inga, -stra, and -ma. The name of the well-known giant Siemens industrial firm probably originated from natives of northwestern Germany.

In eastern Germanic areas, an obvious Slavic influence is shown by the endings of -ski, -ow, -ek, -ke(n), -ak, and -vic. An example here is the family name of the prolific American writer H. L. Mencken.

Sixth, unattached prefixes are important clues. Dutch family names and those of the lower German Rhine sometimes, especially in the older records, use prefixes of the prepositions van, van den, op den, te, and ter, all meaning "from" or "of" a certain locality. An outstanding example is the well-known Op den Graaf family which originated in Germany in Rhenish communities near Krefeld.

For distinction from Dutch names (or lower German Rhine names), the natives of central and eastern Germany occasionally use prefixes of Von (for ordinary citizens) and von (for nobility), and more rarely zu, von der, and vom. The family name of the famous German space scientist, Wernher von Braun, is a good example on two matters. Wernher Magnus Maximilian von Braun, was born: (1) to a German noble family, (2) living in Wirsitz, Posen, a locality now called Wyrzysk, Poznan, well inside Poland. On occasion, Germans were honored with, or assumed the French honorary labels of de, de la, and du before the family name.

Notable representative noble German family names include: von Behr, von Braun, de Haas, von Egloffstein, von Meusebach, von Neumann, von Schack, von Schimmelpfennig, von Schrader, de Schweinitz, von Seckendorff, von Steinwehr, von Steuben, von Vegesack, von Wrede, and von Zinzendorf. Of course, not all members of the same family were entitled to use the von or de, as the case may be.

Other minor noble family names include: Bettendorf (from Nordrhein-Westfalen), Block (from Westfalen), Mallinckrodt (from Schlesien), and Minnegerode (from Mingerode in Niedersachsen), and many others.

On the other hand, suspect names include: de Castro, de Kalb, Von Kapelhoff, Von Kocherthal, Von Stroheim, and Von Tilzer.

Seventh, a host of German given names are easily recognizable, for example: August(us), Conrad, Friederich, Gustav(e), Johann(es), Maximilian, Otto, Ruprecht, and Wilhelm, are very common masculine names in German communities transplanted to the United States, although usually in their English version; i.e., John for Johann, and William, for Wilhelm, etc. The combination of two of these names is a strong clue as to their German origin. Likewise, German feminine names include Anna, Elisabeth, Emma, Katharina, and Ursula.

Jewish names represent special problems when one considers their complex migration history. Many German Jewish names have a characteristic distinction - examples are seen from the list of Jewish clergy which follows. Given names such as Aaron, Felix, Isaac, Isidor, Moses, Samuel, and Solomon are typical Jewish, although not definitively German-Jewish. Many Jewish family names were derived from locality names.

The Warburg family name is a prime example of a family name having been derived from the ancient town of Warburg, near Kassel, Nordrhein-Westfalen. Immigrant Paul Moritz Warburg (1868-1932), and two brothers, Max B. and Felix Moritz, were 12th generation descendants of one "Simon of Cassel", who resided in the town of Warburg in 1559. The town name was adopted by the prominent banking family in later generations. These German-Americans are not related to the occupants of the Castle of Warburg at the same locality.

The complexity of recognizing German-Russian names is seen from a list on notables whose immigrant ancestors were born in Russia. These include family names such as: Adler, Auerbach, Berkman, Bernstein, Billikopf, Bolm, Bronfman, Hesselberg, Epstein, Gershwin, Ginsberg, Goldberg, Goldenweiser, Haldeman, Hirsch, Koenigsberg, Leipzig, Lipman, Loeb, Mayer, Meltzer, Rickover, Rubinstein, Sakel, Schillinger, Schulman, Stern, Weizmann, and Wiener.

Samuel James Meltzer is a good example of this complexity for he was born in 1851 in Ponevyezh, Soviet Republic of Lithuania, recieved an M.D. degree from the University of Berlin in 1882, migrated to the U.S. in 1883, and subsequently had an outstanding medical career in New York until his death in 1921. During his career, Meltzer wrote many articles for publication in medical journals; these articles were about evenly divided between English and German.

Some prominent German-American family names exist as Latinized variants or translations of the German name. Examples in the following chapters include: Hazelius, Kelpius, Pastorius, Preetorius, Roselius, and Wislizenus. The use of Latinized names was a fad which occurred in Germany primarily in the 15th-17th centuries. Fortunately for German linguists, Latin names were adopted at that time in Germany by relatively few highly educated personalities.

The recognition of changes in spelling from the German to English (Anglification) is often a matter of some experience. The following simple examples, in table form, are given from a list of common German family names. According to a 1970 census taken in the Bundesrepublik (West Germany only), the twenty-five most common German family names are:

TABLE 1
25 COMMON GERMAN FAMILY NAMES AND THEIR AMERICAN EQUIVALENTS

in Germany	in America	in Germany	in America
Mueller/Müller	Miller	Klein	Klein, Kline
Schmidt	Smith	Schroeder/Schröder	Shrader
Schneider	Snyder	Schmitz	Smith
Fischer	Fisher	Schmitt	Smith
Meyer	Meyer, Mayer, Myer(s)	Schwarz	Black
Weber	Weber	Wolf	Wolf
Becker	Becker	Neumann	Newman
Wagner	Wagner	Schmid	Smith
Schaefer/Schäfer	Shafer, Schafer	Braun	Brown
Schulz	Shultz	Zimmermann	Carpenter
Hoffmann	Hoffman	Hofmann	Hoffman
Bauer	Bower	Koch	Cook, Cox
Meier	Meyer, Mayer, Myer(s)		

*Data Source: *Wirtschaft und Statistik*, 7/77, p. 450-453

The German-speaking People in America

Basic statistics covering this study are presented in the Table 2 which shows more than 2,400 distinguished German-Americans representing some 1,900 prominent heads of family. Of this group, forty-nine percent were born in the German-speaking countries, or in an administrative area of Germany as defined earlier; these are the first generation Americans.

Another significant group, eighteen percent, form the second generation Americans, many of which retained German as a language and German customs, in part, by virtue of being educated in German universities. The majority of this group married women of German descent.

The third group includes family names of documented, but remote German ancestry (three generations or more after immigration) and comprises sixteen percent of the study group.

TABLE 2
FAMILY NAME CATEGORIES

Occupation	1st Gen Immigrant	2nd Gen Immigrant	3rd and Higher	Immigrant Not Recorded	Total
Artists	92	18	15	15	140
Baseball/Brewers	35	17	12	29	93
Clergy	172	40	61	34	307
Educators	63	19	14	31	127
Engineers	40	18	27	22	107
Entertainment	32	15	4	22	73
Finance/Business	116	85	58	60	319
Government	75	73	64	60	272
Medical	76	39	31	10	156
Music	208	28	5	13	254
Printing	112	37	40	47	236
Science	106	41	26	40	213
Military	56	20	29	27	132
totals	1183	450	386	410	2429
percent of total	49	18	16	17	

The fourth, or remaining group, about seventeen percent, were not defined specifically as German-Americans in the records, although roughly half were cited as being "of German descent", as being Pennsylvania German, etc. In this group, etymological dictionaries, and the seven basic rules cited above, were used to interpret ethnic group. The list is likely within the ninety-eight percent accurancy range.

In this study, family names are arranged into thirteen logical categories, as shown in Table 2. Rarely was an individual name assigned to two different categories although some notable examples occur, such as Dwight D. Eisenhower, whose high military ranking and political status, warranted the dual assignment.

Technology transfer was affected most by two large groups, namely those in the medical professions and in the natural sciences, both groups having relatively high percentages of first generation foreign born and an European education. Other groups, such as the engineers, inventors and corporation founders, also contributed a fair share of technology transfer.

Basic biographical data was obtained from the publications shown in the extensive bibliography at the end of the chapter on finance and business. A general series of biographical sources is given at the end of the book. A relatively minor amount of conflicting data was encountered and, in general, the most recent source was used. For instance, the *Dictionary of American Biography* and *Who Was Who in America* both give the birth date of the prominent editor and political scientist Francis Lieber as being March 18,

1800. However, the more recent *Neue Deutsche Biographie* and the *Encyclopedia Americana* list Lieber's birth date as April 8, 1798.

The data base centers around the *Dictionary of American Biography.* The first twenty volumes of the *DAB* are weighted obviously heavily toward the clergy of 18th century America (to the detriment of the business community), as is to be expected, since this group historically has been the primary record keepers; the various supplements of the *DAB* are much less so. Still, the clery comprises the largest group in the present study, being about thirteen percent of the total.

The current text goes far beyond a mere transfer of biographical data from the *DAB.* Many family names are placed in the context of American and European history. The older volumes of the *DAB* persisted in using archaic locality data; this data was updated and replaced with modern terminology. The lineage of certain key personalities has been re-examined.

On the other end of the recognition scale, individuals who are not even listed in the brief citations of *Who Was Who in America* rarely left a mark in American history.

Many other sets of biographies and countless individual sources also were consulted in order to unbias the categories. Names of prominent women were given special attention. The categories containing entertainment, sports, finances, and business required specific effort to obtain reliable information. The bulk of published information sources are listed in a special section in the back of the book.

The corporate world provided an amazing set of specific data, mostly unpublished, on their respective founders. A subgroup, the many German-American brewers, oddly left few public records, and those records that are available are mostly fragmented.

Jewish names presented some challenging name-change problems, especially in the field of entertainment. Many of these new names were adopted intentionally for business purposes.

Certain Protestant and Catholic family names were changed during the process of immigration. Swiss names were changed when they migrated to Germany and, in many cases, were changed again on the migration to America. A good example is the name Crayenbühl, Grabiel, Krabill, or Krebill. In fact, the *Mennonite Encyclopedia* lists twenty variants for this family name which apparently originated in Kanton Bern, Switzerland. Current German telephone books for the City of Mainz show variants of Gräbel, Krebühl, and Krehbiel. The most common U.S. variants tend to be Graybill, Grable, and Graebel.

When Were the Immigration Periods?

The data base includes dates of immigration for 1416 individuals, or about fifty-eight percent of the total data base. The immigration eras are summarized in table 3.

TABLE 3
IMMIGRATION PERIODS, 1625-1949

Immigration Period	Number of Individuals	Immigration Period	Number of Individuals
1625-1649	7	1820-1829	33
1650-1699	26	1830-1839	95
1700-1709	9	1840-1849	236
1710-1719	27	1850-1859	190
1720-1729	20	1860-1869	103
1730-1739	47	1870-1879	72
1740-1749	39	1880-1889	82
1750-1759	57	1890-1899	49
1760-1769	24	1900-1909	34
1770-1779	22	1910-1919	11
1780-1789	22	1920-1929	24
1790-1799	17	1930-1939	103
1800-1809	18	1940-1949	26
1810-1819	19	total	1416

Several interesting observations are apparent from this rudimentary data tabulation.

Although the first-known Germans in America were a group of two or three (Wm. Unger, Peter Keffler, or Keffer, and Wm. Volday, the latter being from the French part of Switzerland; some sources say "eight Germans or Poles") who accompanied the colony in Jamestown about 1609, they apparently left no trace of accomplishment, nor any known descendants. They likely did not survive the extremely high mortality rate there. Most likely, they filled a specific occupation niche, such as glass-blowers.

Thus, the record begins in 1625 with Peter Minuit. He was born in 1580 in Wesel, Duchy of Kleves, a small city in Germany very close to the Dutch-German border. Minuit became director-general of New Netherlands and later, governor of New Sweden. Historians are divided as to whether the Minuit name originally was of Dutch, German, or even of Walloon origin. The family name is sometimes recorded as Minnewit, etc.

Up to 1683, there were only isolated migrants of notable Germans to America; then the first permanent German settlement was established in Germantown, near Philadelphia. Even then, the group was not large; however, about a half dozen of these pioneering Germantown colonists were the fore-runners of others who acquired some notoriety.

The list of thirty-three 16th century German notables, with arrival dates in America is to be found on Table 4. In this list, many of the names show a strong Dutch influence, as well they might, as they stem from the lower German Rhine. Such names include Updike, van der Beeck, Hardenbroeck, Kunders, Updegraf, and perhaps some others. Still, only the apparent birthplace of the immigrant generation is being considered.

TABLE 4
THIRTY-THREE 16TH CENTURY GERMAN NOTABLES
WITH IMMIGRATION DATES

Date	Name	Origin	Occupation(s)
1625	Minuit	Wesel	Government
1635	Tupper	Hessen	Clergy ancestor
c.1638	Kierstede	Magdeburg	Medical
c.1638	Updike	Wesel	Government ancestor
c.1643	Hack	Köln	Merchant
c.1644	van der Beeck	Bremen	Government
c.1644	Herrman	Prague	Printing
c.1651	Schrick	Nürnberg	Finance
c.1655	de Meyer	Hamburg	Finance
c.1656	Sickles	Vienna	Military ancestor
c.1658	Ebbing	Hamburg	Government
c.1659	Philipse	Elberfeld	Finance
1660	Leisler	Frankfurt	Government
1664	Hardenbroeck	Elberfeld	Government
c.1667	Wagner	unknown	Medical ancestor
1668	Lederer	unknown	Government
1675	Duryea	Mannheim	Sports
1682	Trumbauer	Hannover	Architect ancestor
1683	Pastorius	Sommerhausen	Government
1683	Kunders	Krefeld	Clergy
1683	R. Tyson	Krefeld	Clergy & Medical ancestor
1683	Lukens	Krefeld	Finance ancestor
1683	Updegraf	Krefeld	Clergy ancestor
1685	Levering	Mülheim/Ruhr	Clergy ancestor
1685	C. Tyson	Krefeld	Government ancestor
c.1685	Bachman	Berne	Clergy ancestor
1686	Rittenhouse	Mülheim/Ruhr	Clergy
1690	De Haven	Mülheim/Ruhr	Military
c.1690	Custer	Krefeld	Military ancestor
1694	D. Falckner	Sachsen	Clergy
1694	Kelpius	Siebenbürgen	Government
1695	Pennypacker	Flomborn	Govt. & Military ancestor
1698	Cruger	unknown	Government ancestor

Migration of German-speaking peoples to America during the 1700s was relatively stable, although there was a minor peak period during the thirty-year period of 1730-1759.

The last decade in the 18th century saw a decline of immigrants, a decline which lasted through the French Revolution and the Napoleonic era of 1792-1815.

The thirty-some year period from 1827 to 1859 shows a gradual buildup in migration by intellectuals, as well as by the proletariat as a result of dissatisfaction with the various governments in Europe. In Germany, this dissatisfaction began with dislike of Bavarian governmental control over the areas of Hessen, and Baden, as well as the Palatinate. The student demonstrations in Frankfurt in 1832 were one aspect of this unrest. The main event of the uprisings, the so-called Baden Revolt of 1848, involved armed insurrection. After the military forces supplied by the Prussian Government regained control in Baden, a substantial number of militants slipped across the border to Switzerland, and eventually went to America via French ports.

The main exodus of non-combatants from Europe occurred during the decade of 1840-1849, especially the two year period of 1848-49, and lasted through 1850-1859. The turmoil of the 1840s caused a substantial Jewish element to leave Germany also. Coincidentally, two vital factors came into play: first the railroad transportation network in Germany was just beginning to be important; secondly, the infrastructure in the shipping centers of Bremen and Hamburg also was being developed rapidly.

The predominance of "Rhinelanders" among the German emigrants was noted particularily before the year 1880, an arbitrary date often cited as the division between the departure of the "old emigrants" and the "new emigrants".

The period of 1900 to 1929, which included the 1st World War (1914-1918), followed by rampant inflation in Germany (which peaked in 1924), and a universal economic depression in 1929-1932, is indicated by the lesser number of German migrants.

The onset of Nazi power in the 1930s is reflected from the increased number of notable dissidents, mainly intellectuals, scientists and Jewish peoples, again on the move.

Where Did They Originate

The tabulation of first generation emigrants was used to establish some basic concepts. Point of origin date is available for approximately fifty-eight percent of German-Americans in this study. The data shows that for the entire period of 1625-1949, there was no strong bias toward any part of the German-speaking areas; the migrants went from every nook and cranny. Point of origin is roughly proportional to current population except for the State of Rheinland-Pfalz whose numbers includes a group of thirty-five individuals loosely termed as "Palatines". The state of Hessen also apparently had a slightly disproportionate share of emigrants.

A few individuals, born in Germany to American parents, were not part of the count; these include, for example, actress Katherine Cornell (1893-1974), born in Berlin; and writer Edith Hamilton (1867-1963), born in Dresden. In actual numbers, the area of origin of distinguished German-Americans can be found on Table 5.

In considering prominent German-Americans who came from cities, Wien (Vienna), provided sixty-one, while the Hamburg-Bremen port complex provided fifty-two. Other notable cities were Berlin with thirty-two, and Frankfurt am Main with twenty-seven. Wien and Berlin provided artistic talent, especially musicians. Hamburg and Frankfurt gave businessmen and bankers.

In the Table 5 listing for Switzerland, about two-thirds of the migrants were from predominantly German-speaking Kantons while one-third came from the predominantly French-speaking Kantons. Census figures for Switzerland for 1980 show 6,365,960 residents in that country.

TABLE 5
AREAS OF ORIGIN FOR DISTINGUISHED GERMAN-AMERICANS

German State	Emigrants	1990 Population
Baden-Württemberg	155	9.5 million
Bayern	113	11.1 million
Brandenburg + Berlin	43	6.1 million
Hessen	120	5.6 million
Mecklenburg-Vorpommern	15	2.3 million
Niedersachsen + Bremen	111	7.9 million
Nordrhein-Westfalen	103	16.9 million
Rheinland-Pfalz (Palatinate)	138	3.7 million
Saarland	4	1.1 million
Sachsen	64	4.9 million
Sachsen-Anhalt	23	3.1 million
Schleswig-Holstein + Hamburg	49	4.2 million
Thüringen	31	2.5 million
subtotal	974	78.9 million
Switzerland	77	
Austria	74	
Alsace-Lorraine	56	
Polish (incl. Posen)	43	
Bohemia, Silesia, Moravia	83	
Other eastern areas	48	
total	1355	

The same data set was used to determine the number of so-called "Rhinelanders" going to America. Points of origin within 40 km. (25 miles: a good day's journey on horseback) of the Rhine, between Schaffhausen in Switzerland and Kleves in Germany, were plotted as follows:

TABLE 6
AREAS OF ORIGIN FOR DISTINGUISHED RHINELANDER-AMERICANS

Area	Emigrants
Switzerland	27
Alsace	54
Baden-Württemberg	62
Rheinland-Pfalz	122
Hessen	66
Nordrhein-Westfalen	54
total	385

Thus, in a loose sense, about twenty-eight percent of the study group may be called Rhinelanders. Consequently, there is some merit to the label of the Rhine as the "River of Destiny", especially if one considers that the Rhine was the dominant artery to America before 1850, that is, before the network of railroads, and the harbors of Bremen and Hamburg, became important.

Many much-publicized groups of Germans led the trek to America. Among these were the small, 1683 group of Krefelders (a convenient misnomer), the several thousand 1709-1710 group of Palatines (another convenient misnomer), and the many thousands of 48'ers.

The 48'ers, who emigrated for two decades before 1848, and a decade or so after 1848, for the most part occupied the broad continuum between republicanism, socialism, and communism. The 48'ers carried many degrees of proletarian politics to America. Numerous individuals were characterized by their biographers as "free-thinkers", religious and otherwise. All of these added an element of competition and tended to inject new life into the outmoded political system in America. Lincoln recognized the restless political spirit of the 48'ers, and harnessed much of it in his drive for the presidency and in his anti-slavery campaign.

Migration often was related directly to an impending, or to a real crisis, most notably to the many wars which overran Germany, in particular the Rhineland. The vast majority of migrants were drawn by the search for a better standard of living, by the quest for political and religious freedom, and by the dreams of untold good fortune. The doubters were lured by the quest of a pot of gold at the end of a rainbow.

Rare was the individual who made his way to America alone. The herd instinct was a prominent factor in migration. Often entire families, and related families, formed the nucleus for a community migration. In one well-documented case, the bulk of the residents of an entire village, Niederfischbach (from the state now known as Rheinland-Pfalz) made their way, in 1853, to America. When eighty-five of the 120 residents left Germany, the village of Niederfischbach subsequently disappeared from German maps. Like most such communal groups, the majority settled in one place; in the case of the former residents of Niederfischbach, the new home was Milwaukee.

Chapter Format

The goal of identifying some 2,300 German-Americans with regard to occupational categories is achieved by means of thirteen user friendly directories. For the reader's convenience, the directories are further sub-divided into fields of interest.

Furthermore, the directories are preceded by a brief historical background which embraces the respective occupational catagories. In some cases, background notes also accompany the field catagories. Rather than do a multi-volume compendium of individual biographies, selected profiles give noteworthy characteristics and achievements. In many cases, original German names are shown in parentheses.

In the vast majority of cases, the criteria for listing an individual stems from multi-listing in three or more references cited in the bibliography located at the end of the book. These listings are a reflection of public recognition. A higher degree of selectivity is used for individuals whose careers date from the 20th century. Relatively few individuals still living are included in this book.

Appendices include a glossary of key geographic terms and a list of relatively obscure or rare publications used to identify points of origin.

Contemporary German-American Organizations

This book is dedicated to the many German-American organizations in the United States and Germany which promote good relationships between the two countries.

The *1991 Directory of Historical Organizations in the United and States and Canada* (Nashville, Tenn.) lists numerous such organizations including eighty-two groups dedicated to the history of Jewish immigration to America. Four of the larger and more active Jewish organizations are cited below. Jewish personalities are especially prominent in the areas of entertainment and banking/finance, publishing, and to a somewhat lesser extent in corporate world, particularily in merchandising.

Another very useful publication, although now somewhat dated, is the 127 page booklet by Elizabeth A. Kessel, titled *German American Directory* which was printed in 1986 under the auspices of the U.S. Information Agency, Washington, D.C. This booklet lists hundreds of agencies in the U.S. which are not listed below.

At least forty-five German language newspapers are published periodically in the U.S., most on a weekly basis. The two most important daily newspapers are the *New Yorker Staats-Zeitung und Herold* and the (Chicago) *Abendpost-Sonntagspost*. Likewise, some forty-five radio stations broadcast German language programs in the U.S.

Some twenty Mennonite organizations devoted to keeping records exist in the United States and Canada. The Mennonites were among the earliest of the permanent settlers in the U.S. An amazing number of prominent German-Americans can claim ancestry among the German and Swiss Mennonites and a similar group, the Amish. Historically, the Mennonites in America have kept exceptionally good records of their ancestors. Four of the more active Mennonite groups are listed below.

Other American religious groups which actively study German-American immigration include Brethren in Christ, Church of Jesus Christ of Latter-day Saints (Mormons), Catholic, Evangelical Luthern Church, Moravians, and Seventh Day Baptists.

The most internationally active German-American historical societies, with due apologies to especially active organizations that might have been missed, are the following:

Amana Heritage Society, Amana, IA
American Committee to Promote Studies of the History of the Hapsburg Monarchy, Baton Rouge, LA
American-German Historical Association, Salt Lake City, UT
American Historical Society of Germans from Russia, Lincoln, NE
American Historical Society of Germans from Russia, Edmonton, ALB
American Jewish Historical Society, Waltham, MA
American Schleswig-Holstein Heritage Society, LeClaire, IA
Association for the Advancement of Dutch-American Studies, Grand Rapids, MI.
Association of German Nobility in North America, Benicia, CA
Balch Institute for Ethnic Studies, Philadelphia, PA
Bethel College-Mennonite Library & Archives, North Newton, KS
Catholic Central-Verein of America, St. Louis, MO
Center for Pennsylvania Studies (Millersville Univ.)
Concordia Historical Institute (Luthern), St. Louis, MO
Czech Heritage Preservation Society, Tabor, SD
Danish-American Historical Society, Des Moines, IA
Deutsch-Amerikanischen National Kongress (DANK), Chicago, IL
Die Pommerschen Leute, Oshkosh, WI
Family History Library, Church of Jesus Christ of Latter-Day Saints (Mormons), Salt Lake City, UT (400 plus branch libraries in large U.S. and some European cities)
Frankenmuth Historical Association, Frankenmuth, MI
German-Acadian Coast Historical and Genealogical Society, Inc., Destrehan, LA
German-American Heritage Institute, Forest Park, IL
German-American National Congress (D.A.N.K), Mt. Prospect, IL
German-American Society of Greater Cleveland, OH
German-American Society of Peoria, Peoria, IL
German-Canadian Historical Association, Inc., Montreal, Quebec
German Genealogical Digest, Pleasant Grove, UT
German Genealogical Society of America, Los Angeles, CA
German Heritage Society of Greater Washington, DC
German Historical Institute, Washington, DC
German Information Center, New York, NY
German Interest Group, Chicago Genealogical Society, Tinley Park, IL
German-Palatines to America, Harrisburg, PA
German Queries, Spokane, WA
German Research Association, San Diego, CA
German Society of Pennsylvania, Philadelphia, PA
German Texan Heritage Society (Southwest Texas State University), San Marcos, TX
German-Texan Historical Society, Austin, TX
Germanic Genealogical Society, St. Paul, MN
Germans from Russia Heritage Society, Bismarck, ND
Germantown Historical Society, Philadelphia, PA

Goethe-Institut, Ann Arbor, MI
Goethe-Institut, Atlanta, GA
Goethe-Institut, Beverly Hills, CA
Goethe-Institut, Boston, MA
Goethe-Institut, Chicago, IL
Goethe-Institut, Cincinnati, OH
Goethe-Institut, Houston, TX
Goethe-Institut, New York, NY
Goethe-Institut, St. Louis, MO
Goethe-Institut, San Francisco, CA
Goethe-Institut, Seattle, WA
Goethe-Institut, Washington, DC
Immigrant Genealogical Society, Burbank, CA
Immigration History Research Center (University of Minnesota),
     St. Paul, MI
Indiana German Heritage Society, Indianapolis, IN
Jewish Historical Society of Maryland, Baltimore, MD
Jewish Museum, Manhattan, NY
Johannes Schwalm Historical Association, Inc., Taylors, SC
Krefeld Immigrants & Their Descendants, Sacramento, CA
Lancaster Mennonite Historical Society, Lancaster, PA
Max-Kade German-American Document & Research Center (University of
     Kansas), Lawrence, KS
Max-Kade Institute for German-American Studies (University of
     Wisconsin), Madison, WI
Mennonite Family History, Elverson, PA
Mennonite Historians of Eastern Pennsylvania, Harleysville, PA
Mennonite Historical Library, Goshen, IN
Mid-Atlantic Germanic Society, Baltimore, MD
Moravian Historical Society, Nazareth, PA
National Society German Palatines in America, Camp Hill, PA
Orangeburg German-Swiss Genealogical Society, Charleston, SC
Palatines to America, Columbus, OH
Palatines to America, Indianapolis, IN
Palatines to America, Dillsburg, PA
Pennsylvania German Society, Birdsboro, PA
Pennsylvania German Society, Breinigsville, PA
Polish-American Historical Association, Chicago, IL
Polish Genealogical Society, Chicago, IL
Polish Historical Commission, Pittsburgh, PA
Sacramento German Genealogical Society, Sacramento, CA
Slovenian Genealogical Society, Layfayette, IN
Society for German-American Studies, Bettendorf, IA
Society for the History of Germans in Maryland, Baltimore, MD
Sister Cities International - Town Affiliation Association,
     Washington, DC
Steuben Society of America, Ridgewood, NY (and branches)

Swiss-American Historical Society, Evanston, IL
Swiss-American Historical Society, Norfolk, VA
Swiss Community Historical Society, Bluffton, OH
Swiss Heritage Society, Berne, IN
Texas Wendish Heritage Museum, Giddings, TX
United German-American Committee of the USA, Inc., Philadelphia, PA
Western States Jewish History, Santa Monica, CA

On the other side of the trans-Atlantic migration pipeline, organizations in Germany which actively promote good relationships between the two countries include the DVV (Deutsche Volksportverband e.V.) which operates weekly organized wandering events under the auspices of the IVV (Internationaler Volksportverband e.V.). The DVV has seventeen addresses in Germany. Similarly, the U.S. Information Service - Amerika Haus group has offices in most major German cities, as listed below.

Verlag Degener & Co. published a booklet titled *Aktuelle Themen zur Genealogie, Heft 13, Mitgliederverzeichnis 1992 der DAGV*. The booklet shows sixty-two genealogical organizations active in 1992 in Germany. The names of these worthy organizations are not repeated here.

Other German-American organizations, as well as some highly commercial publishers (Verlag) in Germany, include the following, again with apologies to any that were not identified:

Amerika Haus, Berlin
Amerika Haus, Frankfurt am Main
Amerika Haus, Hamburg
Amerika Haus, Hannover
Amerika Haus, Köln
Amerika Haus, Leipzig
Amerika Haus, München
Amerika Haus, Stuttgart
Carl-Schurz-Haus, Freiburg
C.A. Starke Verlag, Limburg/Lahn
Charles Sealsfield Gesellschaft, Herne (Ruhr)
Düsseldorfer Institut für Amerikanisches Völkerkunde, Düsseldorf
Deutsch-Amerikanisches Institut. Heidelberg
Deutsch-Amerikanisches Institut, Nürnberg
Deutsch-Amerikanisches Institut, Regensburg
Deutsch-Amerikanisches Institut, Saarbrücken
Deutsch-Amerikanisches Institut, Tübingen
Forschungsstelle Niedersächische Auswanderer in den USA (NAUSA), Oldenburg
Friedrich-Gerstäcker-Gesellschaft, Brunswick (Braunschweig)
German Wine Academy, Mainz
Goethe-Institut (main office), München
Hessischen Hauptstaatarchiv, Wiesbaden
Institut für Pfälzische Geschichte und Volkskunde, Kaiserslautern

Interdisziplinärer Arbeitskreis für Nordamerika-Studien, Johannes
  Gutenberg-Universität, Mainz
Karl-May-Verlag & Karl-May-Museum, Bamberg
Kennedy Haus, Kiel
Mennonitische Forschungsstelle, Weierhof, Rheinland-Pfalz
Steuben-Shurz Gesellschaft e.V., Frankfurt am Main
Verlag Degener & Co., Neustadt/Aisch

Art and Artists in America

The early Pennsylvanian Germans left a fine legacy of folk art, most of it either done anonymously or done by an artist whose name does not appear in one of the many standard biographical series. Thousands of artifacts were collected and retained in the Winterthur Museum. The name Winterthur was applied to an estate near Wilmington, Delaware, by James Antoine Bidermann (1790-1865), whose ancestors came from the town of the same name in Kanton Zürich, Switzerland. The Winterthur collection was begun in 1921 by a relative, Henry Francis du Pont (1880-1969), whose family name reflects its obvious French origin.

According to the authoritative 1983 book by Scott T. Swank (ed.), titled *Arts of the Pennsylvanian Germans* (W.W. Norton Co., Philadelphia), the Winterthur collection includes earthenware, glass, metalwork, textiles, fraktur, and books/manuscripts. Approximately eighty percent of the Pennsylvania German folk art can be dated as having been done between 1770 and 1840. The fraktur dates somewhat earlier.

Fraktur was apparently introduced to America by the German-Americans working at the famous Ephrata Cloister in the 1730s.

The Philadelphia Museum of Art contains another notable collection of early Pennsylvania German art. The Philadelphia Museum of Art and the Winterthur Museum published, in 1984, a catalogue of their joint collections under the title *Pennsylvania German Art, Sixteen Eighty Three to Eighteen Fifty*.

In later days, a great quantity of German-American folk art was associated with decorated cabinets, beds, chests, barns and other wooden items which came to be called symbols of Pennsylvanian Dutch (actually Pennsylvanian German).

The famed Conestoga wagon represents another type of Pennsylvania German folk art. This massive freight wagon, which was developed in Lancaster Co., Pa., had its useful period of about 1750 to 1850.

From the formal art standpoint, the 17th century was mainly a matter of survival; little formal art was conceived and virtually no known German artist left any record. The 18th century was a period of transition and adjustment; there are some scattered records of formal art, as for instance, Justus Engelhardt Kühn, who worked in Annapolis, Md., between 1708 and 1717. Businessman David Grim (1737-1826) was but one example of untrained artists who left a sparse, but documented record of early work; Grim made pen and ink sketches of scenes in New York City.

The great German migration to America during the mid-19th century of course was accompanied by numerous temporary and permanent-resident artists who had had formal training. Their record survives today in many museums in the United States as well as in Europe, although European art collections suffered extensive damage during the two World Wars.

In 1903, the University of Harvard dedicated their Germanic Museum, a museum which was devoted to modern German art, especially as it relates to student training. The proposal, which dates 1897, for the establishment of the Museum, was organized by various citizens and given real impetus in 1910 by a substantial cash donation by Adolphus Busch, a German-American brewer from St. Louis. Many other significant monetary donations were made, notably those in 1910 by Hugo Reisinger, son-in-law of Busch, in 1948-1949 by Edmée Busch Greenough, in 1953 by Eda K. Loeb, and in 1988 by Dr. Werner Otto. In 1990, the name of the museum was changed to the Busch-Reisinger Museum. The function of the museum is described in a 1991 booklet titled *The Busch-Reisinger Museum, History and Holdings*.

A relatively quick historical guide to the subject of German-American art, is given in the 1982 book by Matthew Baigell titled *Dictionary of American Art*. For cross checking data and for illustrations, the 1981 book by Milton Rugoff and Gudrun Buettner titled *Encyclopedia of American Art* is also useful. Both books are now somewhat dated.

The subject of art is broken down into six subcategories as given below.

Architects and Designers

German architects seemingly first made their appearance in America with the arrival of Leopold Eidlitz who went to New York in 1843. The family name shows a Slavic influence and indeed Eidlitz was born in Prague, in 1823.

Detlef Lienau also went to New York, this being in 1849. Lienau was from the small town of Ütersen, in Holstein, now Schleswig-Holstein, having been born there in 1818.

Paul Johannes Pelz, from Schlesien (Silesia), was another political refugee, arriving in New York, in 1851. Pelz worked for the U.S. Lighthouse Board from 1872-1877. He created a number of individualistic lighthouses on the East Coast and in the Great Lakes region. Pelz is also noted for his design, with John L. Smithmyer, of the plans for the Library of Congress, initially drawn in 1873, and submitted in modified form in 1892. Construction of the library, in general, followed his plans, but not entirely.

In more recent times, Joseph Urban achieved fame as an architect and stage designer. Urban was in the United States temporarily in 1901 and went permanently in 1911. He is best know in connection with the stage sets of the Ziegfield Follies. Among numerous other projects, Urban also was art director for the Boston Opera Co. from 1911-1914, and later for the Metropolitan Opera in N.Y.

Aline Frankau Bernstein was born in N.Y. and spent her working career, from 1920s to the 1950s, as a stage and costume designer in N.Y.

John Frederick Kiesler, a native of Vienna, went to New York in 1926. Kiesler was involved in various projects, the first of which was an exhibition at Steinway Hall. During the years of 1936-1942, he was the director of scene design at the Juilliard School of Music. Kiesler is known best for his "space stage" and "endless house" themes in stage design.

Walter Adolf Georg Gropius came to America on a permanent basis in 1937, that is, late in his career. He built his reputation as editor of the German magazine *Bauhaus* during the period of 1919-1928; this journal had a large influence on modernizing German, and later American, architecture. Gropius taught at Harvard University from 1938-1952.

Ludwig Mies van der Rohe was another latecomer, arriving either in 1937 or 1938. His architectural work was centered around Chicago.

The directory shows seventeen architects and designers of some renown. Many were associated with the first wave of refugees of the mid-19th century, while another significant group was associated with the refugees of the 1920s and 1930s.

Cartoonists, Illustrators, Genre Painters, Photographers

The best know of this group was Thomas Nast, a cartoonist and political satirist whose work appeared in early issues of *Harper's Weekly*, and from 1859-1886 in the *N.Y. Illustrated News*. Nast went from Landau, in Rheinland-Pfalz, to New York in 1846. Although the concept of Santa Claus was derived long before Thomas Nast began his career, he did much to publicize the American image of Santa Claus with his 1863 illustration of a primitive figure and with his 1881 drawing of a more modern version. Nast is best known, however, for his political cartoons and for his fight via cartoons against the corruption of Tammany Hall, in N.Y. Nast's 1874 illustrations of the Republican elephant and the Democratic donkey were among the earliest formal, printed representations of these political logos. Late in life, Nast was in the diplomatic service and died in 1902, in Guayaquil, Ecuador.

Frederick Burr Opper and Joseph Keppler achieved some fame as caricaturists with the magazine *Puck*, which was founded in 1869. *Puck* was initially written in German for Germans in St. Louis, but was soon converted to English with operations transferred to New York. Keppler was one of the founders of the magazine, which lasted until 1918. Opper joined the staff in 1881. Keppler was born in Wien (Vienna) in 1838 and accompanied his family to Missouri in 1849. Opper was born in Ohio in 1857, the son of native Austrians.

The German Wilhelm Busch (1832-1908) achieved fame with his comic strip characters "Max und Moritz". The appearance of this phenomena in 1865, in book form, was one of the primary bases for the comic books. In America, the German immigrant cartoonist Rudolph Dirks began a popular strip in 1897 which he titled the "The Katzenjammer Kids". These two authors laid the foundation for the widely sucessful growth of American comics in the 1920s and 1930s. The terms katzenjammer, as well as kindergarten, became unaltered loan words in the English language. The former term is perhaps the best translated as hullabaloo. Ironically, even today, German newspapers still do not print comic strips.

The works of immigrant illustrators Joseph Leyendecker (active 1899-1942) and William Koerner (active 1905-1938) were prominently featured in nationally recognized magazines, such as the *Saturday Evening Post*.

The two Reinhart brothers, Charles Stanley and Benjamin Franklin, working in the last half of the 19th century, were sixth generation descendants of ancestors from Alsace-Lorraine, who had arrived in Pennsylvania in 1704. Both of the Reinhart brothers were genre painters, concentrating on scenes from everyday life.

Alfred Stieglitz was born in Hoboken, N.J., in 1864. He was the son of Edward & Hedwig (Werner) Stieglitz who had come from Germany about 1855. Stieglitz became one of America's top-rated photographers and was awarded some 150 medals for his displays at various exhibitions. Stieglitz was noted for his organization of exhibits and for his popularization of this type of art.

Wanda Hazel Gág was born in New Ulm, Minn., in 1893. During the period of 1928-1941, Gág created a reputation as an artist, illustrator, and author of children's stories. One of her first books, in 1928, titled *Millions of Cats*, was a representative example. Gág was a second generation American, her parents having gone from Bohemia to New Ulm, a community known for its high concentration of German-speaking peoples. The family name apparently relfects a Slavic influence.

The directory lists nineteen individuals whose work dates from the mid-19th century and later.

Glassblowers

For over two centuries, the occupation of glassblowing in America was subject to extreme stress because of poor fuel supplies, at first wood and later coal, limited sources of relatively pure quartz sand, the basic raw material, and inaccessible markets.

According to some sources, the first German or Bohemian glass blowers in America were a group of eight individuals accompanying the Jamestown colonists in the period of about 1609. And there the record ends until over a century later.

Caspar Wistar was born in Waldhilsbach, near Heidelburg, Baden-Württemberg, in 1696, and went to Philadelphia in 1717. In 1740, Wistar started a glass manufacturing operation in Salem Co., West Jersey. Wistar was one of the early importers of technology with his use of glass blowers from Belgium, Germany, and Portugal. Wistar died in 1752. A grandson became a physician and is noted in the section on Medicine. The family name appears to have been originally Wüstar.

Henry William Stiegel was born in Köln, Nordrhein-Westfalen, in 1729, and went to Philadelphia in 1750. Stiegel had a wistful career as ironmaster, glassmaker, and townbuilder. First, he bought the Hölz iron manufacturing business in Lancaster Co., Pa. in 1858, and then developed glass making in 1764, in the same area. The town of Manheim, Pa., owes it existence to his operations. By 1774, Stiegel had overextended his credit, went bankrupt, and spent the remainder of his career in menial jobs. He died in 1785. Some of the glass blowers, in particular a group known as the Stanger family, went to work in Glassboro, N.J., about 1780.

Johann Frederick Amelung was born in Germany in 1741, and went to America in 1784. Accompanying Amelung to America were Amelung's family and sixty-eight glass workers. With this considerable group, Amelung founded the town of New Bremen, Md., a town was named after financial backers located in Bremen, Germany. The first glass furnace was operational in 1785, and the second in 1790. However, the operation was discontinued about 1795. Amelung died in 1798. In 1797, part of the workers went to work for Albert Gallatin in New Geneva, Md.

Art Historians, Teachers, Critics of Art

Sylvester Rosa Koehler was born in Leipzig in 1837, and went to the United States in 1849. He is best known as a museum curator, having been connected with the Boston Museum of Fine Arts from 1885-1900. His work included many catalogues of exhibitions of etchings. Among other books, he wrote, in 1883, *Original Etchings by American Artists*.

John Henry Niemeyer was born in Bremen in 1839, and accompanied his family to Cincinnati about 1850. Niemeyer was professor of drawing at the Art Department at Yale University from 1871-1908. One of Niemeyer's works is the 1872 painting of "Gutenberg Discovering Moveable Type."

Aline Milton Bernstein Saarinen was born in N.Y. in 1914, and made her career there. She was an influential art critic whose columns were printed in the *N.Y. Times* beginning in 1947. Saarinen was also an active TV commentator for NBC during the years 1963-1972.

The directory lists ten individuals in this category.

Painters

The directory shows a reasonably large group of sixty-five individuals who bear German family names. Most American historians cite the work of Albert Bierstadt, Emanuel Gottlieb Leutze, and Carl Ferdinand Wimar, all German-Americans who were associated with the Düsseldorf School working in Germany during the mid-19th century. Somewhat later, the München School, which centered around the German-American Frank Duveneck, gained another measure of fame.

Albert Bierstadt was born in Solingen, near Düsseldorf; he arrived in Massaschusetts in the 1830s and achieved fame as a landscape painter, especially of western scenes. Bierstadt studied at Düsseldorf and Rome from 1853-1857. Bierstadt made two trips, one in 1858 and the second in 1863, into the then western reaches of the U.S. These trips form the basis for his paintings centering around the Rocky Mountains, Indians, and buffaloes as primary subject matter. Bierstadt's paintings form an important foundation for the art collection at the Museum of Western Art in Denver.

Karl Bodmer was born in Riesbach, Kanton Bern, Switzerland, in 1809. Bodmer developed a career as an artist and engraver in Europe. He achieved fame in America during the years of 1832-1834 when he accompanied Maximilian Philip Alexander (1782-1867), Prince of Wied-Neuwied on a tour of the Midwest, up the Missouri River as far as Fort McKenzie. Bodmer was one of the earliest Europeans to study and paint Indians tribes. He also made sketches of landscapes, town views, and portraits of Americans. Bodmer's work formed the plates which accompanied the Prince's three volume work published in Koblenz during the years 1839-1841.

Katherina Sophie Dreier was born in Brooklyn in 1877. She was the daughter of Theodor and Dorothy Adelheid (Dreier) Dreier who had gone from Bremen to N.Y. in 1849. Katherine Dreier was active as an artist from 1905-1935. More importantly, she was a patron of art in N.Y. circles until her death in 1952.

Johann Ludwig Krimmel, known in America as John Lewis Krimmel, was born in 1789 in Ebingen, Württemberg. He went to Philadelphia in 1810. Krimmel specialized in portraits, but was also known as the first significant genre painter in America. His 1813 painting titled "Interior of an American Inn" (now in the Toledo Museum) is a representative example. Krimmel was the subject of at least two interesting full-length biographies.

Emanuel Gotlieb Leutze, born in Gmünd, Württemberg in 1816, accompanied his parents from Germany to Virginia about 1820. Lutze grew up in the area of Fredericksburg, Va., and worked mainly in Düsseldorf during the long spell of 1840-1859. He is best known for his oil painting of "Washington Crossing the Delaware", which was dated 1851. Ironically, the original of this famous painting was destroyed in Bremen during World War II. A likeness exists in the Museum of Modern Art in N.Y.

Hilla Rebay deserves special mention as being one of the prime movers in the foundation of the Solomon R. Guggenheim Museum in N.Y. She was born in 1890 in Strassburg, Elsaß (now Alsace) as the daughter of Baron Franz Joseph Rebay von Ehrenwiesen and his wife Antonie von Eicken. Rebay began painting in 1912 and went to N.Y. in 1927. In 1937, she was appointed curator of the Guggenheim Museum which opened in 1939. She was also its first director, beginning in 1952.

Peter Rindisbacher was born in Bern, Switzerland, in 1806 and went to the U.S. in 1821. He lived in St. Louis after 1829 and died there in 1834. Rindisbacher was one of the first to paint the Indians of the Midwest in their natural habitat, as well as scenes of wild animals.

Peter Frederick Rothermel was born in 1817 in Luzerne Co., Pa. He began painting in 1840 and developed a reputation and an historical painting. Rothermal is best known for his 1871 painting "The Battle of Gettysburg", which hangs in Memorial Hall in Philadelphia.

Pierre Eugene Du Simitiere, whose name is obviously French-related, was born about 1736 in Geneva, and went to New York in 1765. He was

known variously as an artist, antiquary, naturalist, and portrait-painter.
Jeremia Theüs, born about 1719 in Switzerland, went to South Carolina around 1739. He achieved some fame there as a portrait-painter.
Edward Troye, born in 1808 in Geneva, went to Philadelphia about 1828. During the period of 1835-1874, Troye specialized in paintings of American blood horses.
Carl Ferdinand Wimar, a native of Sieburg, near Bonn, went to St. Louis in 1843. Wimar studied at the Düsseldorf School from 1852-1857. In the late 1850s, Wimar made several trips up the Missouri River into Indian country. These trips are reflected in his paintings and photographs of the natives. A representative example is the 1859 painting titled "Indians Approaching Fort Benton". Some fifty paintings done by Wimar have been catalogued, of which seventeen were painted in Europe.

Sculptors

William Henry Rinehart, sculptor, was a great grandson of the German-town printer, Ulrich Reinhart, who arrived in America in 1733. The sculptor was born in Maryland in 1825, and died in 1874.
Elisabet Ney, sculptress, was born in Münster, Westfalen in 1833 and went to America in 1871. She eventually transferred her activities to Texas where she achieved local fame; in fact, a museum was established in Austin in her honor. Her works date from about 1850-1907. Ney was christened with the formidable full name of Franzisca Bernardina Wilhemina Elisabeth Ney.
Louis Zoellner was born in Idar, Rheinland Pfalz, in 1852 and went to New York in 1871. He grew up in the Germany's gem cutting center of Idar-Oberstein and was trained in the intricate work of carving cameos. Zoellner had an interesting fifty year career as a master cameo carver and did many cameos of famous U.S. personalities including presidents. He died in 1934, in Brooklyn.
The directory lists twenty-one individuals in this category.

TABLE 7
DIRECTORY OF ARTISTIC TALENTS

Architects & Designers
3. Bernstein, Aline Frankau (1880-1955)
1. Bluemner, Oscar Florians (1867-1938)
1. Breuer, Marcel Iajos (1902-1981)
1. Eidlitz, Leopold (1823-1908)
1. Gropius, Walter Adolf Georg (1883-1969)
1. Gruen, Victor D. (1903-1980)
1. Herter, Christian (1840-1883)
   Ittner, Theodore Carl (1864-1936)
1. Kahn, Albert (1869-1942)
1. Kessler, George Edward (1862-1923)
1. Kiesler, Frederick John (1896-1965)
2. Klauder, Charles Zeller (1872-1938)
1. Lienau, Detlef (1818-1887)
1. Link, Theodore Carl (1850-)
1. Mies van der Rohe, Ludwig (1886-1969)
1. Neutra, Richard Josef (1892-1970)
1. Pelz, Paul Johannes (1841-1918)
5. Trumbauer, Horace (1868-1938)
1. Urban, Joseph (1872-1933)
1. Wachsmann, Konrad (1901-)
3. Walter, Thomas Ustick (1804-1887)

Cartoonists, Illustrators, Genre Painters, Photographers
1. Brödel, Max (1870-1941)
1. Dielman, Frederick (1847-1935)
1. Dirks, Rudolph (1877-1968)
   Ehringer, John Whettin (1827-1889)
1. Farney, Henry E. (1847-1916)
2. Gág, Wanda Hazel (1893-1946)
1. Hahn, William (1827-1887)
3. Keller, Arthur Ignatius (1867-1924)
1. Keppler, Joseph (1838-1894)
1. Koerner, William Henry Detlap (1878-1938)
   Lange, Dorothea (1895-1965)
1. Leyendecker, Joseph Christian (1874-1951)
2. Loeb, Louis (1866-1909)
2. Mosler, Henry (1841-1920)
1. Nast, Thomas (1840-1902)
2. Opper, Frederick Burr (1857-1937)
6. Reinhart, Benjamin Franklin (1829-1885)
6. Reinhart, Charles Stanley (1844-1896)
2. Stieglitz, Alfred (1864-1946)
1. Volck, Adalbert John (1828-1912)

2. Zimmermann, Eugene (1862-1935)
   Zogbaum, Rufus Fairchild (1849-1925)

Glass Blowers
1. Amelung, Johann Friedrich (1741-1798)
1. Stiegel, Henry William (1729-1785)
1. Wistar, Caspar (1689-1752)

Historians, Teachers, Critics of Art, Museum Directors
2. Force, Juliann Rieser (1876-1948)
   Harshe, Robert Bartholow (1879-1938)
1. Koehler, Robert (1850-1917)
1. Koehler, Sylvester Rosa (1837-1900)
1. Neuhaus, Eugen (1879-1963)
1. Niemeyer, John Henry (1839-1932)
1. Oertel, Johannes Adam Simon (1823-1909)
1. Pelikan, Alfred George (1893-)
   Saarinen, Aline Milton Bernstein (1914-1972)
2. Stettheimer, Florine (1871-1944)

Painters
1. Albers, Josef (1888-1976)
2. Anschutz, Thomas Pollock (1851-1912)
2. Baker, George, Augustus (1821-1880)
1. Benziger, August Carl Nicolaus Jakob (1867-1955)
1. Bierstadt, Albert (1830-1902)
2. Blum, Robert Frederick (1857-1903)
   Blumenschein, Ernst L. (1874-1960)
1. Bodmer, Karl (1809-1893)
3. Bohm, Max (1868-1923)
   Cox, Kenyon (1856-1919)
1. Decker, Joseph (1853-1924)
2. Dellenbaugh, Frederick Samuel (1853-1935)
7. Demuth, Charles Henry (1883-1935)
2. Dreier, Katherina Sophie (1877-1952)
1. Du Simitiere, Pierre Eugene (c.1736-1784)
2. Duveneck, Frank (1848-1919)
1. Eckstein, Johann (c.1736-c.1817)
3. Eichholtz, Jacob (1776-1842)
3. Enneking, John Joseph (1841-1916)
3. Feininger, Lyonel Charles Adrian (1871-1956)
1. Frankenstein, Godfrey N. (1820-1873)
1. Frankenstein, John Peter (c. 1816-1881)
1. Füchsel, Herman Traugott Louis (1833-1915)
1. Gaugengigl, Ignatz Marcel (1855-1932)
1. Glarner, Fritz (1894-1972)
   Gottlieb, Adolph (1903-1974)

1. Grosz, Georg (1893-1959)
1. Gutherz, Carl (1844-1907)
1. Haidt, John Valentine (1700-1780)
1. Hofmann, Hans (1880-1966)
1. Holty, Carl Robert (1900-1973)
1. Huge, Jurgen Frederick (1809-1878)
1. Kaufmann, Theodor (1814-1900)
1. Krimmel, John Lewis (1789-1821)
1. Kühn, Justus Englehardt (fl. 1708-1717)
1. Leutze, Emanuel Gottlieb (1816-1868)
1. Lindner, Richard (1901-1978)
   Luks, George Benjamin (1867-1933)
1. Lungkwitz, Hermann (1815-1891)
1. Maentel, Jacob (1763-1863)
   Marr, Carl (1858-1936)
1. Marschall, Nicola (1829-1917)
   Melchers, Gari (1860-1932)
   Miller, Alfred Jacob (1810-1874)
1. Nahl, Charles Christian (1818-1878)
1. Nahl, Hugo Wilhelm Arthur (1820-1881)
1. Niemeyer, John Henry (1839-1932)
1. Petri, Frederick Richard (1824-1857)
3. Rauschenberg, Robert (1925-)
1. Rebay, Hilla (1890-1967)
1. Rindisbacher, Peter (1808-1834)
1. Roesen, Severin (fl. 1847-1871)
1. Roetter, Paulus (1806-1894)
   Rothermel, Peter Frederick (1817-1885)
2. Schreyvogel, Charles (1861-1912)
1. Schussele, Christian (1824-1879)
   Sonntag, William Louis (1822-1900)
1. Theüs, Jeremiah (c.1719-1774)
1. Troye, Edward (1808-1874)
2. Twachtman, John Henry (1853-1902)
1. Ulke, Henry (1821-1910)
1. Vianden, Heinrich (1814-1899)
1. von Iwonski, Carl G. (1830-1912)
1. Weber, Paul (1823-1916)
1. Wimar, Carl Ferdinand (1828-1862)

Sculptors

1. Bitter, Karl Theodore Francis (1867-1915)
   Eberle, Mary Abastenia St. Leger (1878-1942)
1. Eckstein, Frederick (c. 1775-1852)
5. Grafly, Charles (1862-1929)(Graefly)
1. Hesse, Eva (1936-1970)
1. Jaegers, Albert (1868-1925)

1. Jennewein, Carl Paul (1890-1978)
1. Lawrie, Lee (1877-1963)
1. Martiny, Philip (1858-1927)
1. Ney, Elisabet (1833-1907)
2. Niehaus, Charles Henry (1855-1935)
1. Plassmann, Ernst (1823-1877)
4. Rinehart, William Henry (1825-1874)
1. Rosznak, Theodore (1907-1981)
1. Ruckstull, Frederic Wellington (1853-1942)(Ruckstuhl)
1. Schuler, Hans (1874-1951)
1. Schweizer, J. Otto (1863-1955)
6. Shrady, Henry Merwin (1871-1922)
1. Warnecke, Heinz (1895-1983)
1. Zoellner, Louis (1852-1934)

Code:
1. = 1st Generation in America
2. = 2nd Generation
3. = 3rd or more Generation, etc.

Baseball, Brewers, and Other Sporting Personalities

Baseball

Baseball, which was mentioned in records as early as 1714, refers generally to an English game known as "rounders". The game apparently was played in New England in the 1700s.

Although Abner Doubleday was at one time cited as being the heroic founder, in 1839, of America's primary national sport, he is listed now merely as being a stimulus toward organized participation in the game.

In 1845, Alexander J. Cartwright drew up a set of rules for modern baseball which was adhered to by the N.Y. Knickerbocker Baseball Club. The first recorded baseball game was played in Hoboken, N.J., on June 19, 1846.

The National League, which remains the senior league in modern baseball, was established in 1876 with eight charter members, namely Boston, Philadelphia, New York, Hartford, Chicago, Cinncinnati, St. Louis, and Louisville. Interestingly, all but Boston and Hartford are known for their large German immigrant element. The German-Americans in fact provided a number of high profile baseball players.

The American Association was formed in 1882. The first modern World Series was played in 1903.

A tavern owner in St. Louis, one Chris Von der Ahe, is reported as being the first to introduce beer to the ball park. This occurred in 1881 when an early team named the St. Louis Brown Stockings was resident in that city. Other German staples were quickly adapted to the ball park. The pretzel became American in 1856, while the American version of the hamburger dates from 1889, and the American variant of the frankfurter dates from 1894. The uniquely German-American phenomena of the Cracker Jack dates from 1893. Like various other German technology, the original Frankfurt "würstchen" made its appearance at the Chicago World's Fair in 1893. These würstchen were sent to America in cans.

Baseball and breweries may seem at first like an odd combination. However, the most notable association dates from the days of brewer Jacob Ruppert, who bought an interest in the New York Yankees in 1914, and subsequently founded one of the premier baseball teams of all time. Furthermore, in 1919, Ruppert bought a tract of land in New York City from the Astor heirs and initiated construction of Yankee Stadium, a massive sports complex which was completed in 1923. Thus, the famous slogan "the House that Ruth built" should actually be "the House that Ruppert built."

The baseball-brewery owner association was further cemented in the 1950s by the Busch brewery family and the St. Louis Cardinals and by Busch Stadium in St. Louis. More recently, with the advent of the all weather stadium, the major league baseball team called the Milwaukee Brewers also points to the association.

Today, baseball and breweries retain a common thread in million dollar annual baseball salaries and billion dollar brewery and real estate operations.

In the early 20th century, baseball became America's prime symbol of pop culture. And brewers recognized that they made more money by the advertising inherent in a highly visible baseball team and the enormous crowds that sporting activities attracted.

Another key element in baseball was the Black Sox scandal of 1919. Kenesaw Mountain Landis, a jurist of note, was hired in 1920 to become the Commissioner of Baseball and to cleanse the scandal of the proceding year. Landis, in fact, reigned supreme, although fairly, from 1920-1944.

Thus it was that baseball became and remains America's premier sport, paving the way for professional football, basketball, tennis, golf, and the like.

Most of the following seventeen German-American names were taken from the roster of the National Baseball Hall of Fame, located in Cooperstown, N.Y. The selection of members for this organization began only in 1936, and thus includes personalities mainly from the 20th century baseball era. Some of the more colorful personalities are described here in more detail.

Ford Christopher Frick, born in 1894, became a prominent name in baseball executive circles. Frick was president of the National League from 1934-1951 and then became Commissioner of Baseball, a position he held until 1965. Frick was elected to the Baseball Hall of Fame in 1970.

Frank Francis Frisch, better known as Frankie Frisch, was born in New York in 1898, and died in Wilmington, Del., in 1973. Frisch was a professional baseball player of average ability, but gained fame as the manager of the New York Giants from 1919-1926, and the St. Louis Cardinals from 1926-1937. He was the son of immigrants Franz and Katherine (Stahl) Frisch. Frisch was elected to the Baseball Hall of Fame in 1947.

Henry Louis Gehrig, known professionally as Lou Gehrig, was born in New York in 1903, and died from a rare blood disorder, sometimes called "Gehrig's disease," in 1941. He played for the New York Yankees from 1925-1939, and set a record by playing in 2,130 consecutive games. Gehrig was elected to the Baseball Hall of Fame in 1939.

Charles Leonard Gehringer was born in Fowlerville, Mich., in 1903. Gehringer played second base for the Detroit Tigers from 1926-1942. Gehringer was elected to the Baseball Hall of Fame in 1949.

Harry E. Heilmann was born in Detroit in 1894, and played for the Tigers. Heilmann was elected to the Baseball Hall of Fame in 1952.

Charles Herbert Klein was born in Indianapolis in 1904. Klein was elected to the Baseball Hall of Fame in 1980.

Kenesaw Mountain Landis was born in Millville, Ohio in 1866. He was a prominent jurist who made a reputation in 1903 by levying a fine of three million dollars against the Standard Oil Co., which at that time was headed by John D. Rockefeller. Three million dollars was a considerable sum of money in those days. The given names "Kenesaw Mountain" refer to a battlefield location in Georgia where Landis' father was wounded during the Civil War. The family name Landis is a prominent name among the Pennsylvania Germans of Lancaster Co., Pa., and in the Mennonite communities of Switzerland. Landis was elected to the Baseball Hall of Fame in 1944.

Melvin Thomas Ott was born in Gretna, La., in 1908, and died in 1958. Mel Ott was a noteworthy outfielder and home run hitter for the New York Giants from 1926-1938. Ott was elected to the Baseball Hall of Fame in 1951.

George Herman Ruth, Jr., was born in Baltimore, in 1895, and died in New York in 1948. Ruth, who is known professionally as "Babe Ruth", was the son of George Herman and Katherine (Schamberger) Ruth. According to the Babe Ruth Museum in Baltimore, the sometimes quoted family name of "Erhardt" is not considered likely. Ruth started his career with the Baltimore Orioles in 1914, was with the Boston Red Sox from 1914-1920, and was the key player and main crowd drawer on the N.Y. Yankees from 1920-1934. Ruth was elected to the Baseball Hall of Fame in 1936.

Raymond W. Schalk was elected to the Baseball Hall of Fame in 1955. Schalk was born in Harvel, Ill., in 1892.

Albert Fred Schoendienst was born in Germantown, Ill., in 1923. Schoendienst, better known to his many fans as "Red" Schoendienst, was an infielder for the St. Louis Cardinals from 1942-1944, and from 1945-1956.

George Harold Sisler was born in Manchester, Ohio, in 1893. Sisler played second base for the St. Louis Browns from 1915-1926. Sisler was elected to the Baseball Hall of Fame in 1939.

Edwin D. (Duke) Snider was elected to the Baseball Hall of Fame in 1980. Snider was born in 1926.

Charles Dillon Stengel, otherwise known as Casey Stengel, was born in Kansas City, Mo., in 1890. Stengel was a player of moderate ability, who started his coaching/managerial career in Brooklyn in 1932. Stengel was best known as manager of the New York Yankees from 1949-1960, and later for the N.Y. Mets. Stengel was elected to the Baseball Hall of Fame in 1966.

George Edward Waddell was born in Bradford, Pa., in 1876, and died in San Antonio, Tx., in 1914. Waddell's career began with the Pittsburgh Pirates in 1900; thus, he is one of the oldest baseball players on this list. Waddell played for the Philadelphia Athletics from 1902-1907, and with the St. Louis Browns from 1908-1910. Waddell was elected to the Baseball Hall of Fame in 1946.

John Peter Wagner, known as Honus Wagner, was born in Mansfield (now Carnegie), Pa., in 1874. Like Waddell, Wagner's eighteen year career with the Pittsburgh Pirates from 1900-1917 was in the pre-modern era. Wagner was the son of Peter and Katrina (Wolf) Wagner. He was known as the "Flying Dutchman". Wagner was elected to the Baseball Hall of Fame in 1936.

George M. Weiss was elected to the Baseball Hall of Fame in 1971. Weiss was born in New Haven, Conn., in 1895.

Breweries

The first brewing of beer in America is popularily credited to the Englishman Sir Walter Raleigh (1552?-1618) whose "Lost Colony" in Virginia evidently made beer from Indian corn.

Early English settlers appear to have started a small brewery in Jamestown, Va., about 1620.

The Dutch West Indies Company was active in New Amsterdam (which became New York in 1664) by 1632. Records indicate that they began the first commercial brewing in America in 1633. The Dutch name Brouer Straat (translated Brewer Street) referred to the area of interest, a street which is now in lower Manhattan.

The first license to brew beer in America was issued to Captain Robert Sedgwick, in Charleston, Mass., in 1637. The Roger Williams colonists began a brewery in 1638 in Portsmouth, R.I.

A vast, unorganized literature exists which casually mentions beer brewing on a local scale throughout the American colonies during the 17th and 18th centuries. For instance, the Swedish-born Johan Bjornsson Printz (1592-1663), whose lesser noble family originated in Buchau, eastern Germany, who was Governor of New Sweden from 1642-1653, had a small brewery constructed in that colony. Another example is the German emigrant Pieter Keurlis who went to Germantown, Pa., in 1683, and began there a small brewery.

Later English notables who established and maintained small home breweries on their property included William Penn (1644-1718), Samuel Adams (1722-1803), George Washington (1732-1799), and Thomas Jefferson (1743-1826). The Penn operation began about 1683.

The German-Americans early established eastern Pennsylvania as a brewing center. A brewery run by the Moravians near Bethlehem, Pa., ran from 1749 until 1800. Henry Eckert began a brewery in 1763 in Reading, Pa.; this brewery was operated by a succession of other German-Americans until 1827.

By 1810, there were some 150 breweries in America. At that time, the minority were run by German-Americans. Henceforth, however, German brewers became increasingly common as witnessed by the Lauer family in Womelsdorf, Pa. The Lauer operation was actually begun about 1823 by Johann Georg Lauer, the progenitor of the clan in America. After the move of the family to Reading, Pa., in 1826, the operation existed on a commercial base and was run by his son, Frederick Lauer from 1835-1883. The Lauer family had originated in Gleisweiler, a tiny community now in Rhein-land-Pfalz.

Commercial brewing of beer gained impetus about 1829 when lager-type yeast was introduced from Germany. Lager beer, which contains a relative-ly small amount of hops, a flavoring agent containing a bitter, aromatic oil, was also a German import. In 1844, the immigrant Frederick Lauer, long active in Reading, Pa. as mentioned above, brewed larger quantities of lager beer. A statue was erected in 1885 to the memory of Frederick Lauer by the United States Brewers' Association; Lauer was credited for "his unselfish labor for the welfare of the brewing trade."

Franz Ruppert was the founder of the Turtle Bay Brewery, one of the earliest of the many commercial breweries in New York City. This brewery existed from 1834-1867, when it was sold. Franz's descendants then began another brewery as noted below. The Ruppert family name appropriately enough comes from Ruppertsecken, near Rockenhausen, Rheinland-Pfalz. The Ruppert family name was carried to Brooklyn in 1804, that is, during the middle of the Napoleonic Wars.

About 1847, John A. Huck, together with another German brewer John Schneider, began Chicago's first lager brewery.

The influx of German immigrants in the 1840s created the first beer brewing boom. German-led breweries were established throughout the German belt in the northern part of the United States, but especially in New York City. Thereafter, marketing competition became very fierce and very few non-Germans established or maintained breweries in the United States. By 1850, some 431 breweries in the U.S. produced 750,000 barrels of beer.

A prominent German scientist, Justus von Leibig (1803-73) developed new concepts in "animal chemistry," a matter which led to the study of processes of fermentation. In 1857, the famous French scientist, Louis Pasteur (1822-1895), presented his germ theory of fermentation. Pasteur subsequently demonstrated that the spoilage of perishable products could be controlled by a process later called pasteurization. In 1866, Pasteur wrote a pamphlet on pasteurization techniques as applied to wine, and belatedly in 1877, a similar pamphlet for beer brewing. Pasteur's work had already been adapted to the brewing industry.

In 1861, the U.S. Government initiated an income tax system as a means of financing the Civil War. And in 1862, a $1.00 tax was placed upon each barrel of beer. The tax on beer became an important source of income for the Government until the onset of total prohibition in 1919. Because of this act, thirty-seven brewers met in New York City in 1862 to form an organiza-tion which would conduct a joint voice in such matters. The organization was called initially the National Brewers Association, a name which was later changed to the United States Brewers Association, and today is the Beer Institute with offices in Washington, D.C.

The second brewery boom occurred about 1870 when control of fermen-tation in beer making was developed on a commercial scale. Thus, pasteuri-zation made bottling practical. By 1870, the number of breweries had jumped to 3,286 and reached a peak of 4,131 breweries in 1873.

However, the recession of 1873, coupled with intense competition, ever larger breweries, and the beginnings of refrigeration, caused a sharp decline in the number of breweries. By 1880, the number of breweries dropped to 2,741, even though production was up. Moreover, the initial stages of prohibition created pockets of dry areas in the U.S. The temperance movement had begun in Boston in 1826 and was slowly picking up support when, in 1846, Maine became the first state to pass statewide prohibition laws.

In 1875, Valentin Blatz, working in Milwaukee, introduced beer in earthenware containers - this bottled beer created another aspect to the rapidly developing market.

The concentration of German-Americans in 1880 is shown by the level of beer manufacturing, that is, in the key cities of New York, Philadelphia, St. Louis, Cincinnati, Milwaukee, and Chicago, cited here in order of importance. New York's 1880 beer production of almost three million barrels was about five times that of Milwaukee's annual production.

In 1887, a large group of brewers met in Chicago and formed the Master Brewers Association of the Americas. By this time, German-Americas were so dominant in the brewing industry that the proceedings of the Association were conducted entirely in German, a matter which was to last until 1901, and only then was gradually phased out.

By 1920, there were between still 1,500 and 2,000 breweries operating in the United States. Then came total prohibition which ran from 1920-1933, and on top of that, the worst depression in United States' history, which lasted from 1929-1933. The law of survival of the fittest came into play. By the end of 1933, only about 700 breweries remained operational and these were all producing non-alcholic beer and soft drinks. Many of the breweries in New York City never restarted operations with the end of prohibition, preferring to concentrate on real estate and other investment opportunities.

For comparative historic purposes, Milwaukee has had some seventy-five breweries, Chicago about 190 (none major), St. Louis about 102, and Kansas City just sixteen breweries (also none major) in its history. At the turn of the twentieth century, New York City had three major breweries (Ballantines, Ruppert, and Schaefer), but none today.

Since the mid-1930s, there have been nearly constant mergers and reorganizations of breweries. In 1989, the total number of breweries in the U.S. was 215, including fifty-eight breweries in California, a state which benefited from the microbrewery building boom.

Today, six major breweries dominate the market in the United States of which Anheuser-Busch is the largest in the U.S., and also the largest in the world. The others, in order, are Miller, Coors, Stroh's, Heileman, and Pabst.

A bird's eye view shows that family names prominent in the history of Anheuser-Busch were Anheuser and Busch. Family names associated with Miller were Best and Miller. Until well into the 20th century, Coors was associated with various members of the Coors family, Stroh's by the Stroh family, and Heileman with the Heileman family. The firm of Pabst, which was begun by a member of the Best family, was run by the Pabst family, and then by the Uihlein family. Many of the pioneering brewery names listed alphabetically, are as follows.

Eberhard Anheuser (or Anhäuser) was a native of Kreuznach, Rheinland-Pfalz. In 1860, he bought the "Bavarian Brewery" which was established a few years earlier by Georg Schneider in St. Louis. In 1864, Anheuser's son-in-law, Adolphus Busch, became a partner and the name of the brewery was subsequently called Anheuser-Busch.

Emanuel Bernheimer, who was born in Ebenhausen, Bayern, in 1817 went to N.Y. in 1844. In 1850, he and August Schmid formed the Constanz brewery. Operations went through a series of partner changes (James Speyer, Joseph Schmid) and names changes (Lion brewery), and in 1878 was taken over by descendants Simon E. Bernheimer and August Schmid. By 1895, the brewery was the second largest in New York City, producing in excess of 400,000 barrels annually.

In 1844, Jabob Best and his brother Philip Best, founded the Empire Brewery in Milwaukee which was sold to their brewmaster, Frederick Pabst, in 1866. The Best family came to the U.S. from Antwerp, but had their origin in Leipzig. Frederick Pabst was married to Marie Best.

Charles Best who was associated with the Empire Brewery from 1844-1850, began the Plank Road Brewery in Wauwatosa, Wisc., in 1850. This brewery was sold to Frederic Miller either in 1853 or 1855, and survives today as one of the big six under the name Miller's Brewery, a name it acquired in 1920.

Valetin Blatz was born in Miltenberg-am-Main, Bayern, in 1826, and went to the U.S. in 1846. Initially, he was the first brewmaster for Johann Braun's City Brewery in Milwaukee, but in 1851 took over the firm when Braun died, and changed the name to the Blatz Brewing Company. As mentioned earlier, Blatz produced the first bottled beer in America, in 1875. In 1969, the Blatz brewery became a part of Heileman.

The Adolphus Busch family is described more thoroughly in the section entitled "The World of High Finance and Big Business." The Anheuser-Busch Brewery, which got its name in 1862, has headquarters in St. Louis and is today the largest brewery in the world. August A. Busch (1865-1934) led the company during the difficult days of prohibition and the depression of 1929. He had a big hand in the repeal of prohibition. Under the leadership of August A. Busch, Jr. (1899-1989), the Busch family purchased the St. Louis Cardinals baseball team in 1953 and ran that organization as a reasonably successful sideline. The brewery-baseball association provided a strong promotional outlet for the company's primary brand, Budweiser beer. In the 1960s, a prominent St. Louis structure, the Busch Baseball Stadium, was built to house the baseball team. The family name is carried by Busch Gardens in Florida and elsewhere. The Anheuser-Busch brewery in St. Louis is in the National Register of Historic Places, Washington, D.C.

Adolph Coors was born in Rittershausen, near Siegen, Westfalen, in 1847. Coors went to Colorado in 1872, and together with Jacob Schueler, in 1873, founded the Golden Brewery at Golden, Colo. The name was changed in 1933 to the Adolph Coors Brewery. The Coors Brewery is today number 236 on the Fortune 500 list. The Coors Brewery is currently the third largest in the U.S.

George Ehret was born in Hofweiler, Rheinland-Pfalz, in 1835, and went to New York in 1857. Ehret married Anna Hasslocher, the daughter of a German-American brewer, and in 1866, began the Hell Gate Brewery in N.Y. The brewery expanded so rapidly that it was the largest in New York City in 1877, but dropped back to fourth place in 1895. By the turn of the century, Ehret, however, had shifted emphasis to Manhanttan real estate speculation and is reported to have been the second largest holder of New York City property at the time of his death in 1927. Ehret is also noted as having been a prime organizer of the N.Y. Metropolitian Opera which began in 1884.

Gottlieb Heilemann was born in Kirchheim unter Teck, Württemberg, in 1824. Heileman (dropped last "n") went to Milwaukee in 1852. Heileman and John Gund formed the City Brewery in La Cross, Wisc. in 1858. This brewery became the Heileman Brewery in 1872. Heileman died in 1878 and his widow, Johanna Bantle Heileman ran the operation until her death in 1917 (see below).

Johanna Bantle Heileman was born in Württemberg, in 1831. She eventually married Gottlieb Heileman in Milwaukee and managed the Heileman Brewery from 1878-1890, when it was incorporated. At that time, she became the first woman president of a corporation in Wisconsin, and she remained president until her death in 1917. From 1959-1987, Heileman went on a binge of acquiring many small breweries, including Blatz and C. Schmidt breweries as well as a number of bakeries. Heileman is currently the fifth largest brewery in the U.S.

Frederick Koch founded a brewery in Dunkirk, near Buffalo, N.Y., in 1888, and later also a brewery in Trenton, N.J. He produced the well known brand Black Horse Ale.

Frederick Lauer began a brewery in Reading, Pa., in 1826. By 1844, Lauer has boosted production with the introduction of lager beer to such an extent that he was cited as "the father of the American brewing industry". In fact, a statute was erected in his memory in 1885 in Reading, Pa. by the United States Brewers Association.

Jacob Leinenkugel, from Köln, established a small brewery in Chippewa Falls, Wisc. in 1867, and also one in Sauk City, Wisc. The Leinenkugel Brewery was under family operation until 1987 when it was bought by Miller's Brewery.

Francis Xavier Matt, a native of Baden, took over the Columbia Brewery in 1888, in Utica, N.Y., and renamed it the West End Brewing Co. Matt died in 1958. However, the brewery was renamed again as the F.X. Matt Brewery in 1980.

Frederich Miller was born in 1824 and died in 1888. In either 1853 or 1855, Miller took over the Plank Road Brewery in Milwaukee which was begun by Charles Best, son of Jacob Best. Miller Brewery is currently the second largest brewery in the U.S. In recent years, Miller's Brewery was acquired by the Philip Morris Tobacco Co.

Frederick Pabst was born in 1836 in Sachsen and went to the U.S. in 1848. Pabst married into the Best family in Milwaukee and became a master brewer in 1862 for the Empire Brewery. In 1866, Pabst took over the brewery and in 1889 changed the name to the Pabst Brewing Co. Pabst died in Milwaukee in 1904. His son, also Frederick Pabst, was associated with the brewery from 1893-1939. The Pabst brewery organization remains and is currently the sixth largest brewery in the U.S.

Jacob Ruppert, Jr. was born in New York in 1867, as the son of Jacob and Anna (Gillig) Ruppert. He was the grandson of Franz Ruppert, also a brewer. Jacob Ruppert, Sr. founded the Jacob Ruppert Brewery in N.Y., in 1867. In the latter part of the 19th century, the brewery was one of the top three in New York City and marketed the popular Rheingold brand and later the Knickerbocker brand. Both of the Rupperts were heavy and successful investors in New York real estate. The younger Ruppert was also a sportsman who bought the New York Yankees in 1914, and dabbled in yachting, trotters, Boston Terriers, and Saint Bernards. During the dark days of prohibition (1920-1933), the younger Ruppert turned his attention from the brewery, more and more towards sports. He made the Yankees a first rate team with the purchase of Babe Ruth in 1920, and with the acquisition of Lou Gehrig in 1925, as well as other above average players, and thus ushered in the era of modern baseball. Jacob Ruppert, Jr. never married and died in 1939 in New York.

In 1842, the brothers Frederick and Maximilian Schaefer started Schaefers Brewery in N.Y. The two brothers, who went from Wetzlar, Hessen-Nassau, in 1838/1839, purchased the Sebastian Sommers brewery, and commenced operations under the Schaefers name that was to last 140 years. The Schaefer brothers were firm believers of the old German adage that purchase of real estate was a firm investment and had significant holdings in the heart of Manhattan. Under the management of descendants, the brewery moved to Brooklyn in 1916. The brewery was sold to the Stroh's organization in 1947. In 1971, they built a modern plant in Allentown, Pa., but retained the Schaefer Beer label.

Josef Schlitz was born in Mainz and went to the U.S. in the 1850s. In 1856, Schlitz married the widow of August Krug and took over the Krug Brewery which had been founded in Milwaukee in 1849. Schlitz was lost at sea in 1875, and the Schlitz Brewery was inherited by the Uihlein family who retained the Schlitz name. The more prominent members of the Uihlein family, which was very active in Milwaukee banking and real estate, are listed in the directory. The assets of the Jos. Schlitz Brewing Co. were sold to Stroh Brewery in 1982.

Christian Schmidt was a brewer in Philadelphia in 1860. In 1863, Schmidt bought the brewery owned by Robert Courtrenny. The name of the brewery was changed to C. Schmidt & Sons in 1892. In 1987, the brewery was sold to the Heileman's organization.

Georg Schneider was born in 1823 in Pirmasens, Rheinland-Pfalz. He went to St. Louis in 1849 as a political refugee. By 1852, he was brewing beer in St. Louis, but in 1860 sold out to Eberhard Anheuser. Schneider had a number of other ventures, being the publisher of the *Neue Zeit* (1849) in St. Louis, collector of internal revenue in Chicago in 1861, president of the National Bank of Illinois in 1871, and various political roles. He was managing editor of the *Illinois Staats-Zeitung* in Chicago from 1851-1862 and was a prominent Lincoln backer.

Bernhard Stroh was born in Kirn, Rheinland-Pfalz, and went to Detroit in 1850. He established the Stroh's Brewery which today is the fourth largest in the U.S. In 1981-1982, the Stroh organization adsorbed the F. & M. Schaefer Corporation (brewers) of New York and the Jos. Schlitz Brewing Co. of Milwaukee.

Charles Henry Wacker was born in Chicago in 1856. He was the son of Frederick and Catharine (Hummel) Wacker who went from Germany to Chicago in 1854. Wacker had a multi-career as a brewer, an executive in various businesses, and city planner with a hand in the development of the Chicago Loop. As a result of Frederick Wacker's acquisition of part interest in a Chicago brewery in 1857, Charles Henry Wacker became a principal owner in the Wacker & Birk Brewing & Malt Co.. The Wacker name survives today in Wacker Drive, a well-known street in the heart of downtown Chicago.

David G. Yuengling was born in 1806 in Germany. He was one of the earliest German brewers, having started a small brewery in Pottsville, Pa., in 1829. The original German family name was likely Jüngling. Until recent years, the brewery was still owned by members of the Yuengling family and thus was considered the oldest continuously family owned brewery in the U.S.

Other Sports

A mere handful of other sporting personalities are cited below. The listing is confined to those either deceased, or in the case of Jack Nicklaus, to those who made an outstanding contribution to the development of their particular sport.

Maximilian Adelbert Baer, known to his fans as Max Baer, was born Omaha, Nebr., in 1909, and died in 1959. He was world heavyweight boxing champion in 1934-1935.

Hermanus Barkulo Duryea was born in Brooklyn in 1863. He was a descendant of Joose Durie from Mannheim who went, about 1675, to New Utrecht (now Long Island). Duryea was a prominent sportsman who was involved in yachting, horse racing, and skeet shooting.

Amelia Mary Earhart was born in Atchinson, Ks., in 1897. Her grandfather was a Lutheran minister of German descent who went from western Pennsylvania to Kansas in 1856. Earhart was an aviatrix and made her first solo flight in 1920. In 1928, she became the first woman to cross the Atlantic. In 1832, she became the first woman to fly solo across the Atlantic, which she did in about fifteen hours, and in early 1935, she was the first woman to fly solo from Honolulu to the U.S. mainland. Later in 1935, she disappeared on an attempt to fly across the entire Pacific. A statue of Amelia Earhart commemorating these significant events is located in the state capital rotunda, in Topeka, Ks.

Jack William Nicklaus was born in Columbus, Ohio in 1940. In the 1960s and 1970s, Nicklaus established numerous records in the world of professional golf.

William Steinitz was born in Prague, Bohemia, in 1836, and died in N.Y. in 1900. He went to the U.S. in 1883. He was general chess champion of the world from 1866-1896.

John Wise was born in Lancaster, Pa., in 1808. Wise became a pioneering balloonist whose first trip was near Philadelphia in 1835. In 1859, he set a distance record of 809 miles. Wise made made improvements on balloon design and safety, but drowned in Lake Michigan on a balloon flight in 1879.

TABLE 8
DIRECTORY OF SPORTING PERSONALITIES AND BREWERS

Baseball

Frick, Ford Christopher (1894-1978)
2. Frisch, Frank Francis (1898-1973)
2. Gehrig, Henry Louis (1903-1941)
   Gehringer, Charles Leonard (1903-1993)
2. Heilmann, Harry E. (1894-1951)
   Klein, Charles Herbert (1904-1956)
4. Landis, Kenesaw Mountain (1866-1944)
   Ott, Melvin Thomas (1908-1958)
4. Ruth, George Herman, Jr. (1895-1948)
   Schalk, Raymond W. (1892-1970)
   Schoendienst, Albert Fred (1923-)
   Sisler, George Harold (1893-1973)
   Snider, Edwin Donald (1926-)
   Stengel, Charles Dillon (1890-1975)
   Waddell, George Edward (1876-1914)
2. Wagner, John Peter (1874-1955)
   Weiss, George M. (1895-1973)

Brewers

1. Anhäuser, Eberhard (1805-1880), St. Louis
1. Bernheimer, Emanuel (1817-), N.Y.
2. Bernheimer, Simon E. (1849-), N.Y.
1. Best, Jacob (fl. 1844-1853), Milwaukee
1. Best, Charles (fl. 1844-1855), Milwaukee
1. Best, Philip (1814-1869), Milwaukee
1. Blatz, Valentin (1826-1894), Milwaukee
1. Busch, Adolphus (1839-1913), St. Louis
2. Busch, August Anheuser, Sr. (1865-1934), St. Louis
2. Busch, Adolphus, Jr. (1867-1898). St. Louis
3. Busch, Adolphus III (1891-1946), St. Louis
3. Busch, August Anheuser, Jr. (1899-1989), St. Louis
   Busch, Valentin (fl. 1851-1879), Chicago
1. Coors, Adolph Herman Joseph (1847-1929), Golden, Colo.
3. Coors, William K. (1916-), Golden, Colo.
3. Coors, Joseph (1917-), Golden, Colo.
1. Ehret, George (1835-1927), N.Y.
   Griesedieck, Joseph (fl. 1911-1917), St. Louis
   Griesedieck, Alvin (1894-1961), St. Louis
1. Hamm, Theodore (1825-1903), St. Paul, Mn.
2. Hamm, William, Sr. (1858-1931), St. Paul, Mn.
1. Heilemann,Gottlieb (1824-1878), La Crosse, Wisc.
1. Heileman, Johanna Bantle (1831-1917), La Crosse, Wisc.
   Huck, John A. (fl. 1840-1871), Chicago

Hudepohl, Ludwig (fl. 1883), Cincinnati
Hudepohl, Louis II (1843-1902), Cincinnati
Koch, Frederick (fl. 1888) Dunkirk, N.Y.
1. Lauer, Frederick (fl. 1835-1888), Reading, Pa.
1. Leinenkugel, Jacob (fl. 1867-1898), Chippewa Falls, Wisc.
1. Lemp, Johann Adam (1798-1862), St. Louis
1. Lemp, William J., Sr. (1836-1904), St. Louis
2. Lemp, William, Jr. (c.1862-1922), St. Louis
1. Levinger, Moritz (1851-   ), Sioux Falls, S. Dak.
Manger, George (fl. 1844), Philadelphia
1. Matt, Francis Xavier (fl. 1888-1956) Utica, N.Y.
1. Menger, William A. (fl. 1847-1871), San Antonio, Tx.
1. Miller, Frederick (1824-1888), Milwaukee
1. Moerlein, Christian (1818-1897), Cincinnati
1. Muehlebach, George, Sr. (1833-1905), Kansas City, Mo.
2. Muehlebach, George E. (1881-1955), Kansas City, Mo.
1. Pabst, Frederick (1836-1904), Milwaukee
2. Pabst, Frederick, Jr. (1869-1958), Milwaukee
2. Pabst, Gustav G. (c.1867-1921), Milwaukee
2. Ruppert, Franz, (1811-1883), N.Y.
3. Ruppert, Jacob, Sr. (1842-1915), N.Y.
4. Ruppert, Jacob, Jr. (1867-1939), N.Y.
1. Schaefer, Frederick (1817-1897), N.Y.
1. Schaefer, Maximilian (c. 1820-1904), N.Y.
2. Schaefer, Rudolph Jay (1863-1923), N.Y.
1. Schlitz, Josef (1831-1875), Milwaukee
Schmidt, Christian (fl. 1863-1892), Philadelphia
1. Schneider, Georg (1823-1905), St. Louis
1. Seipp, Conrad (1825-1890), Chicago
1. Stroh, Bernhard (1822-1882), Detroit
1. Uihlein, Georg Karl August (1842-1886), Milwaukee
2. Uihlein, Erwin Charles (1886-1968), Milwaukee
2. Uihlein, Joseph Edgar (1875-1968), Milwaukee
2. Uihlein, Robert August (1883-1959), Milwaukee
3. Uihlein, Robert August, Jr. (1916-1976), Milwaukee
1. Wacker, Frederick (fl. 1857-1882), Chicago
2. Wacker, Charles Henry (1856-1929), Chicago
1. Wagner, Johann (fl. 1840), Philadelphia
Weinhard, Henry (fl. 1857-1864), Portland, Ore.
1. Yuengling, David G. (1806-1876), Pottsville, Pa.

Other Sports
3. Baer, Maximilian Adelbert (1909-1959), (Max Baer) boxing
Earhart, Amelia Mary (1897-1937), aviator
3. Duryea, Hermanus Barkulo (1867-1916), yachting
Meyer, Louis (1904-   ), automobile racing
Nicklaus, Jack William (1940-   ), golf

Rathmann, Richard R. (1928-), automobile racing
Schneider, Louis (fl.1927-1932), automobile racing
1. Steinitz, William (1836-1900), chess
Unser, Al (1939-), automobile racing
Unser, Robert William (1934-), automobile racing
Weissmuller, Peter John (1904-1984), swimming
3. Wise, John (1808-1879), balloonist
1. Zuppke, Robert Carl (1879-1957), football coach

Code:

1. = 1st Generation in America
2. = 2nd Generation
3. = 3rd or more Generation, etc.

Pioneering Clergymen and Women

The history of religion in colonial America is largely a history of the various Protestant religions up until the time of the Revolutionary War, and for a considerable time thereafter. Control of the Atlantic migration path was directed by the Dutch merchant fleet during the early part of the 17th century; this fleet was eventually superceded by the English fleet.

With the English occupation of New York in 1664, the English became dominant landlords of the colonies along the eastern coast of North America and remained so for the next century. Neither the Dutch nor the English, both basically Protestant, encouraged either of the two other major religious groups, the Catholics and the Jews, to help settle America.

In fact, the periods of the two Revolutionary Wars, that of 1776-1783 and 1812-1815, as well as the intervening thirty-nine year interval, was marked by a lull in migration to America in which neither Jew nor Catholic was quick to fill the vacuum.

After 1820, however, Jews of many nationalities, many of German birth, and Irish and German Catholics went to America in ever larger numbers.

By mid-19th century, the Jews were to form large groups in major cities such as New York, Philadelphia, Cincinnati, and Chicago. They became major factors in certain businesses such as banking and finance, mercantile, and eventually in the entertainment industry.

During the 18th and 19th centuries, Protestant churches became increasingly fragmented and less and less unified. For instance, during the 19th century, and up until the time of the Civil War, the Lutherans, who were coincidentally mainly German and Scandinavian, divided into more than 100 separate autonomous bodies. The *Dictionary of American Biography* documents a nearly continuous series of squabbles among the Lutherans in America. Eventually, the Lutherans called for unification and did succeed in consolidating somewhat so that about twenty groups exist today. Thus, "Lutheran ", and "Reformed", are often used in a meaningless generic sense.

In the 19th century, Catholics spread throughout America and enjoyed the phenomenal influence of an overall coordination, directed for the most part by the Vatican. In fact, the Roman Catholic Church of today claims some fifty million members in North America and thus has a membership which places it far ahead of any other religious group. Irish and German Catholics were among the early 19th century arrivals. Their ranks were swelled in the latter part of the 19th century by the "new migrants," that is, by the Italians and the old multi-national Austro-Hungarian empire which was composed of the northern Slavs, the southern Slavs, the Magyars (Hungarians), and the Austrians proper, all of which are basically Catholic. All these Catholics tended to form religious and ethnic enclaves in America. This chapter is concerned only with the religion of the various groups of German-speaking persons. Their arrival in America is discussed in a somewhat chronological order. Numerically, the Lutherans (*sensus latus*) comprised twenty-seven percent of the study group; the Roman Catholic, sixteen percent; the Moravians, eleven percent; the German Reformed and Reformed Dutch, eight percent; the Jewish, eight percent; and the sixteen other groups, thirty percent.

Quakers, Mennonites and Amish

Often American publications are written under the mistaken impression that the Quakers, the Mennonites, and the Amish are closely related religious groups. The groups are in fact very distinctly separated religiously, but are grouped together here since during much of their early history, they tended to occupy the same communities in eastern Pennsylvania, intermarried, and periodically crossed the religious boundary from one group to the other.

The Quakers (actually the Society of Friends) began about 1647 in England and to this day remain overwhelmingly English. The first of the large waves of Quakers recruited by William Penn (1644-1718) went to America in 1681. The Mennonites date officially from about 1545 and had their origin in the northern part of the Netherlands, although they later incorporated large numbers of people from all parts of Germany, especially from along the Rhine. The Amish formed a splinter group of the Mennonites about 1693 in the upper part of the Rhine valley, were nearly all German-speaking, and went first to the U.S. about 1620.

The real history of the German clergy in America begins with the arrival of the "thirteen original German colonists" who helped settle Germantown in 1683. Most historians agree that the group of thirteen were originally Mennonites, living in Krefeld in the lower German Rhine, who converted to Quakerism about 1677. Some historians have argued that the basic language of the Krefeld immigrants was Dutch rather than German; at least three original documents attest to this fact.

The arrival of the group of thirteen just after the Frankfort Company representative, Franz Daniel Pastorius and his servants, has been documented many times. Twelve of the group were evidently Quakers, while one seems to have retained his Mennonite background. Pastorius was apparently a Lutheran who favored Pietism, but was sympathetic to the Quakers.

William Penn's Quakerism remained centered in Philadelphia, but spread up and down the coast so that by 1776 it was comprised of 310 churches, all mainly English. In any event, Quakerism was to remain largely an English phenomena, never gaining any significant numbers among later German immigrants. The term Quaker was an informal, but popular name for members of the Society of Friends.

The initial leader of the small German-Quaker group in Germantown, Pa. evidently was Thones Kunders from Krefeld, who provided his home for weekly meetings until the Quaker church was built in 1686.

The German Quakers provided only one other notable in the name of David Brainard Updegraff, born in 1830. He was a seventh generation descendant of one of three Op den Graaf brothers, who were part of the original 1683 colonists in Germantown.

In Germantown, Pa., the Mennonite congregation continued to grow slowly and in a decade or so, outnumbered the Quakers. The first of the notable Mennonites was William Rittenhouse who went to America in 1686. Rittenhouse was followed by Wendel Baumann and Jacob Gottshall (or Jakob Gottschalk), the latter arriving about 1701 and becoming the first real Mennonite preacher in America. In 1708, Gottshall became the first Mennonite bishop in America. About the same time, the Mennonites built their first church.

Pioneer movement continued westward in what was later to be called Montgomery County, Pa. Among the pioneers was Martin Kolb who arrived in America in 1707 and became the first Mennonite preacher at Skippack. He was followed in 1717 by his better known brother Dielman Kolb who helped establish the Mennonite congregation at Salford, also in Montgomery Co.

Another historic personality was Christopher Dock who arrived in America sometime between the years of 1710 and 1714. Dock achieved eventual fame as the "pious Mennonite schoolmaster" who taught at Skippack, Germantown, and Salford through the fifty-three year period of 1718-1771. Dock's 1770 book titled *Schulordnung* (School Management) is the earliest known book published in America about professional education.

Jacob Hertzler was born in Switzerland in 1703, and went to Philadelphia in 1749. He settled in Lancaster Co., Pa. (now Berks Co.) in 1750. Hertzler's role as the first Amish bishop in America reflects both the time of influx and the center of the American part of the Amish community. The Amish were to have a strong Swiss contingent.

The Mennonites and the Amish eventually played an active role in the development of Lancaster County Co., Pa., beginning about 1709. During the following century, a number of splinter groups emerged among the two sects. One such example is the Reformed Mennonite group, founded in 1812 by John Herr.

Throughout American history, Mennonite congregations remained centered in Montgomery and Lancaster counties, in Pennsylvania. In the 18th century, they accompanied the westward spread of pioneers, most notably to Ohio, Indiana, Illinois, and Kansas. Small groups also went northward to western New York and spread across the border into southern Ontario.

John Smith, was a descendant of Christian Smith who came to Pennsylvania from Alsace in 1829. John was born in Illinois, in 1843, and eventually became a Mennonite Bishop. His son, C. Henry Smith, born 1875, was a noted Mennonite historian who lived in the Chicago area.

Christian Krehbiel went from the Palatinate to Ohio in 1850. In 1874, Krehbiel was instrumental in the settlement of about 6,000 Russian Mennonite farmers, mostly of German background, who spread over a five county area in south central Kansas.

In summary, the accompanying directory lists two Amish, two Quakers, and fifteen Mennonites who achieved some lasting fame as Distinguished German-Americans. For instance, the Hershey, Hoover, Kraft and Rittenhouse families have Mennonite forebears.

Today, important Mennonite historical centers and libraries exist at Lancaster, Pa., Goshen, Ind., and North Newton, Ks.

German Baptist Brethren

The Brethren, who were nicknamed the Dunkers, and today are the Church of the Brethren, evidently went to America in 1720. Peter Becker was one of the early leaders.

However, Becker was overshadowed by Alexander Mack, Sr. who brought his family and the remaining entire Brethren group, never very large, from Schwarzenau, in Wittgenstein, (now State of Nordrhein-Westfalen) Germany in 1729. The senior Mack died in 1735 and his son, Alexander, Jr., took over the leadership and was a Brethren minister in America for over fifty years.

Christopher Sower II, son of the famous Germantown printer, and himself a well-known printer, was a member of the Brethren. In fact, Sower's resistance to the Revolution, apparently because of his conservative religion, led to problems with the authorities in Pennsylvania. The entire Sower family is treated more fully in the chapter entitled "The Printing and Publishing World."

Lutherans

In terms of absolute numbers, the Lutherans early formed one of the most prominent of the German religious groups, as noted earlier.

The Lutherans appear to have had their beginning in America with the colony of New Sweden which existed from 1638-1655. The first Lutheran minister in New Amsterdam (later New York) is recorded as one Jan Goetwater whose name, according to some historians, was Dutchified from the German name Johannes Gutwasser. Goetwater arrived in 1657.

Early arrivals in Pennsylvania included the two brothers Daniel and Justus Falckner, the one coming in 1694, and the other in 1700. The brothers made their mark in 1700 when they established the first German Lutheran church in Pennsylvania in an area which later became known as Falckner's Swamp, in the wilds of of what eventually became Montgomery Co. After local political problems, Daniel left Pennsylvania and served as minister to Lutherans in Raritan Valley, N.J., during the years of about 1709 to 1741. Daniel Falckner was also noted as the author of a 1702 book which stimulated immigration to America. Justus' main work was as minister to Dutch and German Lutheran congregations in the Hudson Valley and elsewhere in New York over the period of 1703-1723.

Josua von Kocherthal was born in Fachsenfeld, Württemberg, in 1669. Kocherthal's real name was Josua Harrsch (or Harsch); he assumed the name of Von Kocherthal from his birth place in the Kocher River valley. He was among the early Lutherans when he led a group of fifty others in late 1708 to the Hudson Valley, in New York. In 1710, the group achieved notoriety when they were joined by a much larger group of "Palatines." Initially, 3,086 persons began the 1910 voyage, but some 600 died en route to America and another 250 died soon after landing. Kocherthal died in 1719; his congregation, as mentioned above, was served by Justus Falckner until about 1723 and then by Wilhelm Berkenmeyer.

Wilhelm Christoph Berkenmeyer arrived in America in 1725, and was noted as the only ordained Lutheran pastor in New York before 1743. Berkemeyer married Josua Kocherthal's daughter, Benigna Sibylla Von Kocherthal. Berkenmeyer died in 1751.

Johann Martin Boltzius accompanied a group of "Salzburgers" to Georgia in 1732, and helped develop Lutheranism in that area.

The modern history of Lutherans in Pennsylvania begins with Henry Melchoir Mühlenberg who arrived in Philadelphia in 1742. Mühlenberg reorganized and consolidated the outlying congregations and provided a firm hand in community affairs until he retired in 1779. Three sons became Lutheran ministers and further added to Lutheran prestige in the area. The eldest of the three sons, John Peter Gabriel Muhlenberg, also achieved fame as a general in the Revolutionary forces; in fact, the younger Muhlenberg generations had multiple careers as politicians, college presidents, teachers, and botanists - it was an amazing family whose talents were widespread. One grandson and two great-grandsons were also prominent ministers, two being Lutheran and one joining the Episcopal church. The elder Mühlenberg was noted as a progressive in Lutheran church affairs and, with the aid of his three sons and two sons-in law, John Christopher Kunze and Emanuel Schulze, established a long tradition in this matter. This liberal tradition was to provide a focus of discontent with the arrival in mid-19th century of the large numbers of conservative Lutherans from Germany. The Muhlenberg family has been the subject of numerous family biographies.

Justus Henry Christian Helmuth arrived in Philadelphia in 1769 and for years led a congregation there. The Philadelphia congregation achieved a dubious fame in 1793 when 625 of its members died of yellow fever during an epidemic. Helmuth was also noted as a poet and hymnist.

Paul Henkel was born in North Carolina in 1754 as the fourth generation descendant of Anthony Jacob Henkel who had arrived in in the America in 1717. Paul Henkel became a distinguished Lutheran clergyman and had five sons, all also Lutheran clergymen, who scattered across Tennessee and Ohio. In 1806, a son, Ambrosius Henkel, established a printing house at New Market, Va., which was family operated until 1829, and which was the only Lutheran printing house in America during that period. Henkel family records apparently document about 100 descendants of Paul Henkel who became Lutheran ministers.

Friederich Valentin Melsheimer went to America in 1776 as a German officer mercenary. After 1779, he was exchanged as a prisoner, but stayed in America, and assumed a Lutheran pastorship in Dauphine Co., Pa. Melsheimer's hobby was entomology, which he employed to gather data for a book which became the first book on entomology of America. Melsheimer's entomology book was printed in 1806.

Johannes Andreas August Grabau was a somewhat controversial Lutheran clergyman who accompanied five ships of passengers containing about 1,000 Germans to America in 1839. Most of the newcomers eventually settled in Buffalo, N.Y.

Charles Porterfield Krauth was born in 1823 in Martinsburg, Va. and grew up to become a champion of conservative Lutheranism with congregations in Philadelphia. His much older brother, Charles Philip Krauth, born in 1797, walked a fine line as a Lutheran pastor between the conservatives and the liberals of the Mühlenberg era.

Another leader of the conservatives was Carl Ferdinand Wilhelm Walther who arrived in New Orleans in 1839, and shortly thereafter went to St. Louis. Later, Walther took up residence in Perry Co., Mo., and was instrumental in the 1846 formation of the Missouri Synod which became the symbol of Lutheran conservatism in the Midwest. Walther also helped establish a Synod in Buffalo, N.Y. in 1845, and a Synod in Iowa in 1854.

The father and son combination of Samuel Simon Schmucker (1799-1873) and Beale Melanchthon Schmucker (1827-1888) joined opposing sides of the liberal-conservative Lutheran controversy of the 1840s. The son preferred to bow to the tide of incoming conservative migrants. Both were active in eastern Pennsylvania. The younger Schmucker acquired an impressive library which was eventually acquired by the Philadelphia Theological Seminary.

The accompanying directory shows eighty-two men who achieved some fame in America as Lutheran clergy. The latter arrivals helped pioneer the upper Midwest. In fact, the entire farm settlement between Milwaukee, Wisc. and Butte, Mont. remains dominanted by Scandinavian and German Lutherans to this day. The hill country of Texas, west of Austin, also boasts a strong German Lutheran contingent which dates from the 1840s and 1850s.

Moravians

Between 1742 and about 1830, a constant stream of Moravian bishops, clergy and missionaries traveled from Germany to America. Many completed a tour of ten or so years before returning to Germany, but some left permanent families in America. The missionaries were very active among the various Indian tribes. Some paid a terrible price, for instance, Joachim Seuseman, whose wife was killed in an Indian raid in 1755. Nearly all early Moravians suffered hardships imposed by a primitive American civilization.

Henry Antes was born in Freinsheim, now in Rheinland-Pfalz, in 1701, and went to America with his parents, Philip Frederick and Anna Catherine Antes about 1720. Antes became associated with the "United Brethren" or "Brethren of Skippack", a religion similar to that of the Moravians. By 1740, Antes left the Brethren and became associated with the Moravians. Antes welcomed the arrival in Philadelphia of the Moravian leader Count von Zinzendorf in 1741 and assisted in the purchase of a tract of land which was used in the settlement of Bethlehem, Pa. In 1752-53, Antes also assisted in the purchase of about 100,000 acres of land in the South, along the Yadkin River. This later purchase became the Moravian colony of Wachovia, which was later called Salem, N.C. Henry Antes was a descendant of Baron von Blume, who for political reasons, had hellenized the family name to its Greek equivalent Antes.

One of the earliest Moravians to arrive in America was Augustus Gottlieb Spangenberg who went to Georgia in 1735. The small colony was beset by an inhospitable climate and by medical problems from the start and soon transferred its activities northward to Pennsylvania In 1744, Spangenberg helped reestablish the colony in Bethlehem, Pa., a community which serves as the center of their activity to this day. Spangenberg became a Bishop of the Church.

Peter Boehler went to America in 1738, at first to South Carolina, and eventually to Philadelphia. Boehler was also a Moravian church bishop.

David Zeisberger, went from Europe to Savanah, Ga. in 1739. Zeisberger was an unique individual who gained fame as a Moravian missionary living among the Indians for sixty-two years. Zeisberger helped erect the first church west of the Ohio River, this being in 1771.

The leader of the re-established Moravians, which in Europe was known as the Unitas Fratrum, was Count Nicolaus Ludwig von Zinzendorf. In the 18th century, the Moravians had their headquarters at Herrnhut, near Bertelsdorf, in Sachsen. Zinzendorf went from Herrnhut to Philadelphia in December, 1741 with great plans to unite all Pennsylvania German Protestants into one cohesive group. He stayed in America about thirteen months, long enough to author several books on his philosophy of church unification, but had only a modicum of success in his dreams of a united Protestant church. Von Zinzendorf's daughter achieved notoriety in her own right, as noted in the section on educators.

John Daniel Anders was typical of the "temporary" Moravian Bishops in America. Anders was born and died in Germany, but was in America from 1827-1836.

Later Moravian notables included Lewis David Schweinitz, born 1790, and his son Edmund Alexander de Schweinitz, born 1825, as well as Joseph Mortimer Levering, born 1849. Levering wrote *A History of Bethlehem, Pennsylvania, 1741-1892*. Bethlehem and Lititz, Pa. were to remain the centers of activity of the Moravians, a group which was never large. The directory lists thirty-three notable Moravians.

Reformed Dutch and German Reformed Churches

One of the outgrowths of the Golden Age in the Netherlands was the establishment of a Dutch colony in America, which lasted from 1639-1664, when it was displaced by the English. The Reformed Dutch Church maintained a precarious existence in New York and in the early days was staffed by Dutch clergy. The German Reformed Church was an offshoot of the Reformed Dutch Church.

A German, Theodorus Jacobus Frelinghuysen arrived in 1720, in New York, and was a leader of the Reformed Dutch Church. Frelinghuysen worked mainly in New York in the Raritan Valley of New Jersey.

Another German, Johann Philipp Boehm, also went to America in 1720, and became the primary founder of the German Reformed Church, in Pennsylvania. Historically, the German Reformed Church remained tied to the Reformed Dutch Church, but adapted the German language and German customs to those of its primary constituents in Pennsylvania.

Although the directory list twenty-five individuals of this group, the churches appear to have gone the route of most other religious groups in early America and developed only local importance with splinter groups arising along the way.

For example, one arrival, John Peter Miller, who went to Philadelphia in 1730, was at first associated with the German Reformed Church and later went over to the Seventh Day Baptists at the Ephrata Cloister; Miller is primarily known, however, as the leader of the famous press at the cloister and is discussed in "The Printing and Publishing World" chapter. Another, Philip William Otterbein, a 1752 New York arrival, was at first associated with the German Reformed Church and later helped found the Church of the United Brethren in Christ.

Michael Schlatter went to Pennsylvania in 1746 as a German Reformed Church official. Schlatter received a chaplain's commission in 1757 under the British authorities, but became an ardent patriot during the Revolution, materially assisting in the fight for independence.

The Jews

In 17th century America, there were a small number of Sephardic Jews, that is, Jews with Spanish, Portuguese, and even English backgrounds. The early Jews were not especially distinguished, nor of real concern here.

Migration to America by mostly conservative, northern European Jews saw an increase during the early part of the 18th century to some 3,000 individuals. Around 1728, a synagogue was established in New York, and slightly later, in Newport, R.I.

The migration trend to America by Jews continued slowly until the decade of 1840-49 when some 15,000 Jews, by some estimates, made their way to America. At that time, many Jews of German background joined the migration and brought with them the concept of a distinct type of Reform

Judaism which clashed with the indigenous Orthodox Judaism, particularily in the population centers of New York and Philadelphia.

One of the first notable Germans to arrive in America was Isaac Leeser who went to Richmond, Va. in 1824. There he became a rabbi and editor of Jewish propaganda organs. Throughout his career, Leeser maintained the role of traditional Judaism, that is conservative, in accordance with the wishes of many eastern congregations. Leeser is credited with the first American translation of the Hebrew Bible, and also with the first regular English sermon in synagogue services, both dating from 1853.

Isaac Mayer Wise arrived in America in 1846, settling at first in Albany, N.Y., and later in Cincinnati, Oh. During the 1830s, more than 30,000 Germans, including many Jews, had moved to Cincinnati, and the trend continued during the 1840s and 1850s. After his move to Cincinnati, Rabbi Wise quickly established a liberal attitude among the local Jewish population. His concepts stressed the need to blend in with the other members of the community in factors such as dress and social activity, if not religion. Wise was a moderate reformer as compared to the more conservative Jacob Leeser and the radical reforms advocated by David Einhorn, mentioned below. By the time of his death in 1900, Wise won the title of "Father of Reform Judaism in the United States."

Rabbi Max Lilienthal, had arrived in New York in 1845, where he was the chief rabbi for three congregations. In 1855, he transferred his activity to Cincinnati. Lilienthal served on the Board of Directors of the University of Cincinnati from 1872-1882. He was known for his intense Americanism and for his religious amity.

Rabbi David Einhorn, who arrived in America in 1855, is a good example of the many individuals who were political refugees fleeing from Europe. Born in Dispeck, Bayern, in 1809, Einhorn developed a career as a reform leader in Germany and in Hungary, a career which carried over to his work in the U.S. In America, Einhorn was associated with synagogues in Baltimore from 1855-1861, Philadelphia from 1861-1866, and New York from 1866-1879. His extreme radical views proved too much for the congregation in Baltimore, hence the move to Philadelphia and then to New York.

Bernhard Felsenthal, who arrived in America in 1854, and Maximilian Heller, who arrived in Chicago in 1879, were both prominent rabbis in Chicago. Felsenthal served congregations in Chicago from 1858-1887. He was primarily a conservative reformer of Judaism.

Kaufmann Kohler went to Detroit in 1869 and became an influential rabbi in that city. Kohler was a son-in-law of David Einhorn, and in 1880, after Einhorn's death, published a collected volume of Einhorn's sermons, which as mentioned above, were of the radical reform type.

The directory lists a total of twenty-four prominent Jewish individuals. Most became rabbis with many having varied interests in the field of philosophy, and many having part time occupations as teachers, scholars, writers, and historians.

Roman Catholics

In 1604, a temporary Roman Catholic chapel was established off the coast of Maine, evidently by the French. A more permanent settlement was organized in 1608, in Quebec, and became the base for Jesuit missionaries. In 1669, Jacques Marquette (1637-1675) began the French Catholic push into the Great Lakes region.

George Calvert (ca. 1580-1632), was the first Baron Baltimore and an English Catholic convert; his sons were proprietors of Maryland until 1715. The Calverts paved the way in 1634 for a small British Catholic colony in Maryland. However, Catholicism was banned in general in the colonies from 1654 to 1781.

Spanish Catholic settlements in America date from 1565 when such a colony was settled in St. Augustine, Fla. The Spanish spread along the Gulf Coast into areas that later became Alabama and Mississippi. Spanish Catholics were active also in the southwest, in the area that became Texas and New Mexico.

A French Catholic, Robert Cavalier, Sieur de La Salle (1643-1687) was active in the Mississippi Valley, in the Great Lakes area from 1678 to 1682, and in Louisiana in 1685.

French Catholic settlements were set up in Biloxi in 1697, in Mobile in 1702, and in New Orleans in 1718. The religion spread up the Mississippi River to St. Louis.

The Spaniard, Father Junipero Serra (1713-1784) began his work in California in 1769 and eventually established a series of nine missions scattered along the coast.

Before the Revolutionary War in America, migratory German and Austrian Catholics were encouraged to go to eastern Europe rather than to the west. Some exceptions are as follows.

The enterprising Roman Catholic missionary, Theodore Schneider, seems to have been the first prominent German Catholic in America. Schneider was born in Geinsheim, near Speyer, and went to Philadelphia in 1741.

A German Jesuit missionary, Ferdinand Farmer, original family name Steinmeyer, from Swabia (Bayern) went to America in 1752, and settled in Lancaster, Pa. In 1758, Farmer moved to Philadelphia, and about 1775, organized the first Catholic congregation in New York City.

In 1769, following the Seven Years' War (1756-1763), Britain took much of the territory in America claimed by France and exchanged Florida for Cuba. The Catholics were again forced to curtail activities in these new English territories.

After the Revolutionary War (1776-1783), Catholics began a slow, but general migration to America, led by Bishop John Carroll.

Two other German Catholic missionaries, Lawrence Graessl and Peter Heilbrun, settled in Philadelphia, in 1787.

Anthony Kohlmann, born in Kaiserberg, Alsace, in 1771, was administrator of the Diocese of New York from 1808-1814. At that time, there were about 14,000 Catholics in New York. From 1815-1824, Kohlmann was associated with Georgetown College. Kohlmann left America in 1824 and died in Rome in 1836.

Frederick Rese, who became a Roman Catholic prelate, arrived in Cincinnati about 1824, where he achieved distinction as the first German priest in the Midwest. Rese was followed in Cincinnati in 1831 by Frederic Baraga, a native of Slovenia. Rese (who wrote his name Résé) was born in the province of Hannover to Johann Gotfried & Caroline (Alrutz) Reese. From 1833-1837, he was bishop in Detroit and was the first German bishop there.

New York Catholics welcomed the arrival of John Martin Henni in 1828, John Stephen Raffeiner in 1833, Peter Henry Lembe in 1834, and John Nepomucene Neumann in 1836. The arrival of these four individuals reflects the ever increasing strength of the Catholic element among the German immigrants, and equally important, the shift of the dominant port of disembarkation from Philadelphia to New York. By 1790, New York City was the most populous city in the U.S. with about 32,000 people. The immigrant boom swelled its population to 197,000 in 1830 and to 942,000 in 1870. Significantly, the Erie Canal across New York had been completed in 1825 and provided a key link to the West. The vast expansion of New York port facilities reflected the establishment of this link.

Catholics in Baltimore greeted Joseph Helmpraecht in 1834, while the Catholics of Pittsburgh received Leander Schneer about 1840.

The great tide of Germans in the 1840s and 1850s brought with them a proportionate number of Catholic clergy.

In more recent years, feminine personalities appear to have gained a slight entry into a basically man's world. One notable example is Mary Katherine Drexel, who was born in Philadelphia in 1858. She was the daughter of Frances Anthony and Hannah Jane (Langstroth) Drexel of the former Austrian banking family. Sister Drexel was the founder and leader of a religious order called the Sisters of the Blessed Sacrament for Indians and Colored People, which was organized in 1907. She headed the order until 1937. Sister Drexel was also instrumental in the founding of Xavier University, which was one of the first black universities in the U.S.

There are a total of fifty notable Roman Catholic clergy listed in the following directory.

Protestant Episcopalians

One individual stands out in a group which contained few of German background. He was James Lloyd Breck, born in Philadelphia in 1818. Breck's career was as an Episcopal missionary priest in the then relatively wild territories of Wisconsin and Minnesota. Breck's career spanned the thirty-five year period of 1841-1876.

Eleven Protestant Episcopalians are listed in the directory.

Reformed Presbyterians

One of the earliest of this group was John Joachim Zubly, who went to Purrysburg, S.C. in 1744. In his later years, Zubly gained fame as one of those who opposed a complete break with Great Britain during the events leading up to the Revolutionary War.

Joseph Samuel Christian Frederick Frey was part Presbyterian, part Baptist clergyman, an author, and the son of a Jewish father. Frey went to New York from Bayern in 1816.

Another unique individual was Isidor Loewenthal, son of Jewish ancestors, who arrived in N.Y. as a political refugee in 1846. He became a Presbyterian missionary.

The group of early Presbyterian notables was relatively small, numbering only seventeen individuals as noted in the directory.

United Brethren in Christ

The group was founded about 1767 by Martin Boehm and others; it was one of many splinter groups arising in Lancaster Co., Pa. and never became very large. Boehm was born in Lancaster Co., Pa., as the son of Jacob, a Mennonite from the Palatinate. He grew up as a Mennonite and eventually became a Mennonite bishop, but was a member of the Brethren from 1767, and bishop from 1800 until his death in 1812.

Seven from the United Brethren in Christ are listed in the directory.

Methodists and Methodist Episcopalians

Barbara Heck, maiden name Ruckle, was born in Ireland in 1734 as the daughter of a member of the oft-cited 1709 large Palatine refugee group. She went to New York in 1760, and to Canada about 1776. While in America, she helped launch the Wesleyan movement, and thereby gained the title of "Mother of Methodism in America."

William Nast, born in Stuttgart in 1807, went to Harrisburg, Pa. in 1828. He is cited as the founder of the first German Methodist Church in America, this being in 1838 in Cincinnati. His son was the famous publisher, Condé Nast, listed in "The Printing and Publishing World" section.

Methodism was never very strong among the Germans; only twelve individuals are cited in the directory.

Evangelicals

The Evangelical group is very small, comprising five individuals worthy of some note.

Karl Paul Reinhold Niebuhr, born 1892, died 1971, achieved fame as a historian and liberal Christian through his many publications and newspaper articles. During the period he was at the Union Theological Seminary, from 1928-1960, his influence upon other philosophers was outstanding.

Unitarians

Three Unitarians are listed in the directory.

Disciples of Christ

Samuel Klinefelter Hoshour was born in Heidelburg Township, York Co., Pa., in 1803. He was initially a Lutheran, but converted to the Disciples of Christ and had a varied career as a clergyman and pioneer educator. Hoshour was a fifth generation descendant of the immigrant who went to America from Alsace in the early 18th century. The family name is likely Hausauer derived from the Hausauerbach (Hausauer Brook) in the northern part of Alsace.

Three individuals of this denomination are listed in the directory.

Franciscans

Zephyrin Engelhardt was born in Hildesheim, then in the province of Hannover, in 1851, and went to New York in 1852. He became a Franciscan missionary to the Indians in Kentucky and was a historian of some note, writing a history of the missions in the United States.

Baptists

Four Baptists are listed in the directory. The most noteworthy of the group is Walter Rauschenbusch, born 1861 in Rochester, N.Y., and died there in 1918. Rauschenbusch taught at the Rochester Theological Seminary from 1897-1918. He achieved fame from a 1907 book titled *Christianity and the Social Crisis*. Rauschenbusch's father, the Rev. Augustus Rauschenbusch was a political refugee who went to the U.S. in 1848.

Independent Evangelists

One classic example among individuals of German background stands out. This was William Ashley Sunday, better known to a large following as Billy Sunday. He was the son of a Pennsylvania German, whose family name apparently was Sonntag. Billy Sunday started his career as a baseball player, playing for Chicago, Pittsburgh, and Philadelphia teams between 1883 and 1891. During the period of 1896-1935, he developed an evangelistic career in the Chicago area with an ultraconservative outlook; his most important period was the era of 1910 to 1920.

Communitarians

During American history, more than 200 communes have been formed, mainly in New York, Pennsylvania, and Ohio, but also in many scattered localities elsewhere. Many of these communes were religiously oriented.

The history of these interesting societies has been described in detail by Charles Nordhoff, himself a German-American, in 1875, under the title *The Communistic Societies of the United States* (Harper & Bros., N.Y.). The Nordhoff book was reprinted in 1965 and in 1966. Another early, useful historical source is the 1878 publication by William Alfred Hinds titled *American Communities and Co-Operative Colonies*. Hinds produced a second, revised edition in 1902, and a third, expanded edition in 1908, the latter two published by Charles H. Kerr & Co., Chicago.

One of the earliest communal societies was that formed by Beissel. Johann Konrad Beissel was born in Baden in 1690, and came to America in 1720. In 1732, Beissel founded a colony of Seventh Day Baptists in Ephrata, Lancaster Co., Pa., and was its leader from 1732-1768. The group was related to the German Baptist Brethren, discussed earlier. The Ephrata group was informally known as the Ephrata Brethren, as the Solitary Brethren, as the Ephrata Cloister, and by various other names. The cloister achieved fame for its printing and publishing activities as noted in that section, and also for its music. Beissel's personal fame was as the composer of some 1,000 hymns.

Another early communal society was that of the Schwenkenfelders, named after Kaspar Schwenkfeld, a native of Silesia and an individual who was a 16th century contemporary of Martin Luther. The group went to Philadelphia in 1734. At maximum strength, in 1909, they had about 2,000 followers. Today, they maintain a small, but historically important library in Pennsburg, Pa.

The English Shakers, an outgrowth of the English Quakers, formed their first colony in New York in 1774. The Shakers eventually had about twenty colonies scattered in eight states. These colonies have virtually died out. The Shakers left a well known legacy in their style of furniture which tends toward elegant simplicity.

Johann Georg Rapp was born in Ipfingen, Württemberg, in 1757, and went to Butler, Pa. in 1803. The Harmony Society (Harmonie Gesellschaft) originated in Germany about 1785. Three shiploads of followers came over in 1804, and many others in 1805. The group, which became known as the Harmony Society from its initial location in Harmony, Pa., transferred to a second location in New Harmony, Ind., from 1814-1825, and moved to its final location in Economy, Pa. The society, which went by the informal name of the Rappites, was also very successful financially. However, like many groups of this type, the Harmony Society was a firm believer in celibacy and when the leaders died, the groups tended to become extinct. The Harmony Society died out apparently about 1905.

Joseph Michael Bimeler (original family name Baümler) was born in Württemberg about 1778, and went to Philadelphia in 1817. Bimeler founded the Separatist Society in Zoar, Oh., a society which lasted until about 1898.

Christian Metz was born in Neuwied, along the Rhine, in 1794, and went to Buffalo, N.Y. in 1842. He became the leader of a communistic group called the Community of True Inspiration, better known today as the Amana

Society with its location in Amana, Iowa. When Metz died in 1867, effective leadership in the group was assumed by Barbara Heinemann, who lived until 1883. The community adopted new ethics in 1932. Of the more than 200 communistic groups arising in America, the Amana Society today is the most active and remains one of the most financially successful through its ventures into manufacturing.

Two other German communal societies included the "Ebenezer settlers" who went to West Seneca, N.Y. in the 1840s, and the Bethel German Communal Company at Bethel, Mo. The Bethel Society was founded by Wilhelm Keil in 1844, and had branches in Bethel, Mo. and Aurora, Or. The Bethel community disbanded upon the death of the founder in 1877.

TABLE 9
DIRECTORY OF CLERGY

Amish
1. Hertzler, Jacob (1708-1786)
   Yoder, John K. (1824-1906)

Baptist
2. Bickel, Luke Washington (1866-1917)
1. Rauschenbusch, Karl Augustus (1816-1899)
2. Rauschenbusch, Walter (1861-1918)
10. Tupper, Henry Allen (1828-1902)

Communitarian
1. Beissel, Johann Conrad (1690-1768), Ephrata, Pa.
1. Bimeler, Joseph Michael (c. 1778-1853), Zoar, Oh. (Bäumler)
1. Heinemann, Barbara (1795-1883), Amana, Ia.
1. Keil, Wilhelm (1811-1877), Bethel, Me. & Aurora, Or.
1. Metz, Christian (1794-1867), Amana, Ia.
1. Rapp, Johann Georg (1757-1847), Harmony, Oh.
   & Economy, Pa.

Disciples of Christ
5. Hoshour, Samuel Klinefelter (1803-1883)
1. Loos, Charles (1823-1912)
3. Zollars, Ely Vaughan (1847-1916)

Evangelical
1. Esher, John Jacob (1823-1901)
   Miller, George (1774-1816)
2. Niebuhr, Karl Paul Reinhold (1892-1971)
1. Rieger, Johann Georg Joseph Anton (1811-1869)
2. Seybert, John (1791-1860)

Franciscan
1. Engelhardt, Zephyrin (1851-1934)

German Baptist Brethren (now Church of the Brethren)
1. Becker, Peter (1687-1758)
1. Mack, Alexander, Sr. (1679-1735)
1. Mack, Alexander, Jr. (1712-1803)

Independent Evangelists
3. Sunday, William Ashley (1862-1935)(Sonntag)

Jewish
1. Adler, Felix (1851-1933)

1. Adler, Samuel (1809-1891)
1. Deutsch, Gotthard (1859-1921)
1. Einhorn, David (1809-1879)
1. Felsenthal, Bernhard (1822-1908)
1. Gottheil, Gustav (1827-1903)
1. Grossman, Louis (1863-1926)
1. Gutheim, James Koppel (1817-1886)
1. Heller, Maximilian (1860-1929)
1. Hirsch, Emil Gustav (1851-1923)
1. Jastrow, Marcus (1829-1903)
1. Jastrow, Morris (1861-1921)
1. Kalisch, Isidor (1916-1886)
1. Kallen, Horace Meyer (1882-1874)
1. Kohler, Kaufmann (1843-1926)
1. Krauskopf, Joseph (1858-1923)
1. Leeser, Isaac (1806-1868)
1. Lilienthal, Max (1815-1882)
1. Mielziner, Moses (1828-1903)
1. Schindler, Solomon (1842-1915)
2. Szold, Henrietta (1860-1945)
1. Wise, Aaron (1844-1896)
1. Wise, Isaac Mayer (1819-1900)
1. Wise, Stephan Samuel (1874-1949)

Lutheran
6. Bachman, John (1790-1874)
4. Baugher, Henry Lewis (1804-1868)
1. Berkenmeyer, Wilhelm Christoph (1686-1751)
1. Boltzius, Johann Martin (1708-1765)
1. Deindörfer, Johannes (1828-1907)
1. Demme, Charles Rudolph (1795-1863)
1. Falckner, Daniel (1666-c.1741)
1. Falckner, Justus (1672-1723)
1. Fritschel, Conrad Sigmund (1833-1900)
1. Fritschel, Gottfried Leonhard Wilhelm (1836-1889)
1. Geissenhainer, Frederick Wilbono (1771-1838)
1. Grabau, Johannes Andreas August (1804-1879)
2. Gräbner, August Lawrence (1849-1904)
4. Greenwald, Emanuel (1811-1885)
1. Grossman, Georg Martin (1823-1897)
1. Hartwig, Johann Christoph (1714-1796)
1. Hazelius, Ernest Lewis (1777-1853)
1. Helmuth, Justus Henry Christian (1745-1825)
4. Henkel, Paul (1754-1825)(Henckel)
5. Henkel, Philip (1779-1883)
5. Henkel, David (1795-1831)
5. Henkel, Andrew (1790-1870)

5. Henkel, Charles (1798-1841)
5. Henkel, Ambrose (1786-1870)
1. Heyer, John Christian Frederick (1793-1873)
1. Hoenecke, Gustav Adolf Felix Theodor (1835-1908)
1. Hoffmann, Francis Arnold (1822-1903)
   Horn, Edward Traill (1850-1915)
3. Jacobs. Michael (1808-1871)
1. Keyl, Ernst Gerhard Wilhelm (1804-1872)
1. Kocherthal, Josua Von (1669-1719) (Josua Harrsch
   or Harsch)
2. Krauth, Charles Philip (1797-1867)
3. Krauth, Charles Porterfield (1823-1883)
   Kugler, Anna Sarah (1856-1930)
1. Kunze, John Christopher (1749-1807)
1. Kurtz, John Nicholas (c.1720-1794)
3. Kurtz, Benjamin (1795-1865)
   Lochman, John George (1773-1826)
3. Loy, Matthias (1828-1915)
1. Mann, William Julius (1819-1892)
1. Martin, John Nicholas (c.1725-1795)
2. Mayer, Philip Frederick (1781-1858)
1. Melsheimer, Friederich Valentin (1749-1814)
1. Moldehnke, Edward Frederick (1836-1904)
2. Morris, John Gottlieb (1803-1895)
1. Mühlenberg, Henry Melchoir (1711-1787)
2. Muhlenberg, John Peter Gabriel (1746-1807)
2. Muhlenberg, Frederick Augustus Conrad (1750-1801)
2. Muhlenberg, Gotthilf Henry Ernest (1753-1815)
3. Muhlenberg, Henry Augustus Philip (1782-1844)
4. Muhlenberg, Frederick Augustus (1818-1901)
2. Niebuhr, Helmut Richard (1894-1962)
1. Pieper, Franz August Otto (1852-1931)
1. Quitman, Frederick Henry (1760-1832)
2. Sadtler, John Philip Benjamin (1820-1901)
1. Schaeffer, Frederick David (1760-1836)
2. Schaeffer, Frederick Christian (1792-1821)
2. Schaeffer, David Frederick (1787-1837)
3. Schaeffer, Charles William (1813-1896)
3. Schmauk, Theodor Emanuel (1860-1920)
1. Schmidt, Friedrich August (1837-1928)
1. Schmucker, John George (1771-1854)
2. Schmucker, Samuel Simon (1799-1873)
3. Schmucker, Beale Melanchthon (1827-1888)
2. Schodde, George Henry (1854-1917)
   Schultz, John Christian (to America 1732)
   Seip, Theodore Lorenzo (1842-1903)
   Seiss, Joseph Augustus (1823-1904)

1. Seyffarth, Gustavus (1796-1885)
   Shober, Gottlieb (1756-1838)
1. Spaeth, Philip Friedrich Adolph Theodor (1839-1910)
2. Sprecher, Samuel (1810-1906)
1. Stöckhardt, Karl George (1842-1913)
1. Stoever, John Caspar (c. 1685-1739)
1. Stork, Charles Augustus Gottlieb (1764.1831) (Storch)
1. Stuckenberg, John Henry Wilbrandt (1835-1903)
   Unangst, Erias (1824-1903)
5. Valentine, Milton (1825-1906)
1. Wackerhagen, Augustus (1774-1865)
1. Walther, Carl Ferdinand Wilhelm (1811-1884)
6. Weidner, Revere Franklin (1851-1915)
   Wenner, George Unangst (1844-1934)

Mennonite

5. Bowman, Moses S. (1819-1898)
1. Dock, Christopher (c.1698-1771)
4. Eby, Benjamin (1785-1853)
   Eby, Peter (1763-1843)
   Gingerich, Michael (1792-1862)
1. Gottshall, Jacob (1666-c.1763)
4. Herr, John (1781-1850)
1. Kolb, Dielman (1691-1756)
1. Kolb, Martin (1680-1761)
1. Krehbiel, Christian (1832-1909)
1. Rittenhouse, William (1644-1708)
   Shoemaker, Joseph S. (1854-1936)
2. Smith, John (1843-1906)
3. Smith, C. Henry (1875-1948)
   Yoder, Christian Z. (1845-1939)

Methodist

2. Albright, Jacob (1759-1808)
5. Appenzeller, Henry Gerhard (1858-1902)
4. Boehm, Henry (1775-1875) (Böhm)
1. Cramer, Michael John (1835-1898)
3. Embury, Philip (1728-1773)
1. Heck, Barbara (1734-1804)
1. Jacoby, Ludwig Sigmund (1813-1874)
1. Lyon, John Christian (1802-1868)

Methodist Episcopal

5. Hartzell, Crane (1842-1928)
4. Mood, Francis Asbury (1830-1884)
1. Nast, William (1807-1899)
3. Newman, John Philip (1826-1899)

Moravian

1. Anders, John Daniel (1771-1847)
1. Antes, Henry (1701-1755)
1. Benade, Andrew (1769-1859)
1. Boehler, Peter (1712-1775)
1. Cammerhoff, Johann Christopher Friedrich (1721-1751)
1. Ettwein, John (1721-1802)
1. Graff, John Michael (1714-1782)
1. Grube, Bernhard Adam (1715-1808)
2. Heckwelder, John Gottlieb Ernestus (1743-1823)
1. Herman, Johann Friedrich Gottlieb (1789-1854)
1. Jungman, John George (1720-1808)
1. Klingsohr, John Augustus (1746-1798)
1. Lembke, Francis Christian (1704-1798)
8. Levering, Joseph Mortimer (1849-1908)
   Luckenbach, Abraham (1777-1854)
1. Mack, John Martin (1715-1784)
1. Muenster, Paul (1716-1792)
1. Neisser, George (1715-1784)
1. Nitschmann, David (1696-1772)
1. Post, Christian Frederick (c.1710-1785)
1. Pyrleus, John Christopher (1713-1779)
1. Reichel, Charles Gotthold (1751-1825)
3. Reichel, William Cornelius (1824-1876)
   Reinke, Samuel (1791-1875)
1. Rundt, Charles Godfrey (1713-1764)
1. Schultze, Augustus (1844-1918)
2. Schweinitz, Lewis David (1790-1824)
3. Schweinitz, Edmund Alexander de (1825-1887)
1. Seuseman, Joachim (- 1772)
1. Spangenberg, Augustus Gottlieb (1704-1792)
   Wolle, Peter (1792-1871)
1. Zeisberger, David (1721-1808)
1. Zinzendorf, Nicolaus Ludwig von, Count (1700-1760)

Protestant Episcopal (Episcopal, Episcopalian)

   Breck, James Lloyd (1818-1876)
1. Esher, John Jacob (1823-1901)
3. Kemper, Jackson (1789-1870)
1. Mombert, Jacob Isidor (1829-1913)
4. Muhlenberg, William Augustus (1796-1877)
1. Minnigerode, Karl Friedrich Ernst (1814-1894)
   Nies, James Buchanan (1856-1922)
3. Odenheimer, William Henry (1817-1879)
1. Rieger, Johann Georg Joseph Anton (1811-1869)
2. Schroeder, John Frederick (1800-1857)
4. Tyson, Stuart Lawrence (1873-1932)

Quaker
1. Kunders, Thones (c.1645-1729)
7. Updegraff, David Brainard (1830-1894)

Reformed Dutch & German Reformed Churches
   Apple, Thomas Gilmore (1829-1898)(Appel, Apfel)
   Bausman, Benjamin (1824-1909)
1. Boehm, Johann Philipp (1683-1749)
   Bomberger, John Henry Augustus (1817-1890)
1. Bucher, John Conrad (1730-1780)
6. Dubbs, Joseph Henry (1838-1910)
1. Frelinghuysen, Theodorus Jacobus (1691-c.1748)
5. Gerhart, Emanuel Vogel (1817-1904)
1. Goetschius, John Henry (1718-1774)
4. Good, Jeremiah Haak (1822-1888)
5. Good, James Isaac (1850-1924)
1. Gros, John Daniel (1738-1812)
4. Harbaugh, Henry (1817-1867)
6. Hartranft, Chester David (1839-1914)
1. Helffenstein, John Aalbert Conrad (1748-1790)
1. Hendel, John William (1740-1798)
1. Herman, Lebrecht Frederick (1761-1848)
2. Mayer, Lewis (1783-1849)
1. Meyer, Hermanus (1733-1838)
2. Milledoler, Philip (1775-1852)
1. Otterbein, Philip William (1726-1813)
1. Rieger, Johann Bartholomeus (fl. 1731)
4. Rupp, William (1839-1904)
1. Schlatter, Michael (1716-1790)
1. Weiss, Georg Michael (1696-1763) (Weitzius)

Reformed-Presbyterian
   Beman, Nathan Signey Smith (1785-1871), Presbyterian
   Fisher, Daniel Webster (1838-1913), Presbyterian
1. Frey, Joseph Samuel Christian Frederick (1771-1850),
   Presbyterian
2. Good, Adolphus Clemens (1856-1894), Presbyterian
1. Loewenthal, Isidor (c.1827-1864), Presbyterian
   Machen, John Gresham (1881-1937), Presbyterian
7. Peters, Madison Clinton (1859-1918, Presbyterian
3. Ruffner, Henry (1790-1861), Presbyterian
4. Ruffner, William Henry (1824-1908), Presbyterian
1. Schauffler, William Gottlieb (1798-1883), Congregationalist
2. Schauffler, Henry Albert (1837-1905), Congregationalist
   Schenck, Ferdinand Schureman (1845-1925), Reformed
   Church in America
   Schneider, Benjamin (1807-1877), Presbyterian

3. Stahr, John Summers (1841-1915), Reformed Church
3. Winebrenner, John (1797-1860), Churches of God
   Wisner, William (1782-1871), Presbyterian
1. Zubly, John Joachim (1724-1781), Presbyterian

Roman Catholic
1. Bapst, John (1815-1887) (Jesuit)
1. Behrens, Henry (1815-1895) (Jesuit)
1. Blenk, James Hubert (1856-1917)
2. Drexel, Mary Katherine (1858-1955)
   Dwenger, Joseph (1837-1893)
1. Farmer, Ferdinand (1720-1786) (Jesuit)
1. Flasch, Kilian Caspar (1831-1891)
1. Ganss, Henry George (1855-1912)
1. Gmeiner, John (1847-1913)
1. Graessl, Lawrence (1753-1793)
4. Haas, Francis Joseph (1899-1953)
2. Hecker, Isaac Thomas (1819-1888)
1. Heiss, Michael (1818-1890)
1. Heilbrun, Peter (1739-1816)
1. Helmpraecht, Joseph (1820-1884) (Redemptorist)
1. Henni, John Martin (1805-1881)
1. Jouin, Louis (1818-1890)
1. Katzer, Frederic Xavier (1844-1903)
1. Keller, Joseph Edward (1827-1886)
1. Kohlmann, Anthony (1771-1836)
3. Lambing, Andrew Arnold (1842-1918)
1. Lemke, Peter Henry (1796-1882)
1. Maas, Anthony J. (1858-1927)
1. Marty, Martin (1834-1896) (Benedictine)
1. Menetrey, Joseph (1812-1891) (Jesuit)
1. Messner, Sebastian Gebhard (1847-1930)
2. Michel, Virgil George (1890-1938)
1. Ming, John Joseph (1838-1910)
2. Moeller, Henry (1849-1925)
1. Moosmüller, Oswald William (1832-190l)
   Mundelein, George William (1872-1939)
1. Neumann, John Nepomucene (1811-1860)
   Odenbach, Frederick Louis (1857-1933)
1. Ortznsky, Stephen Soter (1866-1916)
1. Raffeiner, John Stephen (1785-1861)
1. Rese, Frederick (1791-1871)
1. Reuter, Dominic (1856-1933)
1. Riepp, Maria Sybilla (1825-1862)
2. Rigge, William Francis (1857-1927)
1. Roth, John (1726-1791)
1. Saenderl, Simon (1800-1879)

1. Schneider, Theodore (1703-1764)
1. Schneer, Leander (1836-1920)
1. Schrembs, Joseph (1866-1945)
1. Stang, William (1854-1907)
2. Stehle, Aurelius Aloyius (1877-1930)
   Weigel, Gustave (1906-1964)
2. Wigger, Winand, Michael (1841-1901)
1. Wimmer, Boniface (1809-1887)
1. Wolf, Innocent William (1843-1922)
2. Zahm, John Augustine (1851-1921)

Unitarian
3. Weiss, John (1818-1879)
2. Wendte, Charles William (1844-1931)
   Wieman, Henry Nelson (1884-1975)

United Brethren in Christ
4. Berger, Daniel (1832-1920)
2. Boehm, Martin (1725-1812)
4. Flickinger, Daniel Kumler (1824-1911)
4. Kephart, Ezekiel Boring (1834-1906)
4. Kephart, Isiah Lafayette (1832-1908)
2. Kumler, Henry (1775-1854)
2. Newcomer, Christian (1749-1830)

Code:
1. = 1st Generation in America
2. = 2nd Generation
3. = 3rd or more Generation, etc.

Educators and Intellectuals

Ancient Cultures and Languages

A visit to one of the many museums in Germany often shows that the Germans have long been fascinated by the study of ancient cultures and languages. This fascination in part has been stimulated by the traces of ancient Celtic tribes in the southern part of Germany who left their names embedded in the oldest settlements of southern Germany, in Austria, and in some parts of Switzerland.

Later, excavation in Germany of the more abundant remains of the Roman peoples included the stone wall called The Limes. This stone wall was likely as extensive as the well-known, modern day stone wall of China. The Limes did indeed run from about Köln in westernmost Germany to about Vienna in easternmost Austria and served as a barrier between the settlements of the Romans to the south and the nomadic, half-wild Germanic tribes to the north. The Romans occupied many localities cleared by the Celts and added a number of their own, especially along the Rhine. In fact, practically all of the cities along the left bank of the Rhine trace their names back to a Roman origin. Today, the smallest museums in southern Germany proudly display Roman artifacts which were uncovered locally.

In the 19th and 20th centuries, German adventurers explored, or perhaps a better word is re-explored, the countries around the Mediterranean and were intrigued by poorly inhabitated areas of North Africa, such as Libya and Egypt. In Egypt, they acquired some important relics. For example, the famous bust of Nefertiti, Queen of Egypt in the early 14th century B.C., is the masterpiece in Berlin's Ägyptische Museum.

The German-Americans migrating to America in the 19th century retained their interest in ancient cultures and languages. They became very interested in the many Indian cultures scattered across North America. By the 1890s, the popular fiction writer Karl May translated this interest into a lucrative book sales which sold in the millions of copies. May's work is discussed in the Printing and Publishing chapter under Authors.

One of the earliest of these ancient culture students was Charles (Karl) Beck, born in Heidelberg, Baden, who went to America in 1824. Beck was a professor of Latin at Harvard College from 1831-1850. He was an avid promoter of German scholarship in America. Beck's initial trip across the

Atlantic in 1824, from Havre to New York, lasted forty-five days and illustrates the primitive nature of transportation at that relatively late date.

In the linguistic field, George J. Adler, from Leipzig, Sachsen, went to America in 1833. His major contribution to philology was a *Dictionary of the German and English Language* published in N.Y. in 1849. Adler was a professor of Modern Languages at N.Y. University from 1846-1849. Adler suffered from depression and died in 1868.

Albert Samuel Gatschet, from Saint Beatenberg, Switzerland, arrived in the United States in 1868. Gatschet concentrated his academic efforts on the study of Swiss place names of his native land, and on Indian languages of his adopted land.

Edith Hamilton was born to American parents in 1867 in Dresden, Sachsen. She came to the United States some years later, bringing with her an European education in the classics, and in 1896, became headmistress at Bryn Mawr, an important ladies school near Philadelphia.

George Hempl, born in 1859 in Whitewater, Wisconsin, to immigrants from Dresden, Sachsen, gained some renown as a philologist. Hempel worked toward a simplification of the vocabulary and extirpated an unphonetic "e" from his own surname, which then became Hempl. This procedure is the same as that seen in many parts of Bayern today.

Louis Frederick Klipstein was born in Winchester, Virginia. In 1848, the younger Klipstein produced a book titled *A Grammar of the Anglo-Saxon Language*. This book, his main work, was revised and reprinted several times. Klipstein was a grandson of the 1751 immigrant Philipp Klipstein, who came from Darmstadt as a surgeon with a regiment of Hessian troops. Philipp Klipstein is another noted example of the relatively few Germans who fought against the Americans, but were accommodated after the Revolutionary War.

Isaac Nordheimer, from Memelsdorf, Bayern, arrived in New York in 1835. In 1838-41, he wrote *A Critical Grammar of the Hebrew Language*, in two volumes. Nordheimer, although Jewish, was an instructor in sacred literature at Union Theological Seminary from 1838-1842, when he died from the then common hazard of tuberculosis.

Yale University got Swiss immigrant Henry Roseman Lang who taught philology at Yale from 1893-1922. At almost the same time frame, Hugo Karl Schilling, from Saalfeld, Thüringen, was teaching philology, first at Harvard, and later at the University of California.

In 1916, Eduard Prokosch, a 1898 Bohemian immigrant to Milwaukee, Wisconsin, wrote *The Sounds and History of the German Language*.

The directory lists twenty-one individuals in this category.

Educators and Administrators

Harvard University, founded in 1636 at Cambridge, Mass. is the oldest institution of higher learning in the United States. Harvard University was to remain a leader in the field of education, in part through methods cited below.

The prominent German scholar and librarian Christoph Daniel Ebeling (1741-1817), in addition to writing books and doing translations about America during the period of 1772-1815, was an avid book collector. Harvard University acquired his personal library of 3,200 books, 300 folio volumes of American newspapers, and other data in 1818.

The strong interest in German literature at Harvard University dates from the student days of the noted historians George Bancroft (1800-1891), Frederic Henry Hedge (1805-1890), and John Lothrop Motley (1814-1877), all of whom were of English background. After completing basic education at Harvard, the three attended various Universities in Germany, notably the University of Göttingen and the University of Berlin, and returned to the U.S. with their European knowledge. After about 1825, many of their newly gained educational concepts were employed by Harvard and subsequently spread to other universities in the United States.

The popular *Encyclopedia America*, which was published in thirteen volumes from 1829-1833, was edited in Boston by 1827 immigrant Francis Lieber. Lieber initially planned only to translate the famous *Brockhaus Konversations-Lexikon*, but then incorporated original material from American intellectuals. Doubtless, the former Harvard students mentioned above were prime contributors. The first edition of the many editions of the *Encyclopedia Americana* had a run of about 100,000 copies and became a prime source of information for students in most American schools.

The directory gives the names of fifty-four individuals in this group.

In the earlier section on Clergy, Christopher Dock was noted as the "pious Mennonite schoolmaster" who taught elementary school in eastern Pennsylvania from 1718-1771.

Henrietta Benigna Justine von Zinzendorf, later married to Baron Johann von Watteville, accompanied her father, the Moravian leader Count Nicolaus Ludwig von Zinzendorf, to America in 1741. She came again in 1748, and for a three year period of 1784 to 1787, helped found the Moravian Seminary & College for Women at Bethlehem, Pa.

Jacob Rutsen Hardenbergh was born in Rosendale, N.Y., in 1736. In 1758, he was ordained to the ministry of the Dutch Reformed Church, and in 1766, he obtained a royal charter for the founding of Queens' College (now Rutgers University). The opening of the College was delayed by the Revolutionary War during which time Hardenberg was an ardent patriot. Hardenberg was the first president of the College, from 1786-1790.

Johann Heinrich Pestalozzi (1746-1827), born and died in Zürich, Switzerland, devised a system for primary education, which had little following in Europe. The Pestalozzi school had its adherents in America however, notably Johann Heinrich Hermann Krüsi, an 1853 immigrant from Yverdon, Switzerland; and Francis Joseph Nicholas Neef, an 1806 immigrant from Soultz, in the Alsace. The latter had established the first Pestalozzian school in the United States, near Philadelphia, in 1808-1809.

The German term kindergarten was devised in 1837 in Thüringen by Friedrich Wilhelm August Froebel (1782-1852). The practice of kindergarten was applied in fact by a number of German-American proponents, a list which included William Nicholas Hailmann, an 1852 arrival; John Kraus and his wife, Maria Kraus-Boelté, 1851 and 1872 immigrants; the well-known Emma Jacobina Christiana Marwedel, an 1869 arrival; Margarethe Meyer Schurz, 1852 immigrant and wife of the famous Carl Schurz; and Mathilda Kriege, working in Boston from 1868-1872. Sketchy accounts suggest that the first kindergarten in America may have been as early as 1838 and initiated in Columbus, Ohio, by Caroline Louisa Frankenburg. Other accounts report that one of the first kindergarten schools was that prompted by Margarethe Schurz and was set up in Waterville, Wisc. in 1856. The concept of a kindergarten gradually spread throughout the German belt of the U.S. Irma Rombauer, listed in the chapter "The Printing and Publishing World," is reported to have assisted the well-known Susan Blow (1843-1916; English by background) in starting a public kindergarten in St. Louis in 1872.

Frank Louis Soldan, born in Frankfurt am Main, Hessen, went to St. Louis, Mo. in 1863. There he became superintendent of instruction for forty years, from 1868 to 1908.

Herman Schneider, born in Summit Hill, Pa., and educated as an engineer, was a long time (1903-1939) college administrator at the University of Cincinnati. Schneider established a cooperative system of education which included a good working relationship between business and university.

William Albert Wirt, born in Markle, Ind., was the superintendent of schools in Gary, Ind. from 1907 to 1938. He developed the platoon system of class rotation, which is said effectively to have saved 40% building space.

Madeleva (Mary Evaline) Wolff was born in Cumberland, Wisc., in 1887. She was the daughter of August Frederick and Lucy (Arntz) Wolff, the father having come from Germany as a child. Madeleva Wolff became the head of St. Mary's College, at Notre Dame, in 1934, a position she occupied until 1961.

Carrie Bamberger Frank Fuld, was a daughter of Bayern natives, and heiress of I. Bamberger & Co. (located in Newark, N.J.). The company maintained the nation's largest department store from 1893-1928. In 1930, Carrie with her brother, Louis Bamberger, donated $18 million and became co-founders of the Institute for Advanced Study at Princeton. This prestigious organization accommodated a number of 1930's refugees from Germany and counted Albert Einstein as its first professor. Other German-Americans included Abraham Flexner who was the first director of the institute; he led the institute from 1930-1939. Robert Oppenheimer, the famous nuclear physicist, led the institute from 1947-1966.

Historians and Librarians

German-Americans were firm supporters of libraries in the United States. For example, the German intellectuals who settled in Bellevue, Ill., in the 1830s took a significant collection of some 2,000 books written German, French, and Latin. They formed a society called The German

Library Society. The collection is extant and forms an important part of the holdings of the Bellevue Public Library.

The Astor family provided a foundation for the N.Y. Public Library. The Astor Library, which dates from 1854, was incorporated into the N.Y. Public Library following donations from the heirs of Johann Jacob Astor (1763-1848). Later descendants, notably William Vincent Astor (1891-1959), provided millions of dollars for the continued operation of the N.Y. Public Library, which today is one of America's finest.

The historian, Heinrich Armin Rattermann (1832-1923) amassed a personal library of some 7,000 volumes, written mainly in the German language. This set was acquired by the University of Illinois.

About 1944, Yale University acquired the Curt von Faber du Faur library. Von Faber du Faur was an antiquarian who specialized in first editions of German language books. The collection of about 7,000 volumes dates from the 15th through the 19th centuries.

The Beinecke family is another good example, especially Frederick William Beinecke (1887-1971). The family contributed substantially to the Beinecke Rare Book Library, established at Yale University in 1963.

Other important collections of books on Germans, cited in 1927 by that imminent authority Albert B. Faust, include: Library of Congress, Washington, D.C.; German Society of Pennsylvania and Pennsylvania Historical Society, Philadelphia; Zimmermann Library/Lincoln (Germania) Club, Chicago; Missouri Historical Society, Jefferson City; Carnegie Library, Pittsburgh; and the Buffalo (N.Y.) Public Library.

In recent years, the University of Cincinnati with its Blegen Library and the Max Kade Library at the University of Kansas have made determined efforts to build and maintain German-American book collections.

An excellent aide to locating German-American manuscript collections and book collections in American libraries can be found in the 1991 guidebook by Anne Hope and Jörg Nagler titled *Guide to German Historical Sources in North American Libraries and Archives* (German Historical Institute, Washington, D.C.).

Forty-one individuals are included in this group, many of them of exceedingly high profile through their noteworthy publications. The following text is very selective; this list is alphabetical.

Julius Billeter, born and died in Switzerland, lived in the United States periodically from 1882 to 1946. He was atypical for his nationality in that he belonged to the Mormon church. Billeter became an avid Swiss family genealogist who helped start the genealogy section in Salt Lake City, a matter which led eventually to the building, by the Mormons, of the world's largest library for family history.

William Henry Egle was an equally avid Pennsylvanian historian and the first president of the Pennsylvania German Society. Born in 1830 in Lancaster Co., Pa., of Swiss ancestors, Egle was a long time editor of the prominent journal *Pennsylvania Archives*.

Albert Bernhard Faust, American by birth, but historian and professor of German, first at Johns Hopkins and later at Cornell, wrote the book titled

The German Element in the United States. This large and distinguished text was first published in 1909, that is, pre-War, and acquired such a reputation that it was republished, with an addenda, after the War, the last time being in 1927.

Herbert Feis was born in New York in 1893. His 1961 book *Between War and Peace: The Potsdam Conference* won a Pulitzer prize for biography.

Jennie Maas Flexner, whose grandfather came from the Sudeten, which is the mountainous border area separating Germany and former Czechslovakia, was a noted librarian over the years 1912 to 1944. She served at first at the Free Public Library in Louisville, Ky., and later at the much larger N.Y. Public Library.

Friedrich Kapp, born in Hamm, Westfalen, arrived in N.Y. in 1850, and returned to Germany in 1870. He died in Berlin in 1884. However, Kapp wrote several books about the history of German migration to America and also biographies of General von Steuben and General Kalb. More importantly, he achieved fame for his public announcements in America in support of the Union, a matter which was of prime importance in uniting German-Americans behind President Lincoln. Kapp was a lawyer in New York from 1850-1870 and had the position of U.S. Commissioner of Immigration from 1867-1870. Kapp returned to Germany in 1870 where he died in 1884.

Richard Hofstadter was born in Buffalo, N.Y., in 1916. In 1956, Hofstadter received a Pulitzer prize for biography for his book *The Age of Reform.* His 1964 book *Anti-Intellectualism in American Life* won several book prizes.

Marion Dexter Learned, whose family name is not at all German, was a professor of Germanic languages. He taught initially at Johns Hopkins University, and in 1895, occupied the chair at the University of Pennsylvania, a chair formerly filled by Oswald Seidensticker. Learned's several key publications, most notably the 1908 *The Life of Francis Daniel Pastorius,* are available in most large libraries or through interlibrary loan.

Ezra Meeker was born in Huntsville, Ohio in 1830. He was an unusual individualist who farmed in Washington for fifty years, having taken an ox team to Oregon in 1852. Meeker is noted as a historian who wrote an interesting account of his experiences. The account was published in 1907 under the title *The Oregon Trail.* The family name Meeker is not a typical German spelling, perhaps having been changed from Mecker.

John George Nicolay, was born in Essingen, near Landau, in the Palatinate, and arrived in the United States via New Orleans in 1838. Nicolay became private secretary to Abraham Lincoln. After Lincoln's death, he colloborated with John Milton Hay on the ten volume biography of the former President.

Heinrich Armin Rattermann, born in Ankum, near Osnabrück, Niedersachsen, went to Cincinnati, Oh., in 1846, where he remained until his death in 1923. Rattermann collected a personal library of 7,000 volumes, most of it dealing with German-Americans; Rattermann's library eventually was acquired by the University of Illinois.

Israel Daniel Rupp, born in 1803 in Cumberland Co., Pa., as a descendant of an immigrant from Baden, was noted for his pioneering efforts to document the arrival of 18th century German immigrants at the port of Philadelphia. Rupp acquired data on some 30,000 families. The listing was published in Philadelphia in 1856.

John Thomas Scharf was born in Baltimore in 1843 and came of age just in time to enlist in the Confederate forces as a private. Scharf is recognized as a historian mainly through his 1879 book titled the *History of Maryland* which appeared in three volumes. Among other books, Scharf wrote, in 1883, a *History of Saint Louis City and County*. Scharf built up a large collection of Americana which was given to the library at Johns Hopkins University.

Arthur Meier Schlesinger, Jr. was born in Columbus, Oh., in 1917. Schlesinger, whose father is listed under Educators, received a Pulitzer prize for history and another for biography as well as two National Book awards. The first of the Pulitzer prizes was for his 1945 book *The Age of Jackson*. The second Pulitzer prize was for his 1965 book *A Thousand Days*, a work about the Kennedy administration. Schlesinger also wrote a multivolume work titled *The Age of Roosevelt (1957-1960)*, which achieved wide popularity. He was on the Harvard University history faculty from 1946-1961.

Oswald Seidensticker, born in Göttingen, Niedersachsen, went with his father as a political refugee to Philadelphia in 1846. The younger Seidensticker was a professor of German at the University of Pennsylvania from 1867 to 1894. Seidensticker became an authority on much of what was Pennsylvania German and what was German-American. Seidensticker's primary publications, published in 1876 and 1883 were written in German.

Martin Luther Stoever, born in 1820 in Germantown, Pa., was noted for his many biographies including that of the famous Lutheran minister Henry Melchoir Mühlenberg.

Ralph Beaver Strassburger was born in 1883 in Norristown, Pa. aside from being a publisher, Strassburger developed a strong interest in family history, who as senior author sponsored the well-known 1934 book *Pennsylvania German Pioneers*. The book is basically a compilation of ships passenger lists at the port of Philadelphia for the years 1727-1808. William John Hinke, born 1871 in Giershofen, Rheinland-Pfalz, was the junior author and did most of the interpretive work in transcribing passenger names. The two authors estimated somewhat more than 65,000 passengers for the period concerned. This advanced pioneering effort is still useful.

Barbara Wertheim Tuchman, historian, achieved fame in 1958 for her book *The Zimmerman Telegram*. This book became a best seller. She achieved wider recognition in 1962 when her book *The Guns of August* was awarded a Pulitzer Prize. In 1971, she gained another Pulitzer prize for her book *Stilwell and the American Experience 1911-1945*. She was born in N.Y. in 1912, as the daughter of Maurice and Alma (Morgenthau) Wertheim, and died in N.Y. in 1989.

Philosophers

Seven individuals who made contributions to the field of philosophy are listed in the directory. They were all born in Germany except for Suzanne Knauth Langer, whose name is obviously of German origin.

Suzanne Knauth Langer was born in 1895 in N.Y. as the daughter of Antonio and Else M. (Ulich) Knauth. Langer was associated with Radcliff College from 1927-1942. In 1930, she wrote *The Practice of Philosophy*.

TABLE 10
DIRECTORY OF EDUCATORS AND INTELLECTUALS

Ancient Cultures and Ancient Languages
2. Adler, Cyrus, (1863-1940)
1. Adler, George J. (1821-1868)
2. Anthon, Charles (1897-1867)
1. Beck, Charles (1798-1866)
1. Bloomfield, Maurice (1855-1928)
2. Bloomfield, Leonard (1887-1949)
1. Flügel, Ewald (1863-1914)
1. Gatschet, Albert Samuel (1832-1907)
1. Haupt, Paul (1858-1926)
1. Hamilton, Edith (1867-1963)
2. Hempl, George (1859-1921)
1. Hilprecht, Herman Volrath (1859-1925)
3. Klipstein, Louis Frederick (1813-1878)
2. Kober, Alice Elizabeth (1906-1950)
1. Lang, Henry Roseman (1853-1934)
1. Laufer, Berthold (1874-1934)
1. Müller, Wilhelm Max (1862-1919)
1. Nordheimer, Isaac (1809-1842)
1. Prokosch, Edward (1876-1938)
1. Schilling, Hugo Karl (1861-1931)
   Smith, Bryon Caldwell (1849-1877)

Educators and Administrators
1. Berlitz, Maximilian D. (1852-1921)
3. Berlitz, Charles Frambach (1913-)
2. Borchardt, Selma Munter (1895-1968)
3. Bowman, John Bryan (1824-1891)
   Buehler, Huber Gray (1864-1924)
1. Collitz, Hermann (1855-1935)
1. Collitz, Klara Hechtenberg (1863-1944)
2. Eby, Frederick (1874-1968)
2. Flexner, Abraham (1866-1959)
1. Follen, Karl Theodore Christian (1796-1840)
2. Fuld, Carrie Bamberger Frank (1864-1944)
1. Goebel, Julius, Sr. (1857-1931)
1. Gruenberg, Sidonie Matsner (1881-1974)
1. Hailmann, William Nicholas (1836-1920)
1. Harap, Henry (1893-1981)
2. Hardenbergh, Jacob Rutsen (1736-1790)
1. Hendrix, Herman Elert (1880-1948)
1. Hinke, William John (1871-1947)
   Hoffman, David (1784-1854)
   Hollingworth, Leta Anna Stetter (1886-1939)

1. Kraus, John (1815-1896)
1. Kraus-Boelte, Maria (1836-1918)
   Krause, Alvina E. (1893-1981)
1. Krey, August Charles (1887-1961)
1. Krüsi, Johann Heinrich Hermann (1817-1903)
2. Lange, Alexis Frederick (1862-1924)
1. Lazarsfeld, Paul Felix (1901-1976)
   Louderback, George Davis (1874-1957)
1. Malter, Henry (1864-1925)
1. Marwedel, Emma Jacobina Christiana (1818-1893)
   Merk, Frederick (1887-1977)
1. Neef, Francis Joseph Nicholas (1770-1854)
1. Notz, Frederick William Ausustus (1841-1921)
1. Panofsky, Erwin (1892-1968)
1. Pollock, Louise Plessner (1832-1901)
1. Rausch, Frederick Augustus (1806-1841)
2. Reinsch, Paul Samuel (1869-1923)
   Richman, Julia (1855-1912)
1. Roedder, Edwin Carl (1873-1943)
   Sachs, Julius (1849-1934)
   Sadtler, Samuel Philip (1847-1923)
5. Schaeffer, Nathan Christ (1849-1919)
2. Schlesinger, Arthur Meier, Sr. (1888-1965)
3. Schneider, Herman (1872-1939)
1. Schurz, Margarethe Meyer (1833-1876)
   Smith, Charles Alphonse (1864-1924)
1. Stern, Catherine Brieger (1894-1973)
   Snyder, Edwin Reagan (1872-1925)
1. Soldan, Frank Louis (1842-1908)
1. Struck, Ferdinand Theodore (1886-1943)
   Thomas, Calvin (1854-1919)
   Tutwiler, Henry (1807-1884)
   Tutwiler, Julia Strudwick (1841-1916)
1. Ulich, Robert (1890-1977)
1. Watteville, Henrietta Benigna Justine
   von Zinzendorf (1725-1789)
   Wirt, William Albert (1874-1938)
1. Wittkower, Rudolf (1901-1971)
2. Wolff, Madelina (Mary Evaline)(1887-1964)

Historians and Librarians
1. Arendt, Hannah (1906-1975)
   Arndt, Karl John Richard (1903-)
1. Bandelier, Adolph Francis Alphonse (1840-1914)
   Beard, Mary Ritter (1876-1958)
2. Beer, George Louis (1872-1920)
   Bek, William Godfrey (1873-1948)

1. Billeter, Julius (1869-1957)
8. Binkeley, Robert Cedric (1897-1940)(Binggeli)
5. Egle, William Henry (1830-1901)
2. Faust, Albert Bernard (1870-1951)
   Feis, Herbert (1922-1970)
1. Fernow, Berthold (1837-1908)
3. Flexner, Jennie Maas (1882-1944)
1. Francke, Huno (1855-1930)
   Heitman, Francis Bernard (1838-1926)
   Hofstadter, Richard (1916-1970)
   Hone, Philip (1780-1851)
1. Kapp, Friedrich (1824-1884)
3. Kroeger, Alice Bertha (1864-1909)
   Learned, Marion Dexter (1857-1917)
1. Legler, Henry Edward (1861-1917)
1. Nicolay, John George (1832-1901)
   Meeker, Ezra (1830-1928)
   Myers, Albert Cook, (1874-1960)
   Oberholtzer, Ellis Paxson (1868-1936)
1. Rattermann, Heinrich Armin (1832-1923)
1. Ruetinik, Herman Julius (1826-1914)
3. Rupp, Israel Daniel (1803-1878)
2. Sachse, Julius Friedrich (1842-1919)
1. Schaff, Philip (1819-1893)
   Scharf, John Thomas (1843-1898)
3. Schlesinger, Arthur Meier, Jr. (1917-)
   Schmidt, Louis Bernard (1879-1963)
1. Seidensticker, Oswald (1825-1894)
7. Steiner, Bernard Christian (1867-1926)
   Stoever, Martin Luther (1820-1870)
6. Strassburger, Ralph Beaver (1883-1959)
   Tuchman, Barbara Wertheim (1912-1989)
2. Volwiler, Albert Tangeman (1888-1957)
1. von Holst, Hermann Eduard (1841-1904)
   Widener, Henry Elkins (1875-1912)
3. Wister, Sarah (1761-1804)

Philosophers
1. Brokmeyer, Henry C. (1828-1906)
1. Carus, Paul (1852-1919)
2. Langer, Suzanne Katherina Knauth (1895-1985)
1. Lovejoy, Arthur Oncken (1873-1962)
1. Marcuse, Herbert (1898-1979)
1. Marcuse, Ludwig (1894-1971)
1. Tillich, Paul Johannes (1886-1965)

Code:
1. = 1st Generation in America
2. = 2nd Generation
3. = 3rd or more Generation, etc.

Engineers and More Engineers

The world of engineering is one of occasional spectacular results. Whether in bridge building, washing machine or vacuum cleaner manufacture, or automobile racing, German-Americans have contributed their share. Railroads, which in America, had their beginning in 1825 at Hoboken, N.J., had a high point in 1869 with the first transcontinental rail line, and in the years of 1871-1872 during which new rail lines reached a peak. The second half of the 19th century was the age of railroads when vast fortunes were made and lost in this business. However, a new mode of transportation was in the making. German-Americans were in the middle of this speciality.

In 1886, Gottlieb Daimler (1834-1900)), working in Stuttgart, Germany, built a practical internal combustion engine. In the same year, Karl Benz (1844-1929), working in Mannheim, Germany, developed a similar engine. Comparable engines were built in other parts of Europe and in America about the same time or shortly thereafter. By 1895, there were a handful of American made automobiles, but by 1899, there were thousands. The first automobile show was held in New York City in 1900 with thirty-one exhibitors attending. At this show, steam and electric (battery) powered cars showed a slight majority over the gasoline powered cars.

Another German name stands out in the American automobile and truck manufacturing industry. That is Rudolf Christian Karl Diesel, who was born in Paris in 1858, and died in 1913 by drowning while crossing the English Channel. The family name was long established in the Schwaben part of Bayern. In August, 1892, Rudolph Diesel, then resident of Berlin, applied for a U.S. patent; the patent was granted on July 16, 1895. Licenses to manufacture Diesel motors were distributed in the U.S. by brewer Adolph Busch beginning in 1898. In 1912, Busch, with the Gebrüder Sulzer, a large engineering firm in Winterthur, Switzerland, began manufacturing Diesel motors in St. Louis. The Busch-Sulzer Brothers Diesel Engine Company was active from 1911-1939, after which its physical assets were sold to the Nordberg Company of Milwaukee. Today, diesel motors are found in most trucks, buses, and larger boats.

Another milestone was reached in 1911 when the first Indianapolis 500 mile race was held, a factor which indicated a vastly improved level of engineering with regard to engines, tires, and the automobile in general.

Over the next two decades, the Indianapolis 500, notwithstanding World War I, was to prove extremely important in communicating the advances of new technology between Europe and America and vice versa. For instance, in Germany in 1922, Daimler (which became Daimler-Benz in 1926) developed the supercharger. This technology, by which extra oxygen is supplied to the cylinders, thus aiding gasoline combustion, was immediately utilized by American automobile engineers. About the same time, ever higher octane gasoline was developed as were engines to utilize this higher quality gasoline. The development of airplane and boat engines was closely related to that of automobile engines.

And the third era of modern transportation technology centered around rocket development which was initiated in the 1920s in Germany and about the same time in the U.S. and in Russia. The Germans stepped up research prior to and during World War II. After the War, this technology led to outer space travel. Both the Russians and the Americans received a boost from key German scientists in their head-to-head competition to put a man on the moon.

The following discussion begins with the category of Civil Engineers and is followed by that of Electrical Engineers, both groups being fundamental to developing a transportation and industrial infrastructure.

Civil Engineers

Stephen Davison Bechtel was born in Aurora, Ind., in 1900. He joined W.A. Bechtel Co. in 1919 as a civil engineer. His brother, Kenneth Karl Bechtel, was associated with the company from 1921-1945. The Bechtel Company, which was established in 1895 by his father Warren A. Bechtel, operates today as Bechtel Group, Inc., with headquarters in San Francisco. It undertakes massive construction projects, such as pipeline laying and the like, in many foreign as well as domestic locations. The family name is an old Swiss Mennonite name which apparently went to America via the Palatinate. The name has many variants such as Bachtel, Bechtold, and Böchtel.

Adolphus Bonzano was born in Ehingen, Württemberg, in 1830, and went to Philadelphia in 1850, likely as a refugee. Bonzano was an engineer and inventor whose career was primarily with Detroit Bridge & Iron Works. The Bonzano name shows an Italian influence.

Christian Edward Detmold was born in Hannover (now state of Niedersachsen) in 1810, Detmold went to Charleston, S.C., at the relatively early date of 1826. He was a civil engineer who became associated with railroad and building construction, mainly in the state of New York, where he died in 1887.

Frederick Graff was born in Philadelphia in 1774. He was a descendant of Jacob Graff who went to Philadelphia about 1737 from Germany. Frederick Graff became an engineer with the Philadelphia Water Dept. A son, Frederic Graff (1817-1890), likewise was a longtime employee of the Philadelphia Water Dept.

John Edwin Greiner was born in Wilmington, Del., in 1859. Greiner worked as a civil engineer for the Baltimore & Ohio Railroad from 1885-1906, as a bridge-building specialist. In 1908, Greiner founded his own company. He was active from 1908 until about 1939 in this company, Greiner Engineering, Inc. The company participated in the construction of numerous bridges, highway, port development, airports, and the like. Today, Greiner Engineering, Inc. is active worldwide and is listed on the N.Y. Stock Exchange.

Herman Haupt was born in Philadelphia in 1817. Haupt was a civil engineer, author, and inventor who had a varied career in the construction of bridges, railroads, and tunnels. During the Civil War, he declined an appointment as a brigadier general, but did serve the North as superintendent of U.S. railroads during the years of 1862-1863.

John Benjamin Henck was born in Philadelphia in 1815. He was the son of native Germans George Daniel and Caroline (Spiess) Henck. Henck grew up to become the first head of the Civil Engineering Deptartment at Massachusetts Institute of Technology.

Gustav Lindenthal was born at Brünn, Moravia (now the Czech Republic) in 1850. Lindenthal went to Philadelphia in 1874 and later to Pittsburgh and then to New York. Lindenthal was involved in the construction of railways, tunnels, and bridges. He had an office in Pittsburgh from 1877-1890, and after 1890, worked out of an office in New York.

Edward Overholser was born in Sullivan, Ind., in 1869, but moved to Oklahoma City by 1890. Besides being the manager of the Oklahoma City Theatre from 1890-1918, Overholser was in the construction business with his father. Together, they built many of the early buildings in Oklahoma City, such as hotels, and the like. In fact, Overholser came to be known as the "Father of Oklahoma City."

John Augustus Roebling was born in Mühlhausen, Thüringen, in 1806 and went to a small German community called Saxonberg (also called Germania), near Pittsburgh, in 1831. From 1841-1849, Roebling operated a factory in Trenton, N.J., where he perfected the manufacture of steel cables. The factory remained in family hands for three generations. A major achievement was the manufacture of giant steel cable, up to thirty-six inches in diameter, which was required for all large suspension bridges. John Augustus Roebling was one of the prime contractors on the initial stages of the construction of the Brooklyn Bridge.

Washington Augustus Roebling was born in Saxonberg, Butler Co., Pa., in 1837, as the son of Washington Augustus and Johanna (Herting) Roebling. The younger Roebling had a varied career as a civil engineer, a colonel in the Union Army during the Civil War, and as an industrialist. He was chief engineer when the Brookly Bridge was completed in May, 1883, and also contributed to the planning of the Golden Gate Bridge in San Francisco, which however, was not constructed until well after his death. Roebling was a collector of rare minerals whose collection of some 15,000 specimens was given to the Smithsonian Museum. The Roebling family name is borne by the town of Roebling, N.J., southwest of Trenton.

David McNeely Stauffer was born in Mount Joy, Lancaster Co., Pa., in 1845. He was a descendant of John Stauffer who went from Switzerland in 1710 to Pennsylvania. Stauffer was a civil engineer, editor and writer. In 1907, he wrote the book *American Engravers upon Copper and Steel*, a two volume classic in its field. In the U.S., there are numerous Stauffer family descendants, many of whom spell the family name as Stouffer, or some other variant.

David Bernard Steinman was born in New York in 1886. Steinman developed a world-wide reputation as a bridge-builder, the most notable of which was the Mackinac Bridge erected in 1957, and the Salazar Bridge (in Portugal) in 1966.

Joseph Baermann Strauss was born in Cincinnati, in 1870. He was the son of Raphael and Lena (Baermann) Strauss, native Bavarians, who went to Cincinnati in 1854. Joseph Baermann Strauss was associated with the Strauss Engineering Corp. after 1904. He was primarily a bridge builder who designed San Francisco's famous Golden Gate Bridge and otherwise participated in more than 500 bridges.

Charles Louis Strobel was born in Cincinnati, in 1852. He was the son of immigrants Karl and Ida L. (Merker) Strobel. Strobel became a civil engineer associated with the Keystone Bridge Co. from 1878-1885, and later worked independently on steel-framed structures.

Edward Wegmann was born in Rio de Janeiro, Brazil, in 1850. His father, Ludwig Edward Wegmann, of Swiss origin, went to the United States originally in 1831 where he developed an import-export firm. The younger Wegmann became a civil engineer who was associated with the construction of railroads in New England, New York, and Ohio, and from 1884-1914, with the city of New York waterworks.

Lewis Wernawag was born in Riedlingen, Württemberg, in 1769, and went to America about 1786. Wernawag was a pioneer bridge builder who helped construct twenty-nine bridges, all, of course, of the old wooden or stone type. He died in Harpers Ferry, (West) Virginia, in 1843.

Electrical Engineers

Bernard Arthur Behrend was born in Villeneuve, Kanton Vaud, Switzerland, in 1875. Behrend went to the U.S. in 1898, and was a long time prime employee with Westinghouse Electric & Manufacturing Co. in Massachusetts.

William Charles Gotshall was born in St. Louis in 1879. He was an electrical engineer. There are numerous variants on the Gotshall name, a name which is common to the lower German Rhine.

William Joseph Hammer was born in Cressona, Pa., in 1858. He was employed by Edison Co. from 1879-1890 as an electrical engineer.

Reinhold Rüdenberg was born in Hannover (now in the state of Niedersachsen) in 1883, and went to the U.S. in 1939. Rüdenberg taught at Harvard University from 1939-1952, where he worked on electrophysics. He holds several key patents for the electron microscope.

Charles Proteus Steinmetz was born in Breslau, Silesia (now Poland), in 1865. Steinmetz, whose christian name was Karl August Rudolf Steinmetz, went to the U.S. in 1889, where he was an electrical engineer for General Electric Co. from 1893-1923. Steinmetz wrote many books on electrical engineering. He died in Schenectady, N.Y. in 1923.

Gerard Swope was born in St. Louis, in 1872. Swope was associated with General Electric Co. from 1919-1944. He died in N.Y. in 1957.

Inventors, Tinkerers and Mechanical Engineers

Arnold Orville Beckman was born in Cullom, Ill., in 1900. Beckman had a long career as an inventor, scientist, educator, and chemist, all in California. Beckman had a series of companies, the last being Beckman Instruments which he founded in 1935. Beckman invented a pH meter, a spectrophotometer, and a heliopot, all instruments for measuring the chemistry of fluids and solids. He received numerous awards including a spot in the National Inventors Hall of Fame in Akron, Oh. Today, the firm Beckman Instruments is number 378 on the Fortune 500 list.

Emile Berliner was born in Hannover (today in the state of Niedersachsen), in 1851 and went to Washington, D.C., in 1870. Berliner was an inventor who made primary contributions to the gramophone and to the microphone. However, working together with his son Henry Adler Berliner, the two Berliners built three different models of helicopters in the years from 1919-1926.

William Peter Bettendorf was born in Mendotta, Ill., in 1857. Bettendorf became an inventor and manufacturer of farm and railroad equipment. The Bettendorf family name was applied to Bettendorf, Ia. Five villages in Germany bear the name Bettendorf, the largest being near Koblenz.

George E. Clymer, an early American inventor, was born in Bucks Co., Pa., in 1754. While still a teenager, Clymer devised a unique plow and other farm equipment. Somewhat later, he used his talents in helping construct the first permanent bridge across the Schuykill River by devising a suction pump. Clymer is best noted for an improved printing press called the "Columbian." The Columbian was expensive to manufacture and did not sell well in the U.S., but Clymer developed a market for his press in England, the Netherlands, and even in Russia. Clymer was descended from a Swiss family originating in Kanton Geneva. Ancestors apparently went to Philadelphia in 1730. Strassburger & Hinke, 1934, cite 1730 immigrants under the names of "Johannes Cleyner" and "Johan Andres Klemmer."

Christian Dancel was born in "Cassel" (now Kassel, in Hessen), in 1847, and went to New York in 1865. Dancel is known as an inventor of sewing machines for the manufacture of leather shoes.

Rudolf Eickemeyer was born in Altenbamberg, near Bad Kreuznach, Rheinland-Pfalz, in 1831, and went to the U.S. in 1850 as a political refugee. Eickmeyer developed a career as an inventor and manufacturer embracing some 150 patents.

Henry Flad was born in Baden in 1824, and went to Pittsburgh in 1849, as a political refugee. Flad's career in America was to carry him from one project to another, initially with railroads in the east, including service as an engineer in the Civil War, later with St. Louis water supply and public improvement, as an engineer associated with the construction of the Eads Bridge across the Mississippi, and service on the Mississippi River Commission. In each of these areas, Flad developed a number of patents on new or improved types of equipment. For instance, he had patents on water filters, water meters, bridge building equipment, railroad and rapid transit equipment, and on current measuring devices.

John Fritz was born in Chester Co., Pa., in 1822. His father, George, had gone as a child in 1802 to the U.S. from Germany. John Fritz had a career as a mechanical engineer and ironmaster.

Lillian Evelyn Moller Gilbreth was born in Oakland, Calif., in 1878. She was the daughter of William and Annie (Delger) Moller. She married Frank Bunker Gilbreth, also an engineer. Together they conducted motion studies in industry and formed a profitable consulting business in plant efficiency. At the same time, Lillian became a household efficiency expert, advising manufacturers of household appliances on items to increase efficiency.

Jacob Haish was born at Karlsruhe, Baden-Württemberg, in 1826 and went to Pennsylvania, in 1836. Haish became an inventor and manufacturer. One of his achievements was an early type of barbed wire. Haish died in De Kalb, Ill., in 1926.

Herbert Thacker Herr was born in Denver, Colo., in 1876. Herr was employed by the Westinghouse Co., from 1908-1930, and was one of those responsible for the development of air brakes used on railroad cars.

Hermann Hollerith was born in Buffalo, N.Y., in 1860, as the son of German immigrants George and Franciska (Brunn) Hollerith. He was an inventor who pioneered in data processing and tabulating machines. In 1896, Hollerith organized the Tabulating Machine Co., which was incorporated, about 1924, into the firm IBM, a firm that has become a world-wide giant in the manufacture of office equipment.

Charles Franklin Kettering was born in Loudonville, Oh., in 1876. Kettering was an engineer, inventor, and manufacturer whose primary career was with General Motors. He was, in fact, the head of research at General Motors from 1919-1946, as well as a vice-president of the company. Among other things, Kettering helped develop an electric starter for automobiles, and engines which ran on higher octane gasolines. Kettering's name is also known through the famous Sloan-Kettering Institute of Cancer Research, which was started in 1927. Franz Kettering, a possible ancestor, is listed by Strassburger & Hinke, 1934; Franz went to Philadelphia in 1764.

Elmer Carl Kiekhafer was born in Wisconsin as a descendant of 1840s immigrants. In 1939, Kiekhafer bought a small company which made small gasoline motors. Kiekhafer developed a whole series of improvements on the basic motor which was marketed under the name of Mercury Motors and adapted to a variety of uses, especially motor boats.

John Kruesi was born in Speicher, Kanton Appenzell, Switzerland, and went to New York in 1870. Kreusi became a mechanical expert and inventor who improved the Singer sewing machine. He was also superintendent of the Edison Machine Works, and helped to develop electric lighting in New York City.

John George Leyner was born in Boulder, Colo. in 1860, as the son of native German Peter A. Leyner. The younger Leyner became an inventor and manufacturer whose speciality was mining equipment.

John William Lieb was born in Newark, N.J., in 1860. His parents were Wilhelm and Christina (Zens) who went from Württemberg to the U.S. in 1846. The younger Lieb's career was mainly as a mechanical engineer with Edison Electric Co.

Phineas Price Mast was born in Lancaster Co., Pa., in 1825. He became an inventor and manufacturer of farm equipment. The Mast family name is a common one in parts of western Switzerland, where it is often associated with Mennonite communities.

Robert Distler Maurer was born in St. Louis, in 1924. He was an industrial physicist who had worked on optical fibers (revolutionary telephone cables). He was employed by Corning Glass Co. from 1952-1989. His research promoted his award in the National Inventors Hall of Fame, located in Akron, Oh.

Ottmar Mergenthaler was born in Hachtel, near Bad Mergenheim, Baden-Württemberg, in 1854. He went to Washington, D.C. in 1872. Mergenthaler was a maker of watches and scientific instruments, but is best known for his development of the linotype which was first employed in N.Y. in 1884.

Lewis Miller was born in Greentown, Oh., in 1829. He was the third generation in America, his grandfather Abraham having gone from Zweibrücken, Rheinland-Pfalz, to Maryland in 1776. Miller lived most of his life in New York where he invented and manufactured mowing machines and reapers.

Gertrude Agnes Muller was born in 1887. She was the daughter of Victor Herbertus and Catherine (Baker) Muller. Gertrude Muller developed a business centered around the inhouse development of childcare products. She was the president of the business which was called, initially, Juvenile Wood Products Co., from 1924-1954. The company was renamed in 1944 as the Toidey Co.

Frederick Gottlieb Niedringhaus was born in Lübbecke, Westfalen, in 1837, and went to St. Louis in 1855. In 1866, he founded the St. Louis Stamping Co., and later the National Enameling & Stamping Co. In addition to manufacturing, Niedringhaus' career included terms as a congressman.

Charles Piez was born in Mainz, Rheinland-Pfalz, in 1866. Piez's father became a brewer in Newark, N.J., while Piez himself developed a career as a manufacturer (Link Belt Co.) in Chicago. He also served as a U.S. Emergency Fleet Corporation official during World War I. The Piez family name is not at all German and shows an apparent south Slavic influence.

David Rittenhouse was born in Papermill Run, near Roxborough, Pa., in 1732. He was the grandson of Wilhelm Rittenhausen who went to Pennsylvania from the lower German Rhine in 1688. David Rittenhouse became a well-known scientific instrument maker, astronomer, and mathematician. He also gained fame for his work on the early boundary surveys of Pennsylvania, Delaware, Maryland, Virginia, New York, New Jersey, and Massachusetts.

Jacob Schick was born in Des Moines, Iowa in 1877, as the son of an immigrant from Bayern. After an army career lasting from 1898-1910, the younger Schick used his inventive talents on a variety of gadgets which have wide application today. From 1911-1914, Schick developed the "dry razor." By 1923-1924, he patented the (electric) "shaving machine" which went into production in 1931. Schick also developed pencil sharpeners, a mechanical pencil, a card shuffling machine, and various other hand-held devices. Schick was also noted for improving the diesel engine.

Charles Adolph Schieren was born at Neuss, near Düsseldorf, Nordrhein-Westfalen, in 1842. Schieren went with his parents Johann Nikolaus and Wilhelmina (Lagenbach) Schieren, to the U.S. in 1856. The younger Schieren was a manufacturer and inventor whose patents dealt mainly with the construction of leather belting for machinery.

George Otto Schneller was born in Nürnberg, Bayern, in 1843. Schneller went to N.Y. in 1860. He eventually established a factory in Ansonia, Ct., where he devised various techniques to manufacture a variety of brass goods.

Walther Othman Snelling was born in Washington, D.C., in 1880. He was associated with the Trojan Powder Co., from 1917-1954. Snelling eventually held more than 200 patents on various chemical products, including explosives.

Howard Snyder worked for the Maytag Co. in Newton, Ia., and was considered as their head engineer. In 1919, Snyder led the team which developed the "Gyrofoam washer," a product which revolutionized household druggery associated with washing clothes. By 1922, the Gyrofoam washer had sold in the millions.

James Murry Spangler was born, probably in western Pennsylvania, in 1850, but was a longtime resident in northeast Ohio. While still a teenager, Spangler experimented on improvements in farm equipment, notably a hay tedder and rake, equipment which he perfected in 1893. In 1897, Spangler developed a velocipede wagon which worked, but apparently was never put into production. Spangler's real claim to possible fame came with the development, in 1907, of an electric suction sweeper. In 1908, however, Spangler sold the rights of the sweeper to an inlaw, William H. Hoover. The Hoover vacuum cleaner became a lifesaver to businesses and housewives alike.

Carl August Stetefeldt was born in Holzhausen, near Erfurt, Thüringen, in 1838, and went to the U.S. in 1863. Stetefeldt eventually went to California where he became a metallurgist and inventor who contributed to the mining industry, principally in Nevada.

Henry Timken was born at Bremen, in 1831, and went to St. Louis in 1838. Timken's early career was that of the maker of carriages and wagons which featured Timken iron springs. In 1898, he began the production of roller bearings, a process which developed into the Timken Roller Bearing & Axle Co., with headquarters in Canton, Oh. Henry Timken died in 1909, but the firm survives today as number 254 on the Fortune 500 list.

Gustave Whitehead (originally Gustav Albin Weisskopf) was born in 1874, in Leutershausen, Bayern. Whitehead went to Boston in 1895, and apparently conducted one of the first motorized flights, in Fairfield, Conn., on Aug. 14, 1901. Whitehead is reported to have used a steam engine for propulsion of his aircraft and to have flown about 850 meters.

Joseph Zentmayer was born in Mannheim, Baden, in 1826, and went to Cleveland in 1848 as a political refugee. In 1853, Zentmayer went to Philadelphia where he began the manufacturer of scientific instruments, notably microscopes and photographic lenses.

Transportation Engineers

Walter Percy Chrysler was born in Wamego, Kans., in 1875. His father, Henry Chrysler, who was of Canadian birth, was of German ancestry. The younger Chrysler was associated with the automotive industry from the beginning of his career, first with Buick Motor Co. (1912-1920) where he became president in 1916, then Willys Overland Motors, and later Maxwell Motors, the latter firm became Chrylser Motors in 1925. Chrysler died in 1940, but the company today enjoys a position as number eleven on the *Fortune* 500 list. Walter P. Chrysler was an seventh generation German descendant on his father's side, and a third generation German descendant on his mother's side, his mother's maiden name being Breyman. After nearly four decades of research, Chrysler family historians determined that the immigrant ancestor was one Johann Philipp Kreussler (German = Kreußler) who went to N.Y.'s Schoharie Valley in June, 1710. His birthplace is listed as Niederneisen, in an area formerly embraced by Nassau, now in Hessen. Walter P. Chrysler was honored by being named *Time Magazine*'s Man of the Year in 1928. The Chrysler Museum located in Norfolk, Va. and the Chrysler birthplace in Wamego, Kans., also show the many honors this famous automotive engineer received.

William Cramp was born in Philadelphia, in 1807. He was a descendant of Johannes Krampf who went from Baden to America in 1703. Cramp established himself as a ship-builder on the east coast and died in Atlantic City, N.J., in 1879. Charles Henry Cramp, who was born in 1828, carried on his father's shipbuilding business.

Kurt Heinrich Debus was born in Frankfurt am Main, in 1908, and went to the U.S. in 1945. Debus was an aeronautical engineer who was an assistant to Wernher von Braun from 1945-1952. Debus was attached to NASA from 1960-1974.

Friedrich Samuel Duesenberg was born in Kirchheide, Westfalen, in 1876, and went to Iowa, with his mother, three brothers and four sisters in

1884. Two of the brothers, Fred and August (known in the U.S. as "Augie") started their careers as bicycle enthusiasts and mechanics on various farm equipment in Iowa. Eventually, Fred Duesenberg was associated, as was his brother Augie, with the Maytag-Mason Car Co., which was located in Waterloo, Iowa, from 1909-1911. In 1914, the Duesenberg brothers became master mechanics dealing almost entirely with automobile racing and remained in the business of building expensive engines. They worked through a series of companies which were financed by outside partners and had shops in Minneapolis, St. Paul, Chicago, New York, Elizabeth, N.J., Poughkeepsie, N.Y., Newark, N.J., and finally in Indianapolis. Duesenberg engines powered the winning cars in the 1924 and 1925 Indianapolis 500-mile races. The Duesenbergs were among the first Americans to adopt superchargers and other German technology which gave added power to engines. The last financier of Fred (but not Augie) was E. L. Cord who formed the Auburn-Cord-Dusenberg Company which lasted from 1926-1937. This company was designed to build luxury cars, but not racing cars. In 1932, Fred was seriously injured in an automobile accident and died after the last of many bouts with pneumonia. In the years 1926-1937, some 480 custom-built, luxury Duesenberg cars were manufactured, many of which survive today as very expensive collector's items. Duesenberg memorabilia are preserved in the Auburn-Cord-Duesenberg Museum in Auburn, Ind., and in the Motorsports Hall of Fame in Talladega, Ala.

Albert Fink was born at Lauterbach, near Darmstadt, Hessen, in 1827. He went to the U.S. in 1849 as a political refugee. Fink was one of the boom period railroad construction engineers.

James Brown Herreshoff was born in Pappasquaw, near Bristol, R.I., in 1834. A brother, John Brown Herreshoff, was born in 1841. Another brother, Nathanael Green Herreshoff, was born in 1848. The three brothers were the grandsons of Karl Friedrich Herreshoff who went in 1783 from "Prussia" to R.I. The brothers were active as inventors, marine engineers, ship-builders, and yacht designers. In 1863, they formed the Herreshoff Manufacturing Co. in Bristol which was carried on by descendants until 1946. The Herreshoff Co. made, among other things, racing yachts which challenged for the America Cup eight times, and during World War II, torpedo boats. The Herreshoff Marine Museum is still active in Bristol, R.I.

Henry J. Kaiser was born in Sprout Brook, N.Y., in 1882, and died in Honolulu in 1967. Kaiser began a construction firm in 1914 which built highways and dams; the company eventually became the giant Kaiser Industries Corp., which dealt mainly with shipyards and with the construction of merchant ships.

Herman Julius Oberth was born in Hermannstadt, then in Siebenbürgen, now in Rumania, in 1894. His father was a German medical doctor, originally from Sachsen, who directed a local hospital in Siebenbürgen. The younger Oberth achieved fame as one of three pioneering space scientists (the other two included an American and a Russian). His 1923 book *Die Rakete zu den Planeteräumen* (Rockets to Outer Space) was reprinted in 1925, and again in an enlarged 1929 edition and was a best-seller. Oberth was part of the U.S. space team working under von Braun in Alabama in 1955-1958.

Peter Schuttler was born in Wachenheim, near Frankfurt am Main, Hessen, in 1812, and went to the U.S. in 1834. He settled at first in Buffalo, later in Cleveland, and eventually in Chicago. Schuttler became a manufacturer of wagons. The Schuttler wagon was sturdy and weighed about 3,500 pounds; its superior quality caused it to displace the old praire schooner by 1850. The Schuttler wagon was especially popular with the Mormons whose mass migrations westward had begun in 1846.

Ignaz Schwinn was a co-founder, with Adolph Arnold, in 1895 of the Arnold, Schwinn & Co. bicycle firm in Chicago. Schwinn was the president and held that tenure until his death in 1952. In 1908, the company changed its name to Schwinn Bicycle Company. The company, whose initial annual production in 1895 was on the order to 25,000 units, has since manufactured millions of bicycles which over the years adopted many improvements such as balloon tires. The company continues to be a leading U.S. manufacturer of bicycles and fitness products as well as a manufacturer of bicycles in several foreign countries.

Henry Studebaker, the oldest of five brothers born in Gettys Town, Pa. (later Gettysburg, Pa.), was born in 1826. The second oldest was Clement, born in 1831. The third oldest, John Mohler Studebaker was born there in 1833. There were also two other brothers, Peter and Jacob, all of whom became involved in the manufacture of wagons and carriages. The Studebaker brothers were descendants of Clement and Anna Catherine Studebaker who were German Baptists arriving in Philadelphia in 1736. The two oldest brothers formed the H. & C. Studebaker Co. in 1852 in South Bend, Ind., doing general blacksmithing, and in 1857 made the first of hundreds of thousands of wagons which were to provide strong competition for the Schuttler wagon mentioned above. During the Civil War, the U.S. Government was a prime customer. In 1868, a new company, The Studebaker Manufacturing Co., was formed with the brothers Clement, John Mohler, and Peter as principal executives. In 1870, the company established a branch in St. Joseph, Mo. In 1897, they began the first of many experiments with self-propelled vehicles, and by 1902 sold their first electric car. The company switched to selling gasoline powered cars in 1904, and began manufacturing gasoline cars in 1909. The company was incorporated in 1911 as Studebaker Corp. Studebaker was very active in the 1932 and 1933 Indianapolis 500 Mile race by sponsoring five entries each year. The company eventually built the largest vehicle manufacturing plant in the world. Unable to overcome the effects of the 1929 Depression, the company initiated bankruptcy proceedings in 1932 and had their last auto production in 1933. The company was revived in World War II for the production of aircarft engines and amphibious cargo carriers.

Henry Clayton Stutz, was born in Ansonia, Oh., in 1876. Stutz was to become an automobile manufacturer beginning with the Ideal Motor Car Co. about 1910. In 1911, the company entered their first racing car in the Indianapolis 500-mile race, and had entries in 1911-1914, 1919, 1928, and

1930. The Stutz automobile had its peak from 1913-1919. The sporty "Stutz Bearcat" of the 1920s became a collector's item.

Wernher Magnus Maximilian von Braun was born in Wirsitz, Posen (today Poland), in 1912. He was a much desired prisoner of war in 1945 when he was sent to White Sands, N.M. to head up the weak U.S. rocketry effort. Von Braun was the leader of a team which included about forty German scientists. In 1950, von Braun led the spaceship effort in Huntsville, Ala., and he was associated with NASA from 1960-1970. Von Braun died in Alexandria, Va. in 1977.

Webster Wagner, was born in Palatine Bridge, N.Y., in 1817. Wagner became one of the first manufacturer of sleeping cars. His sleeping cars were used primarily by the N.Y. Central Railroad.

George Westinghouse was born in Central Bridge, N.Y., in 1846. He was a descendant of German immigrants from Westfalen. Westinghouse became an inventor and manufacturer of railroad equipment, best known for his part in the development of air brakes in 1869. Although Westinghouse died in 1914, the company was carried on by descendants. The Westinghouse family name evidently stems from the village of Wistinghausen, 16 km east of Bielefeld, Nordrhein-Westfalen. Today, the company is known as the Westinghouse Electric Co., with principal offices in Pittsburgh, Pa., whose emphasis is on electronics and electrical equipment. The company is number thirty-five on the *Fortune* 500 list.

TABLE 11
DIRECTORY OF ENGINEERS, INVENTORS,
BRIDGE-BUILDERS, AND TINKERERS

Civil Engineers

Ammann, Othmar Hermann (1879-1965)
Bechtel, Warren A. (1872-1933)
Bechtel, Stephen Davison, Sr. (1900-1989)
1. Bonzano, Adolphus (1830-1913)
1. Detmold, Christian Edward (1810-1887)
1. Gerhard, William Paul (1854-1927)
2. Goldmark, Henry (1857-1941)
3. Graff, Frederick (1774-1847)
4. Graff, Frederic (1817-1890)
   Greiner, John Edwin (1859-1942)
   Haupt, Herman (1817-1905)
2. Henck, John Benjamin (1815-1903)
1. Hexamer, Ernst (1827-1912)
4. Kneass, Strickland (1821-1884)
4. Kneass, Samuel Honeyman (1806-1858)
   Latrobe, Benjamin, Sr. (1764-1820)
   Latrobe, Benjamin, Jr. (1806-1878)
1. Lindenthal, Gustav (1850-1935)
   Overholzer, Edward (1869-1931)
1. Roebling, John Augustus (1806-1869)
2. Roebling, Washington Augustus (1837-1926)
1. Schleicher, Gustav (1823-1879)
1. Schneider, Charles Conrad (1843-1916)
6. Stauffer, David McNeely (1845-1913)
2. Steinman, David Bernard (1886-1960)
2. Strauss, Joseph Baermann (1870-1938)
2. Strobel, Charles Louis (1852-1936)
2. Wegmann, Edward (1859-1935)
1. Wernewag, Lewis (1769-1843)
1. Wolfel, Paul Ludwig (1862-)

Electrical Engineers

1. Behrend, Bernard Arthur (1875-1932)
   Gotshall, William Charles (1870-1935)
5. Hammer, William Joseph (1858-1934)
1. Rüdenberg, Reinhold (1883-1961)
1. Steinmetz, Charles Proteus (1865-1923)
2. Swope, Gerard (1872-1957)

Inventors, Tinkerers, and Mechanical Engineers

Beckman, Arnold Orville (1900-)
1. Berliner, Emile (1851-1929)

2. Berliner, Henry Adler (1895-1970).
   Bettendorf, William Peter (1857-1910)
1. Broadbeck, Jacob (1821-1910)
2. Clymer, George E. (1754-1834)
1. Dancel, Christian (1847-1898)
1. Eickemeyer, Rudolf (1831-1895)
1. Flad, Henry (1824-1898)
2. Fritz, John (1822-1913)
3. Gilbreth, Lillian Evelyn Moller (1878-1972)
1. Haish, Jacob (1826-1926)
5. Herr, Herbert Thacker (1876-1933)
3. Herreshoff, James Brown (1834-1930)
2. Hollerith, Hermann (1860-1929)
3. Kettering, Charles Franklin (1876-1958)
   Kiekhafer, Elmer Carl (fl. 1939-1961)
1. Kleinschmidt, Edward Ernst (1875-1940)
1. Kruesi, John (1843-1899)
2. Leyner, John George (1860-1920)
2. Lieb, John William (1860-1929)
   Mast, Phineas Price (1825-1898)
   Maurer, Robert Distler (1924-)
   Meisner, Benjamin Franklin (1890-1976)
1. Mergenthaler, Ottmar Friedrich (1854-1899)
3. Miller, Lewis (1829-1899)
3. Muller, Gertrude Agnes (1887-1954)
1. Niedringhaus, Frederick Gottlieb (1837-1922)
1. Piez, Charles (1866-1933)
3. Rittenhouse, David (1732-1790) (Rittinghausen)
2. Schick, Jacob (1877-1937)
1. Schieren, Charles Adolph (1842-1915)
1. Schneller, George Otto (1843-1895)
2. Singer, Isaac Merrit (1811-1875) (Reisinger)
   Snelling, Walter Otheman (1880-1965)
   Snyder, Howard (fl. 1899-1919)
   Spangler, James Murry (1850-1915)
1. Stetefeldt, Carl August (1838-1896)
1. Timken, Henry (1831-1909)
   Uehling, Edward A. (1849-1927)
1. Whitehead, Gustave (1874-1927) (Weisskopf)
1. Zentmayer, Joseph (1826-1888)

Transportation Engineers
2. Boeing, William Edward (1881-1956), aircraft
1. Brill, John George (1817-1888), wagons
7. Chrysler, Walter Percy (1875-1940), automobiles (Kreussler)
5. Cramp, William (1807-1879), ships
6. Cramp, Charles Henry (1828-1913), ships

1. Debus, Kurt Heinrich (1908-1983), aerospace
1. Duesenberg, August Samuel (1879-1955), racing car engines
1. Duesenberg, Frederick Samuel (1876-1932), racing car engines
3. Emanuel, Victor (1898-1960), aircraft
1. Fink, Albert (1827-1897), railroads
3. Fisher, Frederic John (1875-1941), automobiles
3. Herreshoff, John Brown (1841-1915), ships, yachts
3. Herreshoff, Nathanael Greene (1848-1938), ships, yachts
   Hoffman, Paul Gray (1891-1974), automobiles
2. Kaiser, Henry John (1882-1967), merchant ships
   Kindelberger, James Howard (1895-1962), aircraft
1. Oberth, Hermann Julius (1894-1989), aerospace
   Offenhauser, Frederick (1888-1973), racing car engines
3. Rentschler, Frederick Brant (1877-1956), aircraft
1. Schuttler, Peter (1812-1865), wagons
1. Schwinn, Ignaz (1860-1948), bicycles
4. Studebaker, Henry (1826-1895), wagons
4. Studebaker, Clement (1831-1901), wagons
4. Studebaker, John Mohler (1833-1917), wagons, automobiles
4. Studebaker, Peter (1836-1897), wagons
   Stutz, Harry Clayton (1876-1930), automobiles
1. von Braun, Wernher Magnus Maximilian (1912-1977), aerospace
3. Wagner, Webster (1817-1882), railroad cars
3. Westinghouse, George (1846-1914), railroad cars (Wistinghausen)

Code:

1. = 1st Generation in America
2. = 2nd Generation
3. = 3rd or more Generation, etc.

The Entertainment World

In America, the occurrence of notable German-American names in the world of entertainment is mainly a product of the 20th century. Certainly, there were stage actors in the 18th and 19th centuries - all the world is familiar with the assassination of President Lincoln when he was watching a play in Washington, D.C. in 1865. Some German-American names show up in entertainment management in the various biographies for the latter part of the 19th century, but with the exception of actor Richard Mansfield and actress Francesca Janauschek, names of other early actors or actresses do not occur.

The careers of stage producers tended to center naturally around the city of New York, whose large captive audience required live entertainment in the days before movies. On the other hand, the climate of southern California was more conducive to the 20th century phenomena of movie production.

With the advent of radio, silent screen movies and talkies, as well as TV, a host of opportunities for entertainers developed. The German-Americans contributed a fair share of talent to these new entertainment outlets although their role was distinctly lessened by language problems. Few foreign-born actors and entertainers ever fully mastered English, much less entirely overcome the accent problem.

Directors, producers, and managment were not so much affected by language problems. And in the two decades before World War II, they occupied a number of key positions, especially in the movie industry.

For a variety of reasons, the immigrants who settled upon the entertainment industry as a livelihood tended to come to America from eastern areas in the German-speaking countries. One reason was that, historically, the eastern areas were politically unstable, relatively speaking. Another reason was that entertainers were either born in, or attracted to, the key population centers of Berlin and Vienna.

One of the problems in immigration studies, of course, is that actors, actresses, and to a certain extent, directors and management, more often than not assumed pseudonyms, or otherwise altered their names. In a significant number of cases, little clue may be ascertained as to the ethnic origin of the name. A strong attempt is made to record deliberate name changes. Few of the following list require here a detailed description of their basically high-profile careers since they have multiple entries in the references cited in the section on Sources at the end of the book.

Actors

Woody Allen was born in New York in 1935. The popular actor and TV satirist was named originally Alen Stewart Königsberg. Königsberg is a locality name. Towns of that name are located in Bayern and in Hessen.

George Burns was born in New York in 1896. The highly successful radio and TV comedian was named originally Nathan Birnbaum. Birnbaum is a not unusual German name, meaning literally pear tree.

Tony Curtis was born in New York in 1925. The actor was named originally Bernard Schwartz. The German name Schwartz is very common, as is the variant Schwarz. The American equivalent is Black.

Douglas Fairbanks was one of the early 20th century actors, having been born in Denver, in 1883. Fairbanks was named originally Douglas Elton Ulman. The family name probably is a corruption of the German name Uhl(e)man or Ullman.

John Forsythe was born in Penn's Grove, N.J., in 1918. His name originally was John Lincoln Freund. Freund is the German word for friend.

James Garner was born in Norman, Ok., in 1928. The popular TV actor was named originally James Scott Baumgartner. The family name comes from Baumgärtner, meaning nursery man.

Emil Jannings was born in Rorschach, Kanton St. Gallen, Switzerland. Jannings began his career in Hollywood in the initial stages of the talkies in 1927-1929, and had a series of later film appearances there. His original name was Theodor Friedrich Emil Janenz; the family name shows a Slavic influence. It is perhaps related to the Schlesien name Jenisch.

Peter Lorre was born in Rosenberg, Hungary, in 1904. One of several localities in Hungary by this name may apply to Lorre's birthplace. Lorre's original name was Lazlo Löwenstein, which apparently is a combination of Hungarian followed by German. The name Löwenstein is represented also by a community in Württemberg.

Richard Mansfield was born in Berlin in 1854. Mansfield went to Boston in 1872. Likely, the family name was Mansfeld(t) which may have been derived from a community near Eisleben, Sachsen-Anhalt.

Paul Muni was born in Lemberg, Galicia, an area which at the time of his birth in 1895 was under Austrian control. His original name was Meshulom Muni Weisenfreund.

Conrad Veidt was born in Berlin in 1893. Veidt's original name was Konrad Hans Walter Weidt. The family name Weidt is a common one in the area of Rostock, Mecklenburg-Vorpommern.

Clifton Webb, was born in Indianapolis in 1893. His original name was Webb Parmelee Hollenbeck. There are a number of localities in Germany named Hollenbach, Hollenbeck, and Hollenbek.

Louis Robert Wolheim was born in New York in 1881. This stage and screen actor, who had a relatively early career, apparently was a rare entertainment personality who retained his original name.

Actresses

June Allyson was born about 1917. No birth place has been published. The original name of the actress-singer was Ella Geisman. The family was derived apparently from the German Geismann or Geismar. Five towns in Germany are named Geismar.

Mary Astor was born in Quincy, Il., in 1906. Her original name was Lucille Langhanke, daughter of Otto Langhanke. The family name is unusual; -hanke evidently is related to the Slavic Hanek, which is a short-form for Johannes.

Lauren Bacall was born in New York in 1924. Miss Bacall was named originally Betty Joan Perske. The family name is a variant of Perschke which shows a trace of northern Slavic influence.

The very popular actress and singer Doris Day was born in Cincinnati, Oh. She was the daughter of Frederick Wilhelm and Alma Sophia Kappelhoff (or Von Kappelhoff). The full names of the parents imply that they were immigrants from Germany. The family name perhaps is related to one of seven localities in Germany known as Kappel.

Marlene Dietrich was born in Berlin in 1901. Her original name was Maria Magdalena von Losch; her given names were combined and contracted to form Marlene. Marlene Dietrich had a long Hollywood career, beginning in 1930. She became famous with appearances in the movie *The Blue Angel*. Variants of the German family name include Loesch, Lösch, Loesche, and Lösche.

Marie Dressler, a relatively early stage and screen comedian, was born in Coburg, Ontario, in 1871. She was named originally Leila Koerber, whose father, Alexander Rudolph Koerber, was a native of Austria. The family name was originally either Körber or Kerber, names common to Schlesien, Böhmen (Bohemia), and Austria.

Actress Betty Grable was born in St. Louis in 1916. She was named originally Elizabeth Ruth Grable, a name which required no alteration for adaptation to the movie world, although early in her career she used the pseudonym of Francis Dean. Betty Grable was the daughter of Conn and Lillian (Hofmann) Grable. Hofmann is a distinctive German name; the family name Grable may be a variant of the German or Swiss Gräbel, Graebel or Grebel, names which are not especially common.

Actress Francesca Romana Magdalena Janauschek was born in Prague, Bohemia, in 1829. She made appearances in the United States in 1867-1874, and in 1880-1904. Janauschek died in Saratoga Springs, N.Y. in 1904. Related family names in Europe are Jannasch, Janneck, and Jannasch(ek), all of north Slavic or east German origin.

Bertha Kalich was born in Lemberg, Galicia, which at the time of her birth in 1874, was part of Austria. She went to New York in 1894 where she was known primarily as a actress who confined her talents to Yiddish theatre. She retired in 1931 and died in New York in 1939. The family name likely comes from Kalisch, a Slavic locality name.

Hedy Lamarr was born in Vienna in 1914. Lamarr went to Hollywood in 1937, and appeared in films produced there from 1938-1954. She was christened Hedwig Kiesler. The family name is a typical high German name occurring as Kiesel or Kiesler, both stemming from Kies, having to do with gravel or pebbles. The omission of an "e" in Kiesler is typical of family names in Bayern and Austria.

Actress Shelly Winters was born in St. Louis in 1922. Her original name was Shirley Schrift. The family name perhaps was shortened from an occupational name such as Schriftleiter (editor) or Schriftsteller (author).

Jane Wyman was born in St. Joseph, Mo., in 1914. Her original name was Sarah Jane Fulks. Possibly the name Fulks can be interpreted as being derived from German family name Fuchs or Folk.

Actress Loretta Young was born in Salt Lake City in 1913. Her original name was Gretchen Belzer. There are several variants of the family name such as Beltz, Beltzer, Beltzner, all likely a shortened form of Pelzhändler, that is furrier.

Film Directors and Producers

Anne Bauchens was born in St. Louis about 1881. She was the daughter of Otto and Louella (McKee) Bauchens. Bauchens went west to Hollywood, not as an actress, but as a film editor, working at times for Cecil B. DeMille, at times for his brother William C. DeMille, and at times for both jointly. Her long career in editing lasted from more than forty years, from 1917-1959.

William Dieterle was born in Ludwigshafen, Rheinland-Pfalz, in 1893. Dieterle's Hollywood career began in 1930. Related family names are Dieter and Dietrich. The variant Dieterle is common to Schwaben, in Bayern.

Carl Laemmle was born in Laupheim, Baden-Württemberg, in 1867. He went to the United States in 1884. Laemmle began as a pioneer in 1906 in the silent movie service, an outgrowth of which became the large Universal Pictures Corporation. Laemmle died in 1939. The main forms of the family name are Lamm and Lämmle.

Fritz Lang was born in Vienna, in 1890. He went to the Hollywood in 1934 where he was known as a motion picture director and writer. Lang's full name was Fritz Christon Anton Lang.

Ernst Lubitsch was born in Berlin in 1892. Lubitsch went to Hollywood in 1922-23 and thereafter produced numerous pictures of a so-called "witty nature." He died in Hollywood in 1947. Related family names are Lubisch and Lubig, all showing northern Slavic or perhaps Schlesien origin.

Friedrich Wilhelm Murnau was born in Bielefeld, Nordrhein-Westfalen in 1889. Murnau, whose original family name was Plump, was another early film director whose Hollywood career bridged the transition from silent movies to talkies. Murnau died in 1931. In Europe, the family name occurs as Plump or Plümpe, meaning tubby or fat, and is common to low German language areas.

Erich Pommer was born in Hildesheim, Niedersachsen, in 1889. The Hollywood career of Pommer was similar to that of Murnau. The name Pommer occurs commonly in the area around München, in Bayern.

Otto Preminger was born in Wien (Vienna) in 1906. Preminger was a refugee film producer who went to Hollywood in 1935. For the year, 1935-1951, Preminger worked for 20th Century Fox Studios. In 1953, Preminger obtained enough financial backing in order to become an independent producer of films, and until 1980, he produced numerous well-known films.

Max Reinhardt was born in Baden bei Wien (Vienna), Austria, in 1873. Reinhardt went to New York as a refugee about 1938, relatively late in his career. While still in Austria, he was primarily known as a producer of plays. Reinhardt's original name was Max Goldman. The main form of the family name, Goldmann, is used today only by Jewish families.

Irving Grant Thalberg was born in Brooklyn in 1899 as the son of an immigrant father. Thalberg achieved fame as a motion picture director who was associated with the large Metro-Goldwyn-Mayer Co. during the years 1923-1936. The name Thalberg occurs at two localities in Germany.

Erich Von Stroheim was born in Wien (Vienna) in 1885. After his arrival in the United States in 1909, he developed an career as a early motion picture director and actor.

Lois Weber was born in Allegheny, Pa. in 1881. She was a rare female motion picture director as well as a writer and actress. Weber was associated with Universal Pictures and produced dozens of films in the years 1914-1921, and in 1926-1934. The very common family name of Weber is an occupational name referring to weaver.

Billy Wilder was born in Suca, Galicia, in 1906 and went to the United States as a refugee in 1934. Wilder's best known film was *Sunset Boulevard*, produced in 1950. After a long career as a motion picture director, he remains active as a consultant. Wilder's original name was Samuel Wilder. In Europe, the several variants on the family name are Wild(t), Wilde, and Wilder.

Entertainers, Critics, and Pop Musicians

Fanny Brice was born in Manhattan, N.Y.C., in 1891. She was the daughter of Charles and Rose (Stern) Borach, the father being an immigrant from Alsace. Fanny Brice developed a high-profile career, virtually at home in New York, for she was a prominent member of the Ziegfeld Follies from 1910-1936.

Bob Dylan was born in Duluth, Mich., in 1941. The popular folk singer and composer was christened Robert Alan Zimmermann. The relatively common family name is sometimes translated into English as Carpenter, an occupational name.

John Denver was born in Roswell, N.M., in 1943. He was another popular folk singer and composer. Denver's original name was Henry John Deutschendorf, Jr. Even in Europe, this unusual family name is not at all common.

Hedda Hopper was not an entertainer in the direct sense, but for the years 1938-1965 wrote a Hollywood gossip column which tended to be politically inclined toward the ultra-right. She was named Elda Furry, born in Hollidaysburg, Pa., as the daughter of David and Margaret (Miller) Furry, who were reportedly "German Quakers." She had a mediocre career as an actress from 1907-1935, before she encountered success in her second career. By the time Hopper started her gossip column, Louella Parsons, mentioned below, was well along in her similar career. Hopper and Parsons provided much needed competition for each other.

The magician Harry Houdini was born apparently in Budapest, Hungary, in 1874. Houdini traveled often between the United States and Europe and died in Detroit in 1926. His original name was Erik Weisz (or Weiss).

Comedian George Jessel was born in New York in 1898 as the son of Joseph Aaron and Charlotte (Schwartz) Jessel. In Europe, the family name occurs rarely, sometimes as Jeschel.

Lillian Leitzel was born in Breslau, Silesia, in 1892. She came as a circus aerial gymnast to the United States in 1908 and died an accidental death in Copenhagen in 1931. She was christened Leopoldina Mitza Pelikan and had a childhood nickname of Litzl, a name she later used as a family name in her career.

Lotte Lenya, whose original name was Karoline Wilhelmine Blaumauer, was born in Hitzing, near Wien (Vienna), in 1898. She is variously listed as an actress, dancer, and singer. She was married three times, most notably to the composer Kurt Weill, who died in 1950. Lenya's most notable performance was that as the star, in N.Y., of the operetta "The Three Penny Opera".

Louella O. Parsons was born in Freeport, Il., in 1880. After going to Los Angeles in 1925, she became a notorious motion picture columnist whose half-truths inspired fear in the industry and entertained Americans throughout the States. Parsons retired in 1964. Her family name was originally Oettinger, a name which also occurs as Ottinger and Öttinger. There is a town of about 4,000 population in Bayern called Oettingen.

In recent years, none was more famous than the popular von Trapp family group led by Maria Augusta von Trapp. The von Trapps were Austrians who made their first appearance in America in 1938 and a year later became permanent residents.

Stage Management

The Frohman brothers, Charles, Daniel, and Gustave, were born in Sandusky, Oh., as the sons of an immigrant father. The father, Henry, came from Darmstadt, Hessen, in 1854. The brothers, at times operating independently of one another, developed careers as theatrical managers and producers, mainly in New York. The family name was adapted from Frommann, meaning a pious person.

Maurice Grau was born in Brünn, Moravia (then under Austrian administration, now in the Czech Republic), in 1849. He went to New York in 1854 and developed an extensive career as a theatrical agent and operatic impresario, the latter in connection with the New York Metropolitan Opera. He left the Met in 1903 and died in 1907.

Heinrich Conried was born in Bielitz, Galicia, in 1855. Conried was an actor, but was known mainly for producing and directing musicial events, mainly operettas and the like, after his arrival in the United States in 1877/78. Conried directed the Germania Theatre, the Thalia Theatre, and the Irving Palace Theatre, all in N.Y. He was the manager of the Metropolitan Opera House (replacing Grau) in N.Y. from 1903-1908.

Oscar Hammerstein I was born in Stettin, Pommern (now northwest Poland), about 1847, and raised in Berlin. In 1863, he went to the United States. Hammerstein's biographers list him as a musician, inventor, composer, theatrical impresario, and N.Y. opera producer whose primary career was the Hammerstein Opera Co. Hammerstein died in 1919. Hammerstein's famous grandson is cited in the Music Directory. The name Hammerstein is represented by several towns in Germany of the same name.

Theresa Helburn was born in N.Y., in 1887. She was the daughter of native German Julius and Hannah (Peyser) Helburn. She married John Baker Opdycke, but kept the name Helburn for professional reasons. In 1914, she was the principal agent in the formation of the Washington Square Players which eventually became the Theatre Guild of N.Y. Noted successes were the initial productions of Oklahoma and Carousel, both produced during the war years of 1943-1944. Helburn retired from the theatrical business in 1953.

Marc Klaw was born in Paducah, Ky. in 1858, of a father who traced his ancestry to Bavaria. In 1881, Klaw moved to New York where he was employed as a theatrical booking agent by Gustave Frohman. In 1896, Klaw was part of a four man syndicate (Klaw, Erlanger, Frohman, Zimmerman) who developed the "theatrical syndicate," a group which by 1910 had a monopoly on theatrical productions in New York. The several variants of the family name include Klaws, Klaue, and Klaffs, which are derived from Klaus.

Marcus Loew was born in New York in 1870 of parents who came from Wien (Vienna) about 1869. Loew was a well known theatre owner and motion picture producer whose chain of theatres were incorporated into Metro-Goldwyn-Mayer and whose pictures included the famous roaring lion in the introduction. Variants of the family name include Löwe, Löw, and Loew, all being derived from the German name for lion.

Charles Ringling was the leader of five brothers who became circus proprietors about 1882. By 1907, the Ringling Bros. were the dominant entertainers in their field, having absorbed a number of other firms including the famous Barnum & Bailey Co. The brothers eventually moved their headquarters to Sarasota, Fl., a location climatically favorable to their business, and there, expanded into real estate. Florida's west coast owes much of its development to them. Charles Ringling was born in McGregor, Iowa, in 1863. The brothers were the sons of August Frederick Rüngeling who came from near Kassel, Hannover (now Hessen), about 1840.

Samuel Lionel Rothafel was born in Stillwater, Minn., in 1881. He became a theatre manager in New York in 1912-1913. The famous N.Y. "Rockettes" and the "Roxy" motion picture theatres derived their name from his family name. Rothafel was the son of Gustav Rothapfel whose forebears had come from Germany about 1820. The family name translates simply as "red apple."

The most colorful family of all musical promotors, involved Florenz Ziegfeld, who was born in Jever, Oldenburg (now Niedersachsen). Records do not show his birth date (which was probably about 1840), but Ziegfeld arrived in the United States in 1863. Ziegfeld was the president of the Chicago Musical College from 1867-1912. The son by the same name, Florenz Ziegfeld, was born in Chicago in 1869. The younger Ziegfeld eventually moved to New York where, in 1927, he formed the famous Ziegfeld Theatre, whose lavish popular productions gained fame worldwide. The younger Ziegfeld died in Hollywood in 1932, bankrupt as a result of overspending in those economically disastrous times. The family name apparently is derived from Ziegenfeld, meaning goat field.

TABLE 12
DIRECTORY OF THE ENTERTAINMENT WORLD
* Note: Original family names are recorded in parentheses.

Actors
Allen, Woody (1935-) (Konigsberg)
Burns, George (1896-) (Birnbaum)
3. Calhern, Louis (1896-1956) (Carl Henry Vogt)
Curtis, Tony (1925-) (Schwartz)
Fairbanks, Douglas (1883-1939) (Ulman)
Forsythe, John (1918-) (Freund)
Garner, James (1928-) (Baumgartner)
1. Jannings, Emil (1884-1950) (Janenz)
1. Lorre, Peter (1904-1964) (Löwenstein)
1. Mansfield, Richard (1854-1907)
1. Muni, Paul (1895-1967) (Weisenfreund)
1. Veidt, Conrad (1893-1943) (Weidt)
Webb, Clifton (1893-1966) (Hollenbeck)
Wolheim, Louis Robert (1881-1931)

Actresses
Allyson, June (1917-) (Geisman)
2. Astor, Mary (1906-1987) (Langhanke)
2. Bacall, Lauren (1924-) (Perske)
1. Cornell, Katharine (1893-1974)
Day, Doris (1924-) (Kapelhoff)
1. Dietrich, Marlene (1901-1992) (von Losch)
2. Dressler, Marie (c.1869-1934)
Grable, Betty (1916-1973)
1. Hagen, Uta Thyra (1919-)
1. Janauschek, Francesca Romana Magdalena
   (1829-1904)
1. Kalich, Bertha (1874-1939)
1. Lamarr, Hedy (1914-) (Kiesler)
Lamour, Dorothy (1914-1976) (Kaumeyer)
Winters, Shelley (1922-) (Schrift)
Wyman, Jane (1914-) (Fulks)
Young, Loretta (1913-) (Belzer)

Film Directors and Producers
Bauchens, Anne (?1881-1967)
1. Dieterle, William (1893-1972)
1. Laemmle, Carl (1867-1939)
1. Lang, Fritz Christian Anton (1890-1976)
1. Lubitsch, Ernst (1892-1947)
1. Murnau, Friedrich Wilhelm (1888-1931)(Plump)
1. Pommer, Erich (1889-1966)

1. Preminger, Otto Ludwig (1906-1986)
1. Reinhardt, Max (1873-1943)(Goldman)
2. Thalberg, Irving Grant (1899-1936)
1. Stroheim, Erich Oswald (1885-1957) (Von Stroheim)
   Weber, Lois (1881-1939)(Eichelbaum)
1. Wilder, Billy (1906-)
1. von Sternberg, Josef (1894-1969) (Jonas Sternberg)

Entertainers, Critics, and Pop Musicians
3. Berg, Gertrude Edelstein (1899-1966) (Edelstein)
2. Brice, Fanny (1891-1951)
   Denver, John (1943-) (Deutschendorf)
2. Dressler, Marie (1869?-1934) (Koerber)
   Dylan, Bob (1941-) (Zimmerman)
1. Holm, Hanya (1893-1992) (Eckert)
   Hopper, Hedda (1885-1966) (Elda Furry)
1. Houdini, Harry (1874-1926) (Weisz)
2. King, Alan (1927-) (Kniberg)
2. Lahr, Bert (1895-1967) (Irving Lahrheim)
1. Leitzel, Lillian (1892-1931) (Pelikan)
   Merman, Ethel (1909-1984) (Zimmermann)
1. Lenya, Lotte (1898-1981) (Blaumauer)
3. Parsons, Louella O. (1880-1972) (Oettinger)
1. von Trapp, Maria Augusta (1905-1987)

Stage Management
1. Conried, Heinrich (1855-1909)
   Erlanger, Abraham Lincoln (1860-1930)
2. Frohman, Charles (1860-1915)(Frommann)
2. Frohman, Daniel (1851-1940)
1. Grau, Maurice (1849-1907)
1. Hammerstein, Oscar I (c. 1847-1919)
2. Helburn, Theresa (1887-1959)
3. Klaw, Marc, (1858-1936)
2. Lewisohn, Alice (1883-1972)
2. Lewisohn, Irene (1892-1944)
2. Loew, Marcus (1870-1927)
1. Maretzek, Max (1821-1897)
2. Ringling, Charles (1863-1926)(Rüngeling)
3. Rothafel, Samuel Lionel (1881-1936)(Rothapfel)
1. Ullman, Bernhard (?1817-1885)(Uhlman)
2. Ziegfeld, Florenz, Jr. (1869-1932)

Code:
1. = 1st Generation in America
2. = 2nd Generation
3. = 3rd or more Generation, etc.

The World of
High Finance and Big Business

The vast natural resources of the United States provided undreamed of opportunities for those who had the initiative, unbounded energy, and a little bit of luck.

In the early days, there were furs and tobacco growing to exploit. This was followed by local mercantile and international trading. Then came the growing of grains, first in Pennsylvania and New York, later in Ohio, Illinois, and Indiana, and finally in Iowa, Kansas, and Nebraska. Ultimately, fortunes were made in in the east with coal and coke production, iron and steel manufacture, and in the far west with lead, zinc, and silver mining and smelting. And in California, the sugar refiners and citrus fruits did pretty well, too. And finally, the exploitation of oil and gas in Pennsylvania, Oklahoma, Texas, and Louisiana pushed America far into the forefront. Those were just the main natural resources, the cream of the crop.

With the rapidly growing population of the 19th century, service industries such as railroading, finance, banking, and real estate speculation gave rise to spectacular fortunes. After the 1830s, great wealth was directed at, and concentrated in New York City. Much of this wealth was concentrated in Manhattan real estate who value increased by leaps and bounds. Investment in Manhattan real estate was the prime source for the fortunes of a number of German-Americans.

It was almost as if too much came too fast. Some fell by the wayside during the panic years of 1784-1787, 1807-1809, 1818-1822, 1837-1843, 1873-1875, 1893-1896, and especially during the big depression period which began in 1929 and lasted until mobilization for war some ten years later. But survivors persisted through every crisis. The survivors included many big names native to the German-speaking lands. Selected key names are discussed below with honorable mention given to the entire list in the directory.

Bankers, Capitalists, & Financiers

The Frankfurter Wertpapierbörse (Frankfurt Stock Exchange) began in 1585, but for the most of two centuries dealt mainly in German and foreign currency. Sixty-five German cities as well as many of the 300-odd German principalities issued their own coins. Numismatists have catalogued more than 200 different "Talers" issued in Germany during the 17th century. In addition to German coins, trading was in coins from at least nine other European countries. The American dollar takes its name from the German Taler.

Commercial paper dealing in Frankfurt evidently began in the late 17th century. The Saalhof group was formed in 1677 in Frankfurt to purchase an interest in Penn's charter for land in America. This charter was granted to the Englishman William Penn in 1681. The "Frankfort Companie" acquired rights to acreage in 1684 and in 1686 for a total of 25,000 acres. The Frankfurt interests paved the way for the ultimately successful village of Germantown, which today is part of Philadelphia.

In 1717, another Frankfurt group took an option on John Law's charter for the "Compagnie d'Occident" which was granted territory under French control in the Mississippi delta area. Because of over-speculation in these securities, the group headed by Law, a Scotsman, went bankrupt in 1720.

In 1847, the "Mainzer Adelsverein" negotiated (belatedly) with Frankfurt bankers for securities relating to land in central Texas. In 1849, U.S. Government bonds were offered on the Frankfurt stock exchange, and in 1852, the first of many U.S. railroad bonds were offered. These railroad bonds took a backseat to U.S. Government bonds subscribed by Frankfurt brokers during the American Civil War. After the Civil War, securities offered on the Frankfurt Exchange included those for the first transatlantic cable, municipal bonds, U.S. railroad bonds, U.S. Government bonds, and bonds floated by the state of California.

The history of the New York Stock Exchange reflects the history of modern day America. The NYSE had its beginning in 1792 when a group of brokers formally organized trading of bonds. This beginning in the area of Wall Street in lower Manhattan persisted in moderate form until 1817 when the New York Stock & Exchange Board was created. Early trading dealt mainly with stocks and bonds relating to the building of, at first, roads, canals and other public infrastructure. By the 1830s, there was increasing demand for the funding of railroads, a demand which lasted through the 19th century and was particularily heavy in the latter part of the century.

The immigration boom of the 1840s and the 1850s made New York City the nation's financial capital. It occupied the same role that Frankfurt am Main did in Germany. There was in fact extremely close ties between the two cities through the Jewish families who dominated the world of finance. These ties were cemented immensely during the Civil War by the Union forces' need for funds.

In 1863, the NYS&EB changed its name to the NYSE. The NYSE was beginning to mature at this time. Tools such as the telegraph which came into its own about 1853, the first transatlantic cable in 1866, and stock ticker in 1867, and the first telephone in the stock exchange materially advanced trading volumes.

Black Friday, Sept. 24, 1869, was the day when the government intervened in speculative attempts by James Fisk and Jay Gould to corner the gold market. Also in 1869, the NYSE required that all companies on the exchange be registered, a matter which eventually led to the issuance of annual and quarterly reports of listed companies, a registration of outstanding stock, and the like.

Corporations, many of whose growth was stymied for lack of funds until the 1880s, developed the concept of incorporating, selling stock, and using public funds for capitalization. Not withstanding the registration requirements by the NYSE, the period from 1865-1900 was called the Gilded Age (a term used for the title of a 1873 book by Mark Twain, i.e., Samuel Longhorn Clemens, 1835-1910) to denote a free-for-all atmosphere when individuals such as Cornelius Vanderbilt (1794-1877), Daniel Drew (1797-1879), Jay (Jason) Gould (1836-1892), Edward Henry Harriman (1848-1909), and James Fisk, Jr. (1834-1872) used tactics considered unethical today. They accumulated great paper wealth and, in most cases, great material wealth, based in large part on the massive build-up of railroad lines. Many great mansions were contructed in Newport, R.I., by the nabobs of the Gilded Age.

A major element in the financial world was created in 1882 with the founding of Dow-Jones & Co., Inc. by Charles Henry Dow (1851-1902), Edward D. Jones, and Charles M. Bergstresser. In 1889, the company began publishing the *Wall Street Journal* which has become the world's premier financial newspaper and which rivals the *New York Times* and the *Washington Post* for regular news. What the *Wall Street Journal* does so successfully is to cut through the maze of financial gobbledygook and present financial data in a manner which is comprehensible to the average reader. In 1896, the *Wall Street Journal* created the first major industrial stock index. This was an extremely important factor in showing the fluctuation of various groups of stocks within the overall market.

Great industrial fortunes were amassed by the early part of the 20th century as exemplified by names such as Andrew Carnegie (1835-1919), Henry Clay Frick (1849-1919), Andrew Mellon (1855-1937), John Pierpont Morgan (1837-1913), and John D. Rockefeller (1839-1937). Much of this wealth had to do with investments in oil and steel.

Listing requirements on the NYSE were reinforced in the era after the 1907 Panic. And the creation a progressive income tax in 1913 and the Federal Reserve System in 1914 marked the increased role of government in business. But it all came tumbling down on Black Tuesday, Oct. 24, 1929, when the market crashed as a result of unbridled speculation by millions of investors.

Today's great financial brokerage firms of New York City include Goldman, Sachs & Co. (founded about 1882), Kuhn, Loeb & Co. (merged into Lehman Bros. in 1977), and Lehman Bros. (founded about 1852), all of which had their American beginnings in the latter part of the 19th century through the intense efforts of German immigrants.

Certainly not all the financiers were Jewish. In fact, the non-Jewish element runs from Astor to Rockefeller and beyond. Selected individuals from the combined list follows, with the entire list in the directory.

Walter Hubert Annenberg was born in Milwaukee, in 1908. He was the son of Moses Louis and Sadie Cecilia (Friedman) Annenberg. In 1928, Annenberg joined his father's publishing firm, then centered in Philadelphia, which was Triangle Publications. He became head of the firm in 1942 and introduced the very successful magazine Seventeen as well as TV Guide. Annenberg eventually acquired a variety of other interests including real estate and a series of radio and TV stations in and around Philadelphia. In fact, he is currently listed as number eighty on *Fortune* magazine's list of billionaries.

John Jacob Astor, III, was born in New York in 1822. He was the descendant of Johannes Jacob Astor, I, who came to the United States in 1783 from the town of Walldorf, near Heidelberg, in Baden-Württemberg. Astor was the heir to the fortune accumulated by the immigrant ancestor listed below under Merchants. He expanded into real estate and other ventures. The family name is shown on one of New York City's premier hotels, the Waldorf-Astoria, in the city of Astoria, Ore., and at other localities. The family name has been related to the Italian-Piedmonte region where the name was Astore, meaning hawk.

August Belmont was born in Alzei (now Alzey in Rheinland-Pfalz), in 1816. He was the son of Simon and Frederika (Elsaß) Belmont, and was educated at schools in Frankfurt am Main. Belmont went to New York in 1837. There he developed rapidly a multifaceted-career as a financier, capitalist, banker, and political leader. Belmont became one of the first really big banking names in America. The family name is carried in Belmont Race Track in New Jersey, and elsewhere.

George Blumenthal was born in Frankfurt am Main on an undocumented date, apparently in the late 19th century. Like so many bankers, Blumenthal's career started in Frankfurt and ended in New York. He died in 1941. Blumenthal was connected with the Fifth Avenue Bank of New York.

Francis Martin Drexel was born in Dorbirn, Vorarlberg, Austria, in 1792, and went to Philadelphia in 1817. The Drexel name is known world-wide through Drexel & Co., brokers in currency. The family name and the business was propagated by Anthony Joseph Drexel and Joseph William Drexel, sons of Francis Martin Drexel.

Henry Morrison Flagler was born in Hopewell, N.Y. in 1830. He was a descendant of Zachariah Flegler who came from the Palatinate, now state of Rheinland-Pfalz, about 1710. Flagler was an associate of John D. Rockefeller (1839-1937). Together they consolidated the scattered independents in the early oil business and formed Standard Oil, later Standard Oil of New Jersey, the world's largest oil company. Flagler used part of his early fortune in real estate ventures in east Florida. In fact, his promotion of real estate along the east coast of Florida, from Jacksonville south to Key West, initiated one of the Florida real estate booms. Flagler constructed luxury hotels in St. Augustine and Palm Beach, Fla., and elsewhere. The Flagler family name is a prominent street name in downtown Miami and elsewhere. The name is carried also by the Henry M. Flagler Museum in Palm Beach, Fla.

Henry Clay Frick was born in West Overton, Pa., in 1849. He was the son of John W. Frick, of Swiss background, and Elizabeth Overholt Frick, of Palatine Mennonite ancestors. Both the Fricks and the Overholts went to Pennsylvania in the early 18th century. Henry Clay Frick was a coke and steel manufacturer in the Pittsburgh area, who at times, was associated with Andrew Mellon (1855-1937), banker, and Andrew Carnegie (1835-1919), steel manufacturer. Frick acquired the name of the "Coke King." The Frick family name is born by the Frick (art) Collection in Manhattan.

Lewis Gerstle was born in Ichenhausen, Bayern, in 1824. Gerstle was among the early 19th century refugees, arriving in Philadelphia in 1847. His fortune was made in merchandising on the West Coast where he was also a pioneer capitalist.

Marcus Goldman was born in Burgebrach, Bayern, in 1821, and went to N.Y. in 1848. Goldman was a N.Y. banker as from 1869. The giant investment banking firm of Goldman, Sachs & Co. was organized about 1882 when Henry Goldman (c. 1852-1935) and son-in-law Samuel Sachs (1851-1935) officially became representatives of the company. The firm joined the N.Y. Stock Exchange in 1896.

Otto Herman Kahn was born at Mannheim, Baden, in 1867. He went to New York in 1893, where he was associated with the renowned financiers Kuhn, Loeb & Co. Kahn had a close working relationship with Edward H. Harriman, a prominent railroad and real estate man, of New York. Kahn left an indelible record on American Society, having been President of the New York Metropolitan Opera Association for the years 1918-1931. As early as 1903, the Met received a big boost through personal financial contributions from Kahn.

Arthur Lehman was born in New York in 1873 and died there in 1936. His father went to the U.S. in 1850 from Rimpar, near Würzberg, Bayern. The younger Lehman became a partner in the team of the universally-known investment banking firm of Lehman Bros., a position he held from 1898-1936.

Adolph Lewisohn was born in Hamburg in 1849 and went to the U.S. sometime thereafter. Lewisohn has his start as a merchant of horsehair bristles, a venture which proved successful enough for him to expand into mining speculation and banking areas. The family merchant business originated in Holland during the boom days of the 16th century, and was transferred to Germany about 1609. The name apparently went through a series of changes from Levy, to Levysohn, and finally to Lewisohn.

Solomon L. Loeb, was born in Bayern, Germany, in 1828, and went to New York in 1849 as part of the great wave of migrants. Loeb was one of the original partners in the investment banking firm of Kuhn, Loeb & Co. He had two sons, James L. (see below) and Morris L. (1863-1912) who carried on the family business and two daughters, Nina J. and Therese, who married the prominent financiers Paul M. Warburg and Jacob H. Schiff.

James L. Loeb was born in New York in 1867, and was affiliated with the firm of Kuhn, Loeb & Co. from 1888-1901. After 1910, Loeb, a bibliophile, sponsored the Loeb Classical Library which eventually amounted to

360 volumes. In 1913, Loeb moved to an estate in Murnau, Bayern, where he lived until his death in 1933.

Jakob Heinrich Schiff (Jacob Henry Schiff in the U.S.) was born in Frankfurt am Main in 1847. He went to New York temporarily in 1865, and permanently in 1874. Schiff became a full partner of Kuhn, Loeb & Co. from 1875-1920, that is during the railroad boom days and was a driving force in the company's emergence as a prime investment banking firm. Schiff also was heavily involved in the insurance business. He became head of Kuhn, Loeb & Co. in 1885, a position which was aided by his marriage to Therese Loeb. Therese Loeb's mother's name was Kuhn and thus Kuhn, Loeb, and Schiff were directly related. Jacob Schiff also held a high position for many years as the lay head of American Jewry.

Joseph and Jesse Seligman were born in Baiersdorf, Bayern, the older brother in 1819, and the younger in 1827. The older brother went to Philadelphia in 1837 where he was involved initially in clothing merchandising and importing. The younger brother went to Alabama in 1841, and in few years to California. In 1851, the two brothers were part of a family team which formed J. & W. Seligman & Co., bankers, in New York. In 1862, the house of Seligman expanded into international banking as a result of the Civil War. Their effort at selling bonds in Frankfurt am Main provided a tremendous boost for the Union cause.

James Speyer was born in New York in 1861. At the age of 22, he received on-the-job training at the family's banking house in Frankfurt am Main, and subsequently returned to New York. The two brothers, James and Albert, were active partners in the brewering industry, real estate, and other N.Y. interests. The family name undoubtedly is derived from the city in Rheinland-Pfalz of the same name.

Paul Moritz Warburg and Felix Moritz Warburg were born in Hamburg, the older brother in 1868, and the younger brother in 1871. They went to the U.S. in 1902. Both became partners in Kuhn, Loeb & Co. Their ties to the financial world were solidified by marriages, Paul M. to Nina J. Loeb, and Felix M. to Frieda Schiff.

Economists

The directory shows a limited number of individuals in this category. Some came from families which were connected to the banking industry. As a group they occupied a position somewhere between the academic people and the financiers.

Milton Friedman was born in Brooklyn in 1912. His career was spent with the research staff of the Bureau of Economic Research in New York. Friedman won the Nobel Prize for economic sciences in 1975.

Jacob Harry Hollander was born in Baltimore in 1871. Hollander was associated, as an economist, with Johns Hopkins University off and on during the years of 1894-1940.

Lawrence Robert Klein was born in Omaha, Nebr., in 1920. His career was that of economist and educator at the University of Pennsylvania, beginning in 1958. Klein won the Nobel Prize in economic sciences in 1980.

Jacob Schoenhof was born in Oppenheim, Rheinland-Pfalz, in 1839. Schoenhof went to the U.S. in 1861 and developed a career as an economist. He was a strong advocate of free trade.

Theodore William Schulz was born in Arlington, S.D., in 1902. He was an economist at the University of Chicago from 1943-1961, and later, had a variety of positions. Schultz was awarded the Nobel Prize in economic sciences in 1979.

Joseph Alois Schumpeter was born in Triesch, Mähren (Moravia), in 1883. Schumpeter was a refugee who went to the U.S. in 1932. He was an economist at Harvard University.

John Christopher Schwab was born in New York in 1865. His relatively short career was than of an economist and librarian at Yale University. Schwab died in 1916.

Edwin Robert Anderson Seligman was born in New York in 1861. He was an economist at Columbia University from 1904-1931. Seligman was well prepared for his career, being a son of one of the founders of J. & W. Seligman & Co., international financiers. Seligman published many books which emphasized the history of economic thought, especially from the German viewpoint. Seligman was a specialist on tax policies.

George Joseph Stigler was born in Renton, Wash., in 1911. He had a variety of posts, one being at the University of Chicago, beginning in 1958. Stigler received the Nobel Prize in economic sciences in 1982.

Today's Corporate America

Modern corporate America includes a number of large firms whose CEO's are of German-Americans or Swiss-American background. Some examples are: David W. Graebel, Grabel Van Lines, Wausau, WI; Robert P. Hauptfuhrer, Oryx Energy Company, Dallas; Horst Langer, Siemens Corp., N.Y.; Eckhard Pfeiffer, Compaq Computer Corp., Houston; Ewing Marion Kauffman (deceased), Marion Labs (now Marion, Merrell, Dow, Inc., pharmaceuticals); and William Batterman Ruger, head of Sturm, Ruger & Co. (firearms).

Key German products and services in America are prominently displayed in every metropolitan area. A few of the more prominent include Mannesmann industrial products, Lufthansa airlines, and Mercedes-Benz luxury automobiles. All these are distinguished by rather distinctive logos which originated in the early part of the 20th century.

Industry - Top 500 and Large Corporations

The following list of 153 individuals provide exciting examples of rags-to-riches stories. Nearly all of the founders of what latter became large corporations were individualists whose persistence, determination, insight, and good fortune made many of their names a household word. Some went bankrupt on the first or second try; these experiences led to eventual success. And successful they were compared to European standards. Today, most of the following companies remain in business under their own name; some have merged with other companies; a few changed their name. Nearly all are on the N.Y. Stock Exchange, often referred to as the Big Board. Many of the founders are listed in the National Hall of Fame for Business Leadership which maintains a gallery of laureates in Chicago's Museum of Science & Technology. This gallery was initiated in 1975 by *Fortune* magazine and since its inception has 145 individuals, of which twenty-three have family names of easily recognizable German origin. In 1978, Babson College, in Babson Park, Mass. created an An Academy of Distinguished Entrepreneurs which currently cites fifty-two men and women including eight whose family names are of obvious German origin. The *Fortune* magazine list does not duplicate the Babson College list, the former being mainly deceased and the latter being mainly still living.

Virtually all of the following companies provide extremely interesting case studies for today's MBA's. The boom or bust cycle, especially in manufacturing, was repeated many times. The war years of 1861-1865, 1914-1918, and 1941-1945 gave impetuous to economic growth through abnormal demand; the financial crisis years of 1784-1787, 1807-1809, 1818-1822, 1837-1843, 1873-1875, 1893-1896, and 1929-1936 proved challenging for the opposite reason. The major executives in these cycles were those listed below.

When one examines the corporate histories of selected industries such as Brunswick Corp. (sporting equipment, et al., founded 1845), Hart Schaffner & Marx (men's apparel, founded 1872), Hershey Foods Corp. (chocolate, et al., founded 1905), Kroger (food merchandising, founded 1883), Levi Strauss Associates (apparel, founded 1853), Lukens Inc. (iron & steel manufacturing, founded 1817), Maytag Corp. (washing machines, et al., founded 1893), Rohm & Haas (industrial chemicals, founded 1909), or Smucker (jelly and other food products, founded 1897), one finds that virtually all histories start and end with a German and Swiss tradition: quality products. In between, corporate histories cite a mind-numbing array of success factors such as cost effective advertising, eye-catching advertising (slogans, logos, mascots), ear-catching slogans, low overhead, unique products, high margin products, product enhancement, organized research, customer service, utilization of foreign technology, internal product research, crystal clear mission, relatively few product lines, plant efficiency, acquisitions, good packaging, efficient product distribution, horizontal integration, vertical integration, dependable employees, response to consumer demands, and a host of other factors, not to mention good luck. Of course a liberal dose of hard work and attention to detail, bordering on the fanatic, are also characteristics of the German-speaking people. Centuries of European experience, coupled with a grueling migration process, provided the necessary drive to excel.

Very large, privately held companies, whose names reflect a German-American origin, in order of size, include: Koch Industries (Wichita, Ks.);

Goldman, Sachs & Co. (N.Y); Bechtel Group (San Francisco); Levi Strauss & Co. (San Francisco); Anschutz (Denver); Kohler (Kohler, Wisc.); Schreiber Foods (Green Bay, Wisc.); Schottenstein Stores (Columbus, Oh.); J. M. Huber (Edison, N.J.); Zeigler Coal Holding (Fairview Heights, Ill.); Schneider National (Green Bay, Wisc.); Stroh Brewing (Detroit); Snyder General (Dallas); Moyer Packing (Souderton, Pa.); Fred W. Albrecht Grocery (Akron, Oh.); Berwind Corp. (Philadelphia); and Schwegemann Giant Super Markets (New Orleans, La.).

German-American products which have become household names in the 20th century include: Scholl's (foot care products); Calvin Klein (jeans); Eddie Bauer (outdoor gear); Bulova (watches); Fisher (Fisher-Price toys); Fleischmann (yeast and margarine); Hellmann (mayonnaise); Mueller (noodles); Redenbacher (gourmet popping corn); Rempp (Adolph's meat tenderizer); Schick (razors); Sheaffer (pens); Stouffer (frozen foods); Brach (candy); Gebhardt (Tex-Mex foods); Kraft (cheese); Mennen (men's toiletries); and Florsheim (shoes).

And, of course, the old five and ten cent stores of Kress and Kresge hardly exist anymore, having been displaced by giant K-Marts (formerly Kresge's) and even larger discount houses. In recent years, the American phenomena of giant discount houses has been copied in Germany and in other parts of the world.

Huge public service companies, whose founders were German-American, include the State Farm Insurance Companies, and H & R. Block Corporation (income tax preparation).

Modern companies judge each other's success by their ranking on the annual *Fortune* 500 list, and whether or not they are traded on the New York Stock Exchange. A number of these companies whose founders were German-American, are listed alphabetically below.

John Jacob Bausch was born in Süßen, Württemberg, in 1830. Bausch's 1849 trip from Le Havre to N.Y. lasted forty-nine days. Bausch settled in Rochester, N.Y., and in 1853, became one of two founders of the famous optical manufacturing firm of Bausch & Lomb. Bausch was in fact the president of the company for about seventy-five years. In the early days, the company concentrated on eye glasses. In 1874, Bausch & Lomb began the manufacture of microscopes. Later they made search light mirrors, photographic lenses, optical glasses, range finders, and binoculars. The other part of the team, Henry Lomb, was born in Burghaun, Hessen, in 1828. In 1849, Lomb sailed from Bremerhaven, and settled in Rochester, N.Y. Lomb died in 1908. Bausch & Lomb is number 245 on the *Fortune* 500 list.

John Drew Betz was born about 1930. He was head of Betz Laboratories from 1941-1971. The firm was founded in 1925 by L. D. Betz, his father. Betz Labs makes various chemicals for purifying industrial water and waste water, and develops process systems. The company has been on the forefront of environmental protection ecology, or perhaps ahead of it, and has been very successful, ranking today as number 438 on the *Fortune* 500 list. Two villages in Germany bear the name Betzdorf. The prefix "Betz" is used in the name of nine other German villages.

Louis Blaustein was born in Baltimore in 1892. In 1910, with assistance from his father, he founded the American Oil Co., which he headed until 1937. In 1933, it merged with Pan-Am Petroleum & Transport Co. The resulting company eventually changed its name to Amoco Petroleum Co. Amoco is headquartered in Chicago, Ill. and is number fourteen on the *Fortune* 500 list.

John Moses Brunswick was born in Bremgarten, Kanton Aargau, Switzerland. He went to New York in 1834, and later settled in Cincinnati, and still later, in Chicago. The Brunswick Corp. has had a long string of successes in sporting goods, at first manufacturing pool tables (1845), elaborate back bars (1880s), bowling balls (1906), other bowling equipment, most notably automatic pin-setters (1955-1956), and a variety of other equipment. During the years 1958-1962, the Brunswick Corp. also acquired several very successful ventures including Jebco fishing equipment (1961), and Kiekhaefer-Mercury outboard motors (1961). Brunswick Corp. is number 245 on the *Fortune* 500 list.

Adolphus Busch I was born in Kastel (across the Rhine from Mainz), Hessen, in 1839. Busch went to the U.S. in 1857, and in 1861, married Lilly Anhäuser (1844-1928) who was the daughter of Eberhard Anhäuser, St. Louis brewery owner. In 1864, the name of the brewery became the Anheuser-Busch Brewery. In 1876, Busch introduced Budweiser beer, a German name adapted from a town in Czechoslovakia; Budweiser beer was a light beer marketed under the effective slogan the "King of Beers", and was geared to the American taste. Aggressive advertising of this superior product throughout the Midwest, including Texas, made the Anheuser-Busch brewery into the world's largest brewery. Between the years of 1868-1913, Adolphus Busch made the trip to Europe, usually with members of his family, at least twenty times. These trips trips helped him keep up with technological developments, not only in the brewery business, but in a number of other businesses. After Adolphus died in 1913, his wife, Lilly, kept a firm hand on the family fortune until she died in 1928.

August A. Busch, born in St. Louis in 1865, carried the Anheuser-Busch brewery through the difficult prohibition years of 1820-1933. Adolphus Busch III, born in St. Louis in 1891, further expanded the market in Texas, especially Dallas, where the prestigious hotel Adolphus carries his name. The Anheuser-Busch Brewery is number forty-one on the *Fortune* 500 list.

Charles William Engelhard was born in New York in 1917. In 1950, he became president of Engelhard Industries, a precious metals company located in Iselin, N.J., listed today on the N.Y. Stock Exchange.

John Eberhard Faber was born in Stein, near Nürnberg, Bayern. In 1848, Faber brought to America the pencil manufacturing technology which was started in Germany in 1761 by his great-grandfather Casper. The Faber manufacturing firm was set up in New York in 1861. The Company later bought prime forest land in Florida, land which contained the critical supply of cedar used in its main products.

Joseph Fels was born in Halifax Co., Va., in 1854. He was the son of Lazarus and Susanna Freiberg, who were German Jewish refugees settling at first in North Carolina, in 1848. A Fels-Naptha plant was established in Philadelphia, in 1893, as a prelude to a large soap manufacturing complex.

Harvey Samuel Firestone was born in Columbiana, Oh., in 1868. He was a descendant of Nicholas Feuerstein, an Alsatian who went to Pennsylvania in 1753. Firestone formed a rubber manufacturing company in Chicago in 1896. The operations were moved to Akron, Oh., in 1899, and in 1900, the company was named Firestone Tire & Rubber. For many years, Firestone was one of the big three in tire manufacturing. Today, it is a part of Bridgestone/Firestone Inc.

Harry Richard Fruehauf was born in Detroit in 1896. He was the son of August C. and Louise Henriette (Schuchard) Fruehauf. The Fruehauf Trailor Co. was organized in 1910. Roy A. Fruehauf headed the company from 1928-1961. Freuhauf Trailor is headquartered in Detroit, MI.

Joseph Gerber was born in Hiloiman Co., Ontario in 1845. The family moved to Fremont, Oh., in 1874, where they operated the Daniel Gerber Tannery until 1904. Frank Gerber, son of Joseph, was born in Douglas, Mich. in 1873. The family established the Fremont Canning Co. in 1908 in Fremont, MI., with Joseph as president from 1908-1917, although Frank Gerber was the nominal leader. Frank Gerber, the founder, headed the company from 1917-1952. The company's great success came in 1928 when they introduced Gerber's Strained Baby Foods and later expanded into a variety of baby products. The company changed its name to Gerber Products Co. in 1943. In 1993, Gerber Products was number 297 on the *Fortune* 500 list, but recently agreed in principle to be acquired by the Swiss pharmaceutical firm Sandoz.

Meyer Guggenheim was born in Lengau, Kanton Aargau, Switzerland, in 1828. He went to Philadelphia in 1847. Sometime later, he became a mining entrepreneur and formed a company, American Smelting & Refining, whose key asset became the Hugh Anaconda copper mine near Salt Lake City, Ut. Meyer Guggenheim had seven sons, one of whom, Daniel, born in Philadelphia in 1856, eventually headed up the mining consortium. The family name is known through the Guggenheim Museum in New York City.

Otto Haas was born in Stuttgart in 1872. Haas, a born salesman, acquired some experience in accounting. He was in the U.S. from 1901-1906. And in 1909, he returned to the U.S. with some chemical manufacturing processes developed by Otto Röhm, a chemist living in Stuttgart. Setting up shop in Philadelphia, the firm of Rohm and Haas, began the manufacture of industrial chemicals, at first, principally leather softening chemicals. Contact between the research scientists in the U.S. and Germany was halted by World War and for some years after. However, Haas eventually renewed this contact and carried on the vital matter of technology transfer between the two countries. Over the years, they introduced a variety of other chemicals, some developed by internal research in the U.S. and some developed in Germany. The main product in the history of the Rohm & Haas was Plexiglas, an acrylic plastic which resulted primarily from the research of Otto Röhm. In the U.S., Plexiglas manufacture came onstream just in time for World War II. The other part of the team, Otto Röhm (1876-1939), made just one short trip to the U.S., in 1926, in order to clear up some complications of company ownership resulting from a conflict of interest generated by World War I. Rohm & Haas is number 153 on the *Fortune* 500 list.

Henry Harnischfeger was born in Salmünster, today Bad Soden-Salmünster, Hessen, in 1856. His migration in 1872 was from Hamburg to Hoboken, N.J. In 1881, Harnischfeger went to Milwaukee where, in 1884, he formed a partnership with Lonzo Pawling known as the P.& H. Company. The first significant equipment manufactured by the company was an electric overhead crane which was produced in 1888. In 1914, Harnischfeger became sole owner and changed the name corporate name to Harnischfeger Corp., all the while keeping the "P & H" symbol. The company continued to expand, especially in the two world wars and was listed on the N.Y. Stock Exchange in 1971. The company is a supplier world-wide of heavy equipment, such as cranes, fork trucks, and the like. Harnischfeger is number 282 on the *Fortune* 500 list.

The brothers Max and Harry Hart arrived in Chicago in 1858. They had emigrated from Eppelsheim, near Alzey, Rheinland-Pfalz; the trip was from Le Havre to New York. They were to become co-founders, in 1872, manufacturers and owners of the highly regarded men's clothing firm of Hart Schaffner & Marx of Chicago, today listed on the New York Stock Exchange as Hartmarx. Another key figure in the firm was Joseph Schaffner, born in Reedsburg, Oh., in 1848, as the son of German immigrant parents.

Henry Osborn Havemeyer was born in New York, in 1847. He was the son of Frederick Christian & Sarah Osborne (Townsend) Havemeyer who came from Bückeburg, Niedersachsen, about 1806. Havemeyer headed the American Sugar Refining Co. He was associated with a cousin, William Frederick Havemeyer (1804-1874), who also held a term as mayor of New York. Both were capitalists as a result of their sugar refining operations.

Henry John Heinz was born in southside Pittsburgh, Pa., in 1844. He was the son of Johann Heinrich Heinz who went from Kallstadt, near Bad Durkheim, Rheinland-Pfalz, to Pittsburgh in 1840. The younger Heinz started at an early age in the produce business and established a company with a limited produce line which lasted only from 1869-1875. A second company, begun in Pittsburgh in 1876, with a brother and a cousin, had a bigger product line. In 1888, the second company was reorganized and used an expanded produce line which resulted eventually in the now famous slogan of "Heinz 57 Varieties." This company was incorporated in 1905. Today, many of its products, such as catsup and relish, are household names, both in the U.S. and in Europe. In fact, it is a giant corporation, being number eighty on the *Fortune* 500 list.

Frederick Augustus Heinze was born in Brooklyn in 1869. Heinze developed a reputation as the "Montana Copper King." He died in Saratoga Springs, N.Y., in 1914.

Walter Hugo Helmerich II was born in Chicago in 1895, his ancestors having gone from Bad Königshofen, Bayern to the Cincinnati in 1852. In 1920, he organized the Helmerich & Payne Drilling Co. with headquarters in Tulsa, Okla. The company was steadily successful, exploring for oil and gas, primarily in northeastern Oklahoma and Kansas, and investing in Tulsa real estate. The company is listed on the N.Y. Stock exchange.

Milton Snavely Hershey was born in Derry Township, Dauphine Co., Pa. His immigrant ancestors went to Lancaster Co., Pa. from Friedelsheim, near Bad Durkheim, Rheinland-Pfalz, in 1717. One of the ancestors, Benjamin (1697-1789), was a bishop of the Mennonite Church. Milton Hershey learned candy making in Lancaster, Pa., set up shop in Philadephia in 1876, went bankrupt, and received further training in Denver, Colo. He tried his luck in Chicago, New Orleans, and New York. Returning to Pennsylvania in 1886, Milton Hershey formed the Lancaster Caramel Co.; it became highly successful and he sold the company in 1900 for $1 million, keeping the right to manufacture chocolate. At the Chicago International Exposition in 1893, Hershey had the good fortune to encounter some German chocolate-making equipment, which he bought. It was another case of fortuitous technology transfer. The Hershey Chocolate Co. began production in 1905 and was highly successful from start. The Hershey Company admits that key ingredients include an abundance of fresh milk from nearby local sources, good chocolate, a high quality product, and successful packaging. After the death of the founder, the Hershey Chocolate Co. began an aggressive acquisition campaign. Today, Hershey Foods Corp. is number 151 on the *Fortune* 500 list. The Hershey family name was carried to Germany about 1670 from Emmental, Switzerland, where it was Hershi.

Harold Hirsch was born in 1881 in Atlanta, Ga. Hirsch was a lawyer by training, but in 1923 became the founder of Scripto, a manufacturer of writing pens, which he headed until 1939. Scripto, by concentrating on mass production of the most elemental type of ball-point pen, became the leader in its select field. Later expansion into a variety of product lines led to an overall downturn.

William Henry Hoover was born in Stark Co., Ohio in 1849. He was the son of Daniel and Mary (Kryder) Hoover and a descendant of one Johannes Huber who went from Switzerland to America in the period 1710-1724. An ordained minister of the Church of Christ, William Henry Hoover's good fortune in 1908 was to be offered the chance to purchase the rights to the electric suction sweeper which had been developed by an in-law, J.M. Spangler. The offer was accepted and the Hoover vacuum cleaner made history. Hoover made many improvements on the original bulky electric suction sweeper, including an aluminum body, and later, a plastic body. The company today is a part of the Maytag Corporation although the vacuum cleaner is still marketed world-wide under the Hoover name.

George Albert Hormel was born in Buffalo, N.Y., in 1860. He was the son of Johann Georg and Susanna Wilhelmina (Decker) Hormel, the father having gone to Buffalo in 1833 from Schwalbach, near Wiesbaden, Hessen, in 1833, and the mother to Buffalo in 1850 from Neuwied, Rheinland-Pfalz.

By 1891, the younger Hormel had established a meat packing firm in Austin, Minn. which was called George A. Hormel & Co. Later, the firm name became Hormel Foods Corp. Today, the company is number 169 on the *Fortune* 500 list. Their principal line is processed meats, although they carry a variety of other prepared foods.

Max Kade was born in Steinbach, near Schwäbisch Hall, Baden-Württemberg, in 1882. In 1904, he went to New York. He was one of the founders of Seeck & Kade, Inc. in 1909. The company made industrial pharmaceuticals, and after a relatively short but spectacular operation, sold out to Chesebrough-Pond's, Inc. In 1944, Kade formed the Max-Kade-Foundation which was dedicated to supporting a variety of university student activities. Kade died in Switzerland in 1967.

The Klebergs had the good fortune to become associated with the giant King Ranch of Texas when, in 1886, lawyer Robert Justus Kleberg, Sr. married Alice Gertrudis King, daughter of Richard King (1825-1885), founder of the King Ranch. In the years following the marriage, Robert Justus Kleberg, Sr. became a businessman and ranchman who negotiated water wells, a railroad, and cotton gins for the benefit of the area. Robert Justus Kleberg, Jr., born in Corpus Christi, Tx. in 1896, eventually became CEO of the operation. In the 1920s and 1930s, the ranch had expanded to 1,250,000 acres with operations in the U.S. (Tx., Pa., Ky.), Australia, Brazil, Morocco, and Spain. The family name is carried in coastal Kleberg Co., Tx. As shown in the section on Government, the family name comes from Herstelle, Westfalen. Many members of the family acquired a legal background and were active in governmental affairs in Texas.

John Werner Kluge was born in Chemnitz, Sachsen, in 1912. Currently, Kluge is seventh on the *Fortune* magazine world-wide list of billionaires, having been heavily involved in the Metromedia Co., a company which sponsors broadcasting and advertising in the U.S.

Charles Lloyd Lukens was born in 1786 in Horsham, near Philadelphia, Pa. Lukens was a physician, who through marriage with Rebecca Webb Pennock (1794-1854), became owner in 1817 of an iron and steel rolling mill operation. In 1810, the company was called originally the Brandywine Iron Works (from Brandywine, Pa.) although boiler plate was not manufactured until 1818. Lukens died in 1825, but his wife continued the operation with assistance from Salomen Lukens, a brother-in-law. The company name was changed in 1859 to Lukens Rolling Mill. In the years after 1870, the company adopted a whole series of technological innovations including one of the world's largest rolling mills and, in 1964, an all electric melt shop. The firm's name today is Lukens Inc., with primary operations in Coatesville, Pa. The company is number 389 on the *Fortune* 500 list. Charles Lukens was a fifth generation descendant of Johann Lucken who went from Krefeld, Nordrhein-Westfalen to America in 1683.

Daniel Frederic Wilhelm Ludwig Maitag was born in Gandow, Mecklenburg-Vorpommern, in 1831. He went to Cook Co., Ill. in 1848. His son, Frederick Louis Maytag, born 1831 in Illinois, founded the famous Maytag Co. The Maytag Co. actually began in 1893 in Newton, Iowa, as the Parsons Bandcutter Co., and in 1904 changed its name and primary activity to the manufacture of home washing machines. The "wooden tub" era lasted from 1907-1918. Gasoline engine washers were developed for rural customers about 1914; eventually, these were equipped to churn butter, grind meat, and separate cream. The real success of the company came with the development of the Gyrofoam washer with its aluminum body, developed about 1919. The Gyrofoam washer went into full production about 1922 and was produced by the trainloads. Maytag discontinued the manufacture of washing machines during the war years of 1941-1945 in favor of military equipment, but at war's end was practically swamped with orders for a modern wringer. The constant search for a better quality product has put the Maytag Corp. at number 153 on the *Fortune* 500 list.

Edward Mallinckrodt was born in St. Louis, in 1845. He was the son of Emil and Eleanor Didier (Luckie) Mallinckrodt who went from near Dortmund, Westfalen, to America in 1831. In St. Louis in 1867, Edward, Otto and Gustav Mallinckrodt established the concern which was known as G. Mallinckrodt & Co. After Otto and Gustav died, Edward, in 1882, incorporated the company as the Mallinckrodt Chemical Works, which became a well-known manufacturer of industrial chemicals. Eventually, the concern manufactured 1,500 different chemical products and had offices in St. Louis, N.Y., New Jersey, Toronto, and Montreal. Edward acquired the nickname of the "ammonia king".

Oscar Ferdinand Mayer was born in Kösingen, Württemberg, in 1859. He went to Detroit in 1873 and to Chicago in 1876, where, in 1883, he established a meat processing business with his brother Gottfried (1862-1909). The name of the company was originally Oscar Mayer & Bro., but was changed in 1919 to Oscar & Co. Oscar Mayer was president of the company until 1928. His son, Oscar Gottfried Mayer was president from 1928-1955. The company is known for its high quality processed meats, especially the hotdog, which was adapted into a well-known logo and into an automobile mascot. Today, the Oscar Mayer Foods Corp. has corporate offices in Madison, Wisc. Subsidiaries throughout the U.S. process a wide variety of prepared foods.

George Jacob Mecherle was born in Bloomington, Ill., in 1877. Mecherle had an early career as a very successful farmer in central Illinois before starting what became the eminently successful State Farm Insurance Companies, which he headed from 1922-1937. Mecherle was the son of Johann Christian Thomas Mögerle who went from near Heilbronn, Württemberg, to the U.S. in 1852.

After the death in 1902 of her husband and company founder, Gerhard H. Mennen, Elma Christine (Korb) Mennen reigned as president of the company, then named the Gerhard Mennen Chemical Co., until her death in 1916. Her son, second generation German-American William Gerhard Mennen, was president for the period 1916-1965. During the latter's reign, the company produced many well-known consumer products, such as brushless shaving cream, baby oil, and the like. The family had originated, in 1878, in the city of Vegesack, near Bremen, and went at that time to New

Jersey. If one were to give awards for marketing and salesmanship, the Mennen Company would be surely near the top of the award list, although today they are a division of the Colgate-Palmolive Company.

Georg Merck was born into the famous E. Merck Pharmaceutical Company of Darmstadt in 1867, and went to New York in 1887. He married Friedrike Schenck, born in Antwerp, Belgium, who was the daughter of 1848 German political refugee Georg Peter Schenck. The son of the couple, Georg Wilhelm Merck, born in New York in 1894, pioneered the American branch of the giant Merck Pharmaceutical Company which began about 1914 in Rahway, N.J. Georg Wilhelm Merck headed the American branch through World War I and World War II, and until his death in 1957. Historically, there has been a strong interchange of technology between Darmstadt and Rahway. Key employees, for instance, Max Tishler (biochemist, 1906-1989), of the American branch have been honored by the National Inventors Hall of Fame, located in Akron, Oh. Merck is number forty-seven on the *Fortune* 500 list. Thanks to two disastrous wars and destruction of German factories, the U.S. company has considerably outgrown its German counterpart.

Nelson Morris was born in Hechingen, in the Black Forest of Baden-Württemberg, and went to Chicago about 1850. In Chicago, he became a prominent stock breeder and meat packer whose firm was named Morris & Co. In fact, the company at one time was the most extensive cattle feeder in the world with output of cattle rated at about 75,000 annually. Morris died in 1907. He was married to Sarah Vogel. Vogel is doubtless a German name, but Morris evidently has been altered from an unknown German family name, perhaps from Moritz.

John Davidson Rockefeller was born in Richford, N.Y., in 1839. He was a descendant of Johann Peter Rockenfeller who arrived in New Jersey with his second wife in 1723. The Rockefeller family name is derived from a tiny village of Rockenfeld near Neuwied, Rheinland-Pfalz. John D. Rockefeller got his start in the oil business in Ohio about 1865, and in 1870, became one of the founders of Standard Oil of Ohio. By 1899, he became president of Standard Oil (New Jersey) which, even at that time, was one of the largest corporations in the world. Rockefeller died in 1937. A brother, William Rockefeller (1841-1922), likewise was also a prominent industrialist and financier. Several descendants were known for their political careers as listed in the Government section. The Rockefeller Archive Center is located in North Tarrytown, N.Y.

Frederick Hilmer Rohr was born in Hoboken, N.J., in 1896. His father, a sheet metal worker, had gone from Germany to the U.S. in 1896. The younger Rohr moved to southern California, and for the years 1919-1924, was a co-owner of the Standard Sheet Metal Works in San Diego. This business developed into the Rohr Aircraft Corp. whose business boomed with the advent of World War II. Rohr was president of Rohr Industries, Inc., with offices in Chula Vista, Calif., from 1956 until his death in 1965. Today, the company is number 273 on the *Fortune* 500 list.

Charles Michael Schwab was born in Williamsburg, Pa., in 1862, as the grandson of German immigrants who went to America about 1800. Schwab had a meteoric rise in the steel business, becoming president of Carnegie Steel from 1897-1901, and president of U.S. Steel from 1901-1903. He was also head of Bethelem Steel from 1904-1939, as well as head of American Iron & Steel from 1926-1934. However, Schwab attempted to do too much, and got involved in too many smaller enterprises which collapsed during the depression era of the 1930s. He was personally bankrupt by the time of his death in New York in 1939. Today, the Charles Schwab Company is located in San Francisco and is listed on the N.Y. Stock Exchange; it is cited usually as a diversified financial company.

Pauline Agassiz Shaw was born in Neuchatel, Switzerland, in 1841. She was the daughter of the famous scientist Jean Louis Rodolphe Agassiz, listed elsewhere. After coming to the U.S. in 1850, Pauline Agassiz married Quincy Adams Shaw, who was president of Calumet & Hecla Mining.

Jerome Monroe Smucker was born in Wayne Co., Oh., in 1858. He was a descendant of Christian Schmucker who went from Grundewald, Kanton Bern, Switzerland, to Berks Co., Pa. in 1752. The J. M. Smucker Co. was founded from an apple cider operation purchased in 1897 in the fruit-growing area of Orrville, Oh., about seventy-five miles south of Cleveland. An early product was high-quality, home-made style apple butter. Later products included all types of jellies. Production and marketing innovations were always a prime company concern. For instance, special equipment was devised to capture the essences of cooking fruit and return this key element to the product which was sealed in jars having an old-fashioned style of label. Until 1959, Smucker was a family-owned company, but then was listed on the N.Y. Stock Exchange. Its products occupy prime space on grocery store shelves and in many household pantries. The Schmucker family name is maintained in the Schmucker Memorial Library at Gettysburg College, Gettysburg, Pa. The library derives its name from Samuel Simon Schmucker (1799-1873), listed under clergy.

Claus Spreckels was born in Lamstedt, Niedersachsen, in 1828 and went to Charleston, S.C. in 1846. Spreckels eventually went to California where he formed the California Sugar Refinery. He was so successful in processing sugar that he became known as the "Sugar King." There were thirteen children in the Spreckels family of whom John Diedrich (1853-1926), born in Charleston, grew up in California to become a prime mover in the family sugar business.

Edward Riley Stettinius was born in St. Louis, Mo. in 1865. He was the son of Joseph and Isabel (Riley) Stettinius. The father was reportedly of Maryland German stock. The family name shows a Latinized variant of the original name. Edward Stettinius became an industrialist in St. Louis with a primary interest in the Diamond Match Co. During World War I, he was assistant Secretary of War whose primary role was the purchase and coordination of delivery of war supplies.

Levi (or Loeb) Strauss was born in Buttenheim, near Bamberg, Bayern, in 1829. He went to New York in 1847 and became involved in marketing textiles produced by relatives. Levi Strauss & Co. was formed in California in 1853. By 1866, the company had a four story manufacturing plant in San Francisco. The company's canvas pants were successful from the start, but the company really gained attention in 1873 when it produced the first durable pair of outdoor work pants with brass reinforcements. These pants became known as "Levis" and as "Blue Jeans". These were marketed under the sales pitch of being "work clothes for gold-seekers and cowboys." Strauss died in 1902, however, the company became so successful that today it is number one of the top ten apparel makers in the United States and is number ninety-five on the *Fortune* 500 list.

Adolph Heinrich Joseph Sutro was born in 1830 in "Aix-la-Chapelle, Prussia," a designation which translates today to Aachen, Nordrhein-Westfalen. Sutro went to Baltimore in 1850 and then, in 1851, to San Francisco. He became a mining engineer and made a fortune in West Coast mining operations. His multi-faceted career included the development of the Comstock Lode tunnel (1878), San Francisco real estate, and a term as mayor of San Francisco (1894-1896). Sutro was a bibliophile who gathered an impressive collection of incunabula, that is, the first books printed between 1450 and 1500. Most of his collection was willed to the San Francisco Public Library, but unfortunately about half was destroyed during the great San Francisco earthquake of 1906. The Sutro name exists also as a prominent street name in San Francisco.

Henry Villard was born as Ferdinand Heinrich Gustav Hilgard in Speyer, Rheinland-Pfalz, in 1835. He went to New York in 1853 and subsequently to the German-dominated community of Belleville, Ill. Always on the lookout for greener pastures, Villard became a writer, editor, and reporter supporting Lincoln, moved to New York, and later to Cincinnati. In 1881, he became a newspaper owner with his purchase of the *N.Y. Evening Post*. However, Villard's career developed into much more than journalism when he speculated in railroad development, especially the Northern Pacific Railroad, as well as other railroads. Villard made a fortune on these investments. Villard died in Dobbs Ferry, N.Y., in 1900. A son, Oswald Garrison Villard was born in Wiesbaden, Hessen, in 1872, and was also well known in American journalistic circles. The younger Villard was identified as a liberal reformer who ran the *N.Y. Evening Post* from 1897-1918.

Frederick Weyerhaeuser was born in Nieder-Saulheim, Rheinland-Pfalz, in 1834. Weyerhaeuser went to Pennsylvania in 1852, then on to Illinois, and eventually to Minnesota where he died in 1914. Four sons, the last of whom died in 1946, pushed the company lumber business to a premier position. Charles Augustus Weyerhaeuser, the second of the four sons was foremost in the family effort to enhance the business. Today, the Weyerhaeuser Lumber Company, with its head office in Tacoma, Wash., is near the top of the list of U.S. forest and paper products companies, as well as being number fifty-one on the *Fortune* 500 list. The company left its mark in the Charles A. Weyerhaeuser Memorial Museum in Little Falls, Minn.

Harry Lincoln Wollenberg was born in Prescott, Az., in 1886, and died in San Francisco in 1979. He was the son of immigrant Louis Wollenberg who went to New York in 1858 from Dobrojuski, a village in Westpreußen, today in Poland. Harry Lincoln Wollenberg was founder as well as president, and CEO from 1926-1978 of Longview Fibre Co., located in Longview, Wash. Today, Longview Fibre is number 444 on the *Fortune* 500 list; this is a strong measure of success considering the company's relatively late start.

Merchants

Merchants, as a group, went through the same economic cycles as that of the manufacturers. The effects on food merchants were somewhat lessened by the necessity of their products notwithstanding the condition of the economic times. Those with good credit were able to weather the storm, and in some cases, even expand operations from the fire sales provided by those with over-extended credit.

Merchandising giants such as Altmans, Filenes, Gottschalks, Neiman-Marcus, and Wanakers abounded in America's expanding economy. In fact, during the first half of the 20th century, the majority of large merchandisers in America were controlled by former German emigrants and their descendants.

Benjamin Altman was born in New York in 1840, as the son of immigrants from Nürnberg, Bayern, who had arrived in 1835. Altman was first of all a merchant in New York whose fortune allowed him in later years to become a philanthropist and art patron.

John Jacob Astor was born in Walldorf, Baden, in 1763, and went to New York in 1783. After opening a music sales shop in Manhattan in 1786, Astor developed a booming business in the collection and distribution of furs, a business whose assets he passed on to his heirs. Astor's main fortune was accumulated, however, through the speculation on Manhattan real estate. By the time of his death in 1848, the elder Astor had control of one of the biggest fortunes in the United States. As mentioned in the introduction, the Astor family name (originally Astore) was carried from the Italian Piedmonte region to Baden, Germany about 1686, then to America in 1783.

Beatrix Fox Auerbach was born in Hartford, Conn., in 1887. She was the daughter of Moses and Theresa (Stern) Fox. Beatrix married George Auerbach whose father founded Salt Lake City's largest non-Mormon department store. When the Salt Lake City store burned to the ground, they convinced the father to rebuild in Hartford, Conn. Eventually, Beatrix became a key executive in the Hartford store which rapidly developed a reputation for quality goods.

Edward Julius Berwind was born in Philadelphia in 1848. He was the son of Prussian immigrants. Berwind was involved in at least three major fields of coal mining and coal sales, New York City "rapid-transit," and the Pennsylvania railroad.

Moses Herman Cone was born in Jonesboro, Tenn., in 1857. He was the son of Herman and Helen (Guggenheimer) Cone. Cone became a prominent merchant and manufacturer in Tennesee.

Benjamin Williams Crowninshield was born in Salem, Mass. in 1772. He was the great-grandson of Johannes Kaspar Richter von Kronenshelt (or Kronenscheldt), a native of Leipzig. Crowninshield became a prominent merchant and politician in Boston.

Henry Fairchild de Bardeleben was born in 1840, in Autaugaville, Alabama. He was reportedly the grandson of a Hessian officer, mercenary Lt. Franz Ferdinand von Bardeleben, who settled in South Carolina in 1780. Henry Fairchild De Bardeleben married the daughter of Daniel Pratt, then considered to be the wealthiest man in Alabama and subsequently became an Alabama industrialist with interests in coal, coke, iron, and steel. Mercenary Lt. Franz Ferdinand von Bardeleben was separated from service in America in November 1780 and became the German-American progenitor of the family. The family name, in German, von Bardaleben, comes from a tiny community near Braunsberg, formerly in Ostpreußen, now in northern Poland.

Nicholas de Meyer was one of the early merchants in New Amsterdam (now New York), having arrived there about 1655. He was a mayor of the city in 1676, and died there about 1690. Although de Meyer reportedly came from Hamburg, the "de" in the name reflects an influence not typically German and likely was assumed.

Jacob Dold was born in Tuttlingen, Württemberg, in 1825, and went to Buffalo, N.Y. in 1844. Dold became a prominent meat packer in Buffalo.

Edward Albert Filene was born in Salem, Mass., in 1860. He was the son of Wilhelm and Clara (Ballin) Filehne, who were natives of Posen, a district now in western Poland. With a brother, A. Lincoln Filene, he developed Filene's, a prominent Boston department store. The store was in operation by 1891. The family name likely comes from the community of Filehne located in the Bromberg district of Posen.

Francis Fries was born North Carolina, in 1812. He was the son of Johann Christian Wilhelm and Elisabeth (Nissen) Fries, both German immigrants, who settled in the Moravian community of Wachovia, now Salem, N.C.. The younger Fries became a prominent manufacturer and woolen mill owner in Salem.

Lewis Ginter was born in New York in 1824 and died in 1897 in Richmond, Va. Ginter made a modest fortune as a tobacconist. He was the son of Johann & Elisabeth Guenther.

Alain Damascus Goldman was born in St. Louis in 1881. He was associated with Lesser Goldman Cotton Co., and with the large May Department Stores in St. Louis.

Emil Gottschalk was born in Mühlhausen, Thüringen (then Sachsen), in 1861, and went to Sacramento, Calif. about 1862. In 1904, he formed Gottschalks Department Store whose principal locations were in Sacramento and Fresno. The firm is still highly active.

Charles Gratiot was born in Lausanne, Kanton Vaud, Switzerland in 1752. He went to Illinois in 1777, and was a pioneer trader, dealing mainly in furs, but also operated a distillery, a tannery, and a salt works in St. Louis.

He died in St. Louis in 1817. The family name reportedly was of Huguenot, i.e. French, origin.

Bernard Gratz was born in Langendorf, Upper Silesia, in 1738. He went with a brother, Michael, to Philadelphia in 1754. The two brothers became prominent merchants in Philadelphia and Baltimore and were active in coastal shipping and interior trading. They were noted as financiers of the Revolutionary War cause.

David Grim was born in Zweibrücken, Rheinland-Pfalz, in 1737, and went with his parents to New York in 1739. Grim became a N.Y. tavern-keeper, merchant, antiquarian, and early artist. He was the second president of the German Society of New York, this being from 1784-1802.

Charles Frederick Gunther was born in Wildberg, Württemberg, in 1837 and went with his parents to Pennsylvania in 1842. Gunther established a candy manufacturing concern and developed a notable rare book collection.

Georg Nicolaus Hack (Hacke, or Haacke) was born in Köln, Nordrhein-Westfalen, about 1623, and was one of the early settlers in New Amsterdam (later New York). He was a merchant, physician, and tobacco trader. Hack died about 1665, apparently in New York. Descendants changed the family name to Heck.

Michael Hillegas was born in Philadelphia in 1729 and died there in 1804. He was the son of Michael Hillegas who was a native of the Palatinate, now apparently Rheinland-Pfalz. The younger Hillegas became a merchant in Philadelphia and was noted as the first treasurer of the U.S.

Bernard Henry Kroger was born in Cincinnati in 1860. He was the son of Johann Heinrich and Gertrude (Schlebe) Kroger who went to Covington, Ky. from Hannover (now Niedersachsen) in 1827. Kroger learned a valuable lesson from the 1873 recession in America. In 1883, Kroger became co-owner of the Great Western Tea Co. of Cincinnati which had a single store. The next year, Kroger bought out his partner and shortly thereafter expanded to four stores in Cincinnati. Kroger weathered the 1893 recession and even managed to benefit somewhat as competitors fell by the wayside. The company was incorporated as the Kroger Grocery & Baking Co. in 1902, at which time, mainly through acquisition, it had forty stores in Cincinnati. In 1910, the chain was expanded to Hamilton, Dayton, and Columbus, Oh., and in 1912 to St. Louis, Detroit, Indianapolis, Springfield, Oh., and Toledo, Oh. Kroger attributed his success to bulk buying with emphasis on quality foods, advertising, direct cash buying, and the acquisition of those who over-exceeded their credit. Kroger was also a prominent banker in Cincinnati. Fortuitously, he retired from the business in 1928, just before the 1929 market crash. The Kroger family name in Germany was likely Kröger, a low German form, as compared to Krüger, a high German form.

Albert Davis Lasker was born in Freiburg, Baden-Württemberg, in 1880. He was the son of American parents, whose father had gone to the U.S. in 1856. Lasker was an advertising executive who rose to be chairman of Lord & Thomas in Chicago, a firm with which he was associated from 1898-1942.

James Lick was born in Fredericksburg, Pa., in 1796. He was the grandson of Wilhelm Lük. Lick made a fortune investing in California real estate. The family name is preserved in the Lick Observatory in Santa Clara County, California.

Pierre Lorillard was born in New York in 1833 and died there in 1901. He was the son of Peter & Catherine (Griswold) Lorillard, reportedly originally of German stock. Lorillard was a tobacco merchant whose hobbies included a varied interest in sports.

Stanley A. Marcus was born in 1905, in Dallas. He was the son of Herbert and Minnie (Lichtenstein) Marcus. Herbert Marcus, Sr. was one of the three founders of the famous luxury merchandizing chain of Neiman-Marcus which had its origin in Dallas in 1907. The other two founders were Carrie Marcus Neiman and Albert Lincoln Neiman. The company utilized innovations in merchandizing foremost through Old World manufacturing technology imported in the early days from New York, and in later periods, from Europe, especially from France. The Neiman-Marcus stores became famous for their upbeat Christmas catalogues and for devotion to customer service and high quality goods. Both Neiman (pronounced Neeman in the U.S., not Nyman, as in Germany) and Marcus originated in Germany. The Marcus family name went to the U.S., about 1870-1875, from Wronke, a community then in Posen, and now called Vranik, in Poland.

Julius Ochs was born in Fürth, Bayern, in 1826, and went to Louisville, Ky. in 1845. Ochs was an officer in the Union army and became a successful merchant as well as a promoter of civic welfare. Three sons, Adolph Simon Ochs, George Washington Oakes, and Milton Barlow Oakes, all became well-known publishers. The elder Ochs died in Chattanooga in 1888.

Charles F. Orthwein was born in Stuttgart in 1839, and went to Logan Co., Ill. in 1854. Orthwein became a successful grain merchant in St. Louis. In fact, he was primarily responsible for making St. Louis the dominant grain center of the Mississippi Valley. By about 1870, the city was a hub for river and railroad transportation. Orthwein died in St. Louis in 1898.

Margaret Hardenbroek Philipse was born in Elberfeld, near Düsseldorf, Nordrhein-Westfalen. Through Hardenbroek family fortunes and a second marriage to Frederick Philipse, she was in New Netherland (later New York) by 1659. In the colonial days of 1659-1690, she became a prominent merchant and shipowner. The Hardenbroek family name shows an obvious Dutch influence, coming as it does from the lower German Rhine.

Hugo Reisinger was born in Wiesbaden in 1856 and died in Langenschwalbach, Hessen, in 1914. Reisinger was a German merchant who was also an art collector. Reisinger married Edmée, daughter of brewer Adolphus Busch of St. Louis. Reisinger was in the U.S. temporarily in 1882 and 1884, when he organized the first exhibition of modern German art. His name is carried in the Busch-Reisinger Museum at Harvard University.

Heinrich Rosenberg was born in Bilten, Kanton Glarus, Switzerland, in 1824. He went to Galveston, Tx. in 1843. By 1859, Rosenberg, whose American name was Henry, had built the largest retail dry goods store in

Texas. The city of Rosenberg is located near Houston.

Julius Rosenwald was born in Springfield, Ill., in 1862. Rosenwald became a prominent business leader in Chicago, and in fact, about 1895, chairman of the board of the giant Sears merchandising firm.

Paulus Schrick was an early merchant in New Netherlands (now New York), having arrived about 1651. Schrick, who died in 1663, reportedly was from Nürnberg, Bayern.

Alfred Montgomery Shook was born in Winchester, Tenn. in 1845. He was the son of James Keith Shook, who was reportedly of German descent. The younger Shook became a prominent southern industrialist whose main activities were in coal, iron, and steel industries. He died in 1923 in Nashville.

Carl Stoeckel was born in New Haven, Conn., in 1858. He was the son of Gustave Jacob & Mathilda Bertha (Wehner) Stoeckel who came to the U.S. in 1848. The father was associated with the Yale School of Music. The son acquired a fortune and became a patron of music.

Nathan Straus was born in Otterberg, near Kaiserslautern, Rheinland-Pfalz, in 1848. He was the son of Lazarus and Sara (Straus) Straus, and the brother of Isidor & Oscar Solomon Straus. Part of the family went to Georgia in 1852 with the remainder of the family following in 1854. Eventually, the brothers all moved to New York where they became highly successful merchants. In 1888, they were part owners of R. H. Macy in New York, and in 1896, sole owners. They built R. H. Macy into the world's largest department store with branches in many large American cities. Jesse Isidor Straus, who was the son of Isidor, was a long time president of Macy's, beginning in 1919.

Cyrus Leopold Sulzberger was born in Philadelphia in 1858. He was the son of Leopold Sulzberger who went to the U.S. in the early part of the 19th century. Sulzberger became a prominent merchant in Philadelphia and was president of N. Erlanger, Blumgart & Co. from 1900-1932. His sons became prominent N.Y. newspaper men as listed in the section on Publishers.

William Wagner was born in Philadelphia in 1796. He was the son of John & Mary (Ritz) Baker Wagner. Wagner became a prominent merchant in Philadelphia where he donated funds for the Wagner Free Institute of Science.

John Wanamaker was born in Philadelphia in 1838. He was the son of Nelson & Elizabeth (Kochersperger) Wanamaker. The father was reportedly of "German-Scotch" descent while the mother was reportedly of "French Huguenot" descent. In Philadelphia, John Wanamaker was a merchant in mens' clothing in 1861, and expanded into dry goods in 1876. The latter store is cited as the first modern department store existing in America. A branch was established in New York in 1896. A son, Lewis Rodman Wanamaker, born in 1863 in Philadelphia, eventually headed branch offices in Philadelphia, New York, and Paris. This distinctly German family name is a variant of the occupational name of Wannemacher, or Wannenmacher. A "Wanne" apparently was a device for separating the wheat from the chaff.

John David Wolfe was born in New York in 1792. He was the grandson of Johann David Wolfe who came from Sachsen early in the 18th century. In part through his marriage with Dorothea Ann Lorillard, Wolfe built a fortune as a hardware merchant. Wolfe was a benefactor of Protestant churches. A daughter, Catharine Lorillard Wolfe, born in 1828 in New York, inherited a large part of the Wolfe and Lorillard fortunes. Catharine Lorillard Wolfe, who never married, belonged to the Protestant Episcopal Church. In the era 1872-1877, she donated about $4 million to charity, mainly to churches, sciences, and the arts.

Hotels, Transportation and Other Big Business

Among other businesses, the list includes famous German-American names such as the Waldorf-Astoria Hotel in New York, the Ritz-Carlton Hotel in New York, the Adolphus Hotel (built 1912) in Dallas, and the classic Menger Hotel (built 1859) in San Antonio, as well as the Stouffer and Statler Hotel chains.

John Joseph Bernet was born in 1868 in Brant, N.Y. He was the son of Bernard and Emma (Greene) Bernet who came from the French-speaking part of Switzerland. The younger Bernet developed a career in railroads. By 1916, he was president of the N.Y., Chicago, & St. Louis Railroad.

Emil Leopold Boas was born in Görlitz, Lower Silesia, now Sachsen, in 1854. He went to New York in 1873 where he became the general manager for the Hamburg-American Steamship line.

George C. Boldt was born on the Island of Rugen, Mecklenberg-Vorpommern, in 1851, and went to New York in 1864. With the financial backing of the Astors, Boldt was a prime mover in the construction of the Waldorf-Astoria hotel in New York, which opened in March, 1893.

Samuel Cunard was born, apparently in Halifax, Nova Scotia, in 1787, and died in London in 1865. In Halifax, Cunard was a prominent merchant and shipowner, whose ships concentrated on postal service across the Atlantic and on whaling operations. He emigrated to England in 1838, and in 1839 was a principal in the establishment of the British & North American Royal Mail Steam Packet Co. Through the introduction of modern technology, especially propellor driven ships, Cunard's ships became famous for setting trans-Atlantic travel time records. For instance, in 1840, the ship Britannia made the Liverpool-Boston run in 14 days, 8 hours, a new world record. Cunard became a Baron in 1859. Cunard was a descendant of Thones Kunders who was one of the original thirteen Krefeld settlers in Germantown, Pa. in 1683.

Lorenzo Delmonico was born in Marengo, Kanton Ticino, in 1813 and went to New York in 1832. Delmonico took the renowned Swiss cooking to New York where he became a restauranteur and gastronomist. Delmonico died in 1881, but his restaurants are still a part of the better New York eating places.

Jennie Grossinger was born in Baligrod, Galicia (then in Austria), in 1892. She was the daughter of Selig and Malka (Grumet) Grossinger. The family went to N.Y. in 1900. In 1919, the family, of whom Jennie became a key executive, started a small family-type hotel in the Catskill Mountains. In time grew the business grew to a year round, large luxury resort. Part of the success was due to personal service in a first class resort environment. A highly organized system of public relations, first utilized in 1927, also added to their immense success. A measure of their success is that, in 1964, the resort had 1,200 acres, thirty-five buildings, and was averaging some 150,000 guests per year.

Harry Christian Haarstick was born in Hohenhameln, near Hildesheim, Hessen, and went to St. Louis in 1849. In 1869, Haarstick established the Mississippi Valley Transportation Co., and thus became a pioneer in Mississippi river barge transportation.

John Daniel Hertz was born in 1879 in Ruttka, Austria (now in the Czech Republic). In 1915, Hertz founded the Yellow Cab Co., in Chicago. The equally famous Hertz Drive-Ur-Self Corporation was founded in 1924. Hertz died in New York in 1961.

David Eli Lilienthal was born in Morton, Ill. in 1899. He was the son of Leo and Minna (Rosenak) Lilienthal. Lilienthal was involved in business administration. His most notable position was the director of the TVA (Tennessee Valley Authority) from 1933-1946. The TVA built a series of dams which supplied the Midwest with electricity.

Henry Morgenthau was born in Mannheim, Baden, in 1856, and went with his family to the U.S. in 1865. Morgenthau was involved in a variety of business activities, in real estate and in banking, and also in politics. A son Henry Morgenthau, Jr., born in New York in 1891, was the U.S. Secretary of Treasury.

César Ritz was born in Niederwald, Kanton Wallis, Switzerland, in 1850. Ritz, with the help of financial backers, established a chain of luxury hotels world-wide. The Ritz-Carlton was built in New York in 1907. The slogan "putting on the Ritz" derives from these luxury hotels. Ritz evidently never became an American as he died in Küsnacht, Kanton Zürich, in 1907.

Ellsworth Milton Statler was born in Somerset Co., Pa., in 1863. He was the son of William Jackson and Mary (McKinney) Statler, the father being a member of the German Reformed clergy. The younger Statler became a prominent hotel owner, and with financial backing from others, built hotels in Buffalo, St. Louis, Cleveland, Detroit, and Boston. Statler died in New York in 1928.

TABLE 13
DIRECTORY OF HIGH FINANCE AND BIG BUSINESS

Bankers, Capitalists & Financiers

1. Abraham, Abraham (1843-1911)
2. Annenberg, Walter Hubert (1908-)
3. Astor, John Jacob III (1822-1890)
2. Bache, Jules Semon (1861-1944)
1. Baerwald, Paul (1871-1961)
1. Belmont, August (1816-1890)
2. Belmont, August (1853-1924)
1. Blumenthal, George (1858-1941)
2. De Coppert, Edward J. (1855-1916)
1. Drexel, Francis Martin (1792-1863)
2. Drexel, Anthony Joseph (1826-1893)
2. Drexel, Joseph William (1833-1888)
4. Fahnestock, Harris Charles (1835-1914)
4. Flagler, Henry Morrison (1830-1913)
5. Flagler, Henry Harkness (1870-1952)
4. Frick, Henry Clay (1849-1919)
1. Gerstle, Lewis (1824-1902)
1. Goldman, Marcus (1821-1904)
2. Goldman, Henry (c. 1852-1935)
1. Greenebaum, Henry (1833-1914)
2. Guggenheim, Daniel (1856-1930)
1. Kahn, Otto Herman (1867-1934)
2. Kahn, Gilbert Wolff (1903-1975)
1. Kuhn, Abraham (fl. 1867-1887)
1. Hellman, Isais Wolf (1842-1920)
   Hottinger, Henry (1885-1979)
2. Lehman, Arthur (1873-1936)
2. Lehman, Philip (1861-1947)
3. Lehman, Robert (1891-1969)
1. Lewisohn, Adolph (1849-1938)
1. Loeb, Carl M. (1875-1955)
1. Loeb, Solomon L. (1828-1903)
2. Loeb, James Morris (1867-1933)
1. Miller, Albert (1828-1900)
3. Pepper, George Seckel (1808-1890)
   Ream, Norman Bruce (1844-1915)
1. Rentschler, Gordon Sohn (1885-1948)
1. Rohatyn, Felix George (1928-)
1. Sachs, Joseph (1817-c.1875)
2. Sachs, Samuel (1851-1935)
3. Sachs, Walter Edward (1884-1980)
   Salomon, Arthur (fl. 1911)
   Salomon, Herbert (1883-1951)

1. Schiff, Jakob Heinrich (1847-1920)
2. Schiff, Mortimer L. (1877-1931)
   Schwabacher, Albert E. (1888-1964)
1. Seligman, Jesse (1827-1894)
1. Seligman, Joseph (1819-1880)
2. Seligman, Isaac Newton (1855-1917)
1. Sloss, Louis (1823-1902)
1. Speyer, Gustavus (1825-1883)
1. Speyer, Philipp (1815-1876)
2. Speyer, James (1861-1941)
2. Straus, Simon William (1866-1930)
3. Strauss, Lewis Lichtenstein (1896-1974)
1. Warburg, Felix Moritz (1871-1937)
1. Warburg, James Paul (1896-1969)
1. Warburg, Max B. (1867-1946)
1. Warburg, Paul Moritz (1868-1932)
2. Warburg, Frederick Marcus (1897-1973)
1. Wesendonck, Hugo (1817-1900)
5. Widener, George Dunton (1861-1912)
   Wertheim, Maurice (1886-1950)
4. Widener, Peter Arrell Brown (1834-1915)
   Zimmerman, Eugene (1845-1914)

Economists
1. Eckstein, Otto (1927-1984)
2. Friedman, Milton (1912-)
2. Hollander, Jacob Henry (1871-1940)
   Klein, Lawrence Robert (1920-)
1. Schoenhof, Jacob (1839-1903)
   Schultz, Theodore William (1902-)
1. Schumpeter, Joseph Alois (1883-1950)
2. Schwab, John Christopher (1865-1916)
3. Seligman, Edwin Robert Anderson (1861-1939)
2. Stigler, George Joseph (1911-1991)
2. Taussig, Frank William (1859-1940)

Industry - Top 500 and Large Corporations
Baur, Eddie (1898-1986), outdoor apparel
3. Baur, George Frederick (1842-1914), railroads & coal
1. Bausch, John Jacob (1830-1926), optics
2. Bausch, Edward (1854-1944), optics
1. Beinecke, Johann Bernard Georg (1846-), hotels
2. Beinecke, Edwin John (1860-1970), trading stamps
2. Beinecke, Frederick William (1887-1971), advertising
2. Beinecke, Walter (1888-1958), insurance
   Benzinger, Moses (1839-1904), sporting goods
   Betz, John Drew (1930-1990), environmental chemicals

Betz, L. Drew (1895-), environmental chemicals
1. Biderman, Jacques Antoine (1790-1865), gunpowder mfg.
   Blaustein, Louis (1869-1937), oil & gas
   Bloch, Henry Wollman (1922-), tax consulting
1. Bluhdorn, Charles G. (1926-1981), conglomerates
1. Brach, Emil J. (1859-1947), candies
1. Brunswick, John Moses (1819-1886), sporting goods
1. Bulova, Joseph (1851-1935), watches
2. Bulova, Arde (1889-1958), watches
1. Busch, Adolphus (1839-1913), brewing, etc.
1. Busch, Lilly Anheuser (1844-1928), brewing etc.
   (Elisa Anhäuser Busch)
2. Busch, August Anheuser, Sr. (1865-1934), brewing
3. Busch, Adolphus III (1891-1946), brewing
3. Busch, August Anheuser, Jr. (1899-1989), brewing
4. Dietz, Robert Edwin (1886-1970), lighting mfg.
1. Dohme, Charles Emil (1843-1911), pharmaceuticals
1. Dohme, Louis (1837-1910), pharmaceuticals
2. Dohme, Alfred Robert Louis (1867-), pharmaceuticals
1. Dolge, Alfred (1848-1922), piano parts
1. Dreyfus, Camille Edouard (1878-1956), chemicals
1. Englehard, Charles Philip (1867-1950), precious metals
   Engelhard, Charles William (1917-1971), precious metals
1. Erhart, Charles F. (1821-1891), pharmaceuticals
1. Faber, John Eberhard (1822-1879), pencils
2. Faber, Lothar Washington (1861-1943), pencils
2. Fels, Joseph (1854-1914), soap
2. Fels, Samuel Simon (1860-1950), soap mfg.
6. Firestone, Harvey Samuel (1868-1938) (Feuerstein), rubber
   Fisher, Herman Guy (1898-1975), toys
2. Florsheim, Milton Sigmund (-1936), shoes
3. Florsheim, Harold Milton (1899-1987), shoes
2. Fritz, John (1822-1913), steel
   Fruehauf, Harry Richard (1896-1962), trucking
   Fruehauf, Harvey Charles (1893-1968), trucking
   Fruehauf, Roy August (1908-1965), trucking
   Funk, Eugene Duncan, Sr. (1867-1944), plant breeder
   Garst, Roswell (1898-1977), farming
1. Gerber, Joseph (1845-1917), canning
2. Gerber, Frank (1873-1952), baby foods
3. Gerber, Daniel F. (1898-1974), baby foods
   Getz, Oscar (1897-1983), distilling
   Graebel, David W., (contemporary), moving
1. Guggenheim, Meyer (1828-1905), mining
1. Haas, Otto (1872-1960), chemicals & plastics
2. Haas, F. Otto (1915-), chemicals
   Haas, Walter Abraham, Sr. (1899-1979), clothing mfg.

   Haas, Walter Abraham, Jr. (1916-), clothing mfg.
1. Harnischfeger, Henry (1856-1930), building construction
3. Harnischfeger, Henry (1923-1973), heavy equipment mfg.
1. Hart, Abraham (1831-1904), men's clothing
1. Hart, Harry (fl. 1872-), men's clothing
1. Hart, Max (fl. 1872-), men's clothing
2. Havemeyer, William Frederick (1804-1874), sugar refining
3. Havemeyer, Henry Osborn (1847-1907), sugar refining
1. Heckscher, August (1848-1941), zinc & iron
   Hegeman, John Rogers (1844-1919), insurance
2. Heinz, Henry John (1844-1919), food products
2. Heinze, Frederick Augustus (1869-1914), copper mining
   Hellman, Richard (1867?-1971), food products
3. Helmerich, Walter Hugo II (1895-1981), oil & gas
4 Helmerich, Walter Hugo III (1923-), oil & gas
3. Hershey, Milton Snavely (1857-1945), chocolate candy
   Hess, Leon (1914-), oil & gas
2. Hirsch, Harold (1881-1939), pens
5. Hoover, William Henry (1849-1932), vacuum cleaners
6. Hoover, Herbert William (1877-1954), vacuum cleaners
1. Hormel, Johann Georg (1830-), meat packing
2. Hormel, George Albert (1860-1946), meat packing
3. Hormel, Jay Catherwood (1892-1954), meat packing
1. Horstmann, Wilhelm H. (-1852), silk mfg.
1. Isenberg, Paul Heinrich Friedrich Carl (1837-1903), sugar grower
1. Janssen, Henry (1866-1948), textile mfg.
1. Kade, Max (1882-1967), pharmaceuticals
   Kauffman, Ewing Marion, (1916-1993), pharmaceuticals
   Kemper, James Scott, Sr. (1886-1981), insurance
   Kemper, Hathaway G. (1895-), insurance
2. Kleberg, Robert Justus, Sr. (1853-1932), ranching
3. Kleberg, Robert Justus, Jr. (1896-1974), ranching
1. Kluge, John Werner (1912-), broadcasting, advertising
1. Kohler, John Michael, Jr. (1840-1900), toilet fixtures
2. Kohler, Walter Jodok, Sr. (1875-1940), toilet fixtures
3. Kohler, Herbert Vollrath (1891-1968), toilet fixtures
   Kraft, James Lewis (1874-1953) (Krafft), cheese
   Lehrman, Lewis Edward (1938-), conglomerates
   Ling, James Joseph (1922-), electronics
2. Littauer, Lucius Nathan (1859-1944), glove mfg.
1. Lomb, Henry (1828-1908), optics
5. Lukens, Charles Lloyd (1786-1825), steel mfg.
1. Maitag, Daniel Frederic Wilhelm Ludwig (1831-), washing mchns
2. Mallinckrodt, Edward (1845-1928), chemicals
1. Mayer, Oscar Ferdinand (1859-1955), meat packing
2. Mayer, Oscar Gottfried (1888-1965), meat packing
2. Maytag, Frederick Louis (1857-1937)(Maitag), washing machines

3. Maytag, Frederick Louis II (1911-1962), washing machines
2. Mecherle, George Jacob (1877-1951)(Mögerle), insurance
3. Mecherle, Raymond Percy (1904-1954), insurance
1. Mennen, Gerhard H. (1856-1902), toiletries
   Mennen, Elma Christine Korb (-1916), toiletries
2. Mennen, William Gerhard (1884-1968), toiletries
1. Merck, George (1867-1926), chemicals
2. Merck, George Wilhelm (1894-1957), chemicals, pharmaceuticals
1. Miller, Henry (1827-1916) (Heinrich Alfred Kreiser), rancher
1. Morris, Nelson (1838-1907), stock breeder, meat packing
2. Paepcke, Walter Paul (1896-1960), paper products
1. Pfizer, Karl Christian Friedrich, Sr. (1824-1906), chemicals
3. Raskob, John Jacob (1879-1950), multi-co. executive accounting
   Redenbacher, Orville (1907-), gourmet food products
   Rempp, Adolph (1911-), food products
2. Ridder, Herman (1851-1915), advertising
5. Rockefeller, John Davidson (1839-1937)(Rockenfeller), oil & gas
5. Rockefeller, William (1841-1922), oil & gas
2. Rohr, Frederick Hilmer (1896-1965), aircraft components
   Rosenwald, Lessing Julius (1891-1979)
7. Rubicam, Raymond (1892-1978), advertising
   Ruger, William Batterman (1916-), firearms
2. Schaffner, Joseph (1848-), men's clothing
2. Scholl, William Mathias (1872-1968), foot-care products
1. Schumacher, Ferdinand (1822-1908) (Schuhmacher), oatmeal
3. Schwab, Charles Michael (1862-1939), steel
   Schwabacher, James Herbert (1881-1958), paper products
5. Seiberling, Frank Augustus (1859-1955), rubber products
1. Shaw, Pauline Agassiz (1841-1917), mining
   Sheaffer, Walter A. (1846-1946), pens
6. Slaymaker, Samuel Redsecker (1867-1940) (Schleiermacher),
   lock mfg.
4. Smucker, Jerome Monroe (1858-1948), jellies
1. Spreckels, Claus (1828-1908), sugar refining
2. Spreckels, John Diedrich (1853-1926), sugar refining
   Stern, Leonard Norman (1938-), pet supplies
3. Stettinius, Edward Riley (1865-1925), matches
   Stouffer, Vernon Bigelow (1901-1974), frozen foods
1. Strauss, Levi (1892-1902), western wear
1. Sutro, Adolph Heinrich Joseph (1830-1898), mining
   Taubman, A. Alfred (1925-), real estate
   Tisch, Laurence Allan (1923-), broadcasting
1. Villard, Henry (1835-1900), railroads
1. Volker, William (1859-1947), interior decorations
3. Weber, Orlando Franklin (1879-1945), chemicals
1. Weyerhaeuser, Frederick (1834-1914), lumber
2. Weyerhaeuser, John Philip (1858-1934), lumber

2. Wollenberg, Henry Lincoln (1886-1979)
6. Young, Owen D. (1874-1962) (Jung), electrical products
3. Zeckendorf, William (1905-1979), real estate
1. Zellerbach, Anthony (fl. 1850-1869), paper products
2. Zellerbach, Isadore (fl. 1888-1938), paper products
2. Ziegler, William (1843-1905), baking powder
   Ziegler, William, Jr. (1891-1958) (William Conrad Brandt), conglomerates
   Ziff, William Bernard, Jr. (1930-), communications

Merchants

2. Altman, Benjamin (1840-1913)
1. Astor, John Jacob (1763-1848)
3. Auerbach, Beatrice Fox (1887-1968)
   Bamberger, Louis (1855-1944)
1. Baum, Martin (1761-1831)
1. Bernheimer, Charles Leopold (1864-1944)
2. Berwind, Edward Julius (1848-1936)
2. Cone, Caesar (1859-1917)
2. Cone, Moses Herman (1857-1908)
3. Cone, Herman II (1895-1955)
4. Crowninshield, Benjamin Williams (1882-1851)
2. de Bardeleben, Henry Fairchild (1840-1910)
1. de Meyer, Nicholas (fl. 1655-1690)
1. Dold, Jacob (1825-1909)
2. Dold, Jacob C. (1857-1924)
2. Filene, Edward Albert (1860-1937)
2. Filene, A. Lincoln (1865-1957)
2. Fries, Francis (1812-1863)
2. Gimbel, Isaac (1856-1931)
3. Gimbel, Bernard Faustman (1885-1966)
   Ginter, Lewis (1824-1897)
2. Goldman, Alvin Damascus (1881-)
1. Gottschalk, Emil (1861-1939)
1. Gratiot, Charles (1752-1817)
1. Gratz, Bernard (1738-1801)
1. Gratz, Michael (1740-1811)
1. Grim, David (1737-1826)
1. Gunther, Charles Frederick (1837-1920)
1. Hack, Georg (fl. 1623-1665)
   Hellman, Harold (1908-)
2. Hillegas, Michael (1729-1804)
3. Hutzler, Albert David (188?-1965)
1. Hutzler, Moses (1800-1889)
2. Kirstein, Louis edward (1867-1942)
   Klein, Calvin Richard (1942-)
6. Kresge, Sebastian Sperling (1867-1966)

4. Kress, Samuel Henry (1863-1955)
2. Kroger, Bernard Henry (1860-1938)
2. Lasker, Albert Davis (1880-1952)
1. Lehman, Emanuel (1827-1907)
1. Lehman, Meyer (1830-1897)
1. Lehman, Mayer H. (-1918)
   Lick, James (1796-1876) (Lük or Lück)
   Lorillard, Pierre (1833-1901)
2. Marcus, Herbert, Sr. (1878-1950)
3. Marcus, Stanley A. (1905-)
   Neiman, Abraham Lincoln (1880-)
2. Neiman, Carrie Marcus (1883-1953)
1. Ochs, Julius (1826-1888)
1. Ohrbach, Nathan M. (1885-1972)
1. Orthwein, Charles F. (1839-1898)
   Philipse, Margaret Hardenbroek (fl. 1659-1690)
1. Reisinger, Hugo (1856-1914)
1. Rosenberg, Henry (1824-1893)
2. Rosenwald, Julius (1862-1932)
3. Rosenwald, Lessing Julius (1891-1979)
1. Schrick, Paulus (fl. 1651-1663)
2. Shoffner, John Peter (1892-1944)
   Shook, Alfred Montgomery (1845-1923)
2. Stoeckel, Carl (1858-1925)
1. Straus, Lazarus (1809-1898)
1. Straus, Isidor (1845-1912)
1. Straus, Nathan (1848-1931)
2. Straus, Jesse Isidor (1872-1936)
1. Sulzberger, Leopold (1805-1881)
2. Sulzberger, Cyrus Leopold (1858-1932)
3. Wagner, William (1796-1855)
5. Wanamaker, John (1838-1922)(Wannemacher)
6. Wanamaker, Lewis Rodman (1863-1928)
3. Wolfe, John David (1792-1872)
4. Wolfe, Catharine Lorillard (1828-1887)

Hotels, Transportation and Other Big Business
2. Bernet, John Joseph (1868-1935)
1. Boas, Emil Leopold (1854-1912)
1. Boldt, George C. (1851-1916)
5. Cunard, Samuel (1787-1865)
1. Delmonico, Lorenzo (1813-1881)
1. Grossinger, Jennie (1892-1972)
1. Haarstick, Henry Christian (1836-1919)
1. Hertz, John Daniel (1879-1961)
   Jacobs, Walter L. (1895-c.1968)
2. Lilienthal, David Eli (1899-1981)

Luckenbach, Edgar Frederick (1868-1943)
Luckenbach, John Lewis (1867-1942)
Ludwig, Daniel Keith (1897-1992)
1. Menger, William A. (fl. 1847-1871)
1. Morgenthau, Henry (1856-1946)
2. Morgenthau, Henry, Jr. (1891-1967)
Menger, William A. (fl. 1855-1859)
1. Ritz, Cézar (1850-1907)
2. Statler, Ellsworth Milton (1863-1928)
Yoder, Jacob (1758-1832)

Code:
1. = 1st Generation in America
2. = 2nd Generation
3. = 3rd or more Generation, etc.

German-American
Officials in Government

One often finds statements in publications which belittle the role of German-Americans in American politics. Many such accounts cite the varied political activities of immigrant Carl Schurz and then rapidly move on to another subject. In the current book, Carl Schurz, whose most important title was the rank of major general, a non-permanent rank, in the Union forces during the Civil War, is treated more fully in the section on Military. Schurz might just as have well be treated in the section on Printing and Publishing as he was an influential editor on the staff of several prominent German language newspapers.

After the period of Peter Minuit (or Minnewit) who was director general of New Netherlands for a few years beginning in 1626, and later governor of New Sweden, we find a dearth of names in American politics. The next significant politician apparently was Jacob Leisler, who was de facto lieutenant-governor of New York for a period of twenty months, in 1689-1670. After exceeding his authority, Leisler was tried by the British for treason, convicted, and executed.

It is true that German-Americans were very slow to get involved in national politics. Of the fifty-six signers of the Declaration of Independence in August, 1776, none could be included under the label German-American.

The first German-American to be elected a state governor in the United States was Isaac Tichenor who was governor of Vermont from 1797-1807 and from 1808-09. Simon Snyder was elected governor in Pennsylvania from 1808-17, and thus was the first of a long list of so-called Pennsylvania German governors. John Adam Treutlen (or Treutl), apparently born Switzerland, was a provincial governor of Georgia for the short span of 1777-1778; in 1779 Treutlen joined the Continental Army and served as quartermaster general in its fight for independence.

The following documentation of German-Americans includes two U.S. presidents as well as nearly one hundred individuals who attained the title of governor of one of thirty-four States. Among the group of governors, the so-called Pennsylvania Germans head the list with thirteen. Wisconsin is not far behind with nine governors of apparent German-American background.

Another twenty-two prominent German-Americans are cited in the colonizers and frontiersmen category.

Other extensive categories include jurists, lawyers (dealing mainly with governmental affairs), a few mayors of large cities, and senators and congressman. These categories are highly selective and include only those of some prominence.

And finally, "Other Public Officials, Agents, and Reformers" comprise another moderate list of German-Americans who have had an impact on the quality of American life.

Many dissident 48'ers went to America and became leaders of organizazions labeled as "Turnerbund." These individuals were exiles who hoped to return and establish a republican democracy in Germany. When their dreams did not materialize, they contented themselves with promoting socialistic ideas in America. The more prominent 19th century socialists included: Friedrich Hecker, Karl Heinzen, Adolf Douai, Gustav Struve, and Joseph Weydemeyer. Collectively, they led a semi-nomadic life, wandering through the Midwest. Nearly all died in relative obscurity.

In 1878, a law was passed in Germany regulating the activities of Socialists. A new wave of dissident emigration resulted.

In the wild and wooly financial days of the "The Gilded Age" (a term made famous by Mark Twain) after the Civil War, there were few restraints on American business. Railroads boomed, mining flourished, banking operations sky-rocketed, and manufacturers made fortunes, partly at the expense of the working man. Working conditions in general were very poor, especially in the big cities. Labor organizations had little power. Thus in 1886, the workers in Chicago elected to force the issue. The main issue was towards an eight hour day. The notable Haymarket riots of May, 1886, caught everyone's attention. Seven policemen were killed when a bomb exploded in their midst. As a result, eight laborers were subsequently indicted and convicted. Four native Germans, then resident in Chicago, namely August Vincent Theodore Spies, George Engel, Adolph Fischer, and Louis Lingg, were either executed or committed suicide as a result of the conviction. Two other native Germans, Oscar Neebe and Michael Schwab, were sentenced to life imprisonment. Labor unions received a temporary set-back, but in a couple of decades emerged ever stronger and eventually gained the main issues embodied in the Haymarket riots.

In fact, the total of distinguished government and government-related officials is a list of 277 names.

The Push and the Pull

In addition to thousands of newspaper articles and millions of brochures, broadsides, and personal letters, potential German emigrants were bombarded with hundreds of books giving advice, much of it highly commercial, to prospective travellers to America. The 1991 book by Stephen Görisch titled *Information Zwischen Werbung and Warnung: die Rolle der Amerikaliteratur in der Auswanderung des 18. und 19. Jahrhunderts* documents more than 400 such traveller-oriented books.

German newspapers were an important source of immigrant-related news articles and advertisements. In Europe, German-language newspapers numbered fifty-seven in 1701 and had increased to 183 by 1800. Leipzig boasts the first daily German-language newspaper dating from 1650, although Frankfurt, Köln, Öttigen, and Hamburg claim newspapers which appeared several times weekly starting in the decade 1620-1630. The so-called "Mainzer Adelsverein" group of immigrants, who went to Texas in 1844-1847, subsequently has been one of the most publicized group of German-American colonists.

Numbering somewhat more than 7,000 individuals, the Mainzer Adelsverein group in reality is the Nassauer Adelsverein group, from the name of their main sponsor, Duke Adolf von Nassau (1817-1905). The sponsoring society was initiated in 1842 at Biebrich, near Wiesbaden, by fourteen members of the lesser German nobility. By 1845, the total sponsors included thirty-three individuals from twenty-five families of which only one, a Frankfurt banker (L. H. Flersheim), was not nobility. Only four noble families contributed significant funds to the Texas migration. Eventually, Duke Adolf was obliged to resort to the use of Nassau State funds as well as to publicly offered notes sold by Frankfurt bank houses.

Two members of the Nassauer nobility actually went to Texas. Prince Karl von Solms-Braunfels (1812-1875) was in Texas not quite a year and founded the village of Neu-Braunfels. After 1845, Baron Ottfried Hans von Meusebach (1812-1897) spent the remainder of his life there. The two were official representives of the sponsoring society.

As an interesting footnote to the history of the House of Nassau, in 1866, Duke Adolf made the mistake of siding with the Catholic Austrians, who were beaten by the Protestant Prussians. The province of Nassau was adsorbed into Prussia and the duke lost the rule of Nassau, but kept his life.

Colonizers, Promoters, and Frontiersman

Aside from the religious communal societies discussed under Clergy, numerous communities were formed in the 19th century in which the German or Swiss element dominated. The obvious former German community names include: Stuttgart, Ark.; Brunswick, Ga.; Germantown, Ill.; Palatine, Ill.; Schaumberg, Ill.; Bern, Ind.; Frankfort, Ky.; Frederick, Md.; Germantown, Md.; Hagerstown, Md.; New Ulm, Minn.; Bismarck, N.D.; Franconia, N:H.; Hanover, N.H.; East Brunswick, N.J.; New Brunswick, N.J.; Germantown, N.Y.; New Paltz, N.Y.; New Bern, N.C.; Fryburg, Pa.; Germantown, Pa.; Hershey, Pa.; Manheim, Pa.; Boerne, Tx; Groesbeck, Tx.; New Braunfels, Tx.; Fredericksburg, Tx.; Nordheim, Tx.; Fredericksburg, Va.; Hanover, Va.; Bingen, Wash.; Helvetia, W.Va.;, Berlin, Wisc.; Germantown, Wisc.; Kohler, Wisc.; New Berlin, Wisc.; New Glarus, Wisc.; New Holstein, Wisc.; Rhinelander, Wisc.; and many others.

Many 19th century communities do not bear German names; however the German element dominated and most of communities still retain some old world traditions. These include Orangeburg, S.C.; Belleville, Ill.; Ferdinand, Ind.; Waldboro, Maine; St. Cloud, Minn.; Hermann, Mo.; Saint Johnsville, N.Y.; Bowdle, S.D.; Frankenmuth, Mich., and Giddings, Tx. (the latter actually mainly Wendish). In the last century, the German element pervaded large parts of Cincinnati, St. Louis, Milwaukee, and Chicago, and formed the German Village section of Columbus, Oh., and Schoenbrunn Village in New Philadelphia, Oh. And of course, the family name of the noted German naturalist Alexander von Humboldt (1769-1859) provided the name Humboldt County and Humboldt Bay in Calif., as well as the Humboldt River in Nevada, towns in Kansas, Minnesota, and South Dakota, and Humboldt Peak in Colorado.

German place names in some individual states could fill whole chapters of books, as for example, the 1972 book by John Rydjord titled *Kansas Place-Names* (University of Oklahoma Press, Norman).

German-American colonists included in the following discussion are largely those of 17th and 18th century America.

Johann Lederer, who was in America from 1668-1670, is noted as a traveler and explorer. Lederer traversed much of Virginia and the Carolinas, the latter in an attempt to find a route through the Allegheny Mountains. The account of his early travels was published in London in 1672.

The earliest of the notable German colonizers was Franz Daniel Pastorius whose story has been repeated many times. Pastorius, a native of Sommerhausen, near Würzburg, Bayern, arrived in Pennsylvania in 1683, and was instrumental in the success of the small community named Germantown, near Philadelphia. A lawyer by background, Pastorius was the first governmental official in Germantown, and more importantly, taught in Germantown schools from 1698-1718. Pastorius kept hand-written records of early Germantown, and wrote a few articles and poems, a few parts of which were translated and printed decades later. Pastorius died in Germantown either in late 1719 or early 1720. A prominent statue of Pastorius is located in Vernon Park, in Germantown, now part of Philadelphia, Pa.

Johann Kelpius was born in Schässburg, actually deep in Siebenbürgen, then a far flung eastern German outpost, but now in Rumania. Kelpius was the son of Georg Kelp, a Protestant pastor in a small community in Siebenbürgen. The younger Kelp was educated at the University of Altdorf, in Bayern. Kelpius arrived in America in 1694 with about forty Germans in tow. Kelpius and his group belonged to an unique religious organization, generally called the Rosicrucians. Most of the group settled near Germantown, Pa., but eventually dispersed some years after Kelpius' death in 1708.

German religious dominated groups were covered in an earlier section under Clergy. As noted in that section, a large group of German Protestants settled in New York, in the Hudson Valley, between the years of 1708-1710.

In 1710, Jost Hite, whose real name was Hans Jöst Heydt, native of Strasbourg, brought a group of sixteen Dutch and German families to New York. Many of the group moved to Germantown, Pa. in 1716.

Martin Kendig, apparently a Swiss, first went to American in 1710 with six Swiss Mennonite families. The Kendig group was among the early settlers in Lancaster Co., Pa. In 1717, Kendig brought over a much larger group of 363 immigrants.

The story of Baron Christopher de Graffenried, Swiss born adventurer and colonizer, also has been told often. In 1710, the baron led a group of 156 Swiss adventurers to Carolina where they established the town of New Bern (now North Carolina), on the Neuse River, a tributary of Pimlico Sound. In the same year ninety-two "Palatine" families totaling about 650 individuals started across the Atlantic to join de Graffenried's colony; however, about half died at sea. Although, the Baron returned to his native city, Bern, Switzerland, in 1713, the American city of New Bern retains its image as a Swiss colony.

Johann Conrad Weiser, Jr., born in Herrenberg, Württemberg in 1696, was part of the large group of "Palatines" who went to New York in 1710. In 1729, Weiser move to Tulpenhocken, Pa., then deep in Indian country. Weiser became a governmental Indian agent and learned to converse in a number of Indian dialects. He was relatively successful in keeping the peace between the Indians and the immigrant intruders. Weiser died in Pennsylvania in 1760.

Jean Pierre Purrey, born in Neuchatel, Switzerland in 1675, went with a group of about 150 Swiss Protestants to (South) Carolina in 1731. They were joined by some 260 other Swiss in 1734. The groups formed the town of Purreysburgh, but after Purrey's death in 1736, nearly all moved to Georgia.

In 1734, Christian Priber, apparently a native of Sachsen, whose German family name was either Pryber or Preber, founded a communistic colony at Cusawatee in (South) Carolina. When Priber died about 1746 in Frederica, Ga., the colony seems to have disbanded.

As noted earlier, religious groups included the Moravians who went to Georgia in 1735, to (South) Carolina in 1738, and who then migrated to Bethlehem, Pa., in 1744.

Theophile Cazenove was born in Amsterdam in 1740 as the son of a Protestant from the French-speaking part of Switzerland. In 1792, Cazenove became the agent for the Holland Land Company, a group of Dutch investors which acquired millions of acres of land in western New York for real estate speculation. Cazenove was active in Philadelpia apparently only from 1792-1796. The settlement of Buffalo and the remaining parts of Erie Co., N.Y., by thousands of German-speaking peoples, was the result of this land speculation.

Gottfried Duden, who lived in Missouri territory from 1824-1827, returned to Germany as a minor celebrity. The favorable publicity generated in 1829 by the publication of his experiences had a large impact upon thousands of Rhinelanders who eventually settled a wide area around St. Louis. In addition to the substantial German element in St. Louis, nearby Belleville, Ill., and Hermann, Mo. are known for their former German colonies. Duden's primary influence is reflected in the European organizations which were attracted to Missouri, namely, the Giessen Emigration Society, the Mühlhausen Colonization Society, the Osnabrück Colonization Society, the Swiss Colonization Society, and smaller groups from Berlin. Like many lawyers, Duden was a promoter par excellence: Missouri's "mild winter climate" was mild relative to that in northern Siberia, but not to people coming from the Rheinland.

The start of permanent German colonization in Texas generally is attributed to Friedrich Ernst, a native of Oldenburg, Niedersachsen. Ernst settled in an area about fifty miles west-northwest of Houston in 1831. A letter he wrote to friends in was published in north German newspapers and reprinted in book form in 1834. Settlers from Westfalen and Niedersachsen soon thereafter settled the Austin County towns of Industry, Cat Spring, and New Ulm. Ernst died in Texas in 1858.

Frontier colonizers in the Texas hill country during the mid-1840s included the German "Adelsverein" with a reported main body of 5,247 German immigrants (largely from Nassau, now Hessen), which was later expanded to more than 7,000. Baron Ottfried Hans von Meusebach was the second commissioner, in 1845-1847, for the Adelsverein (also called the Society for the Protection of German Immigrants in Texas); he replaced Prince Carl von Solms-Braunfels who was in Texas less than a year in 1844-45. Von Meusebach adopted the American name of John O. Meusebach and died in Texas in 1897.

The followers of the Frenchman Henri Castro were primarily responsible for the settlement in Texas of four or five small communities. Estimates indicate that 2,134 people went to Texas in accordance with Castro's urging, but only 500 or 600 remained there. They were recruited partly from Alsace-Lorraine. The followers of Castro formed several communities of which the largest was Castroville.

One of the most fabulous characters who helped settle the Wild West was Charles Goodnight. He was born in Macoupin Co., Ill. in 1836. Goodnight has been described as a Texas cattleman, Texas ranger, Comanche fighter, trail driver, and frontiersman who "hated hypocrisy, liars, and cow thieves." From 1877-1888, he helped develop one of Texas' largest cattle ranches (the JA ranch named after Irish financier John Adair) which, at one time, covered 600,000 or so acres southeast of Amarillo, in the Palo Duro Canyon area of the Texas Panhandle . The Mexican vaqueros, relatively peaceful Apaches, and not so friendly Comanche Indians of the Panhandle area referred to Goodnight as "Bueno Noche." Today, a small town southeast of Amarillo is called Goodnight. Goodnight evidently was a descendant of Hans Michael Goodknecht who arrived in Philadelphia in 1752. In Europe, the family name was likely Gutknecht. Thus, the translation from Gutknecht to Goodknight and then Goodnight was a rather liberal one since Knecht refers more to a servant rather than to a knight.

Two California pioneers were Johann August Sutter and William Wolfskill. Sutter, born in 1803, apparently in Baden, is famous for his ownership of a large section of land in northern California, near Sacramento, on which gold was discovered in 1848. The discovery, of course, intrigued hordes of fortune seekers to go to California. Wolfskill, born 1798 in Madison Co., Ky., helped establish the citrus fruit land in and around Los Angeles; southern California thus became another type of gold mine.

The railroads were especially active in the last half of the 19th century in the Midwest and West. They actively employed agents with German backgrounds to recruit people in various parts of Germany. Some of the notable agents, for which very little biographical data is available, include the following: Frederick Hedde, agent for Burlington Railroad system in Nebraska; John Hemmeter, agent for the Baltimore & Ohio Railroad; Kent K. Kennan, agent for the Wisconsin Central Railway Co.; Adam Roedelheimer, agent for the Northern Pacific; and Carl B. Schmidt, agent for the Atchinson, Topeka & Santa Fe. The latter very actively recruited Mennonites from Westpreußen who then settled large sections of south-central Kansas.

Governors

The directory lists the names of ninety-three individuals whose names reflect a German-American or Swiss-American background. The various biographies pinpoint the origin of forty-eight names. Thus, some interpretive effort is involved as the origin of the family name of forty-five governors.

The list includes a number of famous families. For instance, the Rockefeller family, which provided governors in Arkansas, New York, and West Virginia, needs little introduction. The Rockefeller family ancestor came to America in 1723.

Madelein May Kunin, governor of Vermont from 1985-1990, has the distinction of being the only woman on the list of governors with a German-speaking background. Kunin was born in Zürich, Switzerland, and came as a refugee to the U.S. in 1940.

Pennsylvania was one of the thirteen original states, dating from 1787. The Pennsylvania Germans include thirteen individuals who occupied the governor's chair, beginning in 1808. Nearly all of these had ancestors who came to America in the 17th or 18th centuries. For instance, the colorful governor, Samuel Whitaker Pennypacker's immigrant ancestor was one Hendrick Pannebecker, former resident of Flomborn, near Alzey, now Rheinland-Pfalz, who went to Philadelphia in 1695. Pennypacker was a reform governor, holding office from 1903-1907.

Among the many governors, Herbert Henry Lehman deserves a special mention for his long career in serving America's most populous state. Lehman was a lt. governor of New York in 1928 and 1930, and governor for the two year terms beginning in 1932, 1934, 1936, and 1938. Additionally, he was a U.S. senator from 1949-1956. Lehman, born in N.Y. in 1878, had an early career as a partner, from 1908-1928, in his family's prestigious N.Y. financial firm, the Lehman Bros.

Surprisingly, the German-belt states of Ohio, Indiana, Illinois, and Iowa did not have many German-Americans as governors. However, Wisconsin, which achieved statehood only in 1848, had nine governors with German-American names. Unexpectedly, five governors of Oregon, which was granted statehood in 1859, and five governors of Vermont (statehood in 1791) have names of apparent German origin. Likely, most of the governors of Oregon are descendants of the surge of pioneers who came over the Oregon trail in the 1840s.

Many of the governors attained prominence in other fields before holding political office. At least three governors, Beaver, Cox, and Hartranft, were generals in the forces of the Union army. Most governors had military service. A majority of governors were lawyers. A minority were businessmen.

Jurists

The directory shows nineteen individuals of which a select few are mentioned.

Mary Margaret Bartelme, was born in Chicago in 1866. She was the daughter of Balthazar, an immigrant from Alsace, and Jeanette (Hoff) Bartelme. Bartelme has a long career as a justice in Chicago's juvenile court.

Judge Louis Dembitz Brandeis was born in Louisville, Ky. in 1856. He was the son of immigrant Adolph Brandeis who was part of the great wave of migrants going to the United States in 1848. Brandeis served in the U.S. Supreme Court from 1916-1939. The family name survives in Brandeis University located in Waltham. Mass.

Judge Felix Frankfurter was born in Vienna, Austria, in 1882, and went to the United States in 1894. Frankfurter was a Professor of Law at Harvard University from 1914-1939, and served on the U.S. Supreme Court from 1939-1962.

Robert Justus Kleberg I was born in Herstelle, Westfalen, in 1803 and went to Texas in 1834. Kleberg was part of a party led by his wife's family, the von Roeders, who were among the first German-American pioneers in Texas, settling in Austin Co. and later in DeWitt Co. The family history which relates all the horrors of shipwreck, high mortality rates from malaria, dysentery, and yellow fever, a marauding Mexican army, and hostile Indians, is admirable. Kleberg was one of the few trained lawyers in Texas before the Civil War. He was made a justice in Austin Co., and a county judge in DeWitt Co. Kleberg was the founder of the Kleberg dynasty, having been the father of four daughters and four sons. Five descendants are listed in the Government and Business sections.

Samuel Freeman Miller was born in Richmond, Ky. in 1816. He was the son of a Pennsylvania German whose family name apparently was either Mueller or Müller. Miller was an associate justice on the U.S. Supreme Court.

Mable Walker Willebrandt was born in Woodsdale, Kans., in 1889. She was the daughter of David William, a Pennsylvanian German, and Myrtle (Eaton) Walker. She married Arthur F. Willebrandt. Mable Willebrandt is best remembered for her role as assistant attorney general of the U.S. during the years 1921-1929, i.e., the heart of prohibition. Although basically neutral about prohibition, she was committed to upholding the law, sentencing many violators to prison terms. For her loyalty to the government, she earned the title of "Prohibition Portia."

John Gabriel Woerner was born in Möhringen, Württemberg, in 1826, and went to Philadelphia in 1833. Some years later, he went to St. Louis where he served as probate judge from 1870-1894. Woerner was part of the group of immigrants, along with Carl Schurz, who were strong Lincoln supporters.

Lawyers

The directory shows thirty-nine lawyers of which nine were foreign born and fifteen were second generation immigrants. Many had varied careers. Some were professors of law. Others were writers. One of the most unusual was Isaac Leopold Rice, native of Wachenheim, Bayern, who went to Philadelphia in 1856 and subsequently became a chess expert in addition to developing a legal career.

Wendell Lewis Willkie, born in Elwood, Ind. in 1892, had the misfortune to be the Republican nominee for U.S. President in 1940 when he ran against the popular incumbent Franklin D. Roosevelt. Still, Willkie persisted in government affairs, and in 1943, wrote the best-seller titled *One World*. In Europe, the Willkie family name was likely Willeke.

Sigmund Zeisler, a native of Bielitz, Silesia, went to the United States in 1883, where he established a strong legal practice in Chicago. Zeisler has a dual reputation as the husband of Fanny Bloomfield, the noted pianist, also from Bielitz.

Mayors of Large Cities

Only seven mayors of representative large cities are listed in the directory. These individuals are not shown in another category.

Rudolph Blankenburg was born in Barntrup, Nordrhein-Westfalen, in 1843, and went to Philadelphia in 1865. Blankenburg was mayor of Philadelphia from 1911-1915, where he was a crusader for the rights of the people and advocated clean municipal government. These actions earned him the nickname of "Old Dutch Cleanser."

John Cruger was born in New York in 1710, the family having come from Germany in 1698. In Europe, the family name must have been either Kruger or Krüger. John Cruger was mayor of New York from 1756-1765.

Emil Seidel was born in Ashland, Pa. in 1864. He was mayor of Milwaukee from 1910-1912, and earned a reputation as a "social politician."

Robert F. Wagner, Jr., was born in New York in 1910. Wagner was mayor of New York from 1954-1965. Wagner's father, a New York senator from 1927-1949, by the same name, had come from Nastätten, Hessen, in 1885.

Presidents

The two German-American presidents, Eisenhower and Hoover, are both descendants of families long established in the United States.

Eisenhower's ancestors arrived in America in 1741 while Hoover's ancestors went to America about 1754. The American ancestor of the Eisenhauer/Eisenhower family is now accepted as originating in the Eiterbach region, some 14 km NE of Heidelberg, Baden. A memorial to the former president, the Dwight D. Eisenhower Library is a popular attraction in Abilene, Ks.

The Hoover name is associated with the Rheinland-Pfalz town of Ellerstadt, near Bad Durkheim. The European version of the Hoover name is Huber, of Swiss origin. The Herbert Hoover Presidential Library is located in West Branch, Iowa.

Senators and Congressman

The directory shows eighteen individuals, only two of whom are discussed here.

The controversial Victor Louis Berger was born in a village reported as "Nieder-Rehbach, Austria" although this village in not shown on current maps of Austria. Likely, the village is somewhere outside of Austria, in the old Austro-Hungarian empire. Berger went to Bridgeport, Conn. in 1878, and subsequently became involved in left-wing politics in Milwaukee, Wisc. Berger was the editor of the *Milwaukee Leader*, a Socialist daily, as of 1911. He was elected to Congress for the term 1911-1913, but denied a seat, convicted and sentenced to prison for political activity. The conviction was later reversed. Berger was again elected to Congress, seated in 1923 and remained in office until 1929, when he died.

Jacob Kappel Javits was born in New York, in 1904. He was the son of Jewish immigrants Morris and Ida (Littman) Javits. The younger Javits developed a career as a liberal Republican official in the state of New York and served as U.S. Senator from 1957-1981. The European origin of the Javits name has not been ascertained; etymologically, it appears to have a Slavic influence.

Other Public Officials, Agents, Reformers

The list of seventy-seven individuals includes a cosmopolitian lot whose widely varied careers are difficult to generalize. Selected representatives are discussed all too briefly here.

Bernard Mannes Baruch was born in Camden, S.C., in 1870. His father, Simon, was a German Jewish immigrant who became a surgeon in the Confederate Army. The younger Baruch joined the firm of A.A. Housman & Co., and speculated in the stock market so successfully that he acquired one third interest in Housman. Baruch is primarily known for his long career, from 1912-1962, as a public official, serving on a number of commissions in both World Wars. In the inter-war period, he was also a key advisor to President Franklin D. Roosevelt (1882-1945).

Elisabeth Christman was born in Germany in 1881 and went with her parents to Chicago about 1885. Elisabeth Christman's early career began as a woman's labor organizer in 1912 with the IGWUA (International Garment Workers Union Association) with which she was associated until 1937. She was also associated with the WTUL (Women's Trade Union League) from 1914-1950.

Hannah Bachman Einstein was born in New York in 1862, the daughter of native Germans. She was a social welfare worker in New York from 1902-1929.

Edna Frischel Gellhorn was born in St. Louis in 1878 and died there in 1970. She married George Gellhorn who had come from Germany in 1899. Edna Gellhorn had an active career, from 1919-1960, as an associate of the LWV (League of Women Voters).

Rebecca Gratz was born in Philadelphia in 1781, her father having gone to America from Upper Silesia in the 1750s. She remained in Philadelphia her entire life where she was a Jewish charitable worker, from 1801-1864.

William Andrew Hirth was born in Tarrytown, N.Y. in 1875 as the son of native Germans. Hirth subsequently moved to Missouri where, in 1917, he began the Missouri Farmer's Association and was an agricultural journalist.

John Edgar Hoover was born and died in Washington, D.C. He was F.B.I. director from 1924-1972. Hoover was the author in 1958 of the book titled *Masters of Deceit*. Evidently, the Hoover family name comes from Switzerland the same as it does for the various other Hoovers in this book, although family ties have not been established.

Henry Alfred Kissinger was born in Fürth, Bayern, in 1923 and went to the U.S. in 1938. Kissinger has had a varied career as professor at Harvard, diplomat, and political scientist. Kissinger was awarded the Nobel Peace Prize in 1973 for his long and extended negotiation of the end of America's most complex war, the Vietnam War (1964-1973).

Gustav Philipp Körner was born in Frankfurt am Main, Hessen, in 1809 and went to Illinois in 1833 as a political refugee, having taken part in the student demonstrations in Frankfurt. He settled in Belleville, Ill., which was a thriving German community at the time. In Bellville, he was associated with other intellectuals, notably in The German Library Society. The family name became Koerner in Illinois. Koerner was a newspaperman, jurist, historian, and statesman, and held the office of lt. governor of Illinois.

Jacob Leisler was born in Frankfurt am Main in 1640. Leisler went to New Amsterdam in 1660. He became de facto lt. governor of New York for a period of twenty months, from 1689-1690. In 1691, Leisler was hanged by the British authorities after being convicted on charges of treason which resulted from his supposedly undue assumption of office. A monument was erected in his memory in New York City.

Henry Morgenthau, Sr. was born in Mannheim, Baden, in 1856, and went with his family to N.Y. in 1865. After establishing himself financially in real estate and banking, Morgenthau joined the ranks of public servants. In 1912-1916, for instance, he was ambassador to Turkey. Henry Morgenthau, Jr., born in N.Y. in 1891, followed in the footsteps of his father. His most notable position was that of cabinet officer when he occupied the office of secretary of treasury from 1934-1943.

Anita Pollitzer was born in Charleston, S.C. in 1894. She was the daughter of Gustave Morris and Clara (Guinzburg) Pollitzer, and the granddaughter of immigrants from Vienna. Anita Pollitzer was an associate of the NWP (National Women's Party) from 1916-1949. The Pollitzer family name is an interesting variation, perhaps related to the family name of Joseph Pulitzer (1857-1911), the well-known publisher.

Walter Philip Reuther was born in Wheeling, W.Va., in 1907. Reuther became prominent as a labor leader and union activist in the automobile industry. He died in Pellston, Mich. in 1970.

Margaret Dreier Robins was born in Brooklyn in 1868, as the daughter of an immigrant from Bremen. Robins became a labor reformer in Chicago where she was president of the Women's Trade Union League from 1907-1913.

Hannah Greenebaum Solomon was born and died in Chicago. She was the daughter of 1840s immigrants from the "Palatinate,' i.e., likely Rheinland-Pfalz. Solomon was a long-time welfare worker in Chicago and president of the National Council of Jewish Women from 1890-1905.

Francis Elias Spinner was born in German Flats, Herkimer Co., N.Y., in 1802. His father, a native of Werbach, Baden, went to the U.S. in 1801. Spinner was treasurer of the U.S. during the crisis period of 1861-1875.

Frances Stern was a long time social worker and dietician in Boston. She was born in Boston in 1873 as the daughter of natives from Albersweiler, Rheinland-Pfalz.

Daniel Updike was born in North Kingston, R.I. about 1693. He held the office of attorney general of R.I. from 1722-1732. Updike was the grandson of Gysbert Opdyck who went from Wesel in the lower German Rhine to New Amsterdam before 1638.

TABLE 14
DIRECTORY OF GOVERNMENT

Colonizers, Promoters, and Frontiersmen
1. Cazenove, Theophile (1740-1811)
1. Duden, Gottfried (1785-1855)
1. Ernst Friedrich (fl. 1831-1858)
1. Follenius, Paul (1799-1844) (Foellen)
1. Graffenried, Christopher, Baron de (1661-1743)
4. Goodnight, Charles (1836-1929)
1. Hager, Jonathan (1719-1775)
1. Herr, Hans (1639-1725)
1. Hite, Jost (1685-1761) (Heydt)
1. Kelpius, Johann (1673-1708)
1. Kendig, Martin (fl. 1710-1717)
1. Krug, Karl (1825-1892)
1. Lederer, Johann (fl. 1669-1670)
1. Münch, Christoph Rudolph Christian (1801-1879)
1. Münch, Friedrich (1799-1879)
1. Pastorius, Franz Daniel (1651-c.1720) (Scepers)
1. Priber, Christian Gotelieb (fl. 1734-1744)
1. Purrey, Jean Pierre (1675-c.1736)
1. Sutter, John Augustus (1803-1880) (Sutor)
1. von Meusebach, Baron Ottfried Hans (1812-1897)
1. Weiser, Johann Konrad, Sr. (1664-1746)
1. Weiser, Johann Conrad, Jr. (1696-1760)
4. Wolfskill, William (1798-1866)

Governors-Arkansas
4. Eagle, James Phillip (1837-1904), 1889-93 (Egle, Egli)
5. Fishback, William Meade (1831-1903), 1893-95
5. Rector, Henry Massey (1816-1899), 1860-62
8. Rockefeller, Winthrop (1912-1973), 1967-71

Governors-California
4. Bigler, John (1805-1871), 1852-56
3. Weller, John B. (1812-1875), 1858-60

Governors-Colorado
4. Buchtel, Henry Augustus (1847-1924), 1907-09
2. Shafroth, John Franklin (1854-1922), 1908-12

Governors-Connecticut
2. Ribicoff, Abraham Alexander (1910-), 1955-61

Governors-Georgia
Schley, William (1786-1858), 1835-37

Governors-Illinois
1. Altgeld, John Peter (1847-1902), 1893-97
   Kerner, Otto (1908-1976), 1961-68

Governors-Indiana
2. Schricker, Henry Frederick (1883-1966), 1941-45, 1949-53

Governors-Iowa
3. Erbe, Norman Arthur (1919-), 1961-63
   Hoegh, Leo Arthur (1908-), 1955-57
2. Kraschel, Nelson George (1889-1957), 1937-39

Governors-Kansas
Hoch, Edward Wallis (1849-1925), 1905-09
Schoeppel, Andrew Frank (1894-1962), 1943-47

Governors-Kentucky
2. Goebel, William (1856-1900), 1900 (assassinated)

Governors-Louisiana
1. Hahn, Georg Michael Decker (1830-1886), 1964-65
   Roemer, Charles Elson III (1943-), 1988-

Governors-Maryland
Mandel, Marvin (1920-), 1969-71, 1979
Schaefer, William Donald (1921-), 1987-

Governors-Michigan
Brucker, Wilber Marion (1894-1968), 1931-32
Sigler, Kim (1894-1953), 1947-49

Governors-Mississippi
2. Quitman, John Anthony (1798-1859), 1835-36, 1850-51

Governors-Montana
Schwinden, Ted (1925-), 1981-89

Governors-Nebraska
3. Crounse, Lorenzo (1834-1909), 1892-94
2. Dietrich, Charles Henry (1853-1924), 1901
6. Shallenberger, Ashton Cockayne (1862-1938), 1909-11
   Tieman, Norbert Theodore (1924-), 1967-71

Governors-Nevada
1. Sadler, Reinhold (1848-1906), 1896-1903

Governors-New Jersey
Hoffman, Harold Giles (1896-1954), 1935-38
3. Meyner, Robert Baumle (1908-), 1954-62
Silzer, George Sebastian (1870-1940), 1923-26
Werts, George Theodore (1846-1910), 1893-96

Governors-New Mexico
2. Seligman, Arthur (1871-1933), 1931-33

Governors-New York
4. Bouck, William C. (1786-1859), 1843-45
7. Hoffman, John Thompson (1828-1888), 1869-73
2. Lehman, Herbert Henry (1878-1963), 1932-42
8. Rockefeller, Nelson Aldrich (1907-1979), 1959-73
2. Sulzer, William (1863-1941), 1913

Governors-North Carolina
Ehringhaus, John Christoph Blucher (1882-1949), 1933-37
Holshouser, James Eubert (1934-), 1973-77
Umstead, William Bradley (1895-1954), 1953-54

Governors-North Dakota
Langer, William (1886-1959), 1933-34, 1937-39

Governors-Ohio
4. Cox, Jacob Dolson (1828-1900), 1866-68
2. Lausche, Frank John (1895-1990), 1945-47, 1949-57

Governors-Oregon
Bowerman, Jay (1876-1957), 1910-11
Goldschmidt, Neil Edward (1940-), 1987-
2. Meier, Julius L. (1874-1937), 1931-35
Snell, Earl Wilcox (1895-1947), 1943-47
Straub, Robert William (1920-), 1975-79

Governors-Pennsylvania
3. Beaver, James Addams (1837-1914)(Bieber), 1887-1891
4. Bigler, William (1814-1880), 1852-55
5. Brumbaugh, Martin Grove (1862-1930), 1915-19
Fisher, John Stuchell (1867-1940), 1927-31
4. Hartranft, John Frederick (1830-1889), 1873-79
2. Hiester, Joseph (1752-1832), 1820-23
6. Pennypacker, Samuel Whitaker (1843-1916), 1903-07
2. Ritner, Joseph (1780-1869), 1835-39
Shafer, Raymond Philip (1917-), 1967-71
2. Shulze, John Andrew (1775-1852), 1823-29
3. Shunk, Francis Rawn (1788-1848), 1844-48

2. Snyder, Simon (1759-1819), 1808-17
2. Wolf, George (1777-1840), 1829-35

Governors-Rhode Island
Licht, Frank (1916-), 1969-73

Governors-South Carolina
3. Miller, Stephan Decatur (1787-1838), 1828-30
   Timmerman, George Bell Jr. (1912-), 1955-59

Governors-South Dakota
3. Bulow, William John (1869-1960), 1927-31
   Kneip, Richard Francis (1933-), 1971-78
   Wollman, Harvey Lowell (1935-), 1978-79

Governors-Tennessee
3. Turney, Peter (1827-1903), 1892-97

Governors-Utah
1. Bamberger, Simon (1847-1926), 1917-21
   Bangerter, Norman Howard (1933-), 1985-
2. Dern, George Henry (1872-1936), 1924-32

Governors-Vermont
Hoff, Philip Henderson (1924-), 1963-69
1. Kunin, Madelein May (1933-), 1985-90
   Snelling, Richard Arkwright (1927-), 1977-85
   Tichenor, Isaac (1754-1838), 1797-1807, 1808-09

Governors- Virginia
7. Kemper, James Lawson (1823-1895), 1874-78

Governors-West Virginia
Kump, Herman Guy (1877-1962), 1933-37
10. Rockefeller, John Davidson (1937-), 1977-85

Governors-Wisconsin
1. Heil, Julius Peter (1876-1949), 1939-45
2. Kohler, Walter Jodok (1875-1940), 1929-31
3. Kohler, Walter Jodok, Jr. (1904-1976), 1951-57
2. Philipp, Emanuel Lorenz (1861-1925), 1915-21
3. Rennebohm, Oscar (1889-1968), 1947-51
1. Salomon, Edward (1828-1909), 1862-64
2. Schmedeman, Albert George (1864-1946), 1933-35
   Schreiber, Martin James (1939-), 1977-79
   Zimmerman, Fred R. (1880-1954), 1927-29

Governors-Wyoming
Herschler, Edgar J. (1918-), 1975-87

Jurists
2. Bartelme, Mary Margaret (1866-1954)
2. Brandeis, Louis Dembnitz (1856-1941)
3. Catron, John (c.1778-1865)
1. Ebbing, Hieronymous (fl. 1658-1673)
1. Frankfurter, Felix (1882-1965)
3. Grimke, John Faucheraud (1752-1819)
2. Kalisch, Samuel (1851-1930)
1. Kleberg, Robert Justus I (1803-1888)
2. Lehman, Irving (1870-1945)
3. Miller, Samuel Freeman (1816-1890)
   Otto, William Tod (1816-1905)
3. Shauck, John Allen (1841-1918)
1. Sulzberger, Mayer (1843-1923)
   Timmerman, George Bell (1881-1966)
2. Von Moschzisker, Robert (1870-1939)
   Wanamaker, Reuben Melville (1866-1924)
4. Willebrandt, Mable Walker (1889-1963)
1. Weiss, Lewis (1717-1796)
1. Woerner, John Gabriel (1826-1900)

Lawyers
2. Anthon, John (1784-1863)
3. Baer, George Frederick (1842-1914)
3. Beck, James Montgomery (1861-1936)
3. Conrad, Charles Magill (1804-1878)
2. Dorsheimer, William Edward (1832-1888)
2. Freund, Ernst (1864-1952)
   Friedman, Lee Max (1871-1957)
1. Hilgard, Theodor Erasmus (1790-1873)
2. Hise, Elijah (1801-1867)
2. Hohfeld, Wesley Newcomb (1879-1918)
2. Holls, George Frederick William (1857-1903)
2. King, Carol Weiss (1895-1952)
3. Kleberg, Edward Robert (1877-1957)
2. Kohler, Max James (1871-1934)
1. Lehmann, Frederick William (1853-1931)
2. Levinson, Solomon O. (1865-1941)
2. Lexow, Clarence (1882-1910)
   Mansfield, Arabella (1846-1911)
2. Marshall, Louis (1856-1929)
3. Marshall, James, 1896-1988)
2. Morawetz, Victor (1859-1938)
2. Pollak, Walter Heilprin (1887-1940)

2. Quitman, John Anthony (1798-1858)
2. Rayner, Isidor (1850-1912)
2. Rellstab, John (1858-1930)
1. Rice, Isaac Leopold (1850-1915)
1. Roselius, Christina (1803-1873)
3. Schell, Augustus (1812-1884)
1. Stallo, Johann Bernard (1823-1900)
   Sterne, Simon (1839-1901)
1. Steuer, Max David (1870-1940)
1. Straus, Oscar Solomon (1850-1926)
   Tiedeman, Christopher Gustavus (1857-1903)
5. Tyson, Job Roberts (1803-1858)
2. Untermyer, Samuel (1858-1940)
3. Willkie, Wendell Lewis (1892-1944)
2. Ward, Hortense Sparks Malsch (1910-1939)
1. Wolf, Simon (1836-1923)
1. Zeisler, Sigmund (1860-1931)

Mayors of Large Cities
1. Blankenburg, Rudolph (1843-1918), Philadelphia
2. Cruger, John (1710-1791), New York
   Kiel, Henry William (1871-1942), St. Louis
2. Seidel, George Lukes Emil (1864-1947), Milwaukee
2. Shoemaker, Benjamin (1704-), Philadelphia
3. Shoemaker, Samuel (1725-1800), Philadelphia
2. Wagner, Robert F., Jr. (1910-1991), New York

Presidents
5. Eisenhower, Dwight David (1890-1969) (Eisenhauer)
6. Hoover, Herbert Clark (1874-1964) (Huber)

Senators and Congressman
3. Barringer, Daniel Moreau (1806-1873)
1. Bartholdt, Richard (1855-1932)
1. Berger, Victor Louis (1860-1929)
4. Borah, William Edgar (1865-1940)
2. Fess, Simeon Davidson (1861-1936)
2. Geyer, Henry Sheffie (1790-1859)
4. Hager, John Sharpenstein (1818-1890)
1. Heilmann, Wilhelm (1824-1890)
2. Javits, Jacob Koppel (1904-1986)
1. Kahn, Julius (1861-1924)
4. Kern, John Worth (1849-1914)
2. Kleberg, Rudolph (1847-1924)
3. Kleberg, Richard Mifflin (1887-1955)
5. Lever, Ashbury Francis (1875-1940)
   Miller, John Franklin (1831-1886)

6. Simmons, Furnifold McLendel (1854-1940)
Waggamann, George Augustus (1782-1843)
1. Wagner, Robert Ferdinand (1877-1953)

Other Public Officials, Agents, Reformers
1. Ameringer, Oscar (1870-1943)
2. Baruch, Bernard Mannes (1870-1965)
Bauer, Catherine Krouse (1905-1967)
Bergh, Henry (1811-1888)
1. Bernays, Edward L. (1891-)
Bernheimer, Charles Seligman (1868-1960)
1. Bollman, Justus Erich (1769-1821)
Cahensly, Simon Peter Paul (1838-1923)
2. Christman, Elisabeth (1881-1975)
2. Cohen, Benjamin Victor (1894-1983)
2. Debs, Eugene Victor (1855-1926)
1. Degener, Eduard (1809-1890)
De Graffenried, Mary Clare (1849-1921)
2. Dreier, Mary Elizabeth (1875-1963)
1. Dubinsky, David (1892-1982)
2. Einstein, Hannah Bachman (1862-1929)
1. Erath, George Bernard (1813-1891)
1. Gallatin, Abraham Alfonse Albert (1761-1849)
Gellhorn, Edna Fischel (1878-1970)
2. Gratz, Rebecca (1781-1869)
5. Hagermann, Herbert James (1871-1935)
2. Hagner, Peter (1772-1850)
1. Hardenbroeck, Johannes (fl. 1664-1665)
Harding, Florence Kling (1860-1924)
2. Herrman, Ephraim George (fl. 1653-1689)
2. Hexamer, Charles John (1861-1921)
2. Hirth, William Andrew (1875-1940)
Hoffman, David (1787-1854)
6. Hoover, John Edgar (1895-1972)
2. Jacobs, Frances Wisebart (1843-1892)
3. Jacobs, Pattie Ruffner (1875-1935)
1. Kissinger, Henry Alfred (1923-)
1. Körner, Gustav Philipp (1809-1896)
3. Kolb, Reuben Francis (1839-1918)
Kuhn, Fritz Julius (1895-1951)
1. Leisler, Jacob (1640-1691)
1. Lieber, Richard (1869-1944)
Linderman, Henry Richard (1825-1879)
6. McCormick, Edith Rockefeller (1872-1932)
3. Meyer, George von Lengerke (1858-1918)
2. Miller, Frieda Segelle (1889-1973)

1. Minuit, Peter (1580-1638)
1. Morgenthau, Henry (1856-1946)
2. Morgenthau, Henry, Jr. (1891-1967)
2. Moser, Christopher Otto (1885-1935)
2. Moskowitz, Bell Lindner Israels (1877-1933)
1. Most, Johann Joseph (1846-1906)
3. Pennypacker, Elijah Funk (1804-1888)
1. Pitzman, Julius (1837-1923)
3. Pollitzer, Anita (1894-1975)
4. Rand, Caroline Amanda Sherfy (1828-1905)
3. Reuther, Walter Philip (1907-1970)
3. Richberg, Donald Randell (1881-1960)
2. Robins, Margaret Dreier (1868-1945)
1. Roelker, Bernard (1816-1888)
   Ruthenberg, Charles E. (1882-1927)
1. Schwimmer, Rosika (1877-1948)
1. Sender, Toni (1888-1935)
2. Solomon, Hannah Greenbaum (1858-1942)
1. Sorge, Friedrich Adolph (1828-1906)
1. Spies, August Vincent Theodor (1855-1887)
2. Spinner, Francis Elias (1802-1890)
   Stern, Edith Rosenwald (1895-1980)
2. Stern, Francis (1873-1947)
1. Stolper, Gustav (1888-1947)
1. Struve, Gustav (1805-1870)
1. Treutlen, John Adam (1726-c.1780)
3. Updike, Daniel (c.1693-1757)
1. van der Beeck, Paulus (fl.1644-1662)
   Wedemeyer, Joseph (1818-1866)
1. Weitling, Wilhelm Christian (1808-1877)
1. Wetzel, Lewis (c.1764-1808)
2. Wirt, William (1772-1834)
2. Wise, Louise Waterman (1874-1947)
2. Woerishoffer, Emma Carola (1885-1911)
   Yerger, George Shall (1801-1860)

Code:

1. = 1st Generation in America
2. = 2nd Generation
3. = 3rd or more Generation, etc.

Medical Sciences in America

The development of modern medicine in America, as in Europe, was a product of the late 19th century. Medicine had remained an art, rather than a science essentially until the invention of the microscope, and even then, the age of advanced microscopic research occurred as late as the period of about 1875 to 1906. That unique period has been called the "Golden Age of Bacteriology." Only then were the medical specialists able to differentiate routinely one disease from another, and more importantly, to provide, in general, effective treatment.

The yellow fever epidemic in Philadelphia in 1793 is a classic example for which no effective treatment was then available. People died by the thousands. There were also less severe, periodic outbreaks of yellow fever in Philadelphia in the periods 1797-1799 and 1802-1805.

Before about 1800, the universal cure and initial preparative treatment of diseases usually involved either bloodletting or the administration of emetics and cathartics, all of which were in general counterproductive. A massive dose of the bitter tasting calomel (mercurous chloride), in combination with jalap and tartarized antimony, was designed to flush the intestines and perhaps unknowingly diluted the effect of concurrent typhus, typhoid, dysentery, and other common internal diseases. The equally distasteful curative treatment of quinine sulfate, arsenious acid, and opium counteracted to some extent the effects of malaria. The last ingredient at least provided some temporary benefit by stimulating a feeling of wellness.

In the interior of the United States, virtually no malaria had been recorded for the years 1670 through 1760. Thereafter, the increasing number of migrants brought with them malaria and many other diseases. In Illinois, the number of cases of malaria increased at alarming rates, so that by 1800 the southern portion of the state had developed a reputation for being decidedly unhealthy. In the swamps and poorly drained farmlands across central and southern Illinois, central Indiana and northwestern Ohio, high rates of malaria incidence continued until the 1870s with malaria disappearing only about 1890.

The great mass of 19th century German immigrants settling in the larger cities of the north were subject to all the horrors of poor sanitation involving haphazard waste disposal, open sewers, crowded tenements, questionable water supplies, and minimal personal cleanliness. In such circumstances, it is little wonder that major cholera outbreaks occurred in the United States in 1832-1834, 1848-1849, 1849-1854, 1866, and 1873.

Typhoid, typhus, dysentery, pneumonia, and tuberculosis were other normal hazzards of tenement life in 19th century America. Often diseases occurred in unison with malnutrition. Scurvy, the deficiency of vitamin C, was a common ailment.

Fortunately, smallpox vaccine had been discovered in 1796 and introduced to America by 1800. In the case of malaria, the effective treatment was a dose of quinine which was isolated from the bark of certain trees grown in Peru and which was in fairly common use in America by 1840. However, the actual cause of malaria was not known until about 1895. The cause of typhoid fever, which was often water borne, and typhus fever, usually louse or flea borne, were identified only in the era of 1909-1910.

With these remarks in mind, the reader will note that there were few medical men of distinction in America in the 1600s and 1700s. And not many in the 1800s, a period in which medicine continued to operate in a near "state of ignorance." The tragedy of medicine, not only in the U.S., but world-wide, was that new technology made a typical individual's learning obsolete within a decade or two after completion of medical school and only the best could keep up to date. Many did not try to keep up and dogmatically passed on erroneous assumptions to the next generation of students. Such a relatively simple tool as the microscope, which was in use for centuries, was little more than a toy until the 1820's when improved lenses were devised. The new lenses were however not that great and, furthermore, staining techniques, serial sections, and all the other accessory technology required for cell study was not yet available. This technology was not to come until the late 1870's. Wilhelm Conrad Röntgens (1845-1923) developed in Würzburg, in 1895, primitive techniques of using X-rays, a technology which became important in America during the next decade.

One noteworthy early physician was Otto Bodo who arrived in America in 1755. As noted in the section on military, Bodo was primarily a surgeon rather than a treater of diseases.

Other prominent family names established in America by the late 1700s, whose descendants later became prominent medical men, were: Gallinger, Gerhard, Keagy, Kuhn, Landis, Leib, Mettauer, Schadle, Schweinitz, Schrady, Steiner, Tyson, Wagner, and Wistar.

One of the earliest medical departments in America was the Harvard Medical School, established in 1783. Another was Dartmouth Medical School set up in 1798, with a one man faculty. The two year's course then normally available did not require a large teaching staff.

For a long time, Europe remained the primary center for either initial or advanced training. The first generation medical men of the 1800s in America were virtually all of the upper middle class who brought with them whatever technology and medical books the best universities in Europe had to offer. The second generation Americans often were sent to European universities to receive their primary medical training, and in a few cases, took American technology to Europe with them.

Esssential background data on the history of medicine is contained in the 1982 book by E. H. Ackerknecht titled simply *A Short History of Medicine* (Johns Hopkins Univ. Press, Baltimore). The 1985 book by R. E. McGrew (ed.) titled *Encyclopedia of Medical History* (McGraw-Hill Book Co., N.Y.) gives basic encyclopedic information on nearly all medical aspects. Concepts about the development of medicine in America are covered in the interesting and well-edited 1991 book by L. S. King titled *Transformations in American Medicine from Benjamin Rush to William Osler* (Johns Hopkins Univ. Press, Baltimore). The latter book notes that Johns Hopkins University in Baltimore became a leading center for medical learning after its establishment in 1893. The book also mentions that two key medical forum were organized in America only in the 19th century, the one being the American Medical Association founded in 1847, and the other being the American Association of Physicians who held their first meeting in 1886. Modern day organizations, such as the Rockefeller Medical Institute, which began operations in 1901, continue to make formal training obsolete within an individual's medical career.

Selective examples of the medical profession in America follow.

General Practice

The term "general practice" is here used arbitrarily as a catch-all term. Many of the group, for example, Eberle, Keagy, Kober, and Pepper, were noted educators in the area of medicine. Others had a mixed career as inventors, explorers, politicians, publishers, and naturalists. The mixed career group hardly kept up with medical developments.

Gustav Brühl was a typical example of that great wave of Germans going to America in 1848. Brühl, from Herdorf, Rheinland-Pfalz, established his residence in the then boom town of Cincinnati.

Frederick Albert Cook was in Hortonville, N.Y., in 1865. Cook (original family name Koch) was a physician and explorer who accompanied several expeditions to the polar regions. In fact, Cook claimed to have reached the North Pole in April, 1908, that is, before Robert E. Peary. The controversy of who reached the pole first raged for years. In the end, Peary was given the credit of this milestone.

Edward Dorsch, from Würzburg, is another example of the mass of 1849 refugees who went to America. Dorsch settled in Detroit. In addition to his medical work, Dorsch achieved some notoriety as a poet.

John Eberle was born in Hagerstown, Md. in 1787. Eberle was one of the founders of Jefferson Medical College in Canonsburg, Pa., where he taught medicine from 1825-1830. In 1831, Eberle reorganized the Medical Dept. at Miami University, Oh., and from 1837, taught medicine at Transylvania University in Lexington, Ky.

Love Rosa Hirschmann Gantt was a second generation immigrant, born in Camden, S.C. in 1875. She spent her career as a physician and public health worker in South Carolina.

John Miller Keagy was born in Strasburg, Lancaster Co., Pa. The Keagy family name is derived from Johannes Keagy, or Keagi, a Swiss who went to America about 1715. In America, Keagy was primarily an educator who promoted the ideas of Pestalozzi toward the field of medicine.

Helen Adams Keller, born in Tuscumbia, Ala. in 1880, needs little introduction. She received a degree from Radcliffe College in 1904, and for many years, was associated with the American Foundation for the Blind. The exact European origin of this particular Keller family name has not been recorded. However, in western Germany, the name Keller is number forty-five on the list of the most common family names. This particular Keller family name evidently comes from Switzerland.

Michael Leib had a varied career as a physician, congressman, and senator. Leib was born in Philadelphia in 1760 as the son of Johann Georg Leib who had come from Strasbourg, Alsace, in 1753. Leib also had an active career as a politician serving as a congressman from Pennsylvania for the years 1799-1806.

Lucy Minnigerode was born in Leesburg, Va. in 1871. She was the granddaughter of Rev. Charles Frederick Ernst Minnigerode, a 1839 dissident emigrant from Darmstadt. Minnigerode was a nurse with the Red Cross, and with the Veterans Bureau, and eventually became superintendent of the Department of Nurses with the U.S. Public Health Service, a role she occupied from 1919-1935.

Arminius Oemler had a varied career as a physician, an agriculturist, and an oyster farm operator in Georgia. He was born in Savannah, Ga., in 1827, as the son of August Gottlieb Oemler, a native of Hettstedt, Sachsen-Anhalt.

John Conrad Otto was born in Woodbury, N.J. in 1774, as the grandson of Bodo Otto of Revolutionary War fame. The younger Otto is noted for his analysis of the yellow fever outbreaks which occurred in Philadelphia in 1797, 1798, 1799, 1802, 1803, and 1805, and also for study of the cholera epidemic which occurred in Philadelphia in 1832. Otto was associated with Pennsylvania Hospital from 1813-1834.

Another noted family was that of William Pepper and his son, also William Pepper. Both were physicians and educators associated with the University of Pennsylvania. The younger William Pepper was part of the Medical Deptartment at the university from 1862-1894 and, after 1864, simultaneously resident physician at the Pennsylvania Hospital. In 1874, the younger Pepper established the concept of a "teaching hospital." In 1881, he became provost at the University of Pennsylvania and for fifteen years continued to improve its program such as increasing the medical course to four years. The Pepper family name comes from one Heinrich Pfeiffer who went from Strasbourg, Alsace to Lebanon Co., Pa. in 1763.

William Taussig was born in Prague, Bohemia, in 1826. He landed in New York in 1847, and eventually settled in St. Louis where he was a physician, banker, and businessman. Taussig is noted as Lincoln supporter and as the president of the Eads Bridge Company, an early bridge across the Mississippi River at St. Louis.

Lillian D. Wald was born in Cincinnati in 1867. She was the daughter of Max D. and Minnie (Schwarz) Wald; both parents came from Jewish families arriving in the United States in 1848. Wald became a public health nurse in New York. With financing with Jacob Henry Schiff (1847-1920) about 1893, she was able to start and operate the Nurses' Settlement on the east side. Lillian Wald remained active in this venture until 1933; this well-known service acquired the name of "Henry Street Visiting Nurse Service." Lillian Wald publicized these efforts with a 1915 book titled *The House on Henry Street* and a 1934 book titled *Windows on Henry Street*. Two other nurses prominent in the Henry Street settlement were Lavinia Lloyd Dock (active 1896-1916), and Margaret Gene Arnstein (1904-1972). The latter used her training at Henry Street before joining the N.Y. Deptartment of Health (1934-1937 and 1940-1943), and the U.S. Public Health Service (1846-1966).

Marie Elizabeth Zakrzewska was born in Berlin in 1829, and went to New York in 1853. She acquired a reputation as a women's emancipation pioneer and physician. She headed the New England Hospital for Women and Children in Boston from about 1862-1899. The family name has an obvious Polish origin.

Homeopathology

In the first half of the 19th century, it became fashionable to call one's self by the distinguished sounding name of homeopathologist. Homeopathology, whose trial and error methods placed it somewhere between outright quackery and medical science, is defined in dictionaries as the application of minute quantities of remedies that in massive doses produce effects similar to the disease being treated. For example, the use of quinine produces an effect similiar to that of malaria. Quinine in very small quantities was thus used to counteract the effects of malaria. By the early 1800s, American physicians used quinine without understanding how malaria was caused. In fact, it was not until 1880 that the malaria parasite was discovered and only in 1895 was this parasite related to the anopheles mosquito.

Homeopathy was founded in Germany about 1807 by Christian Friedrich Samuel Hahnemann (1758-1843). Hahnemann worked in Leipzig from 1811-1835, and thereafter in Paris. His techniques were carried to the United States about 1825, and became popular with the public. The first homepathic association was begun in Philadelphia in 1833. Students of the Hahnemann technique established the Hahnemann Medical College in Chicago before mid-19th century and clinics in various other cities. The American Institute of Homoepathy was founded in 1844. Today, however, not a single school of homeopathy remains.

The pertubations of homeopathy did stimulate the pharmaceutical industry in the U.S., an industry which was well advanced in Germany by the early part of the 19th century. For instance, the ubiquitous, German-developed Bayer asprin made its appearance in America about 1900 and rapidly became a medical panacea.

A half dozen or so prominent German-Americans specialized in homeopathy; virtually all were born in Germany and were active in America during the early part of the 19th century.

Charles Julius Hempel was born in Solingen, Nordrhein-Westfalen in 1811, and went to New York in 1835, where he became an early homeopathic physician.

Constantine Hering was born in Oschatz, Sachsen, in 1800. Hering went to Philadelphia in 1833, where he became a homeopathic physician, as was Hempel above.

Charles Neidhard was born in Bremen in 1809, and went to Philadelphia about 1825. He was an early student of Walter Wesselhoeft, a noted homeopathic physician, and entered that practice in 1836.

Joseph Hippolyt Pulte was born in Meschede, Westfalen in 1811. Pulte went to Allentown, Pa. in 1834, and later transferred his homeopathic activities to Cincinnati.

Charles Gottlieb Raue was born in Niedercunnersdorf, Sachsen, in 1820, and went to Philadelphia in 1848. Raue was a homeopathic physician.

Walter Wesselhoeft was born in Weimar, Thüringen, in 1838. He was one of two brothers who went to the Massachusetts in 1840, where he became a homeopathic physician. The other brother, Conrad, born 1834, in Weimar, was one of the founders, in 1873, of Boston University Medical School. Conrad also worked in the area of homeopathy.

Nervous Disorders

Twenty-one German-Americans are listed in the directory under this field.

Erich Fromm was a well-known psychoanalyst. He was born in Frankfurt am Main in 1900, and went to the United States in 1934. Fromm died in Switzerland in 1980. Fromm wrote, in 1941, the book *Escape from Freedom*, and in 1947, the book *Man for Himself.*

August Valentine Menninger was born in Frankfurt am Main in 1826 and went to America in 1843. He resided initially in Baltimore and later in Cincinnati where he married Katarina Schmidberger, who had emigrated from Bönstadt, Hessen, in 1848. A son who became a medical doctor, Charles Frederick Menninger, was born in Tell City, Ind. In 1882, this son moved to Holton, Kans. Two of his sons, later known as the famous Menninger brothers, Karl Augustus and William Claire, were born in Topeka, Ks. The Menninger Clinic, an innovative physiciatric clinic, began operations about 1919 in Topeka. The family name apparently is related to one of two towns called Menningen in Germany, one being in Baden, and the other in Saarland.

Max Wertheimer was born in Prague in 1880. In Europe, he was a psychologist. As a 1930's refugee, he was associated with the N.Y. School of Social Research from 1933-1943. The family name likely was derived originally from the city of Wertheim in Baden-Württemberg.

Sanitation

Henry Coddington Meyer was born in Hamburg in 1844 as the son of a New York merchant, then resident in Hamburg. After the family returned to the United States, the son became a pioneer sanitary engineer and editor of public health publications.

Edgar Sydenstricker was born in Shanghai, China in 1881. Sydenstricker's career was that of a social and economic investigator with the U.S. Public Health Service from 1915-1928, and with the Milbank Memorial Fund from 1928-1936.

Specialists

John Jacob Abel was born in Cleveland in 1857. During the years 1884-1891, Abel studied at seven different universities in Europe, all of which had German as the basic teaching language. After his European training, Abel was a prominent pharmacologist who had a long career with the University of Michigan (1891-1893), and then at Johns Hopkins University (1893-1932). During his active career of four decades, Abel was a key factor in bringing European technology to America.

Frederick Henry Baetjer was born in Baltimore in 1874. Baetjer was a pioneer roentgenologist (the study of X-rays) at Johns Hopkins Hospital. Baetjer lost four fingers and an eye because of exposure to X-rays, an occupational hazard not recognized in those early days. He was the son of a immigrant from Arsten, near Bremen, who had gone to Baltimore in 1859.

Bernard Samuel Blumberg was born in New York in 1925. In 1976, Blumberg was awarded the Nobel Prize in Medicine for cancer research.

Nathan Edwin Brill was born in New York in 1859. Brill's name is of course associated with the recognition of Brill's disease, which is a mild form of typhus. The family name went to America from the village of Lichtenfels, a locality name in Bayern and also one in Hessen.

Louis Adolphus Duhring was born in Philadelphia in 1845. He was a pioneer dermatologist active in Philadelphia, whose father had come from Mecklenburg in 1818.

Louis Elsberg was born in Iserlohn, Nordrhein-Westfalen, in 1836. The Elsberg family went to Philadelphia in 1849. Elsberg became a laryngologist (throat specialist).

Francis Lawrence Flick was born in Cambria Co., Pa. in 1856. Both parents went to the United States about 1830, the father being a native Alsatian, and the mother being from Bayern. Flick established his practice in Philadelphia where he became a specialist on tuberculosis.

Herman Frasch was born in Gaildorf, Württemberg, in 1851. The family went to Philadelphia in 1868. In Philadelphia, Frasch had a varied career as a pharmacist, chemical engineer, and inventor.

Aaron Friedenwald was born in Baltimore in 1836. His father had gone to the United States from Hessen in 1832. Friedenwald was an opthalmologist. Friedewald is a locality in the northern part of Hessen.

Joseph Goldberger was born in Austria in 1874. The family went to the United States in 1880. Goldberger was a medical research worker who specialized in yellow fever, typhus, and pelagra.

William Wood Gerhard, a fourth generation immigrant, was born in 1809. In 1837, Gerhard recognized that the symptoms of typhus were to be distinguished those of typhoid. Gerhard, working at the University of Pennsylvania from 1838-1872, also was a pioneer investigator of smallpox, cholera, and pneumonia. He was the great grandson of Frederick Gerhard, who, as a Moravian, went in 1737 from Hessen to Berks Co., Pa.

Henry Gradle was born in Friedberg, near Frankfurt/Main, Hessen, in 1855. Gradle went to Chicago in 1868, where he eventually established a medical practice. Gradle was a professor of medicine at Northwestern University from 1879-1906. In 1883, Gradle wrote the book *Bacteria and the Germ Theory of Disease*, which at that time was a landmark and noted as the the first book in the English language on that subject.

Emil Gruening was born in Hohensalza, in 1842. The town was then in West Prussia and is now in western Poland, where it is called Inowroclaw. The family went to the United States in 1862. Gruening was a pioneer opthalmologist and otologist (eye and ear doctor).

Philip Showalter Hench was born in Pittsburgh in 1896. Hench was associated with the famous Mayo Clinic as from 1921. In 1950, he won a Nobel Prize in Physiology for distinguished research.

Alfred Fabian Hess was born in New York in 1875. Hess was a pediatrician and pathologist whose area of interest was scurvy.

Ferdinand Carl Hotz was born in Wertheim, Baden in 1843. Hotz went to Chicago in 1869, where he specialized in opthalmology, and also did pioneering work on plastic surgery.

Henry Robert Murray Landis was born in Niles, Oh., in 1872. Landis became a tuberculosis specialist. The Landis family name is very common around Lancaster, Pennsylvania. The first Landis in America apparently was the Swiss Mennonite pioneer Henry Landis who arrived in 1727.

Karl Landsteiner was born in Baden bei Wien (Vienna) in 1868. He came to the United States in 1922 and was a specialist in serology and immunology in New York from 1922 to 1939. During his long career, Landsteiner gained the title of "father of immunology." In 1930, he was awarded the Nobel Prize in Physiology or Medicine.

John Michael Maisch was born in Hanau, Hessen, in 1831, and went to the United States in 1850 as a political refugee. During the Civil War, he worked in the U.S. Army Laboratory, and in 1866, became a professor at the Philadelphia College of Pharmacy.

Marie Josepha Mergler was born in Mainstockheim, Bayern, in 1851. In 1882, she distinguished herself by becoming the dean of Northwestern University's Women's Medical School. Her medical career started in Chicago. Mergler was a specialist in gynecology.

Paul Fortunatus Mundé was born in Dresden, Sachsen. He went in 1848 to Florence, Mass. as a refugee, where he established a career as an obstretician and gynecologist. Mundé had an unusual career in that he returned to

Europe in 1866-1873 to serve in the Franco-Prussian War. Mundé eventually died in New York in 1902.

John Ruhräh was born in Chillicothe, Oh., in 1872. His father was a native of Bremen. The younger Ruhräh established a career in Baltimore as a pediatrician.

Carl Seiler was born in Switzerland in 1849, and went to the United States sometime before 1871. Seiler was a laryngologist. He died in Reading, Pa. in 1905.

Alfred Stengel was born in Pittsburgh, Pa., in 1868. He was the son of Gottfried Stengel who went to America in 1851 from Landau, Rheinland-Pfalz. The younger Stengel was a pathologist who taught at the University of Pennsylvania.

Karl Von Ruck, was born in Constinantinople, Turkey in 1849. He was the son of George Von Ruck, a native of Stuttgart, Baden-Württemberg. In America, Von Ruck established the Von Ruck Research Laboratory for Tuberculosis.

Clinton Wagner was born in Baltimore in 1837. He became a prominent laryngologist in New York. Wagner's ancestry is reported as a "descendant of Basil who, in 1667, received a grant of land from the Crown in Frederick, Md." Wagner achieved the rank of lieutenant-colonel in the Union army and participated in the Battle of Gettysburg.

Martha Wollstein was born in New York in 1868. She established a career as a pathologist and medical researcher at the Babies Hospital in New York with which she was associated from 1890 to 1935. A locality named Wollstein is a part of the town of Waldkappel in northern Hessen. Other localities are Wöllstein in Rheinland-Pfalz, and Wöllstein in Württemberg. There is also a locality of Wollstein in the former province of Posen, now in western Poland.

Hans Zinsser was born in New York in 1878. He was the son of August and Marie Theresia (Schmidt) Zinsser. The parents went to the United States in 1862, the father being a native of Oberflörsheim, Rheinland-Pfalz, and the mother a native of a small community near Freiburg, Baden. Zinsser had a distinguished career as a physician, bacterologist, immunologist, and author. He was associated with Columbia University and from 1923-1940 with Harvard University. In 1935, Zinsser published a notable book titled *Rats, Lice, and History*. In his book, Zinsser relates the fact that Napoleon's Grand Armee was decimated as much by disease as by the combined effects of cold weather, malnutrition, and actual fighting. Such loss of life was to be repeated in full in the American Civil War.

Surgeons

The title of surgeon was adopted by most medical practioners in the 17th century, although their activities dealt with a broad range of medical treatment. During the early days of no antiseptics, the acutal practice of surgery was a grim business. Three distinguished German-American surgeons, Otto Bocto, Philipp Klipstein and Francis Joseph Mettauer, of the Revolutionary

War are shown in the chapter on the military. Both came as Europeans soldiers and stayed on after the war to found distinguished lines of medical practioners. However, surgical anesthesia was used in America only in 1842, and slowly acquired acceptance. About 1869, the Englishman Joseph Lister (1827-1912) founded antiseptic surgery, another major advancement in this field.

The directory shows fourteen surgeons of some renown.

Carl Beck was born in Neckargemünd, Baden, in 1856. He went to N.Y. in 1881, where he was professor of surgery at the N.Y. Postgraduate School. Beck also served as president of St. Mark's Hospital for twenty-five years. Beck was an early user of X-rays for analysis, and in 1895 wrote the classic book *Roentgen Ray Diagnosis and Therapy*.

Frederick Strange Kolle was born in Hannover, Niedersachsen, in 1872. He went to Brooklyn about 1888, where he eventually became a pioneer in radiography (X-rays), and in plastic surgery.

John Peter Mettauer was born in Prince Edward Co., Va. in 1787. He was a surgeon. Mettauer was the son of Francis Joseph Mettauer, an Alsatian, who had come to America as a surgeon under Jean Baptiste, Comte de Rochambeau. The count was a French army officer who led the French forces in the American Revolution.

George Frederick Shrady was born in New York in 1837. He was the great-grandson of Johan Schrade of Württemberg, who came to America in 1715. Shrady had a surgical practice in New York and also was a prominent medical journalist.

TABLE 15
DIRECTORY OF MEDICAL SCIENCES

General Practice
3. Arnstein, Margaret Gene (1904-1972)
1. Baruch, Simon (1840-1921)
1. Baumgarten, Gustavus E. (1837-1910)
1. Brühl, Gustav (1826-1903)
2. Cook, Frederick Albert (1865-1940)
   Crumbine, Samuel Jay (1862-1954)
1. Dalcho, Frederick (1770-1836)
   Dock, George (1850-1931)
   Dock, Lavinia Lloyd (1858-1956)
1. Dorsch, Edward (1822-1887)
2. Eberle, John (1787-1838)
3. Francis, Samuel Ward (1835-1886)
4. Gallinger, Jacob Harold (1837-1918)
2. Gantt, Love Rosa Hirschmann (1875-1935)
   Haupt, Alma Cecelia (1893-1956)
3. Hoover, Charles Franklin (1865-1927)
4. Keagy, John Miller (1792-1837)
4. Keller, Helen Adams (1880-1968)
1. Kiefer, Hermann (1825-1911)
1. Kierstede, Hans (fl. 1638-1661)
1. Kober, George Martin (1850-1931)
1. Kudlich, Hans (1823-1917)
2. Kuhn, Adam (1741-1817)
1. Kunze, Richard Ernest (1838-1919)
2. Leib, Michael (1760-1822)
1. Mettauer, Francis Joseph (fl. 1780-)
1. Meyer, Willy (1858-1932)
3. Minnigerode, Lucy (1871-1935)
1. Morwitz, Edward (1815-1893)
2. Oemler, Arminius (1827-1897)
3. Otto, John Conrad (1774-1844)
3. Pepper, William (1810-1864)
4. Pepper, William, Jr. (1843-1898)
1. Rapoport, Lydia (1923-1971)
3. Rauch, John Henry (1828-1894)
1. Rominger, Carl Lugwig (1820-1907)
4. Rothrock, Joseph Trimble (1839-1922)
1. Schauffler, Edward William (1839-1916)
1. Schmidt, Ernst (1830-1900)
4. Steiner, Lewis Henry (1827-1892)
1. Sterki, Victor (1846-1933)
1. Taussig, William (1826-1913)
7. Tyson, James Haviland (1841-1919)

2. Wald, Lillian D. (1867-1940)
1. Zakrzewska, Marie Elizabeth (1829-1902)

Homeopathology
1. Hempel, Charles Julius (1811-1879)
1. Hering, Constantine (1800-1880)
1. Neidhard, Charles (1809-1985)
1. Pulte, Joseph Hippolyt (1811-1884)
1. Raue, Charles Gottlieb (1820-1896)
1. Wesselhoeft, Conrad (1834-1904)
1. Wesselhoeft, Walter (1838-1920)

Nervous Disorders
1. Alexander, Franz Gabriel (1891-1964), psychiatry
1. Bettelheim, Bruno (1903-1990), psychology
3. Bronner, Augusta Fox (1887-1966), psychiatry
2. Brunswick, Ruth Jane Mack (1897-1946), psychiatry
1. Bühler, Charlotte Bertha (1893-1974), psychology
1. Frenkel-Brunswik, Else (1908-1958), psychology
1. Fromm, Erich (1900-1980), psychology
1. Fromm-Reichmann, Frieda (1889-1957), psychiatry
1. Hoch, August (1868-1919), psychiatry
1. Horney, Karen Danielsen (1885-1952), psychiatry
3. Menninger, William Claire (1899-1966), psychiatry
3. Menninger, Karl Augustus (1893-1990), psychiatry
1. Meyer, Adolf (1866-1950), psychiatry
1. Münsterberg, Hugo (1863-1916), psychology
2. Rohe, George Henry (1851-1899), psychiatry
1. Sachs, Bernard (1858-1944), neurology
1. Sachs, Hanns (1881-1947), psychoanalysis
2. Spitzka, Edward Charles (1852-1914), neurology
1. Straus, Erwin Walter Maximilian (1891-)
1. Weisenburg, Theodore Herman (1876-1934), neurology
1. Wertheimer, Max (1880-1943), psychology

Sanitation
1. Meyer, Henry Coddington (1844-1935)
Sydenstricker, Edgar (1881-1936)

Specialists
3. Abel, John Jacob (1857-1938), pharmacology
Baer, William Stevenson (1872-1931), orthopedic surgery
2. Baetjer, Frederick Henry (1874-1933), pioneer x-rays
Blumberg, Baruch Samuel (1925-), cancer research
1. Brennemann, Joseph (1872-1944), pediatrics
2. Brill, Nathan Edwin (1859-1925), Brill's disease
2. Dercum, Francis Xavier (1856-1931), neurology

2. Duhring, Louis Adolphus (1845-1913), dermatology
2. Dyer, Isadore (1865-1920), dermatology
1. Elsberg, Louis (1836-1885), laryngology
2. Engelmann, George Julius (1847-1903), gynecology
2. Flick, Lawrence Francis (1856-1938), tuberculosis
2. Francis, John Wakefield (1789-1861), obstetrics
1. Frasch, Herman (1851-1914), pharmacology
2. Friedenwald, Aaron (1836-1902), ophthalmology
4. Gerhard, William Wood (1809-1872), pathology
1. Gescheidt, Louis Anthony (1808-1876), ophthalmology
2. Goldberger, Joseph (1874-1929), yellow fever, typhus
1. Gradle, Henry (1855-1911), bacteriology
1. Gruening, Emil (1842-1914), ophthalmology
   Heitzmann, Carl (1836-1896), anatomy
   Hench, Philip Showalter (1896-1965), physiology
2. Herter, Christian Archibald (1865-1910), biochemistry
2. Hess, Alfred Fabian (1875-1933), pediatrics
1. Hoffman, Frederick Ludwig (1865-1946), medical statistician
1. Hotz, Ferdinand Carl (1843-1909), ophthalmology
2. Huber, Gotthelf Carl (1865-1934), anatomy
1. Jacobi, Abraham (1830-1919), pediatrics
2. Jacobs, Joseph (1859-1929), pharmacology
1. Knapp, Jakob Herman (1832-1911), opthalmology
1. Koller, Carl (1857-1944), opthalmology
6. Landis, Henry Robert Murray (1872-1937), tuberculosis
1. Landsteiner, Karl (1868-1943), serology
1. Loeb, Leo (1869-1959), pathology
1. Loewi, Otto (1873-1961), pharmacology
1. Maisch, John Michael (1831-1893), pharmacology
2. Mall, Franklin Paine (1862-1917), anatomy
2. Mayer, Emil (1854-1931), laryngology
1. Mergler, Marie Josepha (1851-1901), gynecology
3. Miller, Henry (1800-1874), obstetrics
1. Munde, Paul Fortunatus (1846-1902), obstetrics
7. Musser, John Herr (1850-1912), pathology (Messer)
1. Noeggerath, Emil Oscar Jacob Bruno (1827-1895), gynecology
2. Ohlmacher, Albert Philip (1865-1916), pathology
2. Polak, John Osborn (1870-1931), obstretrics
1. Reuling, George (1839-1915), ophthalmology
1. Rice, Charles (1841-1901), pharmacology
2. Ruhräh, John (1872-1935), pediatrics
1. Sander, Enno (1822-1912), pharmacology
4. Schadle, Jacob Evans (1849-1908), laryngology
2. Schamberg, Jay Frank (1870-1934), dermatology
3. Schweinitz, George Edmund de (1858-1938), ophthalmology
1. Seiler, Carl (1849-1905), laryngology
1. Sigerist, Henry Ernest (1891-1957), medical historian

1. Sollmann, Torald Hermann (1874-1965), pharmacology
2. Spitzka, Edward Anthony (1876-1922), anatomy
2. Stengel, Alfred (1868-1939), pathology
1. Von Ruck, Karl (1849-1922), tuberculosis research
7. Wagner, Clinton (1837-1914), laryngology
1. Weber, Gustav Carl Erich (1828-1912), surgery
   Weil, Richard (1876-1917), medical research-cancer
3. Wistar, Caspar (1761-1818), anatomy
2. Wollstein, Martha (1868-1939), pathology
2. Zinsser, Hans (1878-1940), bacteriology

Surgeons
1. Beck, Carl (1856-1911)
2. Bernays, Augustus Charles (1854-1907)
2. Edebohls, George Michael (1853-1908)
4. Gross, Samuel David (1805-1884)
4. Gross, Samuel Weissell (1837-1889)
4. Helmuth, William Tod (1833-1902
1. Herff, Ferdinand Peter (-1912) (von Herff)
1. Kolle, Frederick Strange (1872-1929), plastic surgery
2. Mettauer, John Peter (1787-1875)
2. Ochsner, Albert John (1858-1925)
2. Ransohoff, Joseph (1853-1921)
1. Senn, Nicholas (1844-1908)
1. Schwyzer, Arnold (1864-1944)
5. Shrady, George Frederick (1837-1907)
1. Steindler, Arthur (1878-1959)
3. Teusler, Rudolf Bolling (1876-1934)
1. Walter, Albert C. (1811-1876)

Code
1. = 1st Generation in America
2. = 2nd Generation
3. = 3rd or more Generation, etc.

The World of Pop to Classical Music

In the German-speaking areas of Europe, the world of music revolves today as it did in the past around the key cities of Vienna and Berlin. A great majority of the noted performers listed in the directory were born in the eastern part of Germany, and studied music in one or both of these two centers; in the glorious years between wars, a great many musicians began and spent much of their career either in Vienna or Berlin.

With the large German migration to America in the 19th century, musicians tended to concentrate first and foremost in New York and Boston where they gained the most support both financially and publicly. The prominent German-American business man John Jacob Astor established New York's first music shop in May, 1786, but soon realized that a fortune was more likely to be made in furs and Manhattan real estate.

American Opera

The age of serious music evidently began in New York in 1825 with the presentation of Italian opera at the Park Theatre. In 1833, the Italian Opera House was opened and enjoyed modest success until it burned in 1839. In 1847, the Astor Palace Opera House was opened and carried on Italian opera until its closure in 1852. The next project was the N.Y. Academy of Music opened in 1854, and it presented operas and concerts until 1886, but set a dubious record with a new manager on an annual basis. The N.Y. Metropolitan Opera House opened in 1883. The next year, 1884, Leopold Damrosch initiated German Opera at the Met and thereby established a long tradition for opera lovers. Because of a fire in the 1892-93 season, and subsequent renovation, there was a break in performances. Otherwise, the N.Y. Met has been the mainstay of music in America, both onstage and via radio and TV. The N.Y. Met celebrated its centenary during the 1983-84 season. High finance provided much support, but like virtually all such organizations, the Met has relied on public support for publicity and funds. Currently, the N. Y. Metropolitan Opera Association counts over 100,000 members.

Opera music formed later and lesser cultural roles in Baltimore, Philadelphia, Cincinnati, Chicago, Milwaukee, Minneapolis, and to eventually also in St. Louis and San Francisco. None of these cities had the financial success of New York. The distribution of conductors and other high profile musicians reflects the concentration of German-speaking peoples in the population centers of the United States, except for Boston where English culture demanded the best musicians available, many of whom were of German origin.

American Symphony Music

Individuals interested in the history of symphonic music and classic music in America will do well to read the 1951 book by John H. Mueller titled *The American Symphony Orchestra* (Indiana University Press, Bloomington). Johann Christian Gottlieb Graupner (1767-1836) is cited as a key pioneer who was instrumental in forming an non-permanent orchestra in Boston between 1810 and 1824. Five prominent symphony orchestras were organized in the United States in the 19th century, of which the most important and earliest, was the New York Philharmonic Society, established in 1842. The others, before 1900 were the N.Y. Symphony Society, 1878 (merged with Philharmonic in 1928); Boston Symphony, 1881; Chicago Symphony, 1891; and Cincinnati, 1894.

Mueller further elaborates on the role of German composers, who in fact provided the bulk of classical music played in America. Of the top six composers, four (Beethoven, Brahms, Wagner, and Bach) were German. Mozart, an Austrian, and Tchaikowsky, a Russian, round out the select group. Some fifty-seven composers dominated American symphonic music. Of this latter group, nearly half were Austro-German.

Music lovers in New York benefited from the executive talents and financial resources of many prominent German-Americans. Two notable executives were Henry Harkness Flagler, who was a longtime (1914-1934) supporter of the N.Y. Symphony, and Felix Moritz Warburg, who was a director of the N.Y. Philharmonic Society from 1928-1937. The N.Y. Metropolitian Opera had prime support from George Ehret for its initiation in 1884, and from Otto Herman Kahn, who was a director and an executive leader of the N.Y. Metropolitan Opera from 1903-1931.

The musicians listed below compose a group of 247 individuals, of which eighty-two percent were European born, most in Germany, in the strict sense. Even those from the satellite areas were virtually all German-speaking through long association with German ethnic communities and through training in German musical schools. During the last half of the 19th century, America inherited the cream of the crop not only through the migration of top-flight musicians, but also through training of American born musical talents in the key music centers of Germany.

First rate musicians required first rate musical instruments. Instrument makers either brought technology with them or maintained a constant contact with expert craftsmen in Germany. In America, Germans were prominent both in the manufacture of musical instruments and in their maintenance. String instruments especially required a high degree of maintenance. These basic facts are obvious when one studies the family histories of the Steinway and the Wurlitzer families, among many others.

The Steinert, Wanamaker, and Wurlitzer families, among others, also made important collections of musical instruments, both European and American, which today are interesting from the historical standpoint. Important collections are maintained by Yale University, by the Smithsonian Institution, and by other museums.

The 1986 book titled *The New Grove Dictionary of American Music* is one of the best concise family history sources about musicians. It is a modernized, four volume condensation of a series of editions established in London decades ago and is important for its history of music. The series titled Baker's *Biographical Dictionary of Musicians*, which was begun in 1900, and in 1991 was in its 8th edition, also gives a very comprehensive listing of individuals directly and indirectly associated with the music industry. However, the two works mentioned above do not always agree as to dates and facts, nor do they always agree with the *Dictionary of American Biography*. This factor has to be taken into consideration; in general, one assumes that the latest publishing date supercedes the earlier publishing dates.

Composers

Fifty-two composers are listed in the directory. Many had secondary careers as conductors, organists, music editors, music publishers, teachers, writers, and the like.

The list of composers ranges through hymnologists, composers of popular music, composers of serious music, and in fact, the whole range of categories.

The Germantown mystic Johann Kelpius (1673-1708), who is described more fully under government, produced a seventy page manuscript of hymns. This work was done in the years of 1697-1706. The manuscript is known as the earliest extant musical manuscript compiled in the colonies. It is not clear whether or not Kelpius made any original contribution to this collection. Another hymnologist was David Creamer (described below). Edward Josef Stark was a cantor and composer of synagogue music.

Composers of popular music included Gus Edwards, Fred Fisher, Gus Kahn, Frank Loesser, Theodore August Metz, and Jean Schwartz. Max Hoffman gained a reputation as a ragtime composer.

Composers of semi-classical music and composers of operettas included Ludwig Engländer, Karl Rudolf Friml, Oscar Hammerstein II, Jerome David Kern, Frederick Loewe, Gustav Carl Luders, Sigmund Romberg, Hans Spialek, Maximilian Steiner, Albert Szirmai, and Kurt Weill.

Composers of opera and more serious types of music included Ernest Bloch, Franz Karl Bornschein, Lukas Foss, Rubin Goldmark, Paul Hindemith, Hugo Kauder, Erich Wolfgang Korngold, Gustav Mahler, and Arnold Schoenberg.

The highlights and achievements of a select few of these many composers is described in somewhat more detail.

Fred Fisher (or Fischer), whose name was originally Frederich Breitenbach, was born in Köln, in 1875. He went to N.Y. in 1900. His earliest known compositions date from about 1904. Beginning in 1907, Fisher was involved also with music publishing. Some of his songs are heard periodically, even today. Fisher's songs included the 1913 work "Peg o' my heart", and the popular 1919 work "Dardanella".

Rubin Goldmark was born in New York in 1872 to immigrant Austrian parents. Goldmark was both a composer and teacher of music. He worked for a six year period at the Conservatory of Music in Colorado and from 1911 to 1924 at the New York College of Music. In later years, he was associated with the famous Juilliard School of Music in New York. He died in 1936.

Oscar Hammerstein II was born and died in New York. He was a grandson of Oscar Hammerstein I who had come to the New York in 1863. The younger Oscar, of course, achieved fame as the composer of the lyrics of hit songs such as "Ol Man River" and the many songs that went into the best selling musicals *Show Boat*, *Oklahoma*, and *South Pacific*. In 1950, Hammerstein won a Pulitzer prize for drama for his part in composing the lyrics of *South Pacific* (shared with Richard Rodgers). The immigrant Hammerstein, born in Berlin, is listed in the entertainment-management section. The family name Hammerstein has a counterpart in a city name located in the former West Prussian administrative area of Marienwerder.

Paul Hindemith was born in Hanau, Hessen, in 1895, and came to the United States in 1940. Hindemuth taught at the Yale University Music Department over the years 1940-1953. Hindemith was a composer of the more serious type of music whose works incorporate elements of music theory.

Gus Kahn was born in Koblenz, now in Rheinland-Pfalz, in 1886. Kahn went to Chicago about 1895. Kahn was actually a lyricist, or one who supplies the words for music. Between 1916 and 1928, Kahn colloborated on popular hits such as "Pretty Baby", "Carolina in the Morning", "Toot, Toot, Tootsie", and "Makin' Whoopee".

Mathias Keller is a representative of the 1840's refugees. Keller who was born in Ulm, Württemberg, went to Philadelphia in 1846. He was a composer of more than 100 songs, few of which are remembered today. Keller did write several patriotic songs which inspired the Federal forces in their Civil War effort.

Jerome David Kern, born in 1885 in New York, was another composer of popular songs. His numerous popular hits included some of those in the musical *Show Boat*. Kern was associated with the stage from 1911-1939, and with film music from 1935-1946.

Louis Koemmenich was born in Elberfeld, now in Nordrhein-Westfalen, in 1866, and went to N.Y. in 1890. Koemmenich had a varied career as a composer and musician, but was best noted for conducting singing societies. He was associated with various societies in Brooklyn and New York from 1894-1917.

Gustav Mahler was born in 1860 in Kalischt, Bohemia, and died in Vienna in 1911. Mahler's work in classical music of Austro-German tradition included tours with the N.Y. Metropolitian Opera and the N.Y. Philharmonic Orchestra from 1907-1911. Mahler had a strong influence on many other American musicians.

Theodore Metz was born in Hannover, now in Niedersachsen, in 1848, and went to N.Y. in 1879. Metz's career varied between that of composer and a vaudeville and minstrel show musician. His 1886 song "A Hot Time in the Old Town Tonight" became a stage hit in 1896 and two years later, was used as a rallying song by the American troops involved in the Spanish-American War.

John Frederik Peter was reportedly born in the Netherlands, but was of German ancestry. He was born in 1746 and died in the Moravian community of Bethlehem in 1813. Peter's career varied between composing, playing the organ, and being a minister. From 1770 until his death, he was rated as the most important musician in the varied Moravian communities in America.

Sigmund Romberg, was born actually in Nagykanizsa, now in southern Hungary, in 1887. He went to New York in 1909 where, beginning about 1914, he was a staff composer for the Shubert Brothers. In the early 1930s, Romberg worked mainly in Hollywood. During his career, Romberg was involved in seventy-eight operettas and adapted more than 2,000 songs. Of the operettas, he is best known for his 1924 "Student Prince" and his 1926 "Desert Song".

Arnold Schoenberg, born in Vienna in 1874, became a permanent U.S. resident in 1933. Schoenberg was a conductor and composer associated with the University of California at Los Angeles from 1936-1944, and gained a reputation as the "founder of modern music."

Hans Spialek was born in Wien (Vienna), in 1894 and went to N.Y. in 1924. A long time associate of Broadway theatre, Spialek orchestrated 147 Broadway shows. In later years, he worked as orchestrator, arranger, and composer for radio.

Theodore Moses Tobani was a composer and arranger. Born in 1855 in Hamburg, he went to New York in boyhood, and about 1870 to Philadelphia. During a long career, Tobani composed 550 songs and arranged 4,500 songs. Tobani was also an associate and editor of the music publisher Carl Fischer. Records do not show the origin of the Tobani name, a name not typically German.

Kurt Weill was born in Dessau, Mecklenberg, in 1900. He was a well-known musician and composer who went with other refugees to New York in 1935. Weill is perhaps best known for his 1928 work called *Die Dreigroschenoper*. After Weill's death in 1950, this operetta set performance records in New York from 1954-1961 were the English version was known as *The Threepenny Opera*. Weill's work was promoted by the well-known singer, Lotte Lenya, whom he married in 1926. Lotta Lenya is shown also in the section on entertainment.

Charles Zeuner, born in 1795 in Eisleben, Sachsen, was one of the early European-trained musicians migrating to America. Zeuner went to Boston sometime during the years of 1824-1830; in Boston he was a leader in the field of serious music, being associated with the Handel & Haydn Society from 1830-1839. Prior to his death in 1857, he worked also in Philadelphia. Zeuner's career varied between composing, playing the organ and piano, and various teaching positions.

Conductors

Fifty-two musicians are listed in this category. The highlights of some of their achievements are noted below. The majority had a high profile position with one of the major U.S. music centers.

Henry Berger was born in Potsdam, in 1844. He went to Honolulu in 1872. In Hawaii, Berger was the conductor of the Royal Hawaiian Military Band from 1872-76, and from 1877-1915. During this long career, Berger led 32,000 band concerts, arranged over a thousand musical works and composed hundreds of songs and marches. Like many musicians, Berger simplified his name from Heinrich Wilhelm Berger to simply Henry Berger.

Carl Bergmann was born in Ebersbach, Sachsen, in 1821. He went to New York with the wave of refugees in 1849. In New York, Bergmann was associated with the Germania Musical Society from 1852-1854, and with the N.Y. Philharmonic Society from 1855-1876.

Artur Bodanzky was a Viennese native who went to New York in 1915 where he conducted at the New York Metropolitan Opera. He also conducted at the New Symphony and at the N.Y. Philharmonic during a conducting career that lasted from 1915-1939. Bodansky died in New York in 1939. The Bodansky name evidently has a Slavic origin.

Leopold Damrosch was a leader of the well-known Damrosch musical clan which went to New York in 1871. He was born in 1832 in Posen, an area now in Poland. Damrosch was noted as the director of the N.Y. Symphony Orchestra, occupying that position from 1878 until his death in 1885. A son, Walter Johannes Damrosch, was the conductor for the N.Y. Symphony from 1885-1928.

Arthur Fiedler was born in Boston in 1894, and in 1930, became a conductor of the popular "Boston Pops" Orchestra which he conducted from 1930-1979. Fiedler was also associated with the San Francisco Symphony from 1951-1978. Fiedler died in Boston in 1979.

Wilhelm Gericke, born in Graz, Steiermark, Austria, went to Boston in 1884 where he became the second conductor of the Boston Symphony from 1884-1889, and from 1898-1906. Gericke died in Vienna in 1925.

Boston, which competed with New York for the attraction of famous musicians, enticed Isidor George Henschel, a native of Breslau, Schlesien, to be the first conductor of the Boston Symphony where he conducted during the years 1881-1884. In 1884, Henschel moved to London and worked there for eleven years with the London Symphony where he died.

In London, Henschel was given the official English title of Sir George Henschel.

Victor Herbert deserves special mention and qualification. Actually born in Dublin, Ireland, in 1859, Herbert was raised in Germany during the years of 1866-1886. In 1886, he married the German singer Therese Foerster, and in the same year, went to New York. His long career in America was that of cellist and conductor for the N.Y. Metropolitan Opera., the N.Y. Philharmonic, and the Pittsburgh Symphony.

Erich Leinsdorf, whose original family name was Landauer, is another well-known name of 20th century American musicians. Leinsdorf was born in Vienna in 1912 and went to New York in 1937 as a refugee. He conducted at various places including the N.Y. Metropolitian Opera, the Cleveland Orchestra, the Rochester Philharmonic, and the Boston Symphony.

Charles Münch was born in Strassburg, Elsaß, in 1891. He went to Boston in 1946 and had the role of chief conductor with the Boston Symphony from 1949-1962. Münch was partial to the music of French composers.

Emil Johann Oberhoffer was born in München, Bayern, in 1867. He went to N.Y. in 1885. In 1903, Minneapolis enticed Oberhoffer to conduct the Minneapolis Symphony Orchestra, a position he occupied until 1923.

Eugene Ormandy was born in Budapest, Hungary, in 1899. Ormandy went to the United States in 1920. Ormandy was noted for conducting the Philadelphia Orchestra, beginning in 1936 and lasting until 1980. Ormandy was associated also with the Minneapolis Symphony Orchestra from 1931-1936. Ormandy's name originally was Jeno Blau.

André Previn was born in Berlin, in 1929. Previn went to Los Angeles in 1939 where he had a varied career as conductor, composer, and pianist dealing with popular music. Previn later worked in London, then in Pittsburgh, and most recently in London. The family was originally of Russian Jewish descent as reflected by Previn's original name which was Andreas Ludwig Priwin. Conversion to a French sounding name evidently came during the family's move to Paris in 1938.

Kurt Schindler, born in Berlin in 1882, went to New York in 1905. Schindler established a well-known music school in New York, the Schola Cantorum.

Anton Seidl, born in Pest, Hungary in 1850, went to New York in 1885. Seidl conducted both at the N.Y. Metropolitan and at the N.Y. Philharmonic. He was a strong promoter of Wagnerian music. The Seidl name is interesting for its apparent exterpiration of an "e", a phenomena which is common in Bayern and in Austria.

Johann Friedrich Eduard Sobolewski, born in 1808 in Königsberg, Ost-Preußen, was attracted to Milwaukee in 1859, where he founded the Milwaukee Philharmonic Society Orchestra. He conducted also in Chicago and in St. Louis. Sobolewski was a descendant of an ancient Polish family as the Slavic influence on the family name shows.

Henry Christian Timm, born in Hamburg in 1811, went to New York in 1835. Timm was president of the Philharmonic Society of New York from

1848-1863. He was active as a conductor until 1882.

Christian Friedrich Theodore Thomas was born in Esens, now in Niedersachsen, in 1835. Thomas went to N.Y. in 1845, and had a long career as an American conductor in Brooklyn, New York, and Chicago, lasting from 1845-1891. In America, Thomas was one of the foremost conductors of his time and was especially active in promoting the works of the great German masters. The bulk of the Thomas manuscript library forms an important collection of music in Chicago's Newberry Library.

Bruno Walter was another popular American conductor, having been born in Berlin, in 1876. He joined the refugee crowd migrating to America in 1939 and conducted mainly with the N. Y. Metropolitan Opera and the N.Y. Philharmonic Symphony. His full name was actually Bruno Walter Schlesinger.

Carl Zerrahn was another 1848 member of the Germania Society, a group organized in Berlin for performances in the U.S. in 1848. When the group disbanded in 1854, Zerrahn elected to remain in the U.S. Zerrahn's main work was at Boston where he led the Handel & Haydn Society from 1854-1896.

Music Teachers

The directory shows eleven individuals in this category. Some highlights are as follows.

Frank Heino Damrosch, born in Breslau, Schlesien, went to New York in 1871. Damrosch's primary position was at the Institute of Musical Art from 1905-1933; the institute later became the well-known Juilliard School of Music.

Otto Rudolph Ortmann was born in Baltimore, in 1889. Ortman taught at the Peabody Conservatory in Baltimore from 1917-1941 and at Goucher College from 1942-1957.

Florenz Ziegfeld, Sr. was born in Jever, near Oldenburg, Niedersachsen, date unknown. He evidently went to Chicago in the 1860s. Ziegfeld was the president of the Chicago Musical College from 1867-1916.

Musicologists, Collectors & Critics

Musicologists are devoted to the study of the development of music as well as to the history of music. Collectors of instruments often are also students of the history of music. And critics usually bear a well-rounded knowledge of both aspects. Eleven individuals are listed in the directory.

Jean Beck was born in Guebweiler, Elsaß, in 1881. In addition to teaching music at the University of Illinois from 1911-1914, and at Bryn Mawr College from 1914-1920, Beck developed a strong interest in the philology and history of music. Beginning in 1920, Beck joined the staff of the Curtis Institute. Beck's original name was Johann Baptist Beck.

Alfred Einstein was born in München, Bayern, in 1880. He went to the U.S. in 1939, or at the relatively late age of fifty-nine. Still, Einstein taught musicology at Smith college, Mass. from 1939-1950. He was a cousin to the physicist Albert Einstein.

Karl Johannes Geiringer, was born in Wien (Vienna), in 1899. He went to the U.S. in 1940 and taught musicology at Boston University from 1941-1962. Geiringer was at the University of California, Santa Barbara, from 1962-1972. In 1943, Geiringer wrote *A History of Musical Instruments*.

Henry Edward Krehbiel was born in Ann Arbor, Mich., in 1854. Krehbiel developed a strong reputation as a music critic when he wrote columns for the *Cincinnati Gazette*, 1874-1880, and for the *New York Tribune*, 1880-1923. Among other books, Krehbiel wrote, in 1914, *Afro-American Folksongs* and in 1921, *Life of Beethoven*. Krehbiel developed an extensive music library which was acquired by the N.Y. Public Library.

Curt Sachs was born in Berlin, in 1881. He went to New York in 1937 and from 1937-1959 was musicologist first at N.Y. University and then at Columbia University. Sachs was also a consultant in music matters at the N.Y. Public Library, a library foremost among public libraries in the U.S.

Oscar George Theodore Sonneck was born near Jersey City, N.J., in 1873. Sooneck lived in Germany from about 1875 to 1899. In 1905, he compiled a *Bibliography of Early Secular American Music*. Sonneck was chief of the music division at the Library of Congress from 1902-1917. He held a managerial position with the major music publishing firm of G. Schirmer Co. from 1917-1928. He died in 1928. The Sonneck Society, established in 1975, is interested in music research.

Morris Steinert was born in Scheinfeld, Bayern in 1831. Steinert, whose given name was originally Moritz, went to New York about 1854. He became involved in piano sales under the name of M. Steinert & Sons. The company built up an impressive collection of musical instruments which was willed to Yale University, where it forms a prominent collection.

Emanuel Winternitz was born in Wien (Vienna), in 1898. He was a curator of musical instruments at Harvard's Fogg Museum from 1938-1941, and at the Metropolitan Museum of Art in N.Y. from 1941-1973.

Hugo Worch was born in Potsdam, Brandenburg, in 1855. His father, Christian Worch, was in music sales businesses in Trenton, N.J. and Washington, D.C. as early as 1858. The son began collecting keyboard instruments in the 1880s. By 1914, he had collected some 200 instruments which today form the basis of a noteworthy collection at the Smithsonian.

Music Publishers

Among the earliest German music printed in America were hymnbooks printed in Philadelphia by the Benjamin Franklin (1706-1790) who was of English descent. During the years 1730-1736, Franklin printed three hymnbooks for the Ephrata Community which established its own press in 1743. The Ephrata Press carried on until well into the 19th century with a broad range of printing activities and had a variety of printers as listed in the section on printing and publishing.

The directory shows fifteen publishing firms in America which specialized in music. Most were either begun or carried on by native Germans. The earliest of these specialists was that of Johann Christian Gottlieb Grauper who set up a music printing firm in Boston in 1801 and soon dominated the music market there. The largest and best known music printing firm was G. Schirmer of New York which is described below.

Gustav Schirmer was an early music publisher in New York. He was born in Königsee, Sachsen, in 1829, and went to New York in 1840. Schirmer recorded his trip from Hamburg to New York as lasting forty-six days. The publishing firm was dates from 1848 and in 1854, Gustav became manager. Schirmer and a partner, Bernard Beer, took control of the firm in 1861 with Schirmer becoming sole owner in 1866. After the elder Schirmer died in 1893, the business was reorganized and incorporated as G. Schirmer, Inc. His son, Rudolph Edward Schirmer, carried on the publishing firm's business until about 1917, when Oscar George Theodore Sonneck became manager; Sonneck died in 1928. G. Schirmer, Inc. was acquired by the Maxwell Macmillan Publishing Group in 1968 which still uses the name Schirmer Books for music related items.

Anthony Johnson Showalter was born in Rockingham Co., Va., in 1858. He established a publishing house in Dalton, Ga., in 1884. The firm eventually became the largest music firm in the South, and until 1940, was known as the A.J. Showalter Co. They specialized in hymns and gospel songs. Showalter personally authored more than 100 books on various aspects of music.

Joseph William Stern was born in N.Y. in 1870, his father was an immigrant from Köln. Although a composer, Stern's main contribution was as a music publisher. The company, originally called Sterns & Marks, became the well-known house of Joseph W. Stern & Co.

Instrument Makers

According to Nancy Groce in her 1991 book *Musical Instrument Makers of New York* (City), the 1855 census for New York City lists a total of 836 muscial instrument makers, the majority being German-American, often first generation.

Over the centuries, the modest sized city of Markneukirchen, in Sachsen's Erzgebirge region garnered a reputation as a center for musical instrument manufacture. At least three well-known German-Americans, namely Henry Knopf, Christian Martin, and Wilhelm Mönnig, stem from Markneukirchen.

At least thirty-nine German-American musical instrument makers have been identified as shown in the directory.

Johann Gottlob Klemm was one of the earliest musical instrument makers of German background in America He belonged to the Moravian religious community in Pennsylvania. Klemm went to America from Sachsen about 1733, and was active in the manufacturer of organs from 1739-1762. His largest organ was constructed in 1739 for the Trinity

Church in New York. About 1757, the much publicized David Tannenberg started his apprenticeship with Klemm.

David Tanneberg (or Tannenberger), from Sachsen, went to Bethlehem in 1749, and to Lititz, Pa. in 1765. Over the years of 1758-1804, Tannenberg built more than forty organs, mostly for Moravian churches. However, two of his most notable organs were the larger ones made for the Holy Trinity Lutheran Church in Lancaster, Pa. in 1774, and for the Zion Luthern Church in Philadelphia in 1790. Tannenberg was assisted by his son-in-law, Philip Bachman (1762-1837).

The two Gemünder brothers were natives of Ingelfingen, Württemberg, and arrived in America in 1846. They became well-known violin makers in Boston in 1847 and a few years later, in New York. George Gemünder especially was considered to be one of the finest violin makers of his era and moved to Astoria, N.Y. in 1874, where he was active until his death in 1899. George Gemünder, Jr. (1857-1915) succeeded his father in the business.

Nineteenth century piano manufacturers active in America included Christian Frederick Ludwig Albrecht, Karl Albrecht, Hugo Sohmer, Valentine Wilhelm Ludwig Knabe, George Steck, Henry Engelhard Steinway (originally Steinweg), Charles Maximilian Stieff, Albert Weber, Jacob Zech and Frederick Zech, Sr., all natives of Germany. The transfer of instrument making is a classic case of strong technology transfer.

The most famous of the piano makers were the Steinways. Henry Engelhard Steinway was born in Wolfshagen, now Niedersachsen, in 1797, as Heinrich Engelhard Steinweg. Steinway went to New York in 1850 with most of his family and in 1854 legally changed the family name. Although the elder Steinway had been making pianos since 1836, the firm became big business with the formation of Steinway & Sons in 1853. By 1863, the firm was making some 2,000 pianos per year. A son, Carl Friedrich Theodor Steinway had remained in Germany, but in 1869, he too joined the family firm in New York. This son made many technical improvements, maintained emphasis on high quality, and eventually held twenty patents. Another son, William Steinway, was the businessman in the family and was responsible for Steinway (Concert) Hall being built in N.Y. in 1866. William also oversaw the construction of a factory and company village in Astoria, N.Y., in the 1870s, and the establishment of a factory in Hamburg, Germany in 1880. Additionally, another Steinway Hall was built in London in 1876. By the time of William's death in 1896, the company was in the realm of big business. The firm was sold to CBS in 1972, but Steinway pianos continue to be manufactured under the family name and are one of the top four piano makers sold in the U.S.

Franz Rudolph Wurlitzer was born in Schöneck, Sachsen, in 1831 and went to Cincinnati in 1853. His three sons were born in Cincinnati, in 1871, in 1873, and in 1883. They manufactured a variety of musical instruments and bought instruments from both European and American manufacturers. The Wurlitzer Company began in 1856 when the father, Rudolph Wurlitzer had a small one-man operation. Over the next seventy years, the Rudolph Wurlitzer Co. maintained nearly constant growth, in part through the purchase of the assets of at least three other instrument manufacturers who were located in North Tonawanda, N.Y., Elmira, N.Y., and DeKalb, Ill. The Company achieved notoriety with the introduction, in 1910, of "The Mighty Wurlitzer," a giant theatre organ which contained a wide variety of sound effects. The age of electronics brought electric organs, electric pianos, and, of course, the "jukebox," of which some 750,000 were produced by Wurlitzer. The name Wurlitz is represented by a community in Oberfranken, Bayern.

Pianists

The directory shows twenty-three persons in this category. Twenty-one were born in provinces where German was the common language. One, however, Egon Petri, although born in Hannover, Niedersachsen, was reportedly of "Dutch" background; the name is more suggestive of a French influence, perhaps a Flemish background.

Clara Damrosch Mannes, who was born in Breslau, Lower Silesia, in 1869, was a noted pianist, even though she was in the shadow of her father and two brothers. She went to New York in 1871 and developed her career there. In 1916, she founded, with her husband, David Mannes (1866-1959), the David Mannes Music School in N.Y.

Fannie Bloomfield Zeisler was another famous pianist. She was born in 1863 in Bielitz, Silesia, and went to Wisconsin in 1867. Zeisler developed her career in Chicago, and eventually had a concert career lasting more than fifty years. She worked both as a soloist and in chamber groups and made five European tours during the years 1893-1912.

Organists

Nine individuals are shown in the directory. Some highlights are as follows.

Charles Balmer was born in Mühlhausen, Thüringen, in 1817, and went to the U.S. in 1836. By 1839, he was in St. Louis where he was organist for the Christ Episcopal Church over a period of forty-six years. In 1846, Balmer founded the St. Louis Oratorio Society. In 1848, he was one of the founders of Balmer & Weber Music House, publishers.

Jacob Eckhard, Sr. was born in Eschwege, Hessen, in 1757. Eckhard was a musician who came to America about 1776 with the Hessian troops and after the war, slipped into American society. He is recorded as being organist for churches in Richmond, Va., and in Charleston, S.C., by 1786 and until 1833.

Johannes Herbst was born in Kempten, Bayern, in 1735. He went to Lancaster, Pa. in 1786 as a Moravian minister and organist. In later years, he occupied a similar role at Lititz, Pa. Upon being made a bishop of the church, he was sent to Salem, N.C. Herbst brought a large library of music from Europe which included over 1,000 anthems. As a composer from 1765-1811, he wrote 180 anthems and 145 songs.

Caspar Petrus Koch was born in Karnap, near Essen, Nordrhein-Westfalen, in 1872. He went to Alton, Ill., in 1881 and eventually to Pittsburgh. He was city organist in Pittsburgh from 1904-1954, and organist for the Holy Trinity Catholic Church there for thirty-three years.

Classical and Semiclassical Music Singers

The directory shows fourteen individuals in this group, of which three were born in the United States and eleven in Europe. All of the group had high profile careers, most as opera singers. Some had careers which varied between concert appearances and the more popular and more lucrative stage, radio, and TV presentations. Some individuals, such as Lotte Lenya, are arbitrarily listed in the section on entertainment.

One individual, Minnie Hauk (original name Amalia Mignon Hauck), had a rather unique background. She was born in New York in 1851, as the daughter of a German immigrant carpenter, but spent a migratory childhood in Providence, R.I., Sumner, Ks., and New Orleans, before returning to New York. Hauk eventually married Baron Ernst von Hesse-Warburg, an Austrian who achieved some fame as an author of travel books and as a journalist for the daily, *Neue Freie Press* of Vienna. Minnie Hauk's operatic career started in Brooklyn in 1866, and ended in Chicago in 1891. She toured many parts of Europe. She resided in Berlin after 1918 and died in Switzerland in 1929.

Elisabeth Rethberg was born in Schwarzenberg, Sachsen, in 1894, and went to N.Y. in 1922. Rethberg was the leading soprano of the N.Y. Metropolitan Opera from 1922-1942. She died in Yorktown Heights, N.Y., in 1976.

Ernestine Schumann-Heinck was born in Lieben, near Prague, Bohemia, in 1861. She made her European operatic debut in 1878 and sang for the last time in 1932. She went to New York in 1899 and made many appearances at the N.Y. Metropolitian Opera, as well as in Chicago and other American cities. Schumann-Heinck died in Hollywood in 1936.

Helen Francesca Traubel was born in St. Louis, Mo., in 1899. She was the daughter of Otto Ferdinand and Clara (Stahr) Traubel. She maintained her maiden name as a professional name through two marriages. Helen Traubel began her professional career in 1924 with the St. Louis Symphony. She had earlier requests to join the New York Metropolitan Opera, but did not sing there until 1937. Thereafter, she had a long off and on career at the Met. She was prone to intersperse opera appearances with mundane appearances in nightclubs and movies, a matter which finally led to her last Met appearance in 1953. The family name Traubel is a variant on the German name Traub.

Violinists

The directory lists fourteen high profile individuals, of which four were second generation immigrants, the other ten being born in German-speaking lands. Three of the family names, Kolisch, Kortschak, and Szigeti, show a definite Slavic influence. Immigration dates ranged from 1849 to 1940.

The list shown here is a relatively abbreviated one in the sense that many of those listed under conductors began their careers as violinists. Various other musicians were also proficient violinists.

Bernhard Listemann was born in Schlotheim, Thüringia, in 1841 and went to N.Y. in 1867, where he made his debut in Steinway Hall, this being the year after it opened. Listemann spent a good part of his career in Boston where he was associated with the Boston Symphony. While in Boston, he organized the Listemann Club. In later years, he taught at the Chicago College of Music. Listemann's brother, Fritz (1839-1909), and son, Paul (1871-1950), were also noted violinists. Another son, Franz (1873-1930), was a cellist.

Emil Mollenhauer was born in Brooklyn in 1855. His father Friedrich and uncle, Edward, both violinists, were natives of Erfurt, Thüringen, who went to the U.S. in 1853. The younger Mollenhauer went to Boston in 1884 and until 1927, he was associated at various times with the Boston Symphony, the Germania Orchestra, and the Handel & Hayden Society.

Fritz Scheel was born in Lübeck, Schleswig-Holstein, in 1852, and went to N.Y. in 1893. Scheel helped establish and headed the San Francisco Symphony from 1895-1906. He was associated with the Philadelphia Orchestra from 1900 until his death in 1907.

Other Musical Instruments

Alice Pulay Ehlers was born in Wien (Vienna), in 1887 and went to the U.S. in 1936. Her early career in Europe was that of a harpischord-ist. In the U.S., she taught music at the University of Southern California from 1942-1962.

Wulf Christian Julius Fries was born in Garbeck, near Iserlohn, Nordr-hein-Westfalen, in 1825. Fries went to Boston in 1847 and was active as cellist in the Mendelssohn Quintette Club from 1849-1872.

George C. Krick was born in Germany in 1872. Krick went to St. Louis in 1887. He founded the Germantown Conservatory in 1906 in which he was active until the 1940s. Krick had an extensive guitar collection which was obtained by Washington University in St. Louis.

Johann Christoph Müller was born in Württemberg in 1777. He joined the Harmony (communal) Society in Butler Co., Pa. in 1803. Müller had a multi-talented career as a physician and music director for the society. He was also a flutist, violinist, and pianist and was the society's music director from 1805-1831.

TABLE 16
DIRECTORY OF THE WORLD OF MUSIC

Composers

1. Bloch, Ernest (1880-1959)
2. Bornschein, Franz Karl (1879-1948)
4. Creamer, David (1812-1887)
1. Engländer, Ludwig (1853-1914)
1. Edwards, Gus (1879-1945)
1. Fisher, Fred (1875-1942) (Frederich Breitenbach)
1. Foss, Lukas (1922-)
1. Friml, Karl Rudolf (1879-1972)
2. Goldmark, Rubin (1876-1936)
1. Grobe, Charles (c.1817-1879)
3. Hammerstein, Oscar Greeley Clendenning, II (1895-1960)
1. Heinrich, Antony Philip (1781-1861)
1. Hindemith, Paul (1895-1963)
1. Hoffmann, Max (1873-1963)
1. Josten, Werner Erich (1885-1963)
1. Kahn, Gus (1886-1941) (Gustav Gerson Kahn)
1. Kauder, Hugo (1888-1972)
1. Keller, Mathias (1813-1875)
2. Kern, Jerome David (1885-1945)
1. Kerker, Gustave Adolph (1857-1923)
1. Kitzinger, Frederick E. (1894-1903)
1. Koemmenich, Louis (1866-1922)
1. Korngold, Eric Wolfgang (1897-1957)
1. Kotzschmar, Hermann (1829-1909)
2. Kroeger, Ernest Richard (1862-1934)
2. Loesser, Francis Henry (1910-1969)
1. Loewe, Frederick (1901-1988)
1. Luders, Gustav Carl (1865-1913)
1. Mahler, Gustav (1860-1911)
1. Metz, Theodore August (1848-1936)
1. Peter, John Frederik (1746-1813)
1. Philipp, Adolf (1864-1936)
1. Pisk, Paul Amadeus (1893-)
1. Ritter, Frédéric Louis (1834-1891)
1. Romberg, Sigmund (1887-1951)
1. Schindler, Karl (1882-1935)
1. Schoenberg, Arnold Franz Walter (1874-1951)
2. Schoenefeld, Henry (1857-1936)
1. Schwartz, Jean (1878-1956)
1. Spialek, Hans (1894-1983)
1. Stark, Edward Josef (1858-1918)
1. Steiner, Maximilian Raoul Walter (1888-1971)

2. Stern, Joseph William (1870-1934)
1. Szirmai, Albert (1880-1967)
1. Tobani, Theodore Moses (1855-1933)
1. Toch, Ernst (1887-1964)
1. Troyer, Karl (1837-1920)
1. Weidig, Adolf (1867-1931)
1. Weigl, Karl (1881-1949)
1. Weill, Kurt Julian (1900-1950)
   Zech, Frederick, Jr. (1858-1926)
1. Zeuner, Charles (1795-1857)

Conductors
1. Adler, Kurt Herbert (1905-1987)
1. Anschütz, Karl (1815-1870)
   Beck, Johann Heinrich (1856-1924)
1. Bellstedt, Herman (1858-1926)
1. Berger, Henry (1844-1929)
1. Bergmann, Carl (1821-1876)
1. Bodanzky, Artur (1877-1939)
1. Busch, Fritz (1890-1951)
1. Damrosch, Leopold (1832-1885)
1. Damrosch, Walter Johannes (1862-1950)
1. Eisfeld, Theodor (1816-1882)
2. Fiedler, Arthur (1894-1979)
1. Fiedler, August Max (1859-1939)
1. Gericke, Wilhelm (1845-1925)
1. Hassler, Simon (1832-1901)
1. Henschel, Isidor George (1850-1934)
1. Herbert, Victor (1859-1924)
1. Hertz, Alfred (1872-1942)
1. Klemperer, Otto (1885-1973)
1. Kunwald, Ernst (1868-1933)
1. Leinsdorf, Erich (1912-1993) (Landauer)
1. Muck, Karl (1859-1940)
1. Münch, Charles (1891-1968)
1. Neuendorff, Adolph Heinrich Anton
   Magnus (1843-1897)
1. Nikisch, Arthur (1855-1922)
1. Oberhoffer, Emil Johann (1867-1933)
2. Oehmler, Leo Carl Martin (1867-1930)
1. Ormandy, Eugene (1899-1985) (Jeno Blau)
1. Paur, Emil (1855-1932)
1. Pohlig, Karl (1864-1928)
1. Previn, André George (1929-)
1. Rapee, Erno (1891-1945)
1. Reinagle, Alexander (1756-1809)
1. Reiner, Fritz (1888-1963)

1. Ritter, Frederic Louis (1834-1891)
1. Scheve, Edward Benjamin (1865-1924)
1. Schindler, Kurt (1882-1935)
1. Seidl, Anton (1850-1898)
1. Sobolowski, Johann Friedrich Eduard (1808-1872)
1. Spicker, Max (1858-1912)
1. Steinberg, Hans Wilhelm (1899-1978)
1. Stiedry, Fritz (1883-1968)
1. Stransky, Josef (1874-1936)
1. Strube, Gustav (1867-1953)
1. Szell, Georg (1897-1970)
1. Thomas, Christian Friedrich Theodore (1835-1905)
1. Timm, Henry Christian (1811-1892)
   Wallenstein, Alfred Franz (1898-1983)
1. Wallerstein, Lothar (1882-1949)
1. Walter, Bruno (1876-1963) (Schlesinger)
1. Wolfes, Felix (1892-1970)
1. Zach, Max Wilhelm (1864-1921)
1. Zerrahn, Carl (1826-1909)

Music Teachers
1. Cohen, Frederic (1904-1967)
1. Damrosch, Frank Heino (1859-1937)
1. Ebert, Anton Carl (1887-1980)
1. Greissle, Felix (1894-1982)
1. Merz, Karl (1836-1890)
3. Miessner, William Otto (1880-1967)
   Ortmann, Otto Rudolph (1889-1979)
   Showalter, Anthony Johnson (1858-1924)
   Sonneck, Oscar George Theodore (1873-1928)
1. Steinert, Morris (1831-1912)
1. Ziegfeld, Florenz, Sr. (-1923)

Musicologists, Collectors & Critics
1. Beck, Jean (1881-1943) (Johann Baptist Beck)
1. Einstein, Alfred (1880-1952)
2. Finck, Henry Theophilus (1854-1926)
   (Henry Gottlob Finck)
1. Geiringer, Karl Johannes (1899-)
2. Krehbiel, Henry Edward (1854-1923)
1. Leichentritt, Hugo (1874-1951)
1. Sachs, Curt (1881-1959)
1. Sonneck, Oscar George Theodore (1873-1928)
1. Steinert, Morris (1831-1912)
1. Winternitz, Emanuel (1898-1985)
1. Worch, Hugo (1855-1938)
1. Ziehn, Bernhard (1845-1912)

Music Publishers

Bernstein, Louis (1878-1962)
1. Fischer, Carl (1849-)
1. Fischer, Joseph (1841-1901)
1. Graupner, Johann Christian Gottlieb (1767-1836)
1. Grunewald, Louis (1827-1915)
2. Presser, Theodore (1848-1925)
2. Schirmer, Ernest Charles (1865-1958)
1. Schirmer, Gustav (1829-1893)
2. Schirmer, Rudolph Edward (1859-1919)
1. Schmidt, Arthur Paul (1846-1921)
1. Shapiro, Maurice (1873-1911) .
2. Showalter, Anthony Johnson (1859-1924)
2. Stern, Joseph William (1870-1934)
1. Weber, Carl Heinrich (1819-1892)
1. Werlein, Philip P. (1812-1885)
1. Willig, Georg (1764-1851)

Instrument Makers

1. Albert, Charles Francis, Sr. (1842-1901), violins
1. Albert, John (- 1887), violins
1. Albrecht, Christian Frederick Ludwig (1778-1843), pianos
1. Albrecht, Karl (1759-1848), pianos
2. Antes, Johann (1740-1811), violins, violas
1. Bach, Vincent (1890-1976), brass instruments
   Becker, Carl G. (1887-1975), violins
1. Berteling, Theodore (1821-1890), flutes, clarinets
1. Boucher, William (1822-1899), violins, drums, banjos
1. Eisenbrandt, Heinrich Christian (1790-1861), woodwind, brass
3. Erben, Henry (1800-1884), organs
1. Friedrich, Johann (1858-1973), violins
1. Geib, Johannes Lawrence, Sr. (1744-1819), organs
1. Gemünder, August Martin Ludwig (1814-1895), violins
1. Gemünder, George (1816-1899), violins
   Gretsch, Frederick, Sr. (-1895), string instruments
1. Kilgen, George (-1902), organs
1. Klemm, Johann Gottlob (1690-1762), organs
1. Knabe, Valentine Wilhelm Ludwig (1803-1864), pianos
1. Knopf, Henry Richard (1860-1939), violins
1. Ludwig, William, Sr. (1879-1973), percussion instruments
1. Martin, Christian Friedrich (1796-1873), guitars
1. Meyer, Conrad (-1881), pianos
1. Mönnig, Wilhelm Heinrich (1883-1962), violins
   Reuter, Adolf C. (1880-1971), organs
1. Schwarzer, Franz (1828-1904), zithers
1. Seltmann, Ernst Theodor (1828-1883), brass instruments
1. Sohmer, Hugo (1846-1913), pianos

1. Stein, Adam A. (1844-1922), organs
1. Steck, George (1829-1897), pianos
1. Steinway, Henry Engelhard (1797-1871), pianos
1. Steinway, William (1835-1896) (Steinweg), pianos
1. Steinway, Carl Friedrich Theodore (1825-1889), pianos
1. Stieff, Charles Maximilian (1805-1862), pianos
1. Tanneberger, David (1728-1804), organs
1. Votteler, Gottlieb Ferdinand (1855-1894), organs
1. Weber, Albert (1828-1879), pianos
1. Wurlitzer, Franz Rudolph (1831-1914), wind instruments, drums
2. Wurlitzer, Howard Eugene (1871-1928), pianos, etc.
2. Wurlitzer, Rudolph Henry (1873-1948), violins
2. Wurlitzer, Farny Reginald (1883-1972), organs
1. Zech, Jacob (1832-1899), pianos
1. Zech, Frederick, Sr. (1837-1905), pianos

Pianists
1. Boermann, Carl (1839-1913)
1. Dresel, Otto (c.1826-1890)
1. Faelten, Carl (1846-1925)
1. Ganz, Rudolf (1877-1972)
1. Gebhard, Heinrich (1878-1963)
1. Goldbeck, Robert (1839-1908)
1. Kahn, Erich Itor (1905-1956)
1. Klein, Bruno Oscar (1858-1911)
1. Kunkel, Charles (1840-1923)
   Levant, Oscar (1906-1972)
1. Liebling, Emil (1851-1914)
1. Mannes, Clara Damrosch (1869-1948)
1. Meinecke, Christopher Karl (1782-1850)
1. Perabo, Johann Ernst (1845-1920)
1. Petri, Egon (1881-1962)
1. Rosenthal, Moriz (1862-1946)
2. Schelling, Ernst Henry (1876-1939)
1. Schnabel, Artur (1882-1925)
1. Serkin, Rudolf (1903-1991)
1. Wittgenstein, Paul (1887-1961)
1. Wolfsohn, Carl (1834-1907)
1. Zecker, Richard (1850-1922)
1. Zeisler, Fannie Bloomfield (1863-1927)

Organists
1. Balmer, Charles, (1817-1892)
1. Eckhard, Jacob, Sr. (1757-1833)
2. Erben, Peter (1771-1863)
1. Herbst, Johannes (1735-1812)
1. Koch, Caspar Petrus (1872-1970)

3. Riemenschneider, Charles Albert (1878-1950)
1. Stoeckel, Gustave Jacob (1819-1907)
1. Wetzlar, Hermann Hans (1870-1943)
2. Wolle, John Frederick (1863-1933)

Singers, Classical & Semiclassical
1. Dippel, Andreas (1866-1932), tenor
1. Fischer, Emil Friedrich August (1838-1914), bass
2. Hauck, Amalia Mignon (1851-1929),
   soprano (Minnie Hauk)
1. Heinrich, Max (1853-1916), baritone
1. Janssen, Herbert (1892-1965), baritone
1. Juch, Emma Johanna Antonia (1860-1939), soprano
1. Lehmann, Lotte (1888-1976), soprano
1. Reimers, Paul (1878-1942), tenor
1. Rethberg, Elisabeth (1894-1976), soprano (Sättler)
1. Scheff, Fritzi (1882-1954), soprano
1. Schumann-Heinck, Ernestine (1861-1936), contralto
1. Schwarzkopf, Elisabeth (1915-), soprano
1. Sembrich, Marcella (1858-1935), soprano (Kochanski)
   Traubel, Helen Francesca (1899-1972), soprano

Violinists
1. Busch, Adolf Georg Wilhelm (1891-1952)
2. Dannreuther, Gustav (1853-1923)
1. Eichburg, Julius (1824-1893)
1. Kolisch, Rudolf (1896-1978)
1. Kortschak, Hugo (1884-1957)
1. Kreisler, Fritz (1875-1962)
1. Listemann, Bernhard (1841-1917)
1. Loeffler, Charles Martin (1861-1935)
2. Mollenhauer, Emil (1855-1927)
1. Scheel, Fritz (1852-1907)
1. Schradieck, Carl Franz Heinrich (1846-1918)
2. Spiering, Theodore (1871-1925)
2. Stoessel, Albert Frederic (1894-1943)
1. Szigeti, Joseph (1892-1973)

Other Musical Instruments
1. Ehlers, Alice Pulay (1887-1981), harpischordist
1. Fries, Wulf Christian Julius (1825-1902), cellist
1. Krick, George C. (1872-1962), guitarist
1. Kastner, Alfred (1870-1948), harpist
1. Müller, Johann Christoph (1777-1845), flutist
1. Schuecker, Heinrich (1867-1913), harpist
1. Schuecker, Joseph E. (1886-1938), harpist

Code:
1. = 1st Generation
2. = 2nd Generation
3. = 3rd or more Generation, etc.

The Printing and Publishing World

Centuries before any major settlements existed in America, the Germans had developed a fine-tuned organization of publishing, printing, and marketing. Nearly everyone is familiar with the name of Johannes Gutenberg, born in Mainz, now Rheinland-Pfalz, about 1397 and died there about 1468. Gutenberg's role in the history of printing was to substitute machinery for handicraft and allow mass production to replace the laborious process of making hand copies. Thus, beginning about 1455, printed books became available to a much wider public, not just to the clergy and intellectuals.

Peter Schöffer, a one-time employee of Gutenberg, carried the printing business one step further. Sometime between the years of 1462-1466, Schöffer conceived the idea of printing a list of books he had for sale. The list appeared at the Frankfurt Book Fair as early as 1466. And thus, a major step in the marketing of books was under way.

The European publishing business was given another major impetuous by Martin Luther (1483-1546). Working mainly at Wittenberg, Sachsen-Anhalt, Luther and his team of editors, produced manuscripts which were mass produced in multiple editions. During the 1520s and the 1530s, literally hundreds of thousands of copies of the books, mainly religious works, were printed and distributed to every corner of Germany. The literacy rate in Germany increased accordingly. And the Frankfurt Book Fair, as well as other European book fairs, benefited at the same rate. The Frankfurt Book Fair enjoyed prosperity until about 1618 when the occurrences of wars and epidemics, as well as other factors, contrived to put the fair into decline. By that time, nearly all the elements of modern day publishing and printing were in place. There was, to be sure, some refinement in printing such as the development in the 19th century of lithography, the linotype and later high speed presses, as well as other mechanical improvement. But, here again, the Germans and German-Americans were in the forefront of the developments as we shall see in the following discussion.

The English, of course, with their dominance of the population in 17th and 18th century America, provided the first American printers, who in turn helped to train German-American printers. Two of the key names of Englishmen were Andrew Bradford (1686-1742), printer in Philadelphia, and Benjamin Franklin (1706-1790), printer and financial agent in Philadelphia.

Thus printing in America by German-American printers began about 1738, as noted below in the discussion of the Sower (Sauer or Saur) family. During the 18th century, German-American authors were firmly established in America. Virtually all were concerned with articles and books dealing with American religious aspects. These German-American authors of whom the earliest known printed works date from 1728-1729, were Johann Conrad Beissel, Georg Michael Weiss, and Michael Wohlfart. A fairly extensive list of such religious writers is outlined in the 1989 book titled *The First Century of German Language Printing in the United States of America, 1728-1830* (Niedersächsische Staats - und Universitätsbibliothek, Göttigen; G.J. Bötte and Werner Tannhof, primary editors).

German Language Authors

For whatever reason, whether it be for literary entertainment, as novelists, for political causes, or as writers of travelogues or biographies, writers in general maintain a comparatively high profile because of their profusion of books. Writers of German background have contributed their share to the maze of literature. In addition to the 1991 book by Stephen W. Görisch mentioned earlier under Colonists, the 1988 book by Julian Mikoletzky titled *Die Deutsche Amerika-Auswanderung des 19. Jahrhundert in der zeitgenössischen fiktionalen Literatur* (Tübingen, Max Niemeyer Verlag) is important for its documentation of the numerous authors who wrote books in Germany for the prospective German migrant. Mikoletzky's book, with its extensive bibliography, lists several hundred works written by the many transient German adventurers and political refugees.

During the 19th century, the Germans developed into consummate travelers, went to America, and returned to Germany to write about their experiences. The bulk of this profusion was written in German and widely distributed in Europe. In many cases, the more successful books were translated later into English and then sold in America. Hundreds of books, mostly highly commercial, were written in the 19th century regarding emigration from Germany to various parts of the United States, as well as about immigrant life. Sometimes these books were labeled as travel books, purporting to give advice to the traveller.

Following in the footsteps of the earlier mentioned Gottfried Duden (fl. 1824-1829), two of the more active travel book writers were Traugott Bromme (fl. 1833-1850) and Eduard Pelz (fl. 1842-1872). All three were born in Germany and all died there. All three faded into relative obscurity, with no acknowledgement from German biographers. Their writings, being a complex mixture of fantasy and reality, are now mainly of historic interest. Still, their writing convinced thousands of gullible families to migrate, mainly to the Midwest.

Germans have long sought entertainment through publications dealing with the American Wild West. The German book market exploited this aspect, some of which were realistic travelogues, and others which were pure fantasy.

202 / DISTINGUISHED GERMAN-AMERICANS

For sheer volume of 19th century German language literature concerning America, four names stand out. These were: Karl Anton Postl (alias Charles Sealsfield; fl. 1834-1843), Friedrich Wilhelm Christian Gerstäcker (fl. 1841-1871), Heinrich Balduin Möllhausen (fl. 1860-1905), and Karl May (fl. 1882-1896). Postl was in the U.S. from 1823-1826 and 1827-1832, and also for short periods in 1837, 1850, and 1853. Gerstäcker was in the U.S. from 1837-1843, and for short periods during the intervals of 1849-1852 and 1867-1868. Möllhausen was in the U.S. for a total of about six years between 1849-1858. May made a brief tourist trip to New York in May, 1908.

Karl Anton Postl (alias Charles Sealsfield) was born in Poppitz bei Znaim, Lower Moravia, in 1793. Some biographers identify Sealsfield as the inventor of the ethnographic novel. Sealsfield is generally considered as an ideologue, or one who championed the rights of the American Indians, as well as the rights of various other minority groups. Sealsfield died in Solothurn, Switzerland, in 1864. In the last decade, the collected works of Sealsfield were reprinted, in German, by the Olms Presse, Hildesheim, in twenty-eight volumes under the editorial direction of Karl J. R. Arndt.

Gerstäcker was born in Hamburg, in 1816. His travels included most of the states of the Union, various South and Central American countries, the South Seas, Australia, and parts of Africa. Gerstäcker's writings were a mixture of travelogues and fictional accounts of everyday pioneer experiences. Typical examples are his 1844 book, translated later as *Wild Sports in the Far West*, and his 1848 book translated as *The Pirates of the Mississippi*. Gerstäcker died in 1872 in Brunswick, now Braunschweig, Niedersachsen. Because of his accounts of backwoods life in Arkansas, Gerstäcker was made an honorary citizen of Arkansas in 1957. In 1991, the University of Missouri Press printed selected translations of Gerstäcker's articles under the title *In the Arkansas Backwoods: Tales and Sketches*.

Heinrich Balduin Möllhausen was born in Bonn, in 1825. He made three trips to America, the first time in the company Paul Wilhelm, Duke of Württemberg, a trip which lasted about three years. The second and third were part of the U.S. Army expeditions to explore railroad right of way to the Pacific, and to explore the Colorado River. On these trips, Möllhausen acted as naturalist, topographer, and technical observer. Möllhausen took extensive notes and made sketches. These western U.S. trips, after his return to Germany, formed the basis for forty-five works in 157 volumes and eighty novelettes.

Perhaps no German writer was more commercially successful in promoting and mass producing fantasy tales of the American West than Karl May (1842-1912). May, who was born in Sachsen and who made one short, solitary trip as far west as Buffalo, N.Y., began writing in 1875. His most popular works were written from 1892-1896. Copies of May's novels were produced eventually by the millions in cheap, paperback editions. In the 20th century, virtually every schoolboy in Germany was familiar with the series of Karl May novels. Consequently, May had a great effect in stimulating migration which amounted to approximately 1.5 million German-speaking people going to the United States after 1914.

Although May apparently never admitted directly his source material, one can surmise that he drew on a substantial list of early 19th century German travelogue writers for his imaginative tales. Personal accounts by well-known travelers listed in the publishing directory such as Friedrich Wilhelm Christian Gerstäcker, Heinrich Balduin Möllhausen, Charles Sealsfield (real name Karl Anton Postl), Friedrich Armand Strubberg, Baron Ernst von Hesse-Warttegg, and Frederick Adolph Wislizenus, among several others, doubtless were in May's considerable personal library and were used as his source material. All of these authors spent a good portion of their careers in traveling in America before returning to Europe to publish extensive documentation of their journeys. Additionally, May doubtless had access to the visual arts, notably that of the Düsseldorf School (Albert Bierstadt, Emanuel Gottlieb Leutze, Carl Ferdinand Wimar) and the noted painter-lithographer Karl Bodmer, all of whom are listed in the directory on art.

German nobility was not about to be outdone by the ordinary citizen. Their published accounts collectively were more realistic in nature, and offered scientific aspects, such as it was in those days. Noble travellers to America included Maximilian Philip Alexander (1782-1867), Prince of Wied-Neuwied. The prince's trip up the Missouri River was printed in German in 1839-1841. The trip was also described in some detail in *Nebraska History*.

Bernhard (1792-1862), Duke of Sachsen-Weimar-Eisenach, traveled the Mississippi River in 1825-1826 and published his experiences in 1828. Friedrich Wilhelm Paul (1797-1862), duke of Württemberg, was also aboard a Mississippi steamer in the interval 1822-1824. An account of his journey was printed in 1835.

On the other hand, there were a number of German-American dissidents who used writing to promote various causes. Nineteenth century literary dissidents included Mathilde Franziska Giesler-Anneke, the two Grimké sisters, Angelina Emily Grimké and Sarah Moore Grimké, and Reinhold Ernst Friedrich Karl Solger. Collectively they were for women's rights, against slavery, and for political freedom, among other noble causes.

Contemporary Writers

The following list begins with the earliest American fiction writers, all of whom apparently had a German-American background. The list contains a number of Nobel Prize winners in literature as well as Pulitzer Prize winners in fiction, poetry, and drama. A recent source book on these writers is that by C. H. Holman & William Harmon, 1992, titled *A Handbook to Literature*, Sixth Edition (Macmillan, N.Y.). Bestsellers are given in Daisy Maryles 1993 book titled appropriately *Bestsellers, 1895-1990* (R.R. Bowker, Providence, N.J.).

Owen Wister was an eastern American writer, whose 1902 tale *The Virginian*, was recognized as a classic western novel and became a best-seller. Wister wrote a number of books between 1881-1934, mostly westerns. Wister was born in 1860 in Germantown, Pa., a descendant of 1727 immigrants from the Palatinate.

Orville James Victor, an Ohioan of German and English background, was an author of novels, but primarily a publisher. Victor is credited with inventing, about 1860, the American dime novel.

Second generation immigrant Edward Stratemeyer was a prolific writer of juvenile fiction. His turn of the century series titled *Rover Boys*, and other novels, caught the imagination of American school boys.

Twentieth century English-language novelists included Lillian Hellman, John Richard Hershey, Dorothy Rothschild Parker, Gertrude Stein, John Ernst Steinbeck, Irving Stone, Kurt Vonnegut, Jr., and Thomas Clayton Wolfe.

Twentieth century German-language novelists included Paul Thomas Mann, Bertolt Eugen Brecht, Lion Feuchtwanger, and Erich Maria Remarque, many of whose best works were translated into English for American consumption.

German-American novelists were awarded many writing honors. For instance, in 1962, John Steinbeck, then towards the end of his writing career, was awarded a Nobel Prize in literature. Steinbeck's works included *Tortilla Flat* (1936), *Of Mice and Men* (1938), and that famous 1940 book, *Grapes of Wrath*, which won a Pulitzer Prize for novels. Steinbeck's 1942 book *The Moon is Down* was a best-seller.

Bertolt Eugen Friedrich Brecht was born in Augsburg in 1898. During the 1930s, Brecht fled the oppressive Nazi regime, going first to Scandinavia and later to the U.S. Brecht wrote numerous plays and books, virtually all of which were in German. His notable 1922 book *Trommeln in der Nacht* appeared in English translation in 1966 as *Drums in the Night*. Brecht died in Berlin in 1956.

Pearl Comfort Sydenstricker Buck was born in Hillsboro, W.Va., in 1892. She was the daughter of Absolom & Caroline (Stulting) Sydenstricker, Presbyterian missionaries who raised their daughter in China. Buck was the author of many books, most notedly the 1930 book titled *East Wind: West Wind*, and the 1931 book called *The Good Earth*, both of which reflected her experiences in China. *The Good Earth* was a best-seller and in 1932, won a Pulitzer Prize. Pearl Buck was awarded a Nobel Prize in literature in 1938.

In 1924, Edna Ferber was on the best selling list with her novel *So Big*; this book was awarded a Pulitzer Prize for novels in 1925. Ferber wrote thirteen novels between the years of 1911-1963. Ferber was the daughter of Jacob Charles & Julia (Neumann) Ferber, the father reportedly an immigrant from "Oyeso, Hungary", although this locality is not shown on any 20th century map of Hungary, nor listed in any atlas or gazetteer. The Ferber family name has a likely German variant in Färber.

Lion Feuchtwanger was born in München, in 1884, and went to the U.S. in 1940. Feuchtwanger was a novelist and dramatist. His many books written in the period 1918-1958, virtually all in German, were published in part under the pseudonym of J. L. Wotcheek. A 1926 novel, translated as *Power*, became a best-seller.

Theodor Seuss Geisel was born in Springfield, Mass., in 1904. Geisel, whose parents were both of German origin, achieved fame as a writer of numerous children's book and as a cartoonist. Some of his cartoons had subtle political overtones. While Geisel's career lasted from 1937-1986, his 1957 book *How the Grinch Stole Christmas* was probably the most popular.

Fannie Hurst was born in Hamilton, Ohio in 1889. She was the daughter of Samuel & Rose (Koppel) Hurst whose families came from Bavaria in the 1860s. Hurst's most notable book was printed in 1928 and was titled *A President is Born*. She churned out a variety of articles for magazines as well as being the author of a number of books. In 1940, she was reportedly the highest paid writer in America.

George S. Kaufman was born in Pittsburgh, in 1889. Kaufman was an outstanding playright. His work *Of Thee I Sing* won a Pulitzer Prize for drama in 1932. And in 1937, towards the end of the Great Depression, Kaufman colloborated with Moss Hart (1904-1961) on another Pulitzer winning drama titled *You Can't Take It With You*.

Sidney Kingsley was born in New York in 1906, as the son of Dr. Robert & Sonia ((Smoleroff) Kierschner. In 1934, Kingsley's play titled *Man in White* won a Pulitzer Prize for drama.

Francis Henry Loesser, better known as Frank Loesser, had a varied career as an author, journalist, and song writer. Born in New York in 1910, much of Loesser's career was naturally associated with that city. Loesser composed the popular songs *Baby, It's Cold Outside* and *Heart & Soul*. In 1962, his play *How to Succeed in Business Without Really Trying* (written with Abe Burrows) won a Pulitzer Prize in drama.

Irna Phillips was born in Chicago in 1901. She was the daughter of William S. and Betty (Buxbaum) Phillips, German Jews who went to Chicago in the late 1900s. She was a radio and TV writer during the years 1930-1970, specializing in soap operas. In fact, she earned the title "Queen of the Soap Operas." In the wartime year of 1943, there was such a demand for soap operas that she had five serials being broadcast simultaneously and employed six assistant writers. Phillips pioneered in TV drama during the years 1952-1967. The Phillips name is not a typically German family name, but apparently adapts the German christian name of Philipp or Philippsohn.

In 1929, Eric Paul Maria Remarque wrote the novel *Im Westen Nichts Neues* which was translated for popular English consumption into *All Quiet on the Western Front*. This book was a best-seller. Remarque, a Roman Catholic, was in the United States from 1939 to 1947, when he became a citizen, but returned to Europe shortly thereafter.

Elmer Rice was born in New York, in 1892, as Elmer Leopold (or Lion) Reizenstein. His play *Street Scene* won a 1929 Pulitzer Prize for drama. *Street Scene* reflected the realities of life in the working class district of New York.

Conrad Michael Richter was born in Pine Grove, Pa. in 1890. In 1951, Richter won a Pulitzer Prize for novels for his work *The Town*. Some critics claim that his 1937 book *Sea of Grass* was a better novel.

Irma Louise von Starkloff Rombauer was born in St. Louis, Mo., in 1877. Her father Hugo Maximilian von Starkloff went to the U.S. from Stuttgart, Württemberg, in the 1850s. At the age of twelve, Irma began attending school in Bremen, Germany, where she perfected her German and French. This knowledge aided her greatly in familiarization of Swiss and French cooking recipes, which she used after marriage to St. Louis business man Edgar Roderick Rombauer. Her book *The Joy of Cooking* was first privately printed in 1931 with 3,000 copies. The first printed edition appeared in 1936. After a slow sale start, the book went through a succession of printings with revisions in 1943 and 1952. In fact, the book was eventually wildly successful and housewives everywhere learned modern day cooking with a European flavor. By 1968, the book was in its 18th printing and had sold hundreds of thousands of copies.

Irving Stone (original family name Tennenbaum, a corruption of Tannenbaum) is remembered for his popular and imaginative semi-biographies *Lust for Life* (the life of Vincent Van Gogh) and 1961 best-seller *The Agony and the Ecstasy* (the life of Michelangelo).

Thomas Sigismund Stribling had a long career as an author, dating from 1917-1938. His book *The Store* won a 1933 Pulitzer Prize for novels.

Thorton Niven Wilder was born in Madison, Wisc., in 1897. Wilder was a distinguished author whose book *The Bridge of San Luis Rey* won a 1928 Pulitzer Prize for novels, while his play *The Skin of Our Teeth* won a 1943 Pulitzer Prize for drama.

The directory shows a collective total of fifty-eight German and English language writers in the authors group.

Editors & Critics

Harold Stauffer Bender was associated with Goshen College, Goshen, Ind. from 1924-1962. Bender is classified as an editor, educator, historian, and churchman. Bender is noted primarily as chief editor of the *Mennonite Encyclopedia*, published from 1955-1959.

Charles George Herbermann was born in Saerbeck, Westfalen, and went to New York in 1851. From his personal experiences, he recorded a trying trip of eighty-two days during which time two children in his family died. Herbermann is noted as the editor of *The Catholic Encyclopedia*.

Charles William Henry Kirchhoff, born in 1853 to a father who served in the German Consular Service in San Francisco, became a noted editor of technical journals which included *The Iron Age*.

Francis Lieber was one of the earliest of the great wave of 19th century German dissidents, going as he did to Boston in 1826. Lieber is usually classified as a political scientist, writer, and educator. However, he is best remembered perhaps as the editor of the 1829-1833 edition of the *Encyclopedia Americana*, a work designated as the first of its type published in America. The *Encyclopedia Americana*, which then comprised thirteen volumes, used as a model the 7th edition of the famous *Brockhaus Konver-*

sations-Lexikon and indeed much of the American set was a direct translation from the German. From 1835-1856, Lieber was a professor who taught political science at South Carolina College (now University of South Carolina). With the approach of the Civil War, Lieber moved back to New York, and in 1863, devised the first code of military law written in the United States. Lieber had three sons who are covered in the section on military.

George Washington Oakes (originally Ochs) was born in 1861 in Cincinnati and grew up there to become mayor of Cincinnati. Oakes is known for editing his brother's newspapers, that of the well-known publisher Adolph Simon Ochs.

Wilhelm Rapp was one of the refugees from the 1848-1849 revolution in Germany. Arriving in Philadelphia in 1852, he eventually found editorial positions on the staff of Baltimore's *Der Wecker*, and later on Chicago's *Illinois Staats-Zeitung*.

Jacob Schem was born in Wiedenbruck, Westfalen, and went to the United States in 1851. Schem was editor of the *Deutsch-Amerikanisches Conversations-Lexikon* which appeared in New York in eleven volumes between the years of 1869-1874.

Not all of the immigrants contributed positively to American culture. George Sylvester Viereck, an 1895 arrival, became the editor of the vehemently pro-German journal *The Fatherland*. In 1941, Viereck was indicted and convicted of charges of aiding the enemy. He served five years of a prison term. In 1952, he wrote *Men Into Beasts*, a memoir of his prison experiences, which sold 500,000 copies.

The directory shows a total of twenty-four individuals in the editor & critic group.

Journalists

The long list of forty journalists in the directory includes a fair number of famous names, some known for books and editorals, others known for radio broadcasting.

Mary E. Clemmer Ames was the daughter of Alsatian emigrants. She was born in Utica, N.Y. in 1831 and ultimately became associated with the weekly newspaper *New York Independent* where she was employed as a political writer from 1866-1884. She also wrote three novels. At the time of her peak newspaper career, she was thought to be the highest paid newspaper woman in the U.S.

Theodore Herman Albert Dreiser was born in 1871 in Terre Haute, Ind. Dreiser became notorious as a spokesman for liberal and leftist causes during his occupation as a journalist and novelist. His primary novel *An American Tragedy* was published in 1925. Dreiser wrote a number of novels which were published from 1900-1951.

John Gunther was born in Chicago in 1901. Best known was a reporter and war correspondent, Gunther's extensive travels through Europe provided material for many books, which he wrote between the years 1936-1969. Gunther's 1947 book *Inside U.S.A.* became a best-seller.

The two Hittel brothers, John Schertzer Hittel, and Theodore Henry Hittel, settled in adulthood in San Francisco. The former wrote an early *History of San Francisco* and the latter wrote the *History of California*, both books being published in the late 1800s.

Max Jordan was born in San Remo, Italy, of parents native to Württemberg, Germany. Jordan went to the United States in 1924, and eventually firmly established himself as NBC's representative in Europe, that is, during the troubled period of the 1930's and 1940's.

Hans V. Kaltenborn was born in 1878 in Milwaukee. Kaltenborn became a pioneering news broadcaster covering the period 1922-1958 and spent long periods in radio, first with CBS and then NBC.

Arthur Krock was a political writer for the prestigious *N.Y. Times* for more than three decades, from 1932-1966. His writing won Pulitizer Prizes in 1935 and 1937.

Walter Lippmann was another high profile writer, political journalist, and conservative editor employed by the *N.Y. World* and the *N.Y. Tribune*. Lippmann was born in New York in 1889, the grandson of German Jews who had gone to the U.S. in the 1840s. In 1913, Lippmann wrote the book *A Preface to Politics* which was the most widely known of his many books. Lippmann's journalistic career spanned the period of 1913-1971.

Henry Louis Mencken was near the top of the notorious writers, working both as a journalist and as a writer of some thirty books, some of them massive compilations of linguistic data. Mencken was pro-German in both World Wars, a matter which was tolerated in World War I and decidedly less so in World War II. Mencken's main book was the popular *The American Language* which appeared in 1919 and which was updated with massive supplements and reprinted in several editions up to 1963. Mencken acquired a considerable reputation as a literary critic for the magazine *Smart Set* (1908-1923), and after 1924 for *American Mercury*. Reportedly, Mencken critically reviewed some 2,000 books, both U.S. and European, during the period of 1908-1923. Mencken was the grandson of Burkhardt Ludwig Mencken who went from the area of Leipzig, Sachsen, to the U.S. in 1848.

Miriam Ottenberg was born in Washington, D.C. in 1914 and grew up there to become a first rate reporter for the *Washington Star*. Ottenberg won a Pulitzer Prize for reporting in 1960.

Emil Preetorius was born in 1827 in Alzey, Rheinland-Pfalz. Preetorius was a refugee who went to St. Louis in 1853. There he became associated with the famous editor Carl Schurz and worked on the *Westliche Post* as a journalist and publicist.

Edward Rosewater (family name originally Rosenwasser) from Bukowan, Bohemia, went to Cleveland in 1854 and eventually settled in Omaha, Nebr. Edward Rosewater founded the *Omaha Bee* in 1871, which, under his son Victor, remained in family editorial control until 1920. Both of the Rosewaters were Nebraska politicians who used the newspaper for their platforms. The elder Rosewater especially promoted the rights of the common man.

George Schneider was born in 1823 in Pirmasens, Rheinland-Pfalz. As a refugee, he went to New York in 1849. Eventually, Schneider became a prosperous banker and journalist who edited the *Illinois Staats-Zeitung* which he then used to consolidate the German-born population behind Lincoln.

William Lawrence Shirer was born in Chicago, in 1904. Shirer worked for the *Chicago Tribune*, the *N.Y. Herald,* and for CBS. Shirer's 1941 book titled *Berlin Diary* as well as his 1960 book titled *The Rise and Fall of the Third Reich* became best sellers.

William Franklin Switzler, whose paternal grandparents, as the name implies, came from Switzerland, was born in 1819 in Fayette Co., Ky. Switzler had a dual career as a Missouri legislator and as a journalist-historian in Missouri. The School of Journalism building at the University of Missouri was named in his honor and Switzler acquired the unofficial title of "Dean of Missouri journalists."

Herbert Bayard Swope was born in 1882 in St. Louis. His career as reporter and journalist with the *St. Louis Post Dispatch*, the *N.Y. World*, and the *N.Y. Herald* brought renown as did his 1917 book *Inside the German Empire*. The book won a Pulitzer Prize. The Swope name likely is a corruption of Schwob.

George Wisner achieved fleeting fame as journalist, editor and as an early police reporter. Wisner is best known as co-owner of the *N.Y. Sun* for the years 1833-1835. During that time, the newspaper became the first successful "penny newspaper," which it achieved in spite of competition from much larger New York newspapers.

Poets

On the lighter side of journalistic endeavor is a selective list of eighteen poets. Most of the family names are recognizable as German-American, but a question remains on a couple of names.

John Gnelsenau (or Greenleaf) Neihardt was born in Sharpsburg, Ill., in 1881. Neihardt lived in Nebraska among the Omaha Indiana during the years 1901-1907. He was honored as Nebraska's Poet Laureate in 1921, and worked as an editor on the *St. Louis Post-Dispatch* from 1926-1938. Neihardt is also noted as an author of historical epics as reflected in his 1949 book *A Cycle of the West.* Towards the end of his career, Neihardt was a lecturer at the University of Missouri, from 1949-1966.

Theodore Roethke was born in Saginaw, Mich., in 1908. Roethke's career included terms as an educator at Penn State University from 1936-1943, and at Washington University from 1947-1962. In 1954, his work titled *The Waking* won a Pulitzer Prize in poetry. Roethke was a second generation German-American, his father having gone to the U.S. in 1872.

Leonora Speyer was born in Washington, D.C. in 1872 as the daughter of Count Ferdinand and Julia (Thompson) von Stosch. In 1927, her work titled *Fiddler's Farewell* won a Pulitzer Prize in poetry. In 1937, she became an instructor in poetry at Columbia University.

Henry Timrod was born in Charleston, S.C., in 1828. Timrod's short poetic era nearly coincided with the Civil War, about which his poems were written. Timrod's best poem, published in 1866, was *The Magnolia Cemetery Ode*, which was written as a memorial to slain Confederate soldiers.

Audrey May Wurdemann had a long career, from 1926-1951, as a writer of poems. In 1935, she won a Pulitzer Prize in poetry for her work *Bright Ambush*.

Map-Makers, Lithographers, Metal Engravers, Photographers

Modern map-making techniques were developed in Europe by the Dutch School (1581-1689), the French School (1648-1718), and finally by the German School (1702-1744).

The German-Americans were not especially active map makers in American until well into the 19th century. One important development which occurred, however, was the rediscovery of lithography by the German Alois Senefelder. He perfected the technique of using blocks of limestone, in this case, the famous Solnhofen limestone, in the years 1796-1799. Senefelder worked in the cities of München and Offenbach, in Bayern, thus relatively near the source of Solnhofen limestone quarries. Solnhofen limestone subsequently was imported to America in the early and mid-19th century in large quantities. Also in the mid-19th century, the technology of German lithographers, only a few of whose names are recorded, was used in the printing shops of New York, Philadelphia, and Washington, and to some extent also in St. Louis, Chicago, Cincinnati and Milwaukee. Louis Maurer, a lithographer who worked for the New York firm of Currier & Ives from 1852-1860, is a typical example. After the American Civil War, lithography was displaced by photography, modern printing presses, and other high speed techniqeus of mass reproduction.

The directory shows a selective list of fifteen individuals.

Long before the days of lithography, Augustin Herrman, born about 1605 in Prague, achieved a reputation as a colonial cartographer, merchant, and surveyor. In 1670, Herrman produced a map of Virginia and Maryland which was engraved on metal plates and printed in London in 1673.

Julius Bien was a noted lithographer who was born in 1826 in Naumberg, Hessen. Bien went to New York in 1849. Working primarily in Baltimore and in Washington, D.C., Bien produced literally hundreds of maps for federal and state surveys. Bien's maps were an essential part in the development of the western U.S. A primary example of his work is the atlas series to accompany the U.S. Government-sponsored *1870-1880 Report of the Geological Exploration of the Fortieth Parallel*. Bien was active for the better part of the last half of the 19th century.

August Hoen had a career similar to that of Bien, and in fact, preceded Bien by arriving in the United States in 1835. Hoen (original family name Höhn) is best known for his maps in connection with J.C. Fremont's 1842 exploration of the western part of the United States, another U.S. Government land survey.

Adolph Lindenkohl, who was born in 1833 in Niederkaufungen, Hessen, went to York, Pa. in 1852. Lindenkohl spent nearly fifty years with the U.S. Coast & Geodetic Survey in Washington,D.C., as cartographer and ocean-ographer.

Louis Prang was born in Breslau, then in Schlesien, in 1824, and went to Boston as a political refugee in 1850. In later years, Prang had a varied career. By 1851, he was established as a wood engraver, and by 1856, as a lithographer. Prang began publishing in 1861 under the name of Louis Prang & Co., notably maps and plans of Civil War battles. By 1864, he adapted techniques especially for color reproduction and was noted for chromolithographs, these being reproductions of oil paintings of living art-ists. Prang is even credited by some sources as "inventing" the Christmas card in 1875. A notable Prang publication in 1898 was *The Prang Standard of Color*, a book which promoted uniformity in colors employed in printing processes.

Seymour Schwartz, a physician whose hobby was collecting antique maps, was a joint author, in 1980, with Ralph Ehrenberg of the standard cartographic book *The Mapping of America.*

Some noteworthy names of etchers and engravers in America include Frederick Girsch, Christian Gobrecht, William Kneass, Charles Frederick William Mielatz, and Stephen Alonzo Schoff.

Photojournalists include Alfred Eisenstaedt, Arthur Rothstein, and Edward Jean Steichen. In 1941, Otto Ludwig Bettmann, a 1930s refugee, established in Boca Raton, Fl., a well-known commercial picture archive under the name Bettman Archive, Inc.

Printers and Publishers

Two prime sources of information exist for this group. The first source is a 1965 reprint by Karl J. R. Arndt & May E. Olson titled *German-American Newspapers and Periodicals, 1732-1955. History and Bibliography* (Quelle and Meyer Verlag, Heidelberg) (the book was enlarged and reprinted in 1976 in three volumes as a third edition and updated for the period 1732-1968). This source lists literally hundreds of German language newspapers, state by state, printed in the United States. It was printed by the Johnson Reprint Corp. in New York. In the late 1800s, there were several hundred German language newspapers in print simultaneously in the United States; most ceased publishing prior to World War I.

In the United States, one of the most important newspapers was the *New-Yorker Staats-Zeitung und Herold* which was in existence from 1834 through 1954, and probably is ongoing.

The second source is a 1989 book in two volumes compiled by Gerd J. Bötte, Werner Tannhof, and others, titled *The First Century of German Language Printing in the United States of America, 1728-1830*. The two volumes are often catalogued under the main editor's name who was Karl J. R. Arndt. This compendium shows more than 4,000 book titles (publisher, Niedersächsische Staats- und Universitätsbibliothek, Göttingen). The 1989 book is an expansion of earlier compilations, the most notable of which was that by Oswald Seidensticker and Wilbur H. Oda, working in the 1880s. It does not list newspapers or broadsides.

The two volume *Printing in the Americas*, by John Clyde Oswald (1937, Kennikat Press, Inc., Port Washington, N.Y.) is perhaps the most useful of the older books on printing history, in general, in America.

The early publishers of English background included Andrew Bradford (1686-1742) and Benjamin Franklin (1706-1770), both active in Philadelphia. Bradford printed a few books in German from 1728-1742, while Franklin printed books in German dated from 1730-1756. More importantly, both helped to train printers of German background. In 1732, Benjamin Franklin was the publisher of the short-lived *Philadelphische Zeitung*, one of the earliest German-language newspapers printed in America. The paper was poorly written and edited and was discontinued after a few issues because of the very limited number of subscribers.

The list of notable early German-American printers apparently begins with the Sower family. The original German name undoubtably is Sauer or Saur, and is shown as "Christoph Saur" on the title page of his 1743 Bible, that is, the first German-language Bible known to have been printed in America. Christopher Sower I was born in 1693, apparently in Laasphe a.d. Lahn, Nordrhein-Westfalen (some sources say Ladenburg, near Mannheim, Baden). He went to Philadelphia in 1724, and worked in Lancaster, Pa. from 1726-1738. Sower was a religious or educational leader of the German Baptist Brethren. In 1738, he set up a printing press in Germantown, Pa., which he operated until his death in 1758. Sower's printing type was imported from the Egenolff-Luther type foundry located in Frankfurt am Main. Sower established a paper mill near Philadelphia, in 1744.

Christopher Sower II (active 1759-1777) and Christopher Sower III continued the press until 1777 when they had problems with the Continental authorities because of their Loyalistic and non-supportive tendencies. At that time, Christopher II discontinued printing when most of his property was seized by the American authorities. He moved to Methatchen, Pa., and died there in 1784. Christopher Sauer II, about 1770, apparently became the first in America to start a type foundry.

Christopher III operated a press a few months in Philadelphia and the moved to New York, where he continued printing until about 1779.

Sower descendants established another printing operation in Norristown, Pa., in 1799, which was continued until 1834. However, the operation continued its decline, when the family, not having learned a lesson from their use of anti-war progaganda of the Revolutionary War, also opposed the War of 1812. During the latter war, the printing office was mobbed by local citizenry.

Other early printers were Nicholas Hasselbach, Samuel Keimer, and John Peter Zenger.

The Ephrata Cloister (known also as Der Brüderschaft) in Lancaster Co., Pa. operated a printing press beginning in 1743. John Peter Miller who went to America in 1730 became one of the leaders of Seventh Day Baptists founded in 1732 by Johann Conrad Beissel. The religious group moved to Ephrata in 1735. Miller was translator, proof reader, and head of the press. In 1748, the group translated the *Martyr's Mirror* from the original Dutch, made their own paper, and printed this book of 1,200 pages, which was by far the largest book in the Americas. From about 1745 to 1800, the press printed about 200 different books, the first music sheets printed in America, the Declaration of Independence in seven languages, and during the Revolutionary War, Continental money. Johannes Godfried Zeisiger was a key printer for the Ephrata Press from 1752 to 1770. John Peter Miller, the main translator was fluent in Latin, German, Dutch and later English. The decline of the press began about the time of Miller's death in 1796. However, printers active in Ephrata were Johann Baumann (active 1800-1809), Jacob Ruth (active 1811-1812), and Joseph Bauman (active 1817-1830). The Ephrata community still exists as a town of more than 11,000 population and is mainly of historical interest.

Another Miller, John Henry Miller (also known as Henrich Miller), went to Pennsylvania in 1741 with Count von Zinzendorf. He was also an early printer, editor, and publisher. This Miller operated a newspaper in Philadelphia and was the first to print the announcement of the adoption of the Declaration of Independence.

George Kline (or Georg Klein on some records), who arrived in Philadelphia about 1780, worked in Philadelphia until about 1784. Later he move to Carlisle, Pa. where he was a frontier newspaper editor and book publisher.

Frederick Leypoldt, born in Stuttgart in 1835, went to New York in 1854. In 1873, Leypoldt founded the *Publishers Weekly*, an important publication which, since the days of Leypoldt, has changed hands several times, but remains today at the top of its field.

Eugene Meyer, born 1875 in Los Angeles, became a noted banker. Meyer, bought an interest, in 1933, in one of America's premier newspapers, the *Washington Post*. Meyer is listed as a publisher for the years 1933-1940 and editor and publisher during the period 1940-1946. After 1946, he became chairman of the board, until his death in 1959, of the *Washington Post*. Meyer married Agnes Elizabeth Ernst, a daughter of immigrants native to northern Germany. Through her marriage, Agnes Meyer became, in 1933, part owner of the paper and subsequently developed a part-time career as a journalist and writer for the *Post*. A daughter, Katharine Meyer Graham, was employed by the *Post* from 1939-1945, and in 1963, after the death of her husband, Philip L. Graham, then president of the *Post*, she became president of the Washington Post Co., and CEO in 1973. The European ancestor of Eugene Meyer reportedly came from Alsace in 1859. The Washington Post Company ranks in the realm of big business as it is number 277 on the *Fortune* 500 list.

Anna Behr Uhl purchased the printing firm of Julius Böttcher in 1844. Oswald Ottendorfer, who went as a political refugee to New York in 1850, eventually married Anna Behr Uhl. Together, the Ottendorfers operated the *New Yorker Staats-Zeitung*, which was the most important German language paper of its time, as noted above. The Ottendorfers turned the paper into a highly profitable operation.

In 1890, Herman Ridder became the manager of the *New York Staats-Zeitung*. Not long thereafter, he was the owner of the paper. Ridder also held the important post of director of the Associated Press from 1900-1915. Herman was a second generation German-American, his father of the same name having come from Westfalen sometime prior to 1850. The Ridder family name remains today in the Knight-Ridder publishing chain which is number 198 on the *Fortune* 500 list.

Joseph Pulitzer, born in 1847 in Makó, Hungary, arrived in Boston in 1864 (Makó is about 85 miles southeast of the capital, Budapest). Pulitzer was a mercenary in the Union army, but remained in the army less than a year. In 1878, Pulitzer bought the *St. Louis Post-Dispatch* (actually a combination of two money losing papers), and in 1883, the *New York World*, both papers eventually becoming leaders in their area. Pulitzer competed successfully for newspaper circulation with William Randolph Hearst who bought the *N.Y. Journal* in 1896. Pulitzer died in 1911, but left funds with the Columbia University School of Journalism for the establishment of the Pulitzer Prizes. Joseph Pulitzer II ran the St. Louis *Post-Dispatch* until his death in 1955. The Pulitzer family name is not German, but appears to be derived from a Slavic locality name, possibly from Pölitz (Police), formerly in Pommern, now in Poland, or from Politz (Police) in Bohemia.

Adolph Ochs was born in 1858 in Cincinnati to immigrants from Fürth, Bayern. Ochs was the owner of the *Chattanooga Times* from 1878-1935, and the *New York Times* from 1896-1935. Under Ochs' direction, the *New York Times* became a premier paper in the United States, a ranking which was maintained by the Sulzberger family, mentioned below.

The Sulzberger family of New York came from Germany in the first half of the 19th century, the patriarch of the family being Abraham Sulzberger (1810-1880). Through several generations, the family was successful in merchandising, in textiles, in governmental positions, and in other interests. Arthur Hays Sulzberger was president and publisher of the premier *New York Times* from 1935-1961, and maintained an interest in the paper until his death in 1968. The New York Times Corporation more properly belongs in the realm of big business as it is number 240 in the *Fortune* 500 list.

Alfred A. Knopf was born in New York in 1892. In 1915, he founded the publishing firm which even today bears his name. He was president from 1918-1957, and CEO from 1957-1972. Many famous authors such as H.L. Mencken (1880-1956) were under contract to the Knopf Publishing firm. In fact, Knopf and Mencken enjoyed a very close working relationsip. The first wife of Knopf was Blanche Wolf who succeeded to the presidency of the firm in 1957 and remained president until her death in 1966. Blanche Wolf Knopf, born in 1894, was the daughter of Julius W. and Bertha Wolf who were immigrants from Vienna.

The well-known book publishing firm of Simon & Schuster was established in New York in 1924. Max Lincoln Schuster was born in Kalusz, Austria, and came to the United States in 1897. The Simon family name is likely of German origin also.

Paper Manufacturers & Book Binders

The directory shows three names, of which Miller and Rittenhouse were early paper makers. The Sauer family reportedly also had a paper mill which was located on the Schuykill, in Pennsylvania, near Philadelphia. The third name in the directory, Otto Zahn, was a German immigrant bookbinder of some note who eventually became president of Toof & Co., bookbinders, in Memphis, Tenn.

As stated earlier, the Ephrata Press also made its own paper.

Wood Engravers

The names of five wood engravers are listed in the directory. All operated in the latter part of the 19th century when wood engraving still had some prominence in printing processes.

TABLE 17
DIRECTORY OF THE PRINTING AND PUBLISHING WORLD

Authors
Baum, Vicki Hedwig (1888-1960)
Becker, Marion Rombauer (1903-1973)
1. Brachvogel, Udo (1835-1913)
1. Brecht, Bertolt Eugen Friedrich (1898-1956)
1. Bromme, Traugott (1802-1866)
   Buck, Pearl Comfort Sydenstricker (1892-1973)
1. Erikson, Erik Homburger (1902-1994)
   Ferber, Edna (1885-1968)
1. Feuchtwanger, Lion (1884-1958)
1. Friedman, Lee Max (1871-1947)
   Geisel, Theodor Seuss (1904-1991)
1. Gerstäcker, Friedrich Wilhelm Christian (1816-1872)
   Gerstenberg, Alice (1885-1972)
1. Giesler-Anneke, Mathilde Franziska (1817-1884)
1. Graf, Oskar Maria (1894-1967)
   Griesinger, Theodor (1809-1884)
   Grimké, Angelina Emily (1805-1879)
   Grimké, Sarah Moore (1792-1873)
   Gunther, John (1901-1970)
2. Hellman, Lillian Florence (1907-1984)
3. Helper, Hinton Rowan (1829-1909)
   Herbst, Josephine (1892-1969)
   Hershey, John Richard (1914-1993)
2. Hurst, Fannie (1889-1968)
   Kaufman, George Simon (1899-1961)
   Kaye, Frederick Benjamin (1892-1930)
1. Kiderlen, Wilhelm Ludwig Joseph (1813-1877)
   Kingsley, Sidney (1906-) (Kieshner)
1. Knortz, Karl (1841-1918)
1. Lewisohn, Ludwig (1882-1955)
1. Loher, Franz Von (1818-1892)
   Ludvigh, Samuel Gottlieb (1801-1869)
1. Mann, Paul Thomas (1875-1955)
1. Möllhausen, Heinrich Balduin (1825-1905)
1. Münch, Friedrich (1799-1881)
   Nash, N. Richard (1913-)
1. Neumann, Robert (1897-1975)
   Parker, Dorothy Rothschild (1893-1967)
1. Pelz, Eduard (1800-1876)
2. Phillips, Irna (1901-1973)
2. Plath, Sylvia (1932-1963)
1. Remarque, Erich Paul Maria (1898-1970)
3. Repplier, Agnes (1855-1950)

3. Rice, Elmer Leopold (1892-1967) (Reisenstein)
   Richter, Conrad Michael (1890-1968)
1. Robinson, Therese Albertine Louise von Jakob
   (1797-1870)
2. Rombauer, Irma Louise von Starkloff (1877-1962)
1. Ruppius, Otto (1818-1864)
2. Sandoz, Mari (1896-1966)
   Schriftgiesser, Karl John (1903-1988)
1. Sealsfield, Charles (1793-1864) (Karl Anton Postl)
1. Solger, Reinhard Ernst Fredrich Karl (1817-1866)
2. Smith, Betty (1904-1972) (Wehner)
3. Stein, Gertrude (1874-1946)
   Steinbeck, John Ernst (1902-1968)
   Stempfel, Theodore (1863-1935)
3. Stone, Irving (1903-1989) (Tennenbaum)
2. Stratemeyer, Edward (1862-1930)
   Stribling, Thomas Sigismund (1881-1965)
1. Strubberg, Friedrich Armand (1806-1889)
3. Suckow, Ruth (1892-1960)
2. Tiernan, Frances Christine Fisher (1846-1920)
2. Traubel, Horace L. (1858-1919)
4. Tweed, Blanche Oelrichs Thomas Barrymore (1890-1950)
3. Victor, Orville James (1827-1910)
   Vollmer, Lulu (1898?-1955)
1. von Hesse-Wartegg, Ernst, Baron (1854-1918)
4. Vonnegut, Kurt, Jr. (1922-)
1. von Seckendorff, Gustav Anton (1775-1823)
   West, Nathanael (1902-1940)
1. Wislizenus, Frederick Adolph (1810-1889)
6. Wister, Owen (1860-1938)
   Wolfe, Thomas Clayton (1900-1938)
1. Wollenweber, Louis August (1807-1888)

Editors & Critics

1. Balch, Thomas Willing (1866-1927)
3. Bender, Harold Stauffer (1897-1962)
3. Calverton, Victor Francis (1900-1940) (George Goetz)
1. George, Manfred (1893-1965) (Manfred Georg Cohn)
1. Herbermann, Charles George (1840-1916)
5. Hergesheimer, Joseph (1880-1954) (Hargesheimer)
1. Kirchoff, Charles William Henry (1853-1916)
   Kirchwey, Freda (1893-1976)
   Kenkel, Frederick Philipp (1863-1952)
2. Kobbé, Gustav, (1857-1918)
   Koenigsberg, Moses (1878-1945)
1. Lange, Louis (1829-1893)
1. Lieber, Francis (1798-1872) (Franz Lieber)

1. Mueller, Paul Ferdinand (1857-1931)
3. Oakes, George Washington (1861-1931) (Ochs)
1. Pollak, Gustav (1849-1919)
1. Pollard, Joseph Percival (1869-1911)
2. Pulitzer, Ralph (1879-1939)
1. Rapp, Wilhelm Georg (1828-1907)
3. Ridder, Victor Frank (1886-1963)
1. Schem, Jacob Balthasar Alexander (1826-1881)
3. Spahr, Charles Baryillai (1860-1904)
2. Spingarn, Joel Elias (1875-1939)
1. Thieme, August (1822-1879)
1. Viereck, George Sylvester (1884-1962)

Journalists
2. Ames, Mary E. Clemmer (1831-1884)
1. Bernstein, Herman (1876-1935)
3. Bleyer, Willard Grosvenor (1873-1935)
1. Brentano, Lorenz (1813-1891)
1. Douai, Earl Daniel Adolph (1819-1888)
2. Dreiser, Theodore Herman Albert (1871-1945)
3. Forney, John Wien (1817-1881)
1. Grund, Francis Joseph (1805-1863)
1. Hassaurek, Friedrich (1831-1885)
1. Heilprin, Michael (1823-1888)
1. Heinzen, Karl Peter (1809-1880)
4. Hittell, John Shertzer (1825-1901)
4. Hittell, Theodore Henry (1830-1917)
1. Jordan, Max (1895-1977)
2. Kaltenborn, Hans V. (1878-1965)
   Klauber, Edward (1887-1954)
   Krock, Arthur (1886-1974)
1. Kroeger, Adolph Ernst (1837-1882)
2. Liebling, Abbott Joseph (1904-1963)
3. Lippmann, Walter (1889-1974)
1. List, Georg Friedrich (1798-1846)
3. Mencken, Henry Louis (1880-1916)
1. Müller, Nikolaus (1809-1875)
1. Nordhoff, Charles (1830-1901)
1. Oertel, Johann James Maximilian (1811-1882)
   Ottenberg, Miriam (1914-1982)
1. Preetorius, Emil (1827-1905)
1. Rosewater, Edward (1841-1906)
2. Rosewater, Victor (1871-1940) (Rosenwasser)
   Ruhl, Arthur Brown (1876-1935)
   Schechter, Abel Alan (1907-1989)
1. Schneider, George (1823-1905)
   Seitz, Don Carlos (1862-1935)

Shirer, William Lawrence (1904-1993)
3. Switzler, William Franklin (1819-1906)
2. Swope, Herbert Bayard, (1882-1958)
   (Schwob, Schwab)
1. Villard, Oswald Garrison (1872-1949)
   Wahl, William Henry (1848-1909)
2. Wile, Frederic William (1873-1941)
   Wisner, George (1812-1849)

Poets

1. Bloede, Gertrude, (1845-1905)
2. Cawein, Madison Julius (1865-1914)
2. Hubner, Charles William (1835-1929)
7. Kilmer, Alfred Joyce (1886-1918)
2. Moise, Penina (1797-1880)
   Niehardt, John Gnelsenau (1881-1975)
1. Nies, Konrad (1861-1921)
   Oppenheim, James (1882-1932)
1. Reitzel, Robert (1849-1898)
8. Rittenhouse, Jessie Bell (1869-1948)
2. Roethke, Theodore (1908-1963)
3. Sampter, Jessie Ethel (1883-1938)
3. Saxe, John Godfrey (1816-1887)
2. Schnauffer, Carl Heinrich (1823-1854)
2. Speyer, Leonora (1872-1956)
3. Timrod, Henry (1828-1867)
   Wurdemann, Audrey Mary (1911-1960)

Map Makers, Lithographers, Metal Engravers, Photographers

1. Bettman, Otto Ludwig (1903-)
1. Bien, Julius (1826-1909)
1. Egelmann, Carl Friedrich (1782-1860)
1. Eisenstaedt, Alfred (1898-)
1. Fox, Justus (1736-1805)
1. Girsch, Frederick (1821-1895)
2. Gobrecht, Christian (1785-1844)
1. Gugler, Henry (1816-1880)
1. Herrman, Augustin (c.1605-1686 or c.1621-1686)
1. Hoen, August (1817-1886)
1. Joerg, Wolfgang, Louis Gottfried (1885-1952)
3. Kneass, William (1780-1840)
1. Kollner, Augustus (1812-1906)
1. Kurz, Louis (1833-1921)
1. Lindenkohl, Adolph (1833-1904)
1. Maurer, Louis (1832-1932)
1. Mielatz, Charles Frederick William (1860-1919)
1. Momberger, William (1829-)

1. Prang, Louis (1824-1909)
1. Preuss, George Karl Ludwig (1803-1854)
   Rothstein, Arthur (1915-1985)
4. Schoff, Stephen Alonzo (1818-1904)
   Schwartz, Seymour Ira (1928-)
1. Seifert, Henry (1824-1911)
1. Steichen, Edward Jean (1879-1973)
1. Wissler, Jacques (1803-1887)

Printers & Publishers

1. Annenberg, Moses Louis (1878-1942)
1. Armbrüster, Anton (c.1717-1796)
1. Börnstein, Heinrich (1805-1902)
3. Dryfoos, Orvil Eugene (1912-1963)
1. Fleischmann, Raoul H. (1885-1969)
4. Funk, Isaac Kauffman (1839-1912) (Funck)
1. Glogauer, Fritz (1857-1926)
3. Goddard, Sarah Updike (c.1700-1770)
   Graham, Katharine Meyer (1917-)
   Gruber, Johann (1768-1857)
2. Hart, Abraham (1810-1885)
1. Hasselbach, Nicholas (fl. 1749-1770)
1. Keimer, Samuel (1688-1739)
1. Kline, George (c. 1757-1820)
1. Klopsch, Louis (1852-1910)
   Knopf, Alfred Abraham (1892-1984)
3. Knopf, Blanche Wolf (1894-1966)
1. Kraus, Hans Peter (1907-1988)
1. Levy, Louis Edward (1846-1919)
2. Levy, Max (1857-1926)
1. Leypoldt, Frederick (1835-1884)
2. Meyer, Agnes Elizabeth Ernst (1887-1970)
2. Meyer, Eugene Isaac (1875-1959)
1. Miller, John Henry (1702-1782)
1. Miller, John Peter (1709-1790) (Müller)
   Nieman, Lucius William (1857-1935)
2. Ochs, Adolph Simon (1858-1935)
1. Ottendorfer, Anna Behr Uhl (1815-1884)
1. Ottendorfer, Oswald (1826-1900)
1. Pelz, Eduard (1801-1876)
1. Pulitzer, Joseph (1847-1911)
2. Pulitzer, Joseph II (1885-1955)
2. Ridder, Herman (1851-1915)
3. Schiff, Dorothy (1903-1989)
1. Schuster, Max Lincoln (1897-1966)
   Shuster, William Morgan (1877-1960)
3. Simon, Richard Lee (1899-1960)

1. Sower, Christopher I (1693-1758) (Saur, Sauer)
1. Sower, Christopher II (1721-1784)
2. Sower, Christopher III (1754-1799)
1. Stahlman, Edward Bushrod (1843-1940)
3. Sulzberger, Arthur Hays (1891-1968)
4. Sulzberger, Arthur Ochs, Sr. (1926-)
3. Sulzberger, Iphigene (Ochs) (1892-1990)
2. Tammen, Harry Heye (1856-1924)
2. Wagnalls, Adam Willis (1843-1924) (Wagenhals)
1. Zeisiger, Johann Godfried (fl. 1752-1770)
1. Zenger, John Peter (1697-1746)
   Zimmermann, Herbert P. (1880-1962)

Paper Manufacturers & Book Binders
3. Miller, Warner (1838-1918)
1. Rittenhouse, William (1644-1708) (Rittinghausen)
1. Zahn, Otto (1857-1928)

Wood Engravers
1. Heinemann, Ernst (1848-1912)
1. Juengling, Frederick (1846-1889)
1. Kirchmayer, John (c. 1860-1930)
1. Kruell, Gustav (1843-1907)
1. Wolf, Henry (1852-1916)

Code:
1. = 1st Generation in America
2. = 2nd Generation
3. = 3rd of more Generation, etc.

The Natural Sciences

From the earliest days of the immigrants in America, the biological and physical sciences were a matter of curiosity. Scattered accounts exist as to rudimentary observations made by individuals who were trained neither in botany nor in geology, for instance. These accounts were generally provided by individuals whose university training in Europe provided some background and whose professions allowed them to adopt one of the natural sciences as a hobby.

More advanced observations followed and these often occurred in conjunction with the collection of data, for instance, the collection of many kinds of beetles, or the collection of different types of mollusks. The next step was the classification of this data into a meaningful series of groups.

Classification was not a simple matter and the interpretation of the data required much careful thought. Many false conclusions were based upon interpretation which did not have the benefit of advanced technology, such as optical microscopes, x-ray machines, and scanning electron microscopes of the present time.

The medical profession was at a special disadvantage until well into the 19th century. Trial and error was the rule until the biochemists, the physiologists, the microscopists, the x-ray technologists, and the like provided the tools necessary for diagnosing and understanding the nature of bacteria, viruses, and all sorts of communicable diseases.

The great wave of migrants of the 1840s and 1850s included many men and women with a strong background in the natural sciences, above all, in the biological and geological sciences. These German-Americans were instrumental in helping to develop America's abundant natural resources which the fertile soils and mining localities provided.

The German Weimar Republic, which lasted from 1919-1933, had its problems with trying to recover from World War I and with a runaway economy resulting in hyperinflation. The Third Reich, which was in power from 1933-1945, expelled upwards of 2,500 university trained professionals from its territories. The mass of German, and Austrian refugees of the 1920s and 1930s provided numerous mathematicians and physicists who gave America a head start in the race for the moon and outer space. In the same wave of refugees, the many biochemists and physiologists provided undreamed of medical advances and also changed American eating habits forever. For many Americans, a diet high in salt, sugar, and fat content became taboo.

At any rate, the wonders of the new world posed many challenging problems for those immigrants with a curious mind. The list of notable German-Americans in the biological sciences numbers eighty-six and the list of those in the physical sciences, with its somewhat broader categories, numbers 129. Representatives of the twelve subgroups are noted below with the those of the complete listing receiving honorable mention in the directory. Nobel prize winners are prominent.

Botany

Twenty-four botanists of some note are included here. At least two of the botanists, Engelmann and Lindheimer, were part of the student demonstration in Frankfurt in 1832. Their emigration was the result of suppression of these demonstrations.

John James Dufour was born in Chatelard Vevey, Kanton Vaud, Switzerland about 1793. Dufour, whose name obviously reflects its French origin, went to Kentucky in 1796. Dufour naturally became interested in the growing of grapes in the New World and was a pioneer viticulturist in America.

Georg Engelmann was born in Frankfurt am Main in 1809. Engelmann was another enthusiast caught in the student protests in Frankfurt and went to America in 1832. Engelmann settled in St. Louis and developed a varied career as a physician, botanist, and meteorologist. Today, Engelmann is noted primarily for his work in botany, especially on the collection of data. Englemann was a prime advisor in the organization of the Missouri Botanical Garden which opened in St. Louis in 1859.

Bernhard Eduard Fernow was born in 1851 in Hohensalza, district of Posen, Westpreußen, now known as Inowraclaw, Poland. Fernow went to the U.S. in 1876 and became one of the early advocators of forestry preservation and conservation. Fernow was associated with the U.S. Department of Agriculture, with Cornell University, and other organizations.

George Hansen was born in Hildesheim, former district of Hannover, now Niedersachsen, in 1863. Hansen went to San Francisco in 1887 where he became a premier horticulturist and landscape artist.

George Husmann was born in Meyenburg, Brandenburg, in 1827. Husmann went to Philadelphia in 1837 and shortly therafter, to Hermann, Mo. In Hermann, Husmann became a viticulturist of local renown as well as the author of publications related to grape growing.

Karl Frederic Kellerman was born in Göttingen, Niedersachsen, in 1879. Kellerman became a plant physiologist (the study of life processes) with the U.S. Department of Agriculture in Washington, D.C., where he was employed from 1901-1933. Uniquely, Kellerman was the descendant of one Frederic Kellerman who was a mercenary in the Continental Army during the Revolutionary War.

Ferdinand Jacob Lindheimer was born in Frankfurt am Main in 1801. Like Engelmann, Lindheimer was carried way in the student protests, emigrated at an early date, and settled in the "Latin farmer" community of Belleville, Ill., in 1834. Lindheimer's career varied between that of botany and journalism. He died in New Braunfels, Tx., which was a community dominated by German immigrants. Linheimer's work in Texas earned him the unofficial title "Father of Texas Botany".

Charles Theodore Mohr was born in Esslingen, Württemberg, in 1824. Mohr was part of the great wave of immigrants going to Cincinnati in 1848. Mohr is best known for his work on the botany of Alabama. He died in Asheville, N.C.

Ignaz Anton Pilat was born in St. Agatha, Oberösterreich, Austria, in 1820. Pilat was a political refugee who went to America in 1848. Pilat was a landscape gardner; in fact, much of the landscaping in Central Park, New York City was directed by Pilat. The family name is not recognizable as a German name and is a combination of Slavic and Italian.

Friedrich Traugott Pursch was born in Großenhain, Sachsen, in 1774. Pursch went to Baltimore in 1799 where he became a botanist and horticulturist. He was one of the earliest professional writers on American botany.

John Rock was born in Lauter, Hessen, in 1836. The family name was originally Roch. Rock went to New York about 1850 and later became a prominent California nurseryman.

Filbert Roth was born in Württemberg in 1858 and went to the U.S. in 1871. Roth was an expert on forestry and, in the early days, he was associated with Fernow, mentioned above. From 1903-1923, Roth was at the University of Michigan.

Jacob Weidenmann, born in 1829 in Winterthur, Kanton Zürich, went to New York in 1861. Weidemann established a career as a landscape architect in Hartford, Conn.

Entomology

Augustus Radcliffe Grote was born in Aigburth, near Liverpool, England, in 1841. He was the descendant of one Hugo Grotius, a German. Grote was an entomologist who went to New York in 1846 and returned to Germany in 1884.

Hermann August Hagen was born in Königsburg, a large university city formerly in Ostpreußen, now in Poland, in 1817. Hagen went to Cambridge, Mass. in 1867, where he was attached to Harvard University.

Frederick Knab was born in Würzburg, Bayern in 1865. Knab went to Chicopee, Mass., in 1873. As a specialist in entomology, Knab concentrated on the study of mosquitos of which there are hundreds of species.

Eugene Amandus Schwarz was born in Liegnitz, Silesia, in 1844. Schwarz went to Cambridge, Mass. in 1872. In the years 1881-1928, he was attached to the U.S. Bureau of Entomology in Washington, D.C.

John Bernhard Smith was born in New York, in 1858. He was the son of immigrant "John Smith" (doubtless Johann Schmidt) who came from Bayern in 1853. The younger Smith specialized in the study of salt marsh mosquitoes. Smith married Marie H. von Meske, a daughter of the German immigrant Otto von Meske, a lepidopterist (one who studies butterflies and moths).

Biochemistry, Physiology, Bacteriology, Genetics

The following list of thirty-seven German-American names includes fifteen Nobel Prize winners, many of them Jewish refugees from the 1920-1930s.

Max Bergmann was born in Fürth, Bayern, in 1886. Bermann is typical of the 1933 refugees who went to America. He was associated with the Rockefeller Institute for Medical Research as a biochemist from 1936-1944.

Konrad Bloch was born in Neisse, formerly Upper Silesia, now in Poland, in 1912. He went as a refugee to the U.S. in 1936 and divided his career between the University of Chicago and Harvard University. In 1964, Bloch, a biochemist, was awarded the Nobel Prize in medicine.

Gerty Theresa Radnitz Cori was born in Prague, Bohemia, in 1896 and went to the United States in 1922. She worked on carbohydrate metabolism at Washington University School of Medicine (St. Louis) from 1931-1957.

Carl Djerassi, was born in Vienna in 1923, and went to the U.S. about 1952. Djerassi was an organic chemist who helped to develop oral contraceptives. The name is an unusual one, not at all Germanic. For his work at Stanford University, he is listed in the National Inventors Hall of Fame at Akron, Oh.

Max Delbrück was born in Berlin, in 1906, and went to the United States in 1937. Delbrück's later career was at the California Institute of Technology. In 1969, he was awarded the Nobel Prize in physiology.

Gerald Maurice Edelman was born in New York in 1929 and spent much of his career at Rockefeller Institute for Medical Research. In 1972, Edelman was awarded the Nobel Prize in physiology.

Joseph Erlanger was born in San Francisco in 1874 and died in St. Louis in 1965. Erlanger's career was at Washington University from 1910-1946. In 1944, Erlanger was awarded the Nobel Prize in physiology. The family name is derived from Erlangen, Bayern.

Joseph Leonard Goldstein was born in Sumter, S.C. in 1940. Goldstein is listed as a molecular geneticist whose primary field is cholesterine research. In 1985, he was awarded the Nobel Prize in physiology.

Alfred Day Hershey was born in Owasso, Mich. in 1908. He worked at the Carnegie Institute, Washington, from 1950-1974. In 1969, Hershey, a geneticist, was awarded the Nobel Prize in physiology.

Ida Henrietta Hyde was born in Davenport, Ia. in 1857. She was the daughter of immigrants from Württemburg whose original family name was Heidenheimer. Hyde was a physiologist at the University of Kansas from 1898-1920.

Arthur Kornberg was born in Brooklyn in 1918. Kornberg's career as a biochemist was divided between Washington University and Stanford University. In 1959, Kornberg was awarded a Nobel Prize in physiology.

Joshua Lederberg was born in Montclair, N.J. in 1925. He is listed as a research scientist working at Stanford University, beginning in 1959. In 1959, Lederberg was awarded a Nobel Prize in physiology.

Fritz Albert Lipmann was born in Königsberg, Ostpreußen, in 1899. He went as a refugee to the United States in 1939. In 1953, Lipmann was awarded a Nobel Prize in physiology. Lipmann's later career was that of biochemist at Rockefeller University.

Jacques Loeb was born in Mayen, Rheinland-Pfalz, in 1859. He went to the U.S. in 1891 and established a career as a biologist and physiologist.

Otto Meyerhof was born in Hannover, Niedersachsen in 1884. In 1940, Meyerhof was a refugee who went relatively late to the U.S. where he was associated with the University of Pennsylvania Medical School from 1940 until his death in 1951. Meyerhof received a Nobel Prize.

Andrew J. Moyer was born in Star City, Ind., in 1899. He was associated with the U.S. Dept. Agriculture from 1929-1957. Moyer was a microbiologist who did research on fungi and molds. His work on the mass production of pencillin gained him a place in the National Inventors Hall of Fame in Akron, Oh. The Moyer name is a name common among the Pennsylvania Germans of southeast Pennsylvania.

Hermann Joseph Muller was born in New York in 1890. He was a biologist and geneticist at Indiana University from 1945-1967. In 1946, Muller was awarded a Nobel Prize in medicine.

Marshall Warren Nirenberg was born in New York in 1927. Nirenberg was a biochemist at the National Heart Institute as from 1962. In 1968, he received a Nobel Prize in physiology.

George Davis Snell was born in Haverhill, Mass. in 1903. As from 1934, he was a geneticist at the Jackson Laboratory at Bar Harbor, Me. In 1980, Snell was awarded a Nobel Prize in physiology.

William H. Stein was born in New York in 1911 and became a biochemist at the Rockefeller Institute for Medical Research as from 1938. In 1972, Stein was awarded a Nobel Prize in chemistry.

George Miller Sternberg was born in Otsego Co., N.Y. in 1838. Sternberg has a long career (1861-1902) with the U.S. Army as bacteriologist, epidemiologist, and eventually surgeon-general. Much of his work dealt with yellow fever, malaria, tuberculosis, and typhoid, and with methods for disinfecting Army occupational areas. The family name was derived from immigrants who went from the "Palatinate" in the early 18th century to the Schoharie Valley, N.Y.

Charles Milton Altland Stine was born in Norwich, Conn. in 1882. Stine was an organic chemist who had a long career (1907-1945) with E.I. Dupont de Nemours & Co., eventually being made a vice-president. The American family name is undoubtedly a variant of the German name Stein.

Max Tishler was born in Boston in 1906. Tishler was an biochemist who was employed by Merck & Co., from 1937-1969. Tishler' work on the production of vitamin B2 (riboflavin) earned him a place in the National Inventors Hall of Fame in Akron, Oh. Variants on the family name include Tischer and Tischler.

George Wald was born in New York in 1906 and was associated with Harvard University as from 1934. In 1967, Wald was awarded a Nobel Prize in physiology.

Zoology

Alexander Agassiz was born in Neuchatel, Switzerland in 1835 and went to the U.S. in 1849, or about three years after his more famous father, listed below. The younger Agassiz was known mainly as a zoologist and oceanographer, but also carried on some activities as a mine operator. Much of his work was aboard oceanographic vessels; in fact, he died in 1910 aboard such a vessel on the high seas near England.

Carl H. Eigenmann was born in Flehingen, Baden-Württemberg, in 1863. He went to Rockport, Ind., in 1877. Eigenmann's career was that of zoologist, educator, and ichthyologist.

Charles Frédéric Girard was born in Mülhausen, Haut Rhine, Alsace, in 1822. Girard was a zoologist and physician associated with Harvard University from 1847-1865. The family name shows obvious French ties. Girard died in Paris in 1895.

Richard Benedict Goldschmidt was born in Frankfurt am Main in 1878. Goldschmidt was temporarily in the U.S. in 1914 and permanently from 1936-1958. In the latter period, he was a zoologist specializing in genetics and heredity at the University of California at Berkeley.

Charles Francis Himes was born in Lancaster Co., Pa., in 1838. The family name descended from Wilhelm Heim, a native of the "Palatinate" who went to Philadelphia in 1730.

Louis Francois de Pourtalès was born in French-speaking Kanton of Neuchatel, Switzerland in 1823. He went to the U.S. in 1846 as part of the Agassiz scientific group who were associated with Harvard University and the U.S. Coastal Survey. Pourtalès was a marine zoologist who specialized in deep-sea corals.

Veterinary Science

Raymond Alexander Kelser was born in Washington, D.C., in 1892. Kelser had a remarkable career in veterinary medicine, specializing in microbiology and bacteriology. He was with the Veterinary Corps of the U.S. Army from 1918-1946 and was made a brigadier general in 1942.

Archeology and Anthropology

Franz Boas was born in Minden, Westfalen, in 1858. Boas went to the

U.S. in 1886 and became a prominent anthropologist at Columbia University. Boas, a Jew by background, gained fame through his efforts at belittling the Nazi racial theories of Anglo-Saxon superior intelligence.

Edward Sapir was born in Lauenburg, near Danzig, Pommern, now in Poland. Sapir's family went to the Richmond, Va. in 1889. Sapir's early career was concerned with linguistics, a talent which he subsequently used to study American Indian languages. In fact, during the years 1909-1939, Sapir wrote texts on the linguistics of five different western tribes, of which the last was published in 1967.

Astronomy

Christian Heinrich Friedrich Peters was born in Coldenbüttel, Schleswig-Holstein, in 1813. He went to the U.S. in 1854. Peters is best known for his studies of sun spots. The family name shows obvious north German or Danish ties.

Karl Rudolph Powalky was born in Neudietendorf, near Erfurt, Thüringen, in 1817. He went to the Washington, D.C. in 1873 where he was associated with the U.S. Naval Observatory. The family name shows a Slavic influence.

John Martin Schaeberle was born in Württemberg in 1853 and went to Ann Arbor, Mich. in 1854. Schaeberle was associated with the University of Michigan from 1876-1888, and subsequently joined the staff of the Lick Observatory at Mt. Hamilton, Ca.

Steven Weinberg was born in New York in 1933 under the name of Josey Regenthal Weinberg. Weinberg was an astrophysicist who received the Nobel Prize in physics in 1979. He was on the staff of the University of Texas, beginning in 1982.

Geology, Geodesy, Paleontology

Jean Louis Rodolphe Agassiz was born in Motier-Vully, Kanton Fribourg, Switzerland. He was the son of French Swiss Protestants. His early career included an academic post in Neuchatel. In 1846, the academy in Neuchatel was closed for political reasons (a fore-runner of the widespread 1848 disturbances in Europe) and Agassiz migrated to Boston. In 1848, Agassiz was able to secure positions for himself and several co-workers at Harvard University. Agassiz remained at the university until his death in 1873. Agassiz was one of those renowned naturalists whose broad career centered on geology. During the years 1857-1862, Agassiz wrote four of the planned ten volumes titled *Contributions to the Natural History of the United States*.

Jacob Boll was born in Bremgarten, Kanton Aargau, Switzerland. As a geologist and naturalist, Boll was in the U.S. temporarily in 1870, and from 1874 until his death in 1880. He died in Wilbarger Co., Tx.

Walter Herman Bucher was born in Akron, Oh., in 1889. Bucher had a long time academic career as a structural geologist at the University of

Cincinnati (1912-1939), and at Columbia University (1940-1956). Towards the end of his career, Bucher was a consultant for various divisions of Standard Oil of New Jersey, the world's largest oil company.

Joseph Silas Diller was born in Plainfield, Pa., in 1850, as the son of Mennonites of German and Swiss origin. Diller's career with the U.S. Geological Survey from 1883-1923 dealt mainly with the petrology of igneous rocks and with volcanic processes in the western part of the U.S. The family name descended from one Francis Tueller (listed as "Franz Tieler" in Strassburger & Hinke, 1934) who went to America in 1754.

William Eimbeck was born in Braunschweig (formerly Brunswick), Niedersachsen, in 1841 and went to the Washington, D.C. in 1857. Eimbeck was a geodetic engineer dealing with coastal surveys.

Amadeus William Grabau was born in Cedarburg, Wisc. in 1870. Grabau taught geology, paleontology, and stratigraphy at Rensselaer Polytechnic Institute from 1901-1920. In 1920, Grabau apparently took personal offense at the anti-German feelings in the U.S. and spent the remainder of his career in Peking, China. He died in China in 1946.

Beno Gutenberg, was born in Darmstadt in 1889 and went to the U.S. in 1930. Gutenberg was a seismologist at California Institute of Technology from 1930-1958. His name was applied to the "Gutenberg Discontinuity" which is a deep-seated seismic phenomena seen as the boundary between layers of rock having different densities.

Arnold Henry Guyot was born in Bonvillars, Kanton Vaud, Switzerland, in 1807. Guyot, an associate of Agassiz, went as a geographer to Harvard University in 1848. Guyot's name is applied to "Guyot seamounts" which are oceanographic phenomena noted as flat-topped rises in the sea floor.

Ferdinand Rudolph Hassler was born in Aarau, Kanton Aargau, Switzerland in 1770. He went to Philadelphia in 1805 and in 1816 became the first superintendent of the U.S. Coast Survey. He was a geodesist and mathematician. Hassler was head of the survey from 1816-1819, and again in the renewed survey period of 1832-1845. At the beginning of the survey, Hassler bought books and scientific instruments from Europe, items not available in the states, and thus was among the earliest importers of European scientific technology.

Angelo Heilprin became a noted geologist and paleontologist. Heilprin was born in a village in Hungary in 1853 and was brought to the U.S. in 1856. His father, Michael Heilprin, was apparently born in Polish territory, but took part in the Hungarian Revolution of 1842-1848 and afterwards was a refugee. The exact origin of the family name has not been clarified although it appears more German than Slavic through the spelling of Heilprin.

Eugene Woldemar Hilgard was born in Zweibrücken, Rheinland-Pfalz and was taken by his father, a political refugee, to Belleville, Ill., in 1836. Hilgard was a geologist who became an authority on the soils of the state of Mississippi. His book titled *Geology of the Mississippi Delta* was published in 1870, and was the first authoritative geologic account of the delta. Julius Erasmus Hilgard, who was a brother to Eugene, became a noted geodesist with the U.S. Coast Survey.

George Frederick Kunz was born in New York in 1856. Kunz became a recognized expert on gems and minerals, and wrote several books on the subject. He was associated with the American Museum of Natural History from 1904-1932, and with the jewelers Tiffany & Co. in New York, where he became a vice-president. The gem mineral Kunzite, which is a variety of spodumene with a delicate lavender color, bears his name.

Joseph Leidy was born in Philadelphia in 1823. His grandfather, the immigrant John Jacob Leydig, went to America in 1723 from Wittenberg, Sachsen-Anhalt. Joseph Leidy became a well-known naturalist and paleontologist with the Academy of Natural Sciences in Philadelphia. Perhaps Leidy's most important post was as Professor of Anatomy at the University of Pennsylvania, a post he occupied from 1853-1888. This work is illustrated by his 1861 book titled *Elementary Treatise on Human Anatomy*, which was a landmark in its day. From 1870-1885, Leidy was also Professor of Natural History at Swarthmore College.

Leo Lesquereux was born in Fleurier, Kanton Neuchatel, Switzerland, in 1806. He followed Agassiz to Boston in 1848, and although stone deaf, became an authority on fossil plants, especially plants contained in the coal beds in the geological age known as the Pennsylvania Age from the states of Pennsylvania, Indiana, and Illinois.

Charles Francis Richter was born in Hamilton, Oh., in 1900. Richter became a seismologist working, at first, at the Carnegie Institute in Washington, and later, at the California Institute of Technology. At the latter institute, he was an associate of Beno Gutenberg. Richter devised the scale, which bears his name, for measuring the intensity of earthquakes. The name Richter is a very common German occupational name, having to do with judicial matters.

Karl Ferdinand Roemer was a geologist, born in Hildesheim, Niedersachsen, in 1818. Roemer was in the hill country of Texas for nearly three years, from 1845-1848. His books on the geology of Texas, which contain prized maps of the area, were among the earliest scientific documentation of the rocks of central Texas. Roemer gained the unofficial title "Father of Texas Geology".

Rudolf Ruedemann was born in Georgenthal, Thüringen, in 1864. Ruedemann migrated to the U.S. in 1892, and was associated with the New York State Museum from 1899-1937. Ruedemann developed a reputation as a world authority on fossil graptolites, an unique ancient floating-marine, plant-like organism.

Charles Anthony Schott was born in Mannheim, Baden, in 1826. Schott was among the 1848 immigrant wave going to the U.S. He became a leading geodesist and magnetician in his capacity with the U.S. Coast Survey.

Charles Schuchert was born in Cincinnati in 1858. Schuchert was a paleontologist and historical geologist who had posts at the U.S. National Museum, the U.S. Geological Survey, and at Yale University. Schuchert's reputation was enhanced largely by his publication *Historical Geology of North America*, printed in 1935.

Charles Wachsmuth was born at Hannover, Niedersachsen, in 1829, and went to New York in 1852. By 1854, Wachsmuth was in Burlington, Iowa, where he worked as a paleontologist on the famous fossil crinoids of the Burlington limestone. Wachsmuth produced several elaborate monographs on these bottom-dwelling, plant-like, marine forms.

Inorganic Chemistry

Friedrich August Ludwig Karl Wilhelm Genth was born at Wächtersbach, Hessen, in 1820, and went to Philadelphia in 1848. As a chemist and mineralogist at the University of Pennsylvania and other places, he discovered twenty-four new minerals.

Caesar Augustin Grasselli was born in Cincinnati in 1850, his father having come from Strasbourg, Alsace, in 1836. Grasselli was a manufacturing chemist and successful businessman. The family name shows an Italian influence.

Charles Anthony Goessmann was born in Naumberg, Hessen, in 1827, as Karl Anton Goessmann. Goessmann went to Philadelphia in 1857, where he was employed as a teacher and chemist. He developed several important processes for the refining of sugar and of salt.

Herbert Aaron Hauptman was born in New York in 1917. He became a mathematician and researcher at the Medical Foundation of Buffalo, Inc. In 1985, Hauptman was awarded a Nobel Prize in chemistry.

Georg Augustus Koenig was born in Willstätt, Baden, in 1844, and went to Philadelphia in 1868. Koenig was a chemist and mineralogist at the University of Pennsylvania from 1872-1892, and after 1892, at the Michigan College of Mines.

John Ulric Nef, Jr. was born in Herisau, Kanton Appenzell, Switzerland. He followed his father to Housatonic, Mass., arriving there in 1868. The younger Nef eventually became a prominent chemist at the University of Chicago.

Mathematics

As in grouping for biochemistry and physiology, many of the following eighteen names are those of Jewish refugees of the 1920s and 1930s. Not all of the refugees were Jewish; in at least two instances, they were Roman Catholics who ideology conflicted with that of the Nazi regime.

Florian Cajori was born in St. Aignan, Kanton Grisons, Switzerland, in 1859. He went to Whitewater, Wisc. in 1875. Cajori is noted for his work on the history of mathematics which he developed during his career as a long time instructor at the University of California at Berkeley. The family name shows an obvious Italian influence.

Ernst Alfred Cassirer was born at Breslau, then in Lower Silesia, now a part of Poland. Cassirer fled to England in 1933, and went to the U.S. in 1941. He was at Yale University and at Columbia University until his death in 1945. Cassirer worked on scientific philosophy, developing theories of mathematics, physics, and chemistry.

Max Wilhelm Dehn was born in Hamburg in 1878. He went to the U.S. in 1940, relatively late in his career and worked at St. Johns College from 1945-1952. Dehn was a mathematician who worked on intuitive geometry.

Luther Pfahler Eisenhart was born in York, Pa., in 1876. He was an instructor at Princeton from 1900-1945. Eisenhart contributed numerous articles to journals, most of which dealt with the advancement of knowledge of differential geometry.

Ernest David Hellinger was born in Striegau, Silesia, in 1883. Hellinger fled to the U.S. in 1939, and was an instructor in mathematics at Northwestern University from 1939-1948.

Karl Loewner was born in Lany, near Prague, Bohemia, in 1893. Loewner went to the U.S. in 1939. Part of his career was that of an instructor in mathematics at Stanford University (1951-1963).

Heinrich Maschke was born in Breslau, Silesia, in 1853. Maschke was one of the early mathematicians going to the U.S., in 1891. He had a post at the University of Chicago.

Amalie Emmy Noether was born in Erlangen, Bayern in 1882. She was the daughter of the well-known mathematician, Max Noether. Amalie Noether fled to the U.S. in 1933. She had a short career at Bryn Mawr, dying in 1935, but contributed some important papers on abstract algebra.

Hans Adolph Rademacher was born at Wandsbeck, Schleswig-Holstein, in 1892. Rademacher went to the U.S. in 1933, where he taught mathematics at Swarthmore College and at the University of Pennsylvania (1834-1969).

Tibor Radó was born in Budapest, Hungary in 1895. Radó was an early refugee before the onset of the Third Reich, arriving in the U.S. in 1929. Most of his U.S. career was as an instructor in mathematics at Ohio State (1930-1960). The family name is not German, but more likely Slavic.

Hans Reichenbach was born in Hamburg, in 1891. Reichenbach fled Germany in 1933, working at first in Turkey, and from 1938-1953, at the University of California at Los Angeles. His primary interest was the philosophy of science, involving the fields of mathematics and physics.

Richard Martin Edler von Mises was born at Lemberg, Galicia, in 1883. Von Mises fled to Boston in 1939 and continued a career in probability theories in mathematics at Harvard (1939-1953). In a timely fashion, von Mises also worked on the mechanics of powered flight; this information contributed to the war effort in World War II and later to space flight.

Johann von Neumann was born in Budapest, in 1903. Von Neumann was an instructor in mathematics and mathematical physics at Princeton University from 1930-1957.

Ernest Julius Wilczynski was born in Hamburg in 1876. He went to Chicago about 1890 and eventually became an educator in mathematics, with a specialization in geometry, at the University of Chicago. The family name reflects a north Slavic origin.

Aurel Wintner was born in Budapest, Hungary, in 1903. Wintner was an instructor in mathematics at Johns Hopkins University from 1930 until his death in 1958.

Metallurgy

Albert Arents was born in Clausthal (now Clausthal-Zellerfeld), Niedersachsen, in 1840. Arents went to Massachusetts in 1865. After becoming involved in metallurgy, he was a key figure in lead and silver smelting operations in the Rocky Mountains.

Edward Balbach was born in Karlsruhe, Baden, in 1839. The Balbach family went to the U.S. in 1850.

Frederic Anton Eilers was born in Laufenselden, near Wiesbaden, Hessen. He went to the U.S. in 1859. Like Arents, he was heavily involved in lead and silver smelting operations in the West and acquired the unofficial title of "dean of lead & silver smelting."

John Jacob Faesch was born in Kanton Basel, Switzerland, in 1729, and went to America in 1764. He was an "ironmaster" whose talents were critical to the success of the Revolutionary War.

George Washington Goetz was born in Milwaukee, in 1856. He was the son of German immigrant parents, the father being from Worms, Rheinland-Pfalz, and the mother from Erfurt, Thüringen. Goetz became a prominent metallurgist who specialized in iron and steel.

Peter Hasenclever was born in Remscheid, Nordrhein-Westfalen, in 1716. Hasenclever was in New York from 1764 to 1773, where he contributed to the iron manufacturing industry, then in its pioneering stages. In 1773, Hasenclever went to Silesia.

Heinrich Oscar Hofman was born in Heidelberg, in 1852, and went to the U.S. in 1881. Hofman used his extensive university training as a metallurgist in the lead smelting industry.

Frederick William Matthiessen was born in Altona, Schleswig-Holstein. Matthiessen went to New York in 1857 and was a metallurgist in the zinc industry. He also was a manufacturer whose company, the Western Clock Manufacturing Co., was a producer of the famous "Big Ben" alarm clock which sold in the millions.

Richard George Gottlob Moldenke was born in Watertown, Wisc., in 1864, as the son of Rev. Edward Frederick Moldenke who was cited in the Luthern Clergy section. The younger Moldenke became a noted metallurgist in Pittsburgh, Pa.

Johann Friedrich Overman was born in Elberfeld, Wuppertal, Nordrhein-Westfalen, about 1803. Overman was a metallurgist in the iron industry in Philadelphia. He was killed accidentally in 1852 by inhaling toxic fumes during a smelting process.

August Wilhelm Raht was born in Dillenburg, near Wiesbaden, Hessen, in 1843, and went to the U.S. in 1867. Raht was a top technical employee in the Guggenheim consortium. The consortium had enormous lead & silver smelting operations in Utah and elsewhere.

Physics

Peter Gabriel Bergmann was born in Berlin in 1915 and went to the U.S. in 1936. Bergmann was a theoretical physicist who was an assistant to Albert Einstein (see below) from 1936-1941.

Hans Albrecht Bethe was born in Strassburg, Elsaß, in 1906. Bethe went to the U.S. about 1935, and became a physicist at Cornell University. He was awarded a Nobel Prize in physics in 1967.

Felix Bloch was born in Zürich, Switzerland in 1905 and went to the U.S. in 1934. Bloch was an educator and physicist at Stanford University from 1934-1983. He received a Nobel Prize in physics in 1952.

Albert Einstein, the most notable of the Third Reich refugees, was born in Ulm, Baden-Württemberg, in 1879. In 1933, Einstein became the first academician at the Institute for Advanced Study which was associated with Princeton. In 1921, Einstein had been awarded the Nobel Prize in physics. He died at Princeton in 1955.

Richard Phillips Feynman was born in New York in 1918. He was a physicist at California Institute for Technology as from 1950. Feynman received the Nobel Prize in physics in 1965.

James Franck was born in Hamburg, in 1882. He went to the U.S. in 1935. He was a professor of physical chemistry at Johns Hopkins University from 1935-1938, and at the University of Chicago after 1938. Franck was awarded a Nobel prize in physics in 1925.

Philipp G. Frank was born in Vienna, Austria, in 1884 and fled to the U.S. in 1938. Frank was a professor of physics, of mathematics, and of the philosophy of science at Harvard University from 1938-1954.

Karl Eugen Guthe was born in Hannover, Niedersachsen, in 1866, and went to the Grand Rapids, Mich. in 1892.

Arthur Erich Haas was born at Brünn, Moravia, now Brno, Czechslovakia, and went to the U.S. in 1935. Haas was a Roman Catholic whose parents were Jewish. He was a professor of physics and of the history of physics at the University of Notre Dame from 1936-1941.

Victor Franz Hess was born at Schloss Waldstein, Styria, Austria in 1883, and went to the U.S. temporarily in 1921. A strict Roman Catholic, whose ideology conflicted with that of the Nazis, he went permanently to the U.S. in 1938. Hess was a physicist dealing with cosmic rays and an educator at Fordham University from 1938-1964. He was awarded a Nobel Prize in physics in 1936.

Robert Hofstadter was born in New York in 1915, and was associated with Stanford University, as from 1950. He received the Nobel Prize in physics in 1961.

Rudolf Walther Ladenburg was born in Kiel, Schleswig-Holstein, in 1882, and went to the U.S. in 1931. He was a professor of physics at Princeton from 1931-1950.

Fritz Wolfgang London was born at Breslau, Lower Silesia, now Wroclaw, Poland, in 1900. He was a professor of physics and theoretical chemistry at Duke University from 1939-1954.

Maria Goeppert Mayer was born at Kattowitz, Schlesien, now Katowice, Poland, in 1906. She fled to the U.S. in 1930 where she joined the staff of Johns Hopkins, among other organizations. In 1963, she was awarded the Nobel Prize in physics.

Albert Abraham Michelson was born at Strelno, Westpreußen, now Strzelno, Poland, in 1852. A physicist, Michelson went to the U.S. in 1854 and worked mainly in California. He is known for observations on the velocity of light and for optical interference. Michelson received a Nobel Prize in physics in 1907.

Francis Eugene Nipher was born in Port Bryon, N.Y. in 1847. He was the great-grandson of Michael Niver who went to America from Württemberg in 1756. Nipher was a noted physicist at Washington University in St. Louis.

Julius Robert Oppenheimer was born in New York in 1904. Oppenheimer gained fame as a nuclear physicist at the University of California at Berkeley and at California Institute of Technology (1929-1947). He was also director of the famous Institute for Advanced Science at Princeton from 1947 until his death in 1966. As the leader of the Manhattan Project, Oppenheimer was involved heavily in atomic bomb research.

Isidor Isaac Rabi was born in Rymanow, then in Austrian territory, in 1898 and went to the U.S. as an infant. He was a professor of physics at Columbia University for more than three decades, beginning in 1929. Rabi was awarded a Nobel Prize in physics in 1944.

Burton Richter was born in New York in 1931. He was a physicist at Stanford University, as from 1956. In 1976, Richter was awarded a Nobel Prize in physics.

Floyd Karker Richtmyer was born at Cobleskill, N.Y., in 1881. He was a physicist at Cornell University from 1911-1939. Richtmyer is noted for his pioneering work on X-ray spectra.

John Robert Schrieffer was born at Oak Park, Ill., in 1931. He was a physicist at the University of Pennsylvania, as from 1962. Schrieffer received the Nobel Prize in physics in 1972.

Otto Stern was born in Sohrau, Silesia, in 1888. He fled in 1933 to Pittsburgh where he was a physicist at the Carnegie Institute. In 1943, Stern received a Nobel Prize in physics.

Eugene Paul Wigner was born in Budapest, Hungary, in 1902, and fled to the U.S. in 1930. Wigner received a Nobel Prize in physics in 1963.

TABLE 18
DIRECTORY OF NATURAL SCIENCES

Botany
Braun, Emma Lucy (1889-1971)
1. Dufour, John James (c. 1763-1827)
1. Engelmann, Johann Georg (1809-1884)
1. Fernow, Bernhard Edward (1851-1923)
2. Gideon, Peter Miller (1820-1899)
Goff, Emmett Stull (1852-1902)
1. Hansen, George (1863-1908)
4. Harshberger, John William (1869-1929)
Heller, Amos Arthur (1867-1944)
1. Husmann, George (1827-1902)
Kauffman, Calvin Henry (1869-1931)
1. Kellerman, Karl Frederic (1879-1934)
3. Klippart, John Hancock (1825-1878)
Kraemer, Henry (1868-1924)
1. Lindheimer, Ferdinand Jacob (1801-1879)
1. Mohr, Charles Theodore (1824-1901)
Nehrling, Arno Herbert (1886-1974)
2. Pammel, Louis Hermann (1862-1931)
1. Pilat, Ignaz Anton (1820-1870)
1. Pursh, Friedrich Traugott (1774-1820)
1. Rock, John (1836-1904) (Roch)
2. Roeding, George Christian (1868-1928)
1. Roth, Filbert (1858-1925)
1. Weidenmann, Jacob (1829-1893)

Entomology
1. Grote, August Radcliffe (1841-1903)
1. Hagen, Hermann August (1817-1893)
3. Horn, George Henry (1840-1897)
1. Knab, Frederick (1865-1918)
5. Lintner, Joseph Albert (1822-1898)
1. Schwarz, Eugene Amandus (1844-1928)
2. Smith, John Bernhard (1858-1912) (Schmidt)
4. Thomas, Cyrus (1825-1910)

Biochemistry, Physiology, Bacteriology, Genetics
1. Bergmann, Max (1886-1944), biochemistry
1. Bloch, Konrad Emil (1912-), biochemistry
Cohn, Edwin Joseph (1892-1953), biochemistry
1. Cori, Gerty Theresa Radnitz (1896-1957), biochemistry
1. Delbrück, Max (1906-1981), physiology
1. Djerassi, Carl (1923-), biochemistry
Edelman, Gerald Maurice (1929-), biochemistry

2. Erlanger, Joseph (1874-1965), physiology
3. Ernst, Harold Clarence (1856-1922), bacteriology
1. Fischer, Hermann Otto Laurenz (1888-1960), biochemistry
   Goldstein, Joseph Leonard (1940-), molecular genetics
2. Hahn, Dorothy Anna (1876-1950), biochemistry
1. Hecht, Selig (1892-1947)
2. Hemmeter, John Conrad (1863-1931), physiology
   Hershey, Alfred Day (1908-), genetics
2. Hyde, Ida Henrietta (1857-1945), physiology (Heidenheimer)
2. Koch, Fred Conrad (1876-1948)
6. Kohler, Elmer Peter (1865-1938), biochemistry
   Kornberg, Arthur (1918-), biochemistry
1. Lipman, Fritz Albert (1899-), biochemistry
1. Loeb, Jacques (1859-1924), physiology
1. Loewi, Otto (1893-1961), physiology
2. Mendel, Lafayette Benedict (1872-1935), physiology
1. Meyerhof, Otto (1884-1951), biochemistry
   Moyer, Andrew J. (1899-1959), microbiology
   Muller, Hermann Joseph (1890-1967), genetics
   Nirenberg, Marshall Warren (1927-), biochemistry
2. Novy, Frederick George (1864-1957), microbiology
   Ott, Isaac (1847-1916), physiology
2. Pauling, Linus Carl (1901-1994)
2. Schneider, Albert (1863-1928), bacteriology
1. Schoenheimer, Rudolf (1898-1941), biochemistry
   Snell, George Davis (1903-), genetics
   Stein, William H. (1911-1980), biochemistry
5. Sternberg, George Miller (1838-1915), bacteriology
4. Stine, Charles Milton Altland (1882-1954), biochemistry
2. Tishler, Max (1906-1989), biochemistry
2. Wald, George (1906-), physiology
2. Witthaus, Rudolph August (1846-1915), biochemistry

Zoology

1. Agassiz, Alexander Emmanuel Rodolphe (1835-1910)
1. Eigenmann, Carl H. (1863-1927)
1. Girard, Charles Frédéric (1822-1895)
1. Goldschmidt, Richard Benedict (1878-1958)
4. Guyer, Michael Frederic (1874-1959)
   Haldeman, Samuel Steman (1812-1880)
4. Himes, Charles Francis (1838-1918)
4. Mayor, Alfred Goldsborough (1868-1922) (Mayer)
1. Mayr, Ernst (1904-)
   Nehrling, Henry (1853-1929)
   Nicholas, John Spangler (1895-1953)
1. Pourtalès, Louis Francois de (1823-1880)

Veterinary Science
Kelser, Raymond Alexander (1892-1952)
2. Smith, Theobald (1859-1934)

Archeology, Anthropology
2. Bade, William Frederic (1871-1936)
1. Boas, Franz (1858-1942)
   Goldman, Hetty (1881-1972)
3. Powdermaker, Hortense (1896-1970)
   Reichard, Gladys Amand (1893-1955)
   Richter, Gisela Marie Augusta (1888-1972)
1. Sapir, Edward (1884-1939)
   Van Deman, Esther Boise (1862-1937)

Astronomy
Baade, Wilhelm Heinrich Walter (1893-1960)
Eckert, Wallace John (1902-1971)
1. Peters, Christian Heinrich Friedrich (1813-1890)
1. Powalky, Karl Rudolph (1817-1881)
1. Schaeberle, John Martin (1853-1924)
2. Schlesinger, Frank (1871-1943)
1. Schwarzschild, Martin (1912-)
   Weinberg, Steven (1933-)

Geology, Geodesy, Paleontology
1. Agassiz, Jean Louis Rodolphe (1807-1873)
   Bassler, Raymond Smith (1878-1961)
2. Becker, George Ferdinand (1847-1919)
1. Boll, Jacob (1828-1880)
   Bucher, Walter Herman (1889-1965)
4. Diller, Joseph Silas (1850-1928) (Tueller)
1. Edinger, Johanna Gabrielle Ottelie (1897-1967)
1. Eimbeck, William (1841-1909)
   Fankuchen, Isidor (1905-1964)
2. Foerste, August Frederick (1862-1936)
3. Grabau, Amadeus William (1870-1946)
1. Gutenberg, Beno (1889-1960)
1. Guyot, Arnold Henry (1807-1884)
1. Hassler, Ferdinand Rudolph (1770-1843)
1. Heilprin, Angelo (1853-1907)
1. Hilgard, Eugene Woldemar (1833-1916)
1. Hilgard, Julius Erasmus (1825-1891)
3. Kleinpell, Robert Minssen (1905-1985)
   Krumbein, William Christian (1902-1979)
   Kunz, George Frederick (1856-1932)
4. Leidy, Joseph (1823-1891) (Leydig)
1. Lesquereux, Leo (1806-1889)

5. Marbut, Curtis Fletcher (1863-1935)
2. Meinzer, Oscar Edward (1876-1948)
   Richter, Charles Francis (1900-1985)
1. Roemer, Karl Ferdinand (1818-1891)
1. Ruedemann, Rudolf (1864-1956)
1. Schott, Charles Anthony (1826-1901)
2. Schuchert, Charles (1858-1942)
   Shimer, Hervey Woodburn (1872-1965) (Scheimer)
   Shrock, Robert Rakes (1904-1993)
   Tondorf, Frances Anthony (1870-1929)
2. Twenhofel, William Henry (1875-1957)
2. Ulrich, Edward Oscar (1857-1944)
3. Wachsmuth, Charles (1829-1896)
4. Wieland, George Reber (1865-1953)

Inorganic Chemistry
1. Genth, Friedrich Augustus Ludwig Karl Wilhelm
   (1820-1893)
2. Grasselli, Caesar Augustin (1850-1927)
1. Goessmann, Charles Anthony (1827-1910)
   Hauptman, Herbert Aaron (1917-)
2. Hillebrand, William Francis (1853-1925)
2. Kahlenberg, Lewis Albrecht (1870-1941)
1. Koenig, Georg Augustus (1844-1913)
   Kraus, Charles August (1875-1967)
2. Leffmann, Henry (1847-1930)
2. Loeb, Morris (1863-1912)
1. Nef, John Ulric (1862-1915)
2. Stieglitz, Julius (1867-1937)
2. Volwiler, Ernest Henry (1893-1992)
2. Weber, Henry Adam (1845-1912)
2. Wiechmann, Ferdinand Gerhard (1858-1919)
4. Wurtz, Henry (c.1828-1910)

Mathematics
1. Cajori, Florian (1859-1930)
1. Cassirer, Ernst Alfred (1872-1945)
1. Dehn, Max Wilhelm (1878-1952)
5. Eisenhart, Luther Pfahler (1876-1965)
1. Flügge-Lotz, Irmgard (1903-1974)
1. Geiringer, Hilda (1893-1973)
2. Green, Gabriel Marcus (1891-1919)
1. Hellinger, Ernst David (1883-1950)
1. Loewner, Karl, (1893-1968)
1. Maschke, Heinrich (1853-1908)
1. Noether Amalie Emmy (1882-1935)
1. Rademacher, Hans Adolph (1892-1969)

1. Radó, Tibor (1895-1965)
1. Reichenbach, Hans (1891-1953)
1. von Neumann, Johann (1903-1957)
1. von Mises, Richard Martin Edler (1883-1953)
1. Weyl, Hermann Claus Hugo (1885-1955)
1. Wilczyski, Ernest Julius (1876-1932)
1. Wintner, Aurel (1903-1958)

Metallurgy
1. Arents, Albert (1840-1914)
1. Balbach, Edward (1839-1910)
1. Eilers, Frederic Anton (1839-1917)
1. Faesch, John Jacob (1729-1799)
2. Goetz, George Washington (1856-1897)
1. Hasenclever, Peter (1716-1793)
1. Hofman, Heinrich Oscar (1852-1924)
1. Matthiessen, Frederick William (1835-1918)
4. Moldenke, Richard George Gottlob (1864-1930)
1. Overman, Johann Friedrich (c.1803-1852)
1. Raht, August Wilhelm (1843-1916)

Physics
2. Barus, Carl (1856-1935)
2. Bauer, Louis Agricola (1865-1932)
1. Bergmann, Peter Gabriel (1915-)
1. Bethe, Hans Albrecht (1906-)
1. Bloch, Felix (1905-1983)
   Coblentz, William Weber (1873-1962)
1. Einstein, Albert (1879-1955)
   Feynman, Richard Phillips (1918-1988)
1. Franck, James (1882-1964)
1. Frank, Philipp G. (1884-1966)
1. Guthe, Karl Eugen (1866-1915)
1. Haas, Arthur Erich (1884-1941)
1. Hess, Victor Franz (1883-1964)
   Hofstadter, Robert (1915-1990)
1. Ladenburg, Rudolf Walter (1882-1952)
1. London, Fritz Wolfgang (1900-1954)
3. Mayer, Alfred Marshall (1836-1897)
1. Mayer, Maria Goeppert (1906-1972)
2. Meggers, William Frederick (1888-1966)
1. Michelson, Albert Abraham (1852-1931)
1. Mueller, Erwin Wilhelm (1911-1977)
4. Nipher, Francis Eugene (1847-1926)
2. Oppenheimer, Julius Robert (1904-1967)
1. Rabi, Isidor Isaac (1898-1988)
   Richter, Burton (1931-)

Richtmyer, Floyd Karker (1881-1939)
Schrieffer, John Robert (1931-)
1. Steinberger, Jack (1921-)
1. Stern, Otto (1888-1969)
1. Szilard, Leo (1898-1964)
1. Teller, Edward (1908-)
2. Waidner, Charles William (1873-1922)
1. Wigner, Eugene Paul (1902-)

Code:
1. = 1st Generation in America
2. = 2nd Generation
3. = 3rd or more Generation, etc.

Men and Women at War

Times of Conflict

From the time of the Revolutionary War in 1775-1783 to World War II in 1941-1945, the role of the Germans in five major American wars is decidedly contradictory. During the course of American history, the Germans in general were, in the 18th century, against freedom, then in the 19th century neutral, and later decidedly for, and finally in the 20th century, indirectly against freedom.

In the 17th and 18th centuries, the nobility in Germany, for the most part, were still firmly in control. However, when former Austrian princess Marie Antoinette went to the guillotine in Paris in 1793 through the efforts of the republicans, the tide had turned and a new era dawned. The 1820s and 1830s in Germany were marked by the slow contagion of republicanism which reached its highpoint, however weak and ineffectual in Germany, in 1848. The defeat of the republicans and their allies in 1848 had important consequences which carried over to the United States and indirectly contributed much to the U.S. Civil War. Another new era began in the 1870s, and lasted through two major 20th century wars. Efforts at unifying Germany took the form of various types of nationalism, again with important consequences for the United States.

The Eighteenth Century

In 1714, a peculiar event happened in Europe which was to have important consequences in America. The elector Georg of Hannover became King George I of England. The ongoing and close union of the two houses involved England in German politics for the better part of the century, and vice versa.

The 847 or so "Palatine" families who went to New York in 1710, were soon pressed into military service. In 1711, the German-Americans living along the Hudson Valley formed a group called Palatine Volunteers to Canada. This military group was the size of a company, or about 100 soldiers.

Thereafter, the British regularly conscripted descendants of the N.Y. Palatines for service in America. For instance, various members of the famous Hirchemer (Herkimer, Horchheimer) family were drafted in 1711, 1733 and in 1767.

In 1758, the English General James Wolfe (1727-1759) took an army to Canada to defend English claims against the French. German mercenaries accompanied Wolfe's army and after the war, remained in America. A good example is the Hagermann family of New York who claim descent from one of these soldiers. A Hagermann descendant eventually became the territorial governer of New Mexico, from 1906 to 1907.

During the Revolutionary War of 1775-1783, a considerable number of German mercenaries were in the employ of the English government. The House of Hannover was primarily responsible for providing these mercenaries, the majority of which came from "Hesse-Cassel" or "Hesse-Hanau." Some 12,000 of the Hessian troops were commanded by General Leopold Philip de Heister (1707-1777), and after his early recall, by Barton Wilhelm von Knyphausen (1716-1800).

The total number of Germans sent to America during that war, by reliable estimates, was about 30,000 men, a considerable number for that time. About 5,000 former soldiers remained in America after the war, of which at least half went to receptive communities in Canada. The fate of most of the 2,500 or so German soldiers remaining in America has never been adequately accounted for: doubtless, many quietly assumed new roles, married local girls, and settled into American society. One notable example, Philipp Klipstein (or Klippstein), a surgeon, settled in Westchester, Va. after the War. Unconfirmed reports of other American family names which were derived from Hessian soldiers serving in the British forces included: De Bardeleben (German = von Bardaleben), Eckhard (or Eckhardt), Kellerman(n), Hise (German = Heis, Heisse), Knisely (German = Kneissel), Ludwig, Melsheimer (German = Meltzheimer), Snyder (German = Schneider), and Wangenheim (von Wangenheim).

The German participation in the Revolutionary War was not confined to the large Hessian contingent. In 1780, Count Christian von Forbach (1752-1817) led the Régiment Royal Deux-Pont as part of an approximately 5,000 man army which fought on the American side. This regiment, consisting of about 1,000 men from the area of Zweibrücken in the southern part of the Pfalz, took part in the critical Battle of Yorktown, Va. They helped capture a vital part of the English army, consisting of some 8,000 English and Hessian soldiers. After the war a small number of the Zweibrücken regiment remained in America as, for instance, John Jakob Ernst Klippart.

French soldiers, led by Marquis de Lafayette (1757-1834) and by Count de Rochambeau (1725-1807), played a decisive role in the American fight for freedom. Lafayette served the American forces from 1777-1783 and became a major general. Rochambeau served from 1780-1783 and became a lieutenant general. In the last major battle of the Revolutionary War, at Yorktown, Lafayette had at his command some 2,000 men, while Rochambeau had about 5,000 men under his command. Many of these forces were French, some with German names. In one well documented case, one by the German family name of Francis Joseph Mettauer, from Alsace, went to

America with Rochambeau in 1780 as a surgeon and stayed on to found a prominent American family by that name.

Two brothers, Bernard Gratz, merchant of Baltimore, and Michael Gratz, merchant of Philadelphia, played an important role in helping to finance the Revolutionary War. They had gone to the America about 1754. Both brothers are listed in the chapter on finance. Another financier, Haym Salomon from Lissa (perhaps either the city in Schlesien or the village in Posen) was another prominent German-American. In America, about 1773, Salomon became a Philadelphia merchant and reportedly later loaned $650,000 to the new American government, an enormous sum in those days. The money was never repaid even though often claimed by his descendants; Salomon himself died as a debtor.

Headless Hessian Soldier or Reality?

In 1819-1820 when Washington Irving (1783-1858), of English origin, wrote his tale "The Legend of Sleepy Hollow," along with other tales, he unwittingly promoted a tradition which was to prove often false and sometimes downright embarassing. In this tale, which was set in New York's Hudson Valley, a "headless Hessian trouper" was one of the main characters. Since that time, an amazing number of Americans have claimed descent from a Hessian officer, headless or not.

The myth of being descended from a Hessian officer is exemplified by the reported lineage of the Custer family, a family which supplied several well known members to the Union forces in the Civil War, and later to the Indian Wars. In this myth, the ancestral Custer (or Kuster) was long thought to be one Emanuel Custer, a supposed Hessian officer serving under the British forces during the Revolutionary War. Grandsons of an Emanuel Custer were documented, properly, as being the famous George Armstrong Custer and Thomas Ward Custer, both killed in one quick battle with the Sioux Indians in Montana in 1876. For nearly a century, descendants of Emanuel Custer could claim membership in the Headless Horseman Society. A few still do!

The first biographies of George Armstrong Custer, written in 1876, perpetuated the myth. Since then, the myth was carried by many prominent German-American historians, including that in a 1909 book by the recognized German-American authority Albert B. Faust. In the third edition of his monumental *The German Element in the United States*, dated 1927, Faust finally admitted that Emanuel may not have been the immigrant ancestor. So strong was the myth, however, that the normally reliable *Dictionary of American Biography*, in 1930, continued to recognize Emanuel Custer as a Hessian soldier, and as the immigrant ancestor.

After nearly a century of research, Custer family historians (notably Milo Custer and Chester E. Custer) provided reasonably firm evidence, albeit in privately printed publications, that Emanuel fought on the American side in the Revolutionary War, was not Hessian, was not an officer, and was not an immigrant. The real immigrant was one Paulus Küster who went to Germantown, Pa., about 1690.

Now, of course, it is possible to search the nearly complete, six volume register of Hessian soldiers, whose volumes were compiled from 1972-1987 by members of the Archivschule Marburg. This computerized listing shows seven individuals under the German family name Kuester, but none by the given name Emanuel. A search of lists of the 2,459 mercenaries in the Ansbach-Bayreuth troops, which was published by Erhard Städtler in 1956, likewise shows no Küster among the deserters, turncoats and opportunists.

The Nineteenth Century

During the second war for independence, the War of 1812 (1812-1815), Germans appeared to have played no major role and therefore were essentially neutral. The Germans were, in fact, recovering from the effects in Europe of the French Wars of Independence and the Napoleonic Wars which combined, lasted from 1792-1815.

Marks of Excellence

The United States was relatively late in developing its own army and navy. The prestigious U.S. Military Academy, often referred to simply as "Westpoint," was not established formally until 1802, and the U.S. Naval Academy at Annapolis was not authorized until 1845. Thereafter, with some notable exceptions, in order to attain the rank of general or admiral in the regular forces, it was mandatory to have attended either Westpoint or Annapolis.

Another measure of military achievement is being granted the Medal of Honor, America's highest medal award. The Medal of Honor was first awarded to Union soldiers and sailors during the Civil War of 1861-1865. Through the Vietnam War, which lasted until 1973, only 3,394 individuals received the award, according to the authoritative 1985 book titled *Above and Beyond, A History of the Medal of Honor from the Civil War to Vietnam* (Boston Publishing Co., Boston, Mass.).

Of the total awards, about 270 names are recognizable as German-American. One imagines that many more names have been altered during the course of time to obscure their ethnic origin. Distinguished German-American recipients of the Medal of Honor and dates of their heroic action include: 2nd Lt. Thomas W. Custer (1865), Col. John F. Hartranft (1861), Col. Galusha Pennypacker (1861-1865), 1st Lt. Frederick Phisterer (1863), Capt. Theophilus F. Rodenbough (1861-1865), 1st Lt. Theodore Schwan (1861-1865), Major General Daniel E. Sickles (1863), Major General Julius Stahel (1864), Major Ernst M. P. von Vegesack (1862), Major John Green (1873), 1st Lt. Marion P. Maus (1890), 1st Lt. Edward V. Rickenbacker (1917-1918), Sargeant Herman Hannekin (1919-1920), and 1st Lt. Christian F. Schilt (1928).

Some received the award decades after the fact, as for instance, Lt. Schwan, whose award was given in 1898 for combat service in 1864. In

1901, Schwan was promoted to Brigadier General, and in 1916, to Major General, USA.

The Impact of the Baden Revolt

Indirectly, the so-called Baden Revolt in Germany in 1848-49, together with civil unrest in Austria, in Switzerland, in Croatia and other parts of Europe, had a major role for the fate of America. The massive number of German migrants to America in the 1840s and 1850s provided America with many dissidents who were to support both directly and indirectly the Union cause in the American Civil War of 1861-1865.

Actual fighting in the Baden Revolt began in the area of Heidelberg in 1848 and ended with the twenty-three day seige of the castle at Rastatt in July, 1949. The Prussians were victorious. Most of the rebels survived, fleeing to Switzerland. The Swiss were cordial initially, but some months later were anxious to have the Germans move on. An agreement was reached with French authorities for a goodly number of rebels to be transported from Le Havre to New York. In one well documented case, 600 rebels boarded the ship Havre in the French port of Le Havre on September 1, 1850, and reached New York twenty-two days later.

Of course, these migrants overtaxed employment opportunities in New York as well as the city's infrastructure and again were encouraged to move. Many went to Buffalo, to Pittsburgh, and to Cincinnati, where they settled. However, encouraged by good wages in these localities, they soon provided for friends and relatives in multiple numbers to join them. Once again, the new communities could not contain all the entrants and the Germans spread further, to Louisville, to St. Louis, to Chicago, and to smaller places in between. Eventually they moved in droves to Milwaukee and to Minneapolis.

Many rebel leaders went to America along with the troops. The most noteworthy of these leaders was Carl Schurz. There were a host of others who all played a major role in uniting the Germans, many of whom spoke little English, behind Lincoln's drive for the presidency and behind the Union cause when war was declared. At the beginning of the Civil War, regiments from New York, Ohio, Indiana, and Illinois were composed entirely of Germans. There were also many Pennsylvania German volunteers whose ancestors had settled there in the previous century.

The Civil War: Brother Against Brother

The Civil War produced several types of Union generals. Some twenty-four German-Americans merited the title of major general as a result of their service in the Union army, a title which was then the army's highest rank. Eight of these individuals were foreign-born. But they were far from being of the same rank. The well-defined pecking order ranged from the Regular Army (abbreviated USA), down through the Volunteers (abbreviated USV), the National Guard, the Militia, and "Brevet" major general. Numerous German-Americans were brigadier generals in the Union army and at least three who served in the Civil War eventually became admirals.

German-American financiers in New York likewise played a major role in selling bonds in the key financial centers of Frankfurt and Hamburg. Key men in this effort were Solomon L. Loeb, Jacob Henry Schiff, Jesse Seligman, and Joseph Seligman; these men are cited in some detail in the financial section.

Even though some nine individuals with German names served as generals in the Confederate forces, the relatively few Germans living in the South had barely perceptible impact on the outcome of the war.

The Twentieth Century: Where Poppies Grow

Descendants of the five million plus German migrants of the 19th century were once again called upon to show their loyalty to the new homeland, twice, in World War I, and in World War II. They were to provide a nearly solid front. Doubtless, many cousins fought tooth and nail against each other. The financiers in New York, many of them descendants of former German Jews, were also united in this front. In the end, of course, might and reason prevailed.

Although the Americans supported the Allied effort in World War I from its beginning in 1914, American soldiers were not committed to combat until 1917. One of those dying in World War I, the eternal optimist, Alfred Joyce Kilmer, had written a deceptively simple little poem which appealed to millions of ordinary Americans. Kilmer had a fair element of German blood in his veins as biographers maintain, for he was a seventh generation descendant of one Georg Kuhlmann who went from "Hesse-Cassel" to New York in 1710. The Kilmer poem, first published by Putnam Publishers, N.Y., in 1913, reads (first stanza only):

I think that I shall never see
A poem as lively as a tree

A tree whose hungry mouth is prest
Against the earth's sweet flowing breast;

A tree that looks at God all day,
And lifts her leafy arms to pray;

A tree that may in Summer wear
A nest of robins in her hair;

Upon whose bosom snow has lain;
Who intimately lives with rain.

Poems are made by fools like me,
But only God can make a tree.

Sergeant Kilmer was killed in action on July 30, 1918, at Chateau Thierry, in France.

The Germans had their war hero too in the person of Freiherr Manfred Albrecht von Richthofen, the German aviator who downed eighty Allied planes. The legendary "Red Baron" was held in awe by school boys everywhere, even in America, where to this day he remains as somewhat of a cult hero. First lieutenant von Richthofen was killed in combat on the unlucky day of April 21, 1918, near Amiens, France.

For these two heroes, World War I ended just a few months too late. The Armistice was signed on November 11, 1918.

Ironically, in 1915, the Scottish-Canadian John McCrae (1872-1918) wrote an equally simple little poem which had foreseen the deaths of these two heros and that of many others. The McCrae vision reads:

> In Flanders fields the poppies blow
> Between the crosses, row on row,
> That mark our place; and in the sky
> The larks, still bravely singing, fly
> Scarce heard amid the guns below.
>
> We are the Dead. Short days ago
> We lived, felt dawn, saw sunset glow,
> Loved and were loved, and now we lie
> In Flanders fields.
>
> Take up our quarrel with the foe:
> To you from failing hands we throw
> The torch; be yours to hold it high.
> If ye break faith with us who die
> We shall not sleep, though poppies grow
> In Flanders fields.

Each May, the European wild poppy, known in scientific terms as *Papaver rhoeas*, springs into vivid full bloom throughout the countryside of Germany. The flowers occur in bright orange-red to scarlet colors, and thus often blood-red, in patches of a half dozen or so, or occasionally as a field of thousands of blooms. They are a reminder of the past, the present, and the future. An old German proverb says that each wild poppy reflects a fallen soldier. In the United States, Veteran's Day is marked by the sale of artificial wild poppies. Because of these events, the European wild poppy approached a status symbol almost as an American national flower.

Perhaps McCrae had a premonition. He also did not survive the end of the World War I. Lt. Colonel McCrae was a physician attached to an Allied military hospital in Boulogne, France, and died of pneumonia on Jan 28, 1918. Be that as it may, let us examine the role of typical German-Americans in the various American wars.

German Mercenaries in the British Armies (1756-1778)

Henry Bouquet joined the ranks of British troops. The family name reflects the family's origin from the village of Rolle, in the French-speaking part, being Kanton Vaud, Switzerland. Bouquet was sent to America in 1756. Among other duties, he helped build "Forbes Road," one of the first man-made trails across Pennsylvania.

Count Carl Emil Kurt von Donap, commander of a Hessian brigade in America under the British, was killed in combat at the battle of Fort Mercier at Red Bank, N.Y., on Oct. 25, 1777.

John Reed was another soldier of fortune who apparently was a German mercenary in the employee of George III, King of England from 1760 to 1820. Sometime during the Revolutionary War, Reed seems to have deserted the ranks of Hessen soldiers and settled in North Carolina. Reed married Sarah Kiser, who came from a German immigrant family. Reed was reportedly unable to read and write, but discovered the Reed gold mine who production from 1803-1845 amounted to some $10 million. Reed died in 1845 in North Carolina.

John David Schöpf, from Wunsiedel, Bayern, was sent to America in June, 1777 as a surgeon in the Ansbach regiment and remained in the British army for six years. After release from service, he traveled for two years through the eastern part of the United States, collecting data for a travelogue which was published in 1788 in Erlangen, Bayern. Schöpf's work included some of the earliest description of American geology. Schöpf died in 1800, in Germany.

Revolutionary War (1775-1783)

American battle deaths during the Revolutionary War are cited in one case as being 4,435, and in another case as 7,174. Total service deaths may have been as high as 25,674, a figure which includes substantial fatalities from disease, cold weather, and malnutrition. The German-American contribution to this war includes the following individuals, most of whom survived.

John Philip De Haas, born about 1735 in Holland, was the descendant of Baron Christian de Haas of Brandenburg, Prussia. De Haas went in 1737 as an infant with his father to Philadelphia who later settled in Lancaster Co., Pa. De Haas attained the rank of brigadier general during the Revolutionary War.

Nicholas Herkimer was born in 1728 in Herkimer, N.Y. His father had come from the Palatinate about 1725. Herkimer also attained the rank of brigadier general and died in August, 1777 of battle wounds. The family name obviously is altered from Herchheimer.

Daniel Hiester had a varied career as farmer, businessman, congressman, and brigiadier general in the militia. Hiester was born in Montgomery Co., Pa. of as German immigrant father who had come from Elsoff, Westfalen, in

1737. Biographers occasionally use the preferred German spelling of Heister.

Johann Kalb was born in Erlangen, Bayern in 1721 and went to Philadelphia on two occasions, in 1768 and 1777. During the latter trip he was given the rank of general and died in 1780 in New Jersey of battle wounds. Kalb apparently assumed the title of "Baron de Kalb" as a result of his prior service with French military forces.

Christopher Ludwick was born in Giessen, Hessen in 1720. He was noted as a ardent patriot having arrived in Philadelphia about 1753. Ludwick achieved the title of superintendent of bakers in the Continental Army. Legends relate that Ludwick convinced hundreds of Hessen mercenaries to desert their employ in the English army.

Mary Ludwig Hays McCauley, Revolutionary heroine better known as "Molly Pitcher," was the daughter of Johann Georg Ludwig Haas (or Heis) who had come from the Palatinate in 1752. In 1778, at the Battle of Monmouth, Molly Pitcher was reported to have delivered water to the thirsty troops until her husband was wounded whereupon she took up his arms and continued the battle. At least one account indicates that there were various "Molly Pitchers" in the Revolutionary War of which McCauley was the best known. At any rate, a monument was erected at the Monmouth Battlefield State Park in Freehold, N.J. in the honor of this distinguished German-American.

John Peter Gabriel Muhlenberg was the son of the famous immigrant Luthern minister, cited in the section on clergy. Muhlenberg achieved the rank of major-general.

Otto Bodo, born in 1717 in Scharzfels am Harz, Niedersachsen, arrived in America in 1755. Bodo became the senior surgeon in the Continental Army and served six years. Several generations of Bodo descendants have been acknowledged as accomplished physicians.

Baron Friedrich Wilhelm Ludolf Gerhard Augustin von Steuben was a professional soldier who arrived in America during the dark days of the early part of the war. Von Steuben was given the title of inspector general by Washington and made responsible for training and organizing a motley crowd of non-disciplined troops. Von Steuben was born in Magdeburg, Sachsen-Anhalt, and died in 1794 in New York. The Steuben House Museum is located at River Edge, Bergen Co., N.J. A Steuben Monument was erected in 1910 in Washington, D.C.

Henry Wisner was born in 1720 in New York as the son of a Swiss immigrant who had arrived in 1714. In 1774, Wisner became a member of the Continental Congress; he made a large contribution in the drive for independence through his ownership of powder mills in Ulster and Orange Counties, N.Y.

David Ziegler was a pioneer and soldier who arrived in Pennsylvania in 1774. Born in Heidelberg in 1748, Ziegler served with the Continental Army from 1776-1783 and with the U.S. Army from 1784-1792.

War of 1812 (1812-1815)

Few prominent German-American names are recorded for this war. One exception is that of George Michael Bedinger. He was the grandson of Adam Büdinger, an early immigrant from Alsace. Bedinger, born in 1756 in York Co., Pa., acquired a reputation as a soldier and pioneer, and, later, congressman of Pennsylvania.

Civil War - Union Forces (1861-1865)

One of the most interesting and concise summaries of the Civil War was printed in 1990 under the editorship of Frances H. Kennedy. The book title is *The Civil War Battlefield Guide* (Houghton Mifflin Co., Boston). This book shows Union deaths as 364,511, and Union wounded as 281,881. Many deaths were the result of disease (often described as "camp fever"), cold weather, malnutrition and other indirect factors. The Civil War was a tragedy which pitted West Point class mates against each other. One often cited case is that of Union General George Armstrong Custer who fought many skirmishes against Confederate General Thomas Lafayette Rosser.

On occasion, the Civil War pitted close relative against close relative. The sons of immigrant Franz Lieber, cited in the section on government, were one such case. Two of his sons, Hamilton and Guido Norman, fought on the Union side. Hamilton lost an arm in combat; after the war, Guido Norman remained in the army and eventually became a brigadier general, USA. A third son, Oscar Norman (1830-1862) fought on the Confederate side and was killed at Williamsville, Va.

The Civil War was an American war in which generals faced the same hazards as regular troups. German-Americans who were either killed or wounded in combat, or who died of war related injury or illness included Union Generals: Louis Blenker, Henry Bohlen, William High Keim, Alexander von Schimmelpfennig, and Samuel Koscinzko Zook. In some ways, those who died in battle were the lucky ones. Countless others lost arms and legs (i.e., Generals Theophilus Francis Rodenbough, Daniel Edgar Sickles, Hugo Wangelin, and Max Weber) and thus had to adapt to a strange and occasionally terrifying new world. A goodly number acquired malaria, yellow fever, and other tropical diseases which tormented them for life. The majority of generals were wounded in combat, some several times.

The directory shows eighty prominent German-Americans in this group of which twenty-one were foreign born. Most prominent of those foreign born were: Louis Blenker, Friedrich Karl Franz Hecker, August Valentine Kautz, Konrad Krez, William C. Kueffner, Peter Joseph Osterhaus, Frederick Pfisterer, Carl Schurz, Franz Sigel, John Eugene Smith, Alexander von Schimmelpfennig, Alexander von Schrader, and August Willich.

Blenker, Hecker, Krez, Osterhaus, Schurz, Sigel, von Schimmelpfennig and Willich were all prominent leaders in the Baden Revolt of 1848-1849; they escaped to America in the early 1850s where their experience was used to great advantage in the Civil War. Most became generals in the Union army.

Peter Osterhaus was rated as one of the better officers. Osterhaus and John Eugene Smith led the successful charge in the Battle of Missionary Ridge, near Chattanooga, a battle which marked the beginning of the end of Confederate hopes for success. Osterhaus served from 1861-1866 and achieved status as a major general of the Volunteers. After the war, he served as a consul in Lyon, France, and later in Mannheim, Germany. He was promoted to brigadier general, USA, in 1905.

Carl Schurz was not an especially able military man, but after arrival in America in 1852, he initially had a law office in Milwaukee and then achieved a remarkable career as a skilled politician and newspaper man. Schurz was a close associate of Lincoln and convinced hundreds of thousands of German-Americans to support Lincoln in his drive for the presidency. In the Army, Schurz's popularity lay with the rank and file enlisted men; he had little popularity among the professional soldiers, especially with the West Point graduates. Schurz was rewarded with the rank of major general, Volunteers (a non-permanent rank), the army's highest possible rank at that time. Schurz worked for the abolition of slavery, black suffrage, just treatment of minority groups, civil service reform, and anti-imperialism. After the Civil War, Schurz was a U.S. senator from Missouri from 1869-1875. His enormous influence was partly due to his association, from 1865 to 1897, with key newspapers and journals as correspondent, editor, and part owner. These included the *N.Y. Tribune*, *Detroit Daily Post*, *St. Louis Westliche Post*, *N.Y. Evening Post*, and *Harpers Weekly*. When Lincoln was assassinated in 1865, Schurz's shining star faded just a bit, and when his wife died following complications of the birth of their fifth child in 1876, the luster was considerably diminished. Schurz's last important public office was from 1877-1881 when he was U.S. Secretary of the Interior. Various busts and monuments have been erected in Schurz's honor; these include those in Philadelphia, New York City, and Oshkosh, Wisc. Schurz was also commemorated in the 1983 Great American postage stamp series.

A number of noble German military officers were "on loan" from the Prussian military forces. These included Louis von Blessingh, Frederick W. von Egloffstein, and Georg von Schack.

Adolph Wilhelm August Frederick von Steinwehr was also of the German nobility. Von Steinwehr participated in the Mexican War of 1846-1848, married an Alabama girl, and had a varied career as a "Latin farmer" in Connecticut, professor of military science at Yale, and U.S. Government engineer. He was a brigadier-general in the Union army from 1861-1865.

Samuel Peter Heintzelman was born in 1805 in Manheim, Lancaster Co., Pa. and eventually acquired forty-three years of military service, from 1826-1869, thus serving through the Mexican War and the Civil War. Heintzelman achieved the rank of major general, Volunteers, during the Civil War, and was retired as major general, USA.

August Valentine Kautz, born 1828 in Ispringen, Baden, went with his family to Ohio in 1832. Kautz fought in the Mexican War and then attended

West Point. He served in the army continuously from 1852-1918 and eventually held ranks of brevet major general, USA, and major general, Volunteers. A brother, Albert, became an admiral in the navy.

William C. Kueffner, born in Mecklenburg, fought in 110 Civil War engagements; his service was one of the longest continuous combat records. Kueffner was wounded four times. In the Civil War, Kueffner had the rank of brevet brigadier general.

Franz Sigel was born in 1824 in Sinsheim, Baden and went as a political refugee to New York in 1852. Sigel moved to St. Louis where he was a strong Lincoln supporter and helped win over Missouri for the Federal cause. Although his talent in the military field was at best mediocre, he was rewarded with a position of brigadier general, and eventually major general, Volunteers during the Civil War. A monument to Sigel was erected in New York.

James Addams Beaver, Jacob Dolson Cox (originally Koch), John Frederick Hartranft, Union Civil War officers, are listed also in the government directory as governors of various states.

Galusha Pennypacker was part of the illustrious Pennypacker family long established in Pennsylvania. His grandfgather had fought in the Revolutionary War while his father was an officer in the Mexican War. Pennypacker served in the U.S. Army from 1861-1883, was the Civil War's youngest general, at age twenty, and received the Medal of Honor for his deeds. Pennypacker's rank was that of brigadier general, with brevet major general, Volunteers.

Edward Selig Salomon, born 1836, died 1913, was one of nine Jewish generals in the Civil War. Salomon commanded a Union regiment from Illinois which contained many Jewish soldiers, of which a majority originated in the Chicago area. After the war, Salomon was a governor of Washington territory.

Daniel Edgar Sickles was born in N.Y. in 1825. His ancestry has been traced to one Zacharias Sickles who went to America from Wien (Vienna) about 1656. Sickles had a spectacular career, became a brigadier general, USV, in Sept. 1861, and a major general, USV, in Nov, 1862. He lost a leg in combat at Gettyburg, Pa., and was awarded a Medal of Honor. Sickles was retired as a major general USA in 1869, and was military governor of the Carolinas from 1865-1867. After retirement, among other posts, he was U.S. minister to Spain, from 1869-1873.

Simon Snyder, born in 1839 in Selinsgrove, Pa., saw army service from 1861-1902. He eventually achieved the rank of brigadier-general.

Al Sieber was another interesting immigrant, whose biography lists him as "soldier, army scout." Sieber was in the Union army from 1862-1865 and the U.S. Army from 1871-1890, the latter era being associated with the Apache Indian Wars. Sieber is credited with being wounded twenty-nine times and with the killing of some fifty Indians.

The one heroine in the Civil War group was Barbara Hauer Frietschie, born in 1766 in Lancaster, Pa. and died in 1862 in Frederick, Md. Frietschie (or Fritchie, locally) was the legendary patriotic heroine depicted in John

Greenleaf Whittier's poem as "Barbara Fritchie," Union flag waver. The poem was published in Oct., 1863, in the *Atlantic Monthly*.

George Armstrong Custer, a Union major general, Volunteers, in the Civil War, was killed in combat at the Battle of Little Bighorn, Montana, in 1876. The famed Custer family luck had run out. All of Custer's band of 225 men died during the skirmish. These included brothers Thomas W. Custer and Boston Custer, as well as a brother-in-law and a nephew. At his death, Thomas W. Custer was almost as well-known as his older brother, having been awarded two Medals of Honor during combat in the Civil War. The Custer family name was brought to Germantown, Pa., by one Paulus Küster, about 1690, from Kaldenkirchen, in the lower German Rhine. The National Park Service maintains the Custer Battlefield National Monument at Crow Agency, Montana. The contemporary artist Eric von Schmidt's painting of oil on canvas shows a thirteen foot long battle field scene under the title here "Here Fell Custer." This painting, which was preceded by hundreds of paintings by other artists of the Custer battle scene, is currently on display at the Ulrich Museum at the Wichita State Univ., Ks. The current catalogue of the University of Nebraska Press lists a dozen or so in-print books devoted to interpreting the military lives of the Custer family.

Major, later brevet brigadier general, Ernst von Vegesack, although born in Sweden, was one of the few native Europeans to receive the Medal of Honor, America's highest honor. He fought for the Union cause, in 1862-1863. The Vegesack family name comes from the city of Vegesack, near Bremen.

Civil War - Confederate Forces (1861-1865)

Confederate casualties were similiar to those of the Union forces. *The Civil War Battlefield Guide* gives an estimate of about 260,000 dead and 194,000 wounded, but notes that the records are very erratically preserved.

Confederate generals killed during the Civil War included Otho Fench Strahl and Felix K. Zollicofer.

The directory lists fourteen notable German-Americans in this group, of which nine were long-time residents in the South.

Rufus Barringer and Robert Frederick Hoke are representative of German-American descendants born in North Carolina. Barringer participated in seventy-six engagements and was wounded three times; he achieved the rank of brigadier general. Hoke became a major general.

James Lawson Kemper, born in Virginia in 1823, was a major general in the Confederate forces, and later became governor of Virginia. Kemper was a descendant of John Kemper who was an original settler in Spotwood's Germania settlement in the northeastern part of Virginia. The colony evidently began about 1714 on a 70,000 acre tract, centering around present day Fredericksburg, granted to Alexander Spotswood (1676-1740).

Christopher Gustavus Memminger was born in Naihingen, Württemburg in 1803, and went to South Carolina about 1806. Memminger was put in the difficult role of secretary of treasury of the Confederate Cabinet, a role he served from 1861-1864. A relatively small number of Confederate bonds were floated on the Frankfurt financial market. The Confederates had somewhat better success on the London financial market.

Johann August Heinrich Heros von Borcke was one of the few Prussian officers acquired by the Confederate forces. Von Borcke became major general J.E.B. Stuart's chief of staff and attained the rank of colonel. He was seriously wounded.

Immigrant John Andreas helped start the German Colony Society at Walhalla, S.C. in 1848. He had the rank of brigadier general in the S.C. Milita.

World War I (1914-1918)

As mentioned earlier, American involvement in fighting began only in 1917. American battlefield deaths have been reported by the Department of Defense as being 116,516.

This extremely abbreviated list of German-Americans shows only twelve personalities, of which two are discussed briefly.

John Joseph Pershing, born in 1860 near Laclede, Mo., was a descendant of Frederick Pfoerschin who went to America from the Alsace sometime before 1750. "Black Jack" Pershing achieved the title of general of the armies of the U.S. In 1932, Pershing's book *My Experiences in the World War* received a Pulitzer prize for biography. Pershing's birth place, in Laclede, Mo., is now a State Historic Site.

Edward Vernon Rickenbacker, born in 1890 in Columbus, Oh., achieved fame on several accounts. Rickenbacker drove racing cars in the Indianapolis Speedway races in 1911, 1912, and 1917. In World War I, he became an ace pilot with 22 downed German planes to his credit. He was awarded the Medal of Honor. And finally, he had a remarkable career as an Eastern Airlines executive from 1938-1953. Rickenbacker died in Zürich, Switzerland in 1973. At least six localities in Switzerland are named Rickenbach, one of them likely being the family ancestral home.

World War II (1941-1945)

The Department of Defense shows 405,399 Americans as having been killed in battle during World War II, with total participation in the millions. Only two German-American individuals of this extremely large group are mentioned.

The career of Dwight David Eisenhower is relatively well-known by the average American: he was a five-star general and supreme commander of the Allied Expeditionary Force in Western Europe during World War II, and 34th president of the U.S., from 1953-1961. In 1948, Eisenhower's book *Crusade in Europe* was a best seller. Eisenhower was a fifth generation descendant of Johann Nicol Eisenhauer who landed in Philadelphia in 1741. The Eisenhauer name is commonly assciated with the hilly, wooded area known as the Odenwald, between Heidelberg and Darmstadt. Although

President Eisenhower was born in Denton, Tx, the state of Kansas claimed him as a native son and erected a memorial and museum in his honor in Abilene. A statue of Eisenhower is on display at the State Capitol Rotunda in Topeka, Kansas.

Chester William Nimitz was born in 1885 in the Germanized colony of Fredericksburg, Tx. Nimitz's grandfather immigrated in 1884 from Bremen and spent a short two years in South Carolina before moving on to the hill country of Texas. Chester Nimitz achieved fame as a five-star admiral, having command of the naval military forces in the Pacific during World War II.

TABLE 19
DIRECTORY OF MEN AND WOMEN AT WAR

German Mercenaries in the British Army
1. Bouquet, Henry (1719-1765)
1. Klipstein, Philipp (1751-)
1. Reed, John (1757-1845)
1. Schöpf, Johann David (1752-1800)
1. Wangenheim, Frederick Adam Julius, Baron
     (1747-1800)

Revolutionary War
1. De Haas, John Philip (c. 1735-1786)
1. de Woedtke, Frederich Wilhelm (c.1740-1776)
1. de Zeng, Frederick Augustus (1756-1838)
2. Herkimer, Nicholas (1728-1777) (Herchheimer)
2. Hiester, Daniel (1747-1804)
1. Kalb, Johann (1721-1780)
1. Ludwick, Christopher (1720-1801)
1. Lutz, Nicholas (1740-1807)
2. McCauley, Mary Ludwig Hays (1754-1832),
     "Molly Pitcher"
2. Muhlenberg, John Peter Gabriel (1746-1807)
1. Otto, Bodo (1711-1787)
1. Schott, Johann Paul (1754-1839)
1. Steuben, Friedrich Wilhelm Ludolf Gerhard
     Augustin von, Baron (1730-1794)
1. Weissenfels, Frederick H., Baron (1738-1806)
2. Wisner, Henry (1720-1790)
1. Ziegler, David (1748-1811)

War of 1812
3. Bedinger, George Michael (1756-1843) (Büdinger)
2. Barringer, Paul (fl. 1812-1814)
1. de Barth, John Baptiste,
     Baron de Walbach (1766-1857)

Civil War - Union Forces
1. Adams, Charles (c. 1845-1895)
2. Ammen, Daniel (1819-1898)
2. Ammen, Jacob (1807-1894)
3. Beaver, James Addams (1837-1914)
1. Blenker, Ludwig (1812-1863)
1. Bohlen, Henry (1810-1862)
1. Burger, Louis (1821-1871)
     Chrysler, Morgan Henry (1822-1890)
4. Cox, Jacob Dolson (1828-1900)

7. Custer, George Armstrong (1839-1876) (Küster)
7. Custer, Thomas Ward (1845- 1876)
5. De Haven, Edwin Jesse (1816-1865)
   Deitzler, George Washington (1826-1884)
1. Engelmann, Adolph (1825-1890)
2. Ernst, Oswald Herbert (1842-1926)
1. Flagler, Daniel Webster (1835-1899)
2. Frietschie, Barbara Hauer (1766-1862)
   Guenther, Francis Luther (1838-1918)
   Harbach, Abraham Alexander (1841-1933)
4. Hartranft, John Frederick (1830-1889)
   Hartsuff, George Lucas (1830-1874)
   Hazen, William Babcock (1830-1887)
1. Hecker, Friedrich Karl Franz (1811-1881)
3. Heintzelman, Samuel Peter (1805-1880)
   Ingalls, Rufus (1820-1893)
1. Kautz, August Valentine (1828-1895)
1. Kautz, Albert (1839-1907)
   Keim, William High (1813-1862)
   Knipe, Joseph Farmer (1823-1901)
1. Koltes, John A. (1823-1862)
1. Krez, Konrad (1828-1897)
1. Kueffner, William C. (? -1893)
2. Kuhn, Joseph Ernst (1864-1935)
   Lauman, Jacob Gartner (1813-1867)
2. Lieber, Guido Norman (1837-1923)
3. Marchand, John Bonnet (1808-1875)
2. Mayer, Brantz (1809-1879)
3. Mervine, William (1791-1868)
4. Michler, Nathaniel (1827-1881)
1. Moor, Augustus (1814-1883)
   Myer, Albert James (1829-1880)
3. Negley, James Scott (1826-1901)
1. Osterhaus, Peter Joseph (1823-1917)
6. Pennypacker, Galusha (1844-1916)
1. Phisterer, Frederick (1836-1909)
4. Poe, Orlando Metcalfe (1832-1895)
4. Raum, Green Berry (1829-1909)
3. Rodenbough, Theophilus Francis (1838-1912)
   Roehr, Henry E. (fl. 1861-65)
   Salomon, Edward Selig (1836-1897)
1. Salomon, Friedrich Sigel (1826-1897)
1. Salomon, Karl Eberhard (1822-1881)
4. Schley, Winfield Scott (1839-1909)
   Schriver, Edmund (1812-1899)
1. Schurz, Carl Christian (1829-1906)
1. Schwan, Theodore (1841-1926)

7. Sickles, Daniel Edgar (1825-1914)
1. Sieber, Al (1844-1907)
1. Sigel, Albert (1827-1884)
1. Sigel, Franz (1824-1902)
   Smith, Gustavus Adolphus (1820-1885)
1. Smith, John Eugene (1816-1897)
2. Snyder, Simon (1839-1912)
1. Stahel, Julius (1825-1912)
1. Tafel, Gustav (1830-1908)
1. von Blessingh, Louis (fl. 1861-65)
1. von Egloffstein, Frederick W., Baron (c.1824-1898)
1. von Schack, Georg (? -1887)
1. von Schimmelpfennig, Alexander (1824-1865)
1. von Schrader, Alexander (1821-1867)
1. von Steinwehr, Adolph Wilhelm August Frederick, Baron (1822-1877)
1. von Vegesack, Ernst Mathais Peter, Baron (fl. 1861-65)
   Wagner, George Day (1829-1869)
1. Wagner, Louis (1838-1914)
1. Wangelin, Hugo (1818-)
1. Weber, Max (1824-1901)
2. Weitzel, Godfrey (1835-1884)
1. Willich, August (1810-1878)
5. Wistar, Isaac Jones (1827-1905)
   Zeilin, Jacob (1806-1880)
   Zook, Samuel Kosciuzko (1821-1863)

Civil War - Confederate Forces
   Andreas, John (fl. 1848-)
   Armistead, Lewis Addison (1817-1863)
3. Barringer, Rufus (fl. 1861-65)
5. Hoke, Robert Frederick (1837-1912)
   Imboden, John Daniel (1823-1895)
7. Kemper, James Lawson (1823-1895)
1. Memminger, Christopher Gustavus (1803-1888)
2. Snyder, John Francis (1830-1921)
   Strahl, Otho Fench (1831-1864)
1. von Borcke, Johann August Heinrich Heros (1835-1895)
1. Wagener, John Andreas (1816-1876)
   Weisiger, David Addison (1818-1899)
4. Zollicoffer, Felix Kirk (1812-1862)

World War I
2. Eberle, Edward Walter (1864-1929)
2. Falk, Otto Herbert (1865-1940)
2. Haan, William George (1863-1924)

5. Heintzelman, Stuart (1876-1935)
   Kempff, Louis (1841-1920)
7. Kilmer, Alfred Joyce (1886-1918)
   Maus, Marion Perry (1850-1930)
5. Pershing, John Joseph (1860-1948) (Pfoerschin)
2. Rickenbacker, Edward Vernon (1890-1973)
   Spaatz, Carl (1891-1974) (Spatz)
4. Sibert, William Luther (1860-1935)
   Ziegemeier, Henry Joseph (1869-1930)

World War II
5. Eisenhower, Dwight David (1890-1969)
3. Nimitz, Chester William (1885-1966)

Code:
1. = 1st Generation in America
2. = 2nd Generation
3. = 3rd or more Generation, etc.

Biographical Sources

American Library Association, 1968-1981, *The National Union Catalog, Pre-1956 Imprints.* (also supplements for years 1956-1982, 451 vols.) London: Mansell Publ., 740 vols.

Anonymous, 1875-1912, *Allgemeine Deutsche Biographie.* Leipzig & München: Verlag von Duncker & Humblot, 56 vols.

Anonymous, 1984, *The Encyclopedia Americana, International Edition.* Danbury, Conn.: Grolier Inc., 30 vols.

Anonymous, 1943-1985, *Who Was Who in America, Index, 1607-1993.* Vols. I-X, and Historical Vol. Chicago: Marquis Who's Who, Inc.
_____, 1910-11, *Who's Who in America*: ibid.
_____, 1954, ibid.
_____, 1962-63, ibid, vol. 32
_____, 1978-79, ibid, 2 vols., 37th ed.
_____, 1990-91, ibid, 2 vols., 46th ed.
_____, 1993, *Index to Marquis' Who's Who Books*: ibid, 500 p.

Anonymous, 1958-1994, *Who's Who of American Women.* Chicago: Marquis Who's Who, Inc. (18 editions)

Anonymous, 1957-1990, *Neue Deutsche Biographie.* Berlin: Duncker & Humblot, Berlin, 16 vols.-to-date.

Anonymous, 1898-1979, *The National Cyclopaedia of American Biography.* New York: James T. White Co., 58 vols., permanent series; also current series. (early volumes reprinted by University Microfilms, Ann Arbor, MI, 1967).

Anonymous, 1970, *The New York Times Obituaries Index, 1858-1968.* New York: The N.Y. Times, 1136 p.

Anonymous, 1991, *Biographical Dictionary of Mathematicians.* New York: Charles Scribner's Sons, 4 vols.

Anonymous, 1993, *Cumulative Index, Contemporary Authors*. Vols. 1-138; *Contemporary Authors New Revision Series*. Vols. 1-39, Detroit, Mi.: Gale Research, Inc., 392 p.

Anonymous, 1993, *The National Inventors Hall of Fame*. Arlington, Va.: U.S. Dept. Commerce, Patent & Trademark Office, 77 p., illus.

Asimov, Isaac, 1982, *Asimov's Biographical Encyclopedia of Science and Technology*. Garden City, N.Y.: Doubleday & Co., Inc., 941 p.

Baillie, Lauren, 1993, *American Biographical Index*. London: K.G. Saur, 6 vols.

Barthel, Manfred, 1986, *Lexikon der Pseudonym*. Düsseldorf: Econ Verlag, 272 p., illus.

Bender, H.S. (ed.), 1955-1959, *The Mennonite Encyclopedia*. Scottdale, Pa.: Mennonite Publ. House, 4 vols.

Benz, Wolfgang & Hermann Graml (eds.), 1988, *Biographisches Lexikon zur Weimarer Republik*. München: Verlag C.H. Beck, 392 p.

Bishop, E. L. (ed.), et al., 1978-1992, *Dictionary of Literary Biography*. Detroit: Gale Research Inc., 124 vols.
_____, 1984-1992, *Dictionary of Literary Biography, Documentary Series*: ibid, 10 vols.

Block, Maxine (ed.), et al., 1940-1993, *Current Biography*. New York: H.H. Wilson Co., 55 vols., Cumlative Index 1940-1970, 1971-1980, 1981-1990, 1991-1993.

Boatner, Mark M. III, 1976, *Encyclopedia of the American Revolution*. New York: David McKay Co., Inc., 1290 p.
_____, 1991, *The Civil War Dictionary*. revised edition. New York: Random House, Inc., 974 p.

Böttcher, Kurt, et al., (eds.), 1992, *Lexikon Deutschsprachiger Schriftsteller*. Hildesheim: Georg Olms Verlag, 2 vols.

Bowden, H.W., (ed.), 1977, *Dictionary of American Religious Biography*. Westport, Ct.: Greenwood Press, 572 p.
_____, 1993, ibid. revised and expanded edition. London: Greenwood Publ. Group., 720 pp.

Buhle, Mari Jo, Paul Buhle, & Dan Georgakas, 1990, *Encyclopedia of the American Left*. Chicago: St. James Press, 928 p.

Bull, Donald, Manfred Friedrich & Robert Gottschalk, 1984, *American Breweries.* Trumbull, Ct.: Bullworks, 400 p.

Bunch, Bryan & Alexander Hellemans, 1993, *The Timetables of Technology.* New York: Simon & Schuster, 490 p.

Burke, W.J., Will D. Howe, & I.R. Weiss, 1964, *American Authors and Books. 1640 to Present Day.* rev. ed. New York: Crown Publishers, Inc., 834 p.

Chicago, Judy, 1985, *The Dinner Party, 999 Kurzbiographien berühmter Frauen*: Verein "Die Dinner Party in Deutschland". Frankfurt/Main, 230 p. (translated from the English original by numerous individuals).

Claus, Sybille (ed.), 1983, *International Biographical Dictionary of Central European Emigrés 1933-1945.* vol. 3, Index. München: K.G. Sauer, 281 p.
_____, & Beatrix Schmidt, 1980, *Biographisches Handbuch der deutschsprachigen Emigration nach 1933. Bd. I, Politik, Wirtschaft, Öffentliches Leben*: ibid, 875 p.

Conzen, Kathleen Neils, 1980, *Germans.* Harvard Encyclopedia of American Ethnic Groups, p. 405-425. Cambridge, Mass.: Belknap Press.

Cunz, Dieter, 1973, *They Came from Germany.* New York: Dodd, Mead & Co., 178 p.

Debus, A.G. (ed.), 1968, *World Who's Who in Science.* Chicago: Marquis Who's Who Inc., 1855 p.

Delaney, J.J., & J.E. Tobin, 1961, *Dictionary of Catholic Biography.* London: Robert Hale Ltd., 1245 p.

Durnbaugh, D.F. (ed.), 1983-1984, *The Brethren Encyclopedia.* Ambler, Pa.: The Brethren Encyclopedia, Inc., 3 vols., 2126 p.

Dyck, C. J. & D. D. Martin (eds.), 1990, *The Mennonite Encyclopedia,* Vol. 5 (A-Z). Scottdale, Pa.: Herald Press, 961 p.

Falk, Peter Hastings, 1985, *Who was Who in American Art (Biographies of American Artists active from 1898-1947).* Madison, Ct.: Sound View Press, 707 p.

Faust, P.L., (ed.), 1986, *Historical Times Illustrated Encyclopedia of the Civil War.* New York: Harper & Row, 850 p.

Fink, G.M., (ed.), 1984, *Biographical Dictionary of American Labor.* Westport, CT: Greenwood Press, 767 p.

Fischel, Jack & Sanford Pinsker (eds.), 1992, *Jewish-American History and Culture. An Encyclopedia.* New York: Garland Publ., Inc., 710 p.

Friederichs, Elisabeth, 1971, *"Lebensbilder" Register, Alphabetisches Verzeichnis der in der deutschen regionalen "Lebensbilder"- Sammelbänden behandelten Personen.* Neustadt/Aisch: Verlag Degener & Co., 177 p.
_____, 1985, ibid, Bd. 2, ibid, 223 p.

Garraty, J.A., & J.L. Sterstein (eds.), 1974, *Encyclopedia of American Biography.* New York: Harper & Row, 1241 p.

Gillispie, C.C. (ed.), 1970-1976, *Dictionary of Scientific Biography.* New York: Charles Schribner's Sons, 14 Vols.

Gordon, J. M., 1989, *Encyclopedia of American Religions.* 3rd ed. Detroit: Gale Research Co., 1102 p.

Halpenny, Francess G. (ed.), et al., 1966-1991, *Dictionary of Canadian Biography, 1000-1900.* Vols. 1-12 & Index. Toronto: Univ. Toronto Press.

Halsey, W. D. & Emanuel Friedman, (eds.), 1985, *Collier's Encyclopedia.* New York: Macmillan Educational Company, 24 vols.

Harding, Anneliese, 1986, German-American Contributions to Art. *Eagle in the New World,* p.166-180. College Station, Tx.: Texas A & M Press.

Hege, Christian, et al. (eds.), 1913-1967, *Mennonitisches Lexikon.* Vols. 1-2, privately printed; Vols. 3-4, Karlsruhe: Verlag von Heinrich Schneider.

Heitman, Francis B. 1903, *Historical Register and Dictionary of the U.S. Army (from 1789-1903).* Washington, D.C.: Government Printing Office, Washington, D.C.; Vol. 1, 1069 p.; Vol. 2, 626 p. (reprinted 1965 by Univ. Illinois Press).

Hitchcock, H.W., & Stanley Sadie (eds.), 1986, *The New Grove Dictionary of American Music.* London: Macmillan Press, 4 vols.

Honegger, Marc, & Gunther Massenkeil (eds.), 1987, *Das grosse Lexikon der Musik.* Freiburg im Breisgau: Verlag Herder, 8 vols.

Ingham, John (ed.), 1983, *Biographical Dictionary of American Business Leaders.* Westport, Ct.: Greenwood Press, 4 vols.

Jackson, Michael, 1977, *Das grosse Buch vom Bier*. Bern: Hallweg Verlag, 255 p., illus.

Jacques Cattell Press (ed.), 1965, *American Men of Science. The Physical and Biological Sciences.* 11th ed., (Suppl. 4, 1968). New York: R.R. Bowker Co., 6 vols.
_____, 1968, *American Men of Science. The Social and Behavioral Sciences.* 11th ed. (Suppl. 1, 1970): ibid, 2 vols.
_____, 1982, *Directory of American Scholars.* 8th ed.: ibid, 4 vols.

James, E. T., et al. (eds.), 1971, *Notable American Women, 1607-1950. A Biographical Dictionary.* Cambridge, Mass.: Belknap Press - Harvard Univ. Press, 3 vols.

Johnson, Allen, et al. (eds.), 1928-1937, *Dictionary of American Biography.* New York: Charles Schribner's Sons, 20 vols. + Index, 1928-1937; Suppl. One, 1944; Suppl. Two, 1958; Suppl. Three, 1973; Suppl. Four, 1974; Suppl. Five, 1977; Suppl. Six 1980. Also reprinted in 1946 as Centenary Edition. 1990 updates comprise 10 base volumes and 8 supplements with 18,000 biographies and a comprehensive index volume.
_____, 1980, *Concise Dictionary of American Biography.* 4th ed.: ibid, 1 vol., 1,140 p.

Jones, Henry Z., Jr., 1985, *The Palatine Families of New York.* Universal City, Ca.: H. Jones Pub., 2 vols., 1298 p.
_____, 1991, *More Palatine Families. Some Immigrants to the Middle Colonies 1717-1776 and their European Origins, plus New Discoveries on German Families who Arrived in Colonial New York in 1710*: ibid, 592 p.

Kaufman, Martin, Stuart Galishoff, & Tockl L. Savitt, 1984, *Dictionary of American Medical Biography.* Westport Ct.: Greenwood Press, 2 vols., 1027 p.

Kichen, Steve & Tina Russo McCarthy (eds.), 1993, The 400 Largest Private Companies in the U.S. Behind the Green Door. *Forbes Magazine*, Dec. 6, 1993: p. 168-230 (intermittently paged).

Kutsch, K.J., & Leo Riemens, 1987, *Grosses Sängerlexikon.* Bern: Francke Verlag, Bern, 2 vols., 3451 p. (note also revised & expanded ed., 1993).

Lamar, Howard R. (ed.), 1977, *The Reader's Encyclopedia of the American West.* New York: Thom Y. Crowell Co., 1306 p.

McHenry, Robert, (ed.), 1984, *Webster's American Military Biographies.* New York: Dover Publ., Inc., 548 p.

McKerns, J.P., (ed.), 1989, *Biographical Directory of American Journalism*. Westport, Ct.: Greenwood Press, Inc., 820 p.

McNeil, Barbara, (ed.), 1993, *Biography and Genealogy Master Index*. Detroit: Gale Research Inc., 1293 p. (lists 450,000 names)

McNeil, Ian, 1990, *An Encyclopaedia of the History of Technology* London: Routledge, 1062 p.

Martin, Justin & Lorraine Tritto, 1993, The Fortune 500. The Largest U.S. Industrial Corporations. *Fortune International*. (April 19,1993) vol. 127, no. 8, p. 100-168. Amsterdam: Time Warner Publ. B.V.

Martin, Werner, 1988, *Verzeichnis der Nobelpreisträger 1901-1987*, 2nd revised & expanded ed. München : K.G. Saur, 382 p.

Maurer, J.F., (ed.), 1981, *Concise Dictionary of Scientific Biography*, New York: Charles Schribner's Sons, 773 p.

Ohles, John F., (ed.), 1978, *Biographical Dictionary of American Educators*. Westport, Ct.: Greenwood Press, 3 vols., 1666 p.

Opitz, G.B., (ed.), 1986, *Mantle Fielding's Dictionary of American Painters, Sculptors and Engravers*. 2nd ed. Poughkeepsie, N.Y.: Apollo Book, 1081 p.

Pallot, James, (ed.), 1991, *The Encyclopedia of Film*. New York: Putnam Publ. Group, 596 p.

Porter, D.L., (ed.), 1986, *Biographical Dictionary of American Sports. Baseball*. Westport, Ct.: Greenwood Publishing Group, Inc., 730 p.

Robinson, A.M., (ed.), 1989, *The Notable Women in the American Theatre: A Biographical Dictionary*. London: Greenwood Publ. Group, 993 p.

Rogers, Alison & Marlene McCampbell, 1993, The Billionaires List. *Fortune International*, (June 28, 1993), vol. 127, no. 13, p. 32-52. Amsterdam: Time Warner Publ. B.V.

Root, Anne & John Wyatt, 1993, Fortune's Service 500 (Companies). *Fortune International*. (May 31, 1993) vol. 127, no. 11, p. 114-168. Amsterdam: Time Warner Publ. B.V.

Rosenblatt, J.T., (ed.), 1987, *Who's Who in World Jewry*. 6th ed. New York: Who's Who in World Jewry Inc., 631 p.

Ross, Cecil & Geoffrey Wigoder, (eds.), 1970, *The New Standard Jewish Encyclopedia.* London: W. H. Allen, 2027 p.

Sadie, Stanley (ed.), 1980, *New Grove Dictionary of Music and Musicians.* London: Stockton Press, 20 vols.

Santifaller, Leo, & Eva Obermayer-Marnach, (eds.), 1957-1988, *Österreiches Biographisches Lexikon 1815-1950.* Graz-Köln: Verlag Herman Böhlaus Nachf., 10 vols-to date (A-Sav).

Schapsmeier, E.L., & F.H. Schapsmeier, 1975, *Encyclopedia of American Agricultural History.* Westport, Ct.: Greenwood Press, 467 p.

Schlessinger, B.S. & June H. Schlessinger, (eds.), 1986, *The Who's Who of Nobel Prize Winners.* Phoenix: Oryx Press, 212 p.

Schultz, A.R., 1984, Biography: Prominent Americans of German Descent: in *German-American Relations and German Culture in America: A Subject Bibliography, 1941-1980.* Millwood, N.Y.: Kraus Int. Publ., p. 957-1008.

Sicherman, Barbara & Carol Hurd Green, (eds.), 1980, *Notable American Women The Modern Period.* Cambridge, Mass.: Belknap Press of Harvard Univ. Press, 773 p.

Sifakis, Stewart, 1987, *Who was Who in the Civil War.* New York: Facts on File, 768 p.

Slonimsky, Nicolas, (ed.), 1991, *Baker's Biographical Dictionary of Musicians.* 8th ed. New York: G. Schirmer, Inc., 2,624 p.
_____, 1993, *The Concise Baker's Biographical Dictionary of Musicians.* New York: Music Sales Corp. (Schirmer Books), 1,407 p.

Sobel, Robert, John Raimo, & Marie Marmo Mullhaney, (eds.), 1978-1988, *Biographical Directory of the Governors of the United States, 1789-1988.* Westport, Ct.: Meckler Books, 6 vols.

Spiller, R.J., J.G. Dawson III, & T.H. Williams, (eds.), 1984, *Dictionary of American Military Biography.* Westport, Ct.: Greenwood Press, 3 vols., 1368 p.

Stenzel, Dorothea & Günter Stenzel, 1992, *Das große Lexikon der Nobelpreisträger.* Hamburg: Verlag Dr. Kovac, 321 p.

Stetler, Susan L., (ed.), 1989, *Almanac of Famous People.* 4th ed. Detroit: Gale Research Ind., 2 vols., 2078 p.

_____, 1994, *Almanac of Famous People*. 5th ed. Detroit: Gale Research, 2 vols., 1659 & 1056 p.

Strauss, H.A., & Werner Röder, (eds.), 1983, *International Biographical Dictionary of Central European Emigres 1933-1945*. Vol. 2, Part 1, (A-K), Vol. 2, Part 2, (L-Z), The Arts, Sciences and Literature. München: K.G. Saur, 1316 p.

Strassburger, R.B. & Hinke, W.J., 1934, *Pennsylvania German Pioneers*. Norristown: Pennsylvania German Soc., 2 vols. (reprint by Genealogical Publ. Co., Baltimore, 1966)

Sturm, Heribert, (ed.), 1979, *Biographisches Lexikon zur Geschichte der Bohmischen Länder*. München: R. Oldenbourg Verlag, 2 vols.

Theime, Ulrich & Felix Becker, 1940-1949, *Allgemeines Lexikon der Bildenden Künstler*. Leipzig: Verlag E.A. Seeman, 37 vols.

Thrapp, D.L. (ed.), 1990, *Encyclopedia of Frontier Biography*. Lincoln: University of Nebraska Press, 3 vols., 1696 p.

Walk, Joseph, 1988, *Kurzbiographien zur Geschichte der Juden 1918-1945*. München: K.G. Sauer, 452 p.

Wigoder, Geoffrey, 1991, *Dictionary of Jewish Biography*. New York: Simon & Schuster, 567 p., illus.

Wilson, J.G., & John Fiske (eds.), 1887-1889, *Appleton's Cyclopaedia of American Biography*. New York: D. Appleton & Co., 6 vols.

Yenne, Bill, 1986, *Beers of North America*. (1992 revised & expanded ed.) Stamford, Ct.: Longmeadow Press, 208 p., illus.

Zucker, A.E., 1950, Biographical Dictionary of the Forty-Eighters. *The Forty-Eighters, Political Refugees of the German Revolution of 1848*. New York: Columbia Univ. Press, 379 p., illus.

Corporate Histories

Alberts, A.R., 1971, *The Good Provider (History of H. J. Heinz Co.)*. New York: Houghton Mifflin Co., 267 p.

Anonymous, 1924, Captain Henry Lomb. *Bausch & Lomb Mag.* vol. 1, no. 1: p. 3, 4, 14.

Anonymous, 1926, John Jacob Bausch -- 1830 - 1926. *Bausch & Lomb Mag.* vol. 3, no. 7: p. 3-15.

Anonymous, 1967, *Kuhn Loeb & Co., A Century of Investment Banking*. New York: Kuhn Loeb & Co., 52 p.

Anonymous, 1984, *A Centennial History of the Harnischfeger Corporation*. Milwaukee: Harnischfeger Corp., 30 p., illus.

Anonymous, 1992, *Unabridged Biography of Arnold O. Beckman*. Fullerton: Beckman Instruments, Inc., 9 p.

Anonymous, 1992, *A Profile of Hershey Foods Corporation*. Hershey: Hershey Foods Corp., 24 p., illus.

Anonymous, 1992, *Rohr. A Pioneer in Aeronautics*. Chula Vista: Rohr, Inc., 9 p., illus.

Anonymous, 1993, *Biographical Data of the Helmerich Family*. Tulsa: misc. sources, in part privately printed, Helmerich & Payne, Inc., 42 p.

Anonymous, 1993, *Growth through Innovation. A Brief History*. New York: Pfizer Inc., 27 p., illus.

Anonymous, 1993, *Siemens '93. A Review of Siemens Businesses in the USA*. New York: Siemens Corp., 32 p., illus.

Anonymous, 1993?, *Barney Builds a Business. The Story of the Founding of the Kroger Co.* Cincinnati: The Kroger Co., 23 p.

Anonymous, 1993?, *Levi Strauss, A Biography*. San Francisco: Levi Strauss & Co., 6 p.

Anonymous, 1993?, *Schwinn Bicycle Company, A History of Quality, Service and Progress*. Chicago: Schwinn Bicycle Co., 5 p.

Arnsberg, Paul, 1969, *Jakob Heinrich Schiff, von der Frankfurter Judengasse zur Wallstreet*. Frankfurt am Main: Waldemar Kramer Verlag, 57 p.

Bausch, J.J., 1905, *The Story of My Life*. Rochester: publisher not cited, 53 p., illus.

Brandon, Ruth, 1977, *A Capitalist Romance. Singer and the Sewing Machine*. Philadelphia: J.B. Lippincott Co., 240 p.

Blum, G.H., 1993, *Biographical Data of Emil Gottschalk*. Fresno: Gottschalks, 1 p.

Cassidy, Pamela & Harrison, E.C., 1988, *One Man's Vision: Hershey, The Story of Chocolate Town, U.S.A.* Hershey: Hershey Foods Corp., 20 (unnumbered) p., illus.

Cochran, Thomas C., 1948, *The Pabst Brewing Company*. New York: New York Univ. Press, 451 p., illus.

DiOrio, E.L., c.1990, *Lukens, 1810-1990. Remarkable Past - Promising Future*. Coatesville, Pa.: Lukens' Corporate Affairs Div., 38 (unnumbered) p., illus.

Doughtery, Richard, 1966, *In Quest of Quality. Hormel's First 75 Years*. St. Paul: North Central Publ. Co., 357 p.

Downward, Wm. L., 1980, *Dictionary of the History of the American Brewing and Distilling Industries*. Westport, Conn.: Greenwood Press, 269 p.

Ebner, Fritz, & Lerch, Leopold (eds.), 1968, *Merck, 1668-1968. Von der Merckshen Engel-Apotheke zum pharmazeutisch-chemischen Großbetrieb*. Darmstadt: E. Merck, 142 (unnumbered) p., numerous photos.

Ebner, Fritz et al., 1991, *Johann Heinrich Merck (1741-1791). Ein Leben für Freiheit und Toleranz*. Darmstadt: E. Merck, illus.

Ellis, W.D., 1987, *With a Name Like . . .* Orrville, Oh.: J. M. Smucker Co., 161 p., illus.

Felise, Verra (undated), *The Life of Henry Harnischfeger*. Milwaukee: no publ., 14 p.

Fucini, J.J. & Fucini, Suzy, 1985, *Entrepreneurs. The Men and Women Behind Famous Brand Names and How They Made It*. Boston: G.K. Hall & Co., 297 p.

Gardner, D.S., 1982, *Marketplace: A Brief History of the New York Stock Exchange*. New York: Office of the Secretary, NYSE, 22 p., illus.

Hernon, Peter & Ganey, Terry, 1991, *Under the Influence (Anheuser-Busch Dynasty)*. New York: Simon & Schuster, 347 p.

Hobbs, J.B., 1987, *1987, Corporate Staying Power*. Lexington, Ma.: D.C. Heath & Co., 179 p., tabs.

Hochheiser, Sheldon, 1986, *Rohm and Haas. History of a Chemical Company*. Philadelphia: Univ. Pennsylvania Press, 231 p., illus.

Kogan, Rick, 1985, *Brunswick. The Story of an American Company from 1845 to 1985*. Skokie, Il.: Brunswick Corp., 140 p., illus.

Krebs, Roland and P.J. Orthwein, 1953, *Making Friends in our Business. 100 Years of Anheuser-Busch*. St. Louis: Cuneo Press, 450p., illus.

Langworth, R.M., 1985, *The Complete History of the Chrysler Corporation, 1924-1985*. New York: Beekman House.

Lemmerhirt, Richard H., 1973, *Kohler 100. Bold Craftsmen*. Kohler, Wisc.: Kohler Co., 39 p., illus.

Lief, Alfred, 1954, *The Mennen Story*. New York: McGraw-Hill Books, Inc., 89 p., illus.

Longstreet, Stephen, 1952, *A Century on Wheels, the Story of Studebaker*. New York: Henry Holt & Co., 121 p., illus.

Lynch, Peter & Rothchild, John, 1990, *One Up on Wall Street*. New York: Simon & Schuster, 399 p.

Marcus, Stanley, 1993, *Minding the Store*. New York: Plume Books, Penguin Group, 277 p., illus., new ed. (The Neiman-Marcus Corp.).

Masson, Irmalotte & von Wiest, Ursula, 1991, *Die Levi-Strauss-Saga*. München: Th. Knaur Nachf., 248 p. (reprint of 1978 ed.)

Michel, Wilhelm & Wolff, Paul, 1937, *E. Merck, Darmstadt*. Frankfurt/Main: Chemischen Fabrik E. Merck, Darmstadt, H. L. Brönners, Druckerei, 90 p., numerous photos, map.

Peters, T.J. & Austin, Nancy, 1985, *A Passion for Excellence*. New York: Random House, 437 p.

Peters, T.J. & Waterman, R.H., Jr., 1982, *In Search of Excellence: Lessons from America's Best Run Companies*. New York: Harper & Row, 360 p.

Precourt, Geoffrey (ed.), 1993, *Hertz: Going the Extra Mile*. Park Ridge, N.J.: The Hertz Corporation, 175 p., illus.

Schriftgiesser, Karl, 1955, *The Farmer from Merna. A Biography of George J. Mecherle and a History of the State Farm Insurance Companies of Bloomington, Illinois*. New York: Random House, Inc., 243 p., illus.

Soto, Carolyn (ed.), 1986, *Beers of North America*. Greenwich: Bison Books Corp., 191 p., illus.

Weiss, E.R., 1985, *Merck: A Family of Spirit*: no pub. found, p. 32-34, illus.

Condensed List of Geographic References

Anonymous, 1981, *GOF-Ortsverzeichnis von Österreich*. Wien: GOF-Verlag, Gustau O. Friedl, 397 p., index, map (9,000 localities).

Brilmayer, Karl Johann, 1905, *Rheinhessen*: Verlag von Emil Roth, 513 p., map (reprinted by Verlag Weidlich, Würzburg, 1985)

Cohen, Chester G., 1989, *Shtetl Finder, Gazetter*. Bowie, Md.: Heritage Books, Inc., 145 p.

Demandt, Karl, 1980, *Geschichte des Landes Hessen*. 2nd ed. Kassel: Bärenreiter Verlag, 719 p., 9 maps.

Dolch, Martin & Albrecht Greule, 1991, *Historisches Siedlungsnamenbuch der Pfalz*. Speyer: Verlag der Pfälzischen Gesellschaft, 554 p., index map.

Haller, C.R., 1993, *Across the Atlantic and Beyond*. Bowie, Md.: Heritage Books, Inc., 324 p., index, maps.

Hellwig, Fritz, Wolfgang Reiniger & Klaus Stopp, 1984, *Landkarten der Pfalz am Rhein, 1513-1803*. Bad Kreuznach: Druckerei Förner GmbH, 274 p., 100 map photos.

Henne-Am-Ryn, Otto (ed.), 1874, *Ritters Geographisch-Statistisches Lexikon*. 6th ed. Leipzig: Verlag von Otto Wigand, 1733 p. (1983 reprint by Verlag Pomp & Sobkowink, Essen).

Hoffmeyer, L., 1901, *Unserer Preußen. Die Entwickelung des Preußischen Staates, insonderheit unter der zweihundert jährigen Königsherrschaft der Hohenzollern*. Breslau: F. Hirt, 368 p., maps.

Hupp, Otto, 1896/1898, *Königreich Preußen. Wappen der Städte, Flecken und Dörfer (Ostpreußen, Westpreußen, Brandenburg, Pommern, Posen, Schlesien)*. Bonn: Kulturstiftung der Deutschen Vertriebenen, 184 p., illus., map (reprint ed. 1985).

Kartographischen Institut Bertelsmann, 1984, *Bertelsmann Atlas International*. Gütersloh: Verlagsgruppe Bertelsmann GmbH, 630 p., large format (maps of Germany at scale of 1:800,000).

Kessler, Wolfgang (ed.), 1982, *Bücherei des Deutschen Ostens, Bestandkatalog. Band 1: Nordostdeutschland*. Herne: Stadtbücherei Herne, 436 p., illus., maps.

_____, 1982, *Bücherei des Deutschen Ostens, Bestandkatalog. Band 2: Brandenburg/Preußen, Nordosteuropa*. Herne: ibid, 454 p., illus.,maps.

_____, 1984, *Bücherei des Deutschen Ostens, Bestandkatalog. Band 3: Schlesien*. Herne: ibid, 540 p., illus., maps.

_____, 1987, *Bucherei des Deutschen Ostens, Bestandkatalog. Band 4: Böhmischen Lander, Südosteuropa*. Berne: ibid, 602 p., illus., maps.

_____, 1990, *Martin-Opitz-Bibliothek, Herne, Bestandskatalog. Bd. 5, Historische Deutsche Ostgebiete Preussen*. Herne: Stiftung Martin-Opitz-Bibliothek, 500 p., illus., maps.

Köbler, Gerhard, 1988, *Historisches Lexikon der deutschen Länder*. München: Verlag C. H. Beck, 639 p.

Kratsch, Johann Friedrich, 1843-1845, *Lexicon der sämmtlichen Ortschaften der Deutschen Bundesstaaten*. Naumberg: Verlag von Eduard Zimmermann, 3 volumes, 827 p., 820 p., & 856 p.

Müller, Joachim, 1985/86, *Müllers Grosses Deutsches Ortsbuch, Bundesrepublik Deutschland*. 22nd ed. Wuppertal: Post- und Ortsbuchverlag: Postmeister a.O. Friedrich Müller, 957 p., (110,000 localities).

Neumann, Gustav, 1883, *Geographisches Lexicon des Deutschen Reichs*. Leipzig: Verlag des Bibliographischen Instituts, 2 vols., 1416 p.

Oesterley, Hermann, 1962, *Historisch-gepgraphisches Wörterbuch des deutschen Mittelalters*. Aalen: Otto Zeller Verlagsbuchhandlung, 807 p. (reprint of 1883 edition).

Penzler, Johannes (ed.), 1905, *Ritters Geographisch-Statistiches Lexikon: Erster Bd. (A-K)*. Leipzig: Verlag von Otto Wigand, 1248 p.

_____, 1905, *Ritters Geographisch-Statistiches Lexicon: Zweiter Bd. (L-Z)*. Leipzig: ibid, 1359 p.

Rehm, Max, 1991, *Reichsland Elsaß-Lothringen. Rigierung und Verwaltung 1871 bis 1918*. Bad Neustadt a.d. Saale: Verlag Dietrich Phaehler, 160 p., illus., map.

Schnieper, Claudia & Robert Schnieper, 1983, *Neues Schweizerisches Ortslexikon*. München: C.J. Bucher, 347 p., (postal index map)

Scobel, Albert (ed.), 1912, *Andrees Allgemeiner Handatlas: Jubiläumsausgabe.* 5th ed. Bielefeld & Leipzig: Verlag von Velhagen & Klasing, 139 main maps (scale 1:500,000), 161 secondary maps, large format, 189 p.

Seltzer, L.E. (ed.), 1962, *The Colombia Lippincott Gazetter of the World.* New York: J. B. Lippincott Co., 2148 p.

Satzinger, Walter (ed.), 1981, *Geographisches Namenbuch Bundesrepublik Deutschland. Band I.* Frankfurt/Main: Institut für Angewandte Geodäsie, 738 p.

Schützeichel, Rudolf, 1988, *Bibliographie der Ortsnamenbücher des deutschen Sprachgebietes in Mitteleuropa.* Heidelberg: Carl Winter - Universitätsverlag, 1206 p.

Stewart, G.R., 1970, *American Place-Names.* New York: Oxford Univ. Press, 550 p.

Sturm, Heribert, 1983, *Ortslexikon der Böhmischen Länder 1910-1965,* München: R. Oldenbourg Verlag, 955 p.

Uetrecht, E., (ed.), 1913, *Meyers Orts- und Verkehrs-Lexikon des Deutschen Reichs: Bd. 1, (A-K).* 5th ed. Wien: Bibliographisches Institut, 1092 p.

_____, 1913, *Meyers Orts- und Verkehrs-Lexikon des Deutschen Reichs: Bd. 2, (L-Z).* 5th ed. Wien: ibid, 1246p + 28 p. + 74 p., maps (210,000 localities).

Verderhalen, Fritz, 1970, *Kleiner historischer Städt-Schlüssel für Deutschland und die ehemaligen deutschen Gebiete.* Neustadt/Aisch: Verlag Degener & Co., 50. p.

von Reitzenstein, Wolf Armin, 1986, *Lexikon bayerischer Ortsnamen.* München: Verlag C.H. Beck, 456 p.

Zelenka, Ales & Tony Javora, 1986, *Sudetendeutsches Wappenlexikon. Ortswappen aus Böhmen, Mähren und Sudetenschlesien.* Passau: Verlag Passavia, 448 p., 330 coats-of-arms, maps.

Abridged Glossary of European Localities

Allenstein (German) - Olsztyn (Polish). A city formerly in East Prussia, now in Poland.

Alsace (French, English) - see Elsaß (German).

Baden - A pre World War II state extending along the east side of the Rhine. Principal cities were Karlsruhe, Heidelberg, and Mannheim.

Baden-Württemberg - A current German state. Combined from old states of Baden and Württemberg. Principal city is Stuttgart.

Bas-Rhin (French) - Lower Alsace (English), capital is Strasbourg. Northern province of Alsace.

Bayern - A current German state (English = Bavaria). Principal city is München; other key cities are Regensberg, Nürnberg, and Wurzburg. Bayern historically has been the largest and one of the politically important States in Germany. Seven subdivisions of Bayern are: Oberbayern, Niederbayern, Oberpfalz, Oberfranken, Mittelfranken, Niederfranken, and Schwaben.

Bayern-Pfalz - Before World War I, the old area of the "Pfalz", which see, as administered by Bayern. Sometimes called the "lower Pfalz", as distinguished from the Oberpfalz.

Böhm(en) (German) - Bohemia (English), main cities are Prague, Pilsen, and Budweis. In 1648, the kingdom of Bohemia was larger than the dukedom of Austria. A province now in the Czech Republic.

Brandenburg - A state in eastern Germany, capitol is Potsdam. The state of Brandenburg surrounds Berlin, an independent state.

Breslau (German) - A city formerly in lower Silesia. Wroclaw (Polish), a city now in southern Poland.

Brünn (German) - Brno (Czech). A city formerly in Moravia now in the Czech Republic.

Brunswick - The former name for Braunschweig, a city now in Niedersachsen.

Czechoslovakia - A country in central Europe which came into existence in 1918. Formerly composed of the old countries of Bohemia, Moravia, Slovakia and parts of Silesia. Since 1993, this territory has been subdivided into the Czech Republic (Bohemia, Moravia) and Slovakia.

Danzig (German) - Gdansk (Polish). A key city now on the north Polish coast.

Dillenburg - A German city and county formerly in Nassau, now in Hessen. Noted as representative of several hundred Nassau migrants in the 1709-1710 group of "Palatines" who migrated to America.

Eger (German) - Erlau (Czech). A town and province in westernmost Czech Republic. Also a city in northern Hungary.

Elsaß (German) - Alsace (French & English), principal city is Strasbourg, now in northeastern France. Elsaß was under German rule from 870-1648, 1871-1919, and 1940-1945. It was tied to Lothringen in 1871.

Frankfurt an der Oder (German) - Slubice (Polish). An east German city at the German/Polish border.

Frankfurt am Main - A key German financial capital; in state of Hessen.

Freiburg (German) - Fribourg (French), a Kanton & city in Switzerland. Not to be confused with Freiburg im Breisgau, Baden.

Galizien (German) - Galicia (English). A former province, now divided into a western part in southern Poland with principal cities of Krakow (Krakau), Bielsko (Bielitz), etc., and an eastern part, now in Ukraine-Russia with principal city of Lvov (formerly Lemberg).

Genève (French) - Geneva (English) & Genf (German). A key Swiss city.

Habsburger Monarchie - Included, in general, at various times, territories of Bohemia, Moravia, Slovakia, Austria, and Hungary. The Habsburgs provided rulers of Austria from 1271-1918. Hapsburg in English.

Hannover (German) - Hanover (English). Refers both to a current city and an old term for a district which is now roughly the southeast part of the state of Niedersachsen.

Haut-Rhin (French) - Upper Alsace (English). Southern province of Alsace. A key city is Mülhausen (French = Molhouse).

Hesse-Darmstadt (English) - A 1567-1866 term for the southern part of Hessen; area around the industrial city of Darmstadt. See map in Demandt, 1980.

Hessen - A current German state, (English = Hesse). Principal city is Wiesbaden; also now contains financial capital of Frankfurt am Main.

Hesse-Kassel - A 1567-1866 term for the northern part of Hessen; around the city of Kassel (English, Cassel). See map in Demandt, 1980.

Hohensalza (German) - Inowroclaw (Polish). A city in the province of Posen (Polish = Poznan), now in Poland.

Hohenzollern - A pre World War II district in the southern part of Württemberg, which see.

Insterburg (German) - Chernyakhovsk (Russian). A city formerly in East Prussia, now in Russia.

Kassel (German) - Cassel (English). A city now in northernmost Hessen.

Kattowitz (German) - Katowice (Polish). A city formerly in Upper Silesia, now in southern Poland.

Königsberg (Prussian) - Kalingrad (Russian). A large university city formerly in East Prussia, now in Russia (there is also a Königsberg NE of Berlin).

Krefeld - A town near Köln, Nordrhein-Westfalen. Noted for group of Protestant emigrants who settled Germantown, Pa. in 1683.

Kreuzberg (German) - Kluczbork (Polish). A city formerly in Upper Silesia; now in southern Poland.

Krisheim - A village west of Worms, Rheinland-Pfalz. Noted for group of Protestants who went to Germantown, Pa. in 1685. See 1993 book by author. Since 1794, called Kriegsheim.

Krotoschin (German) - Krotoszn (Polish). A city in Posen (Polish = Poznan), now in western Poland.

Lemberg (German) - Lvov (Russian). A large city formerly in western Galicia, now in Ukraine-Russia.

Liegnitz (German) - Legnica (Polish). A city formerly in western Lower Silesia, now in southwest Poland.

Lothringen (German) - Lorraine (French & English), principal city is Metz. Since 1919, a state in northern France.

Luban (German) - Luban (Polish). A city formerly in Silesia now in southern Poland.

Mähren (German) - Moravia (English). A province adjacent to Bohemia and now forming part of Czech Republic. Principal cities are Brünn & Olmütz. A key area for origin of 18th century Protestant migrants.

Mecklenburg-Vorpommern - A current German state. Principal city is Schwerin.

München (German) - Munich (English), capital of Bayern (Bavaria).

Nassau - A former province, now a part of western Hessen. The ruling House of Nassau dates from 1125 to 1866. The many territorial changes were directly related to deaths and marriages in the family. The modern concept of the dukedom embraces the period of 1806 to 1866. Key cities were Wiesbaden, Limburg, Nassau and Dillenburg. See maps for years 1785 and 1815 in Demandt, 1980.

Neisse (German) - Nysa (Polish). A city formerly in Upper Silesia, now in southern Poland.

Neusalz (German) - Nova Sol (Polish). A city formerly in Lower Silesia, now in southern Poland.

Niedersachsen - A current German state (English = Lower Saxony) occupying much of northwest Germany. Principal city is Hannover. Niedersachsen surrounds Bremen, an independent state.

Niederschlesien (German) - Lower Silesia (English). A province now in southern Poland. Capital was Breslau.

Nordrhein-Westfalen - A current German state, principal city is Düsseldorf. Also contains the Ruhr industrial areas.

Oberschlesien (German) - Upper Silesia (English). A province now in southern Poland. Capital was Oppeln.

Österreich (German) - Austria (English). Capital is Wien (Vienna).

Olmütz (German) - Olomouc (Czech). A city formerly in Moravia, now in the Czech Republic.

Oppeln (German) - Opole (Polish). Former capital of Upper Silesia, now in southern Poland.

Ortnice (German) - Ortynyczi (Polish). A city formerly in Galicia, now in southern Poland.

Ostpreußen - A former state, now divided between Russia and Poland. The main cities were Königsberg, Allenstein, Insterburg, Gumbinnen.

Palatinate - Roughly the southeastern, or Pfalz portion, of the current state of Rheinland-Pfalz; see next entry. In some cases, the 1709-10 migrants from Baden (perhaps rightly so), from Hessen (erroneously), and other Rhineland areas were considered to be "Palatines". See 1708-1712 Homann map in Hellwig, Reiniger & Stopp, 1984.

Pfalz - A part of Rheinland-Pfalz, now includes wine district called Rheinpfalz. The key cities are Kirchheimbolanden, Kaiserlautern, Zweibrücken, Landau, and Speyer. See map in Dolch & Greule, 1991.

Pinne (German) - Pniewy (Polish). Formerly in Posen, now in western Poland.

Pommern (German) - Pomerania (English), an old term for Vorpommern. The principal cites were Stettin, Köslon, & Stralsund.

Posen (German & English) - Poznan (Polish), both a city and a province. The principal cities were Posen and Bromberg. Now in western Poland.

Prachatitz (German) - Prachatice (Czech). A city formerly in southern Bohemia, now in the Czech Republic.

Prag (German) - Praha (Czech) & Prague (English). The capital of the Czech Republic.

Preßburg (German) - Bratislavia (Slovakian). The capital of Slovak.

Prussia - Basically a term for the states in eastern Germany which had military power from 1675-1918, and eventually administrative control over the better part of northern Germany. Just prior to World War I, the primary territories included: Rheinland, Hessen-Nassau, Hessen, Westfalen, Hannover, Schleswig-Holstein, Mecklenburg, Pommern, Brandenburg, Sachsen, West-Preußen, Ost-Preußen, Posen, and Schlesien. See maps in Hupp, 1896-1898; and Uetrecht, 1913.

Rheinhessen (German) - The northern part of current state of Rheinland-Pfalz. A wine district as well as a railroad district known as Rheinhessen. Principal cities are Bingen, Mainz, Worms, & Alzey. See map in Brilmayer, 1905.

Rheinland-Pfalz - current German state, principal city is Mainz (older literature refers to area as the Pfalz, in part).

Rhenish Bavaria (English) - Bayern-Pfalz (German), roughly the Palatinate, which see. Sometimes also called incorrectly Rhenish-Palatinate.

Rhenish-Prussia - An old term for parts of current state of Rheinland-Pfalz and parts of Nordrhein-Westfalen.

Rosenberg (German) - Susz (Polish). A city formerly in Galicia, now in southern Poland. (Note: there are many other villages by the name of Rosenberg in German-speaking areas of Europe).

Sachsen - A current German state (English - Saxony). Principal city is Dresden, although Leipzig is a key city, historically.

Sachsen-Anhalt - A current German state (English = Saxony-Anhalt). Principal city is Magdeburg.

Schlesien (German) - Silesia (English). Principal German cities were Oppeln, Breslau, Liegnitz; a province mainly now in Poland.

Schleswig-Holstein - A current German state. Principal city is Kiel.

Schubin (German) - Szubin (Polish). A city formerly in Posen (Polish = Poznan), now in northwest Poland.

Schwäbisch Alb (German) - Swabian Alps (English). A low range of hills, trending northeast-southwest, in the Württemberg portion of Baden-Württemberg.

Schwaben (German) - Swabia (English). A province in southern Bayern.

Siebenbürgen (German) - Transylvania (English). A district now in Rumania.

Sohrau (German) - Zary (Polish). A city formerly in Upper Silesia, now in southern Poland.

Stettin (German) - Szczecin (Polish). A city formerly in the province of Pommern, now in northwest Poland.

Strassburg (German) - Strasbourg (French). The capital of Alsace, which see, and also capital of Bas-Rhin province.

Strelno (German) - Strzelno (Polish). A city formerly in Posen (Polish = Poznan), now in Poland.

Sudeten - A semi-circular, mountaineous area separating Germany and the former Czechslovakia. Annexed by Germany in 1938 and returned to Czechoslovakia after the World War II.

Thüringen - The current German state (English = Thuringia). Principal city is Erfurt.

Warschau (German) - Warszawa (Polish) & Warsaw (English). The capital of Poland.

Westfalen (German) - Westphalia (English). Now part of Nordrhein Westfalen, which see.

Westpreußen - A former German state, the main cities were Danzig and Marienwerder. See Prussia.

Wien (German) - Vienna (English). The capital of Austria and of Niederösterreich (English = Lower Austria).

Wirsitz (German) - Wryzysk (Polish). A city formerly in Posen (Polish = Poznan), now in western Poland.

Württemberg - A pre World War II state, now part of Baden-Württemberg. Principal cities are Stuttgart and Heilbronn.

Zwittau (German) - Svitavy (Czech). A city formerly in Moravia, which see.

Everyname Index

This index excludes the directory of names at the end of each chapter.

HELMPRAECHT, Joseph 62
HELMUTH, Justus Henry Christian
56
HEMMETER, John 151
HEMPEL, Charles Julius 170
HEMPL, George 76
HENCH, Philip Showalter 172
HENCK, Caroline 89 George
Daniel 89 John Benjamin 89
HENKEL, Ambrosius 56 Anthony
Jacob 56 Paul 56 57
HENNI, John Martin 62
HENSCHEL, Isidor George 185
George 184
HERBERMANN, Charles George
206
HERBERT, Victor 185
HERBST, Johannes 190
HERCHHEIMER, 249
HERING, Constantine 170
HERKIMER, Nicholas 249
HERR, Herbert Thacker 92 John 54
HERRESHOFF, James Brown 96
John Brown 96 Karl Friedrich 96
Nathanael Green 96
HERRMAN, 17 Augustin 210
HERSHEY, 8 55 Alfred Day 225
Benjamin 124 John Richard 204
Milton 124 Milton Snavely 124
HERSHI, 8
HERTING, Johanna 89
HERTZ, John Daniel 136
HERTZLER, Jacob 54
HESS, Alfred Fabian 172 Victor
Franz 234
HESSELBERG, 12
HEYDT, Hans Jost 148
HIESTER, 9 Daniel 249
HILGARD, Eugene Woldemar 229
Ferdinand Heinrich Gustav 129
Julius Erasmus 229
HILLEGAS, Michael 132
HIMES, Charles Francis 227
HINDEMITH, Paul 181 182
HINKE, William John 81
HIRCHEMER, 243
HIRKIMER, 243

HIRSCH, 12 Harold 124
HIRTH, William Andrew 155
HISE, 243
HITE, Jost 148
HITTEL, John Schertzer 208
Theodore Henry 208
HOEN, August 210
HOFF, Jeanette 152
HOFFMAN, 13 Max 181
HOFFMANN, 13
HOFMAN, Heinrich Oscar 233
HOFMANN, 13 Lillian 104
HOFSTADTER, Richard 80 Robert
234
HOHENZOLLERN, 3 3 4 5 10
HOHN, August 210
HOKE, Robert Frederick 254
HOLLANDER, Jacob Harry 117
HOLLAR, 10
HOLLENBECK, Webb Parmelee
103
HOLLER, 10
HOLLERITH, Franciska 92 George
92 Hermann 92
HOOVER, 55 153 Daniel 124
Herbert 154 John Edgar 155
Mary 124 President 8 William H
94 William Henry 124
HOPPER, Hedda 107
HORCHHEIMER, 243
HORMEL, George A 125 George
Albert 124 Johannes Georg 124
Susanna Wilhelmina 124
HOSHOUR, Samuel Klinefelter 64
HOTZ, Ferdinand Carl 172
HOUDINI, Henry 107
HOUSMAN, A A 154
HUBER, 8 J M 120 Johannes 124
HUCK, John A 42
HUHNE, Bernhard 3 3
HUMMEL, Catharine 47
HURST, Fannie 205 Rose 205
Samuel 205
HUSMANN, George 223
HYDE, Ida Henrietta 225
IRVING, Washington 244
IVES, 210

ROMBAUER, Edgar Roderick 206
Irma 78 Irma Louise 206 Irma
Louise Vonstarkloff 206
ROMBERG, Sigmund 181 183
RONTGENS, Wilhelm Conrad 166
ROOSEVELT, Franklin D 154
ROSELIUS, 13
ROSENAK, Minna 136
ROSENBERG, Heinrich 133 Henry
133
ROSENEASSER, Edward 208
ROSENWALD, Julius 134
ROSEWATER, Edward 208 Victor
208
ROSSER, Thomas Lafayette 251
ROTH, Filbert 224
ROTHAFEL, Samuel Lionel 109
ROTHAPFEL, Gustav 109
ROTHERMEL, Peter 32
ROTHSTEIN, Arthur 211
RUBENKAMP, 10
RUBINCAM, 10
RUBINSTEIN, 10 12
RUCKLE, Barbara 63
RUDENBERG, Reinhold 90
RUDOLF I, 3
RUDOLPH, King and Emperor of
Germany 3
RUEDEMANN, Rudolf 230
RUGER, 10 William Batterman 118
RUHRAH, John 173
RUNGELING, August Frederick
109
RUPP, Israel Daniel 81
RUPPERT, 39 42 43 Anna 46 Franz
42 46 Jacob 38 46 Jacob Jr 46
Jacob Sr 46
RUTH, 39 Babe 40 George Herman
40 George Herman Jr 40 Jacob
213 Katherine 40
SAARINEN, Aline Milton
Bernstein 31
SACHS, 114 120 Curt 187 Samuel
116
SAKEL, 12
SALOMON, Edward Selig 253
SAPIR, Edward 228
SAUER, 201 212 Christopher II 212

SAUR, 201 Christoph 212
SCHADLE, 166
SCHAEBERLE, John Martin 228
SCHAEFER, 13 43 F 47 Frederick
46 M 47 Maximilian 46
SCHAFER, 13
SCHAFFNER, Hart 119 Joseph 123
SCHALK, Raymond W 40
SCHAMBERGER, Katherine 40
SCHARF, John Thomas 81
SCHEEL, Fritz 192
SCHEM, Jacob 207
SCHENCK, Friedrike 127 Georg
Peter 127
SCHICK, 120 Jacob 94
SCHIEREN, Charles Adolph 94
Johann Nikolaus 94 Wilhelmina
94
SCHIFF, Frieda 117 Jacob 117
Jacob H 116 Jacob Henry 117
169 247 Jakob Heinrich 117
Therese 116 117
SCHILLING, Hugo Karl 76
SCHILLINGER, 12
SCHILT, Christian F 245
SCHINDLER, Kurt 185
SCHIRMER, G 187 188 Gustav 188
Rudolph Edward 188
SCHLATTER, Michael 59
SCHLEBE, Gertrude 132
SCHLEIERMACHER, 10
SCHLESINGER, 10 Arthur Meier
Jr 81 Bruno Walter 186
SCHLITZ, Jos 46 47 Josef 46
SCHMID, 13 August 44 Joseph 44
SCHMIDBERGER, Katarina 170
SCHMIDT, 13 C 45 47 Carl B 151
Christian 46 Johann 225
SCHMITT, 13
SCHMITZ, 13
SCHMUCKER, 9 Beale
Melanchthon 57 Christian 128
Samuel Simon 57 128
SCHNEER, Leander 62
SCHNEIDER, 13 120 243 Georg 44
47 George 209 Herman 78 John
42 Theodore 61
SCHNELLER, George Otto 94